A
Second
Anthology
of
Atheism
and
Rationalism

Recent titles in
The Skeptic's Bookshelf

A
Second
Anthology
of
Atheism
and
Rationalism

Edited and with
Introductions by
Gordon Stein, Ph.D.

PROMETHEUS BOOKS
Buffalo, New York

For Sam, With Love

Published 1987 by Prometheus Books
700 East Amherst Street, Buffalo, New York 14215

Copyright © 1987 by Gordon Stein
All Rights Reserved

Library of Congress Cataloging-in-Publication Data

A Second anthology of atheism and rationalism.

  (The Skeptics bookshelf)
  Includes bibliographies.
  1. Atheism. 2. Rationalism. I. Stein, Gordon.
II. Series.
BL2747.3.S373   1987   211′.8   87-7378
ISBN 0-87975-415-X

Printed in the United States of America

Acknowledgments

I would like to thank George H. Smith for calling a few of the items in this anthology to my attention. I would also like to thank Eve Triffo for indefatigable criticism of countless poems, both fine and not so fine. Thanks also to the publishers who gave permission to reprint items still under copyright. As requested, specific acknowledgment is hereby given to the following:

Lawrence Ferlinghetti, from *A Coney Island Of The Mind*. Copyright © 1958 by Lawrence Ferlinghetti. Reprinted by permission of New Directions Publishing Corporation.

Macmillan Publishing Company for permission to reprint "Christianity and Slavery" from Edward A. Westermarck's *Christianity and Morals*. Copyright © 1939 by Macmillan & Co.

Corliss Lamont for permission to reprint "Life Without Immortality" from *The Illusion of Immortality*. Copyright © 1959 by Corliss Lamont.

I would also like to thank the National Secular Society and the Rationalist Press Association for permission to reprint from their copyrighted materials.

Preface

When *An Anthology of Atheism and Rationalism* was first published in 1980, there were a number of sections that had to be omitted for lack of space. With the passage of time, additional topics were suggested. The major omitted topics were immortality/life after death and ethics/morality, which are now represented. Among the topics new to the present volume but not holdovers from the first, is one on atheist poetry. This section has been one of the most difficult to compile because it was felt that uncovering obscure poems by well-known nonbelieving poets would be better than gathering a group of second-rate works by unknowns. As a result, there are virtually unknown poems by Keats, Shelley, Swinburne, Browning, Kipling, Byron, and a multitude of good but lesser-known poets. This is surely some of the finest quality atheist poetry ever printed.

The reasons for offering a second anthology of the best of atheist and rationalist writing remain the same as those which justified publication of the first volume. The first reason is that such writings are quite hard to find amid the plethora of less suitable materials. Even the largest of libraries do not have most of the materials from which the selections presented here have been taken. Again, access to what is perhaps the finest collection of such materials in the world has greatly aided my task. There is very little contemporary material that measures up to the high standards we have come to expect from earlier works on the important topics that define how we live our lives.

The importance of the topics outlined and of presenting an opposing view to what the public is usually provided, constitute the second reason for offering this collection. Finally, these writings gain importance because they were some of the first attempts to formulate many of the ideas we now accept as common sense. Such things as equal rights for women, evolution, the abolition of slavery, higher criticism of the Bible, birth control, and separation of church and state, were advocated in the atheist and rationalist literature well before they were even seriously considered by more traditional thinkers.

Most atheists and rationalists have their favorite writings: those that influenced them in some important way, or ones they found moving enough to read over and over again. I have not necessarily tried to identify the most widely known of these items: first because they are sufficiently accessible to have been widely read, at least within the atheist/rationalist camp; second, although they may be inspirational, they often do not clearly state the important ideas that I want to make more readily available to the public. I hope that some of my choices will become the reader's new favorites, as has been reported to me many times about the selections in the first volume. I will give only one example of how I have put this principle into action: *The Rubiyat* of Omar Khayyam. This poem is one of the most familiar and yet atheistic poems in English. I have not included it because it is readily available elsewhere, although it is mentioned in the introduction to the section on poetry.

The plan of this book is identical to that of the first volume in all areas except the poetry section. In the rest of the sections, there is an introductory essay, which attempts to review the scope and history of the subject at hand, followed by a short biographical sketch of each author, along with a brief history of the particular selection's publication. The selection is then presented. In the poetry section, because of the relatively large number of short pieces, the overview and author sketches have been combined.

Some of the selections have been edited to remove long and extraneous digressions or dated references that no longer make sense. All editing is indicated by the presence of an ellipsis mark (. . .). I have taken care that the editing has not changed the sense of any of the pieces. It is hoped that this volume will form a suitable companion to the first *Anthology,* and that together they will cover the entire spectrum of the best of atheist and rationalist writing.

G.S.

Contents

PART THREE: ATHEIST AND RATIONALIST POETRY

PART FOUR: IMMORTALITY/LIFE AFTER DEATH

PART FIVE: DEBATES AND DIALOGUES ON UNBELIEF

PART SIX: ETHICS AND UNBELIEF

Part One

The "Benefits" of Religion

Introduction

Quite aside from whether a particular religion is "true" or not, many people add the idea that *regardless* of the lack of factual support, all religions give hope and comfort, and that therefore they are good. It is exactly this question and its varying aspects that concerns the selections in this section. Not a great deal has been written that directly addresses the truth or falsity of the proposition that what gives hope and comfort to people, though it be totally false, is still a good thing. Many of the issues involved in this evaluation *are* discussed in the selections that follow.

Obviously, *some* of the world's religions are factually false: the presence of contradictions within and between religions clearly shows that *all* religions cannot be true. Which are true (if any) and which are false is not the subject of the present section, and need not be discussed here. What *is* important, however, is the fact that we can all agree that *some* of the religions of the world are factually false, and therefore cannot deliver what they promise (whether it be heaven, nirvana, or whatever). Let us then concentrate upon those religions whose claims are false (without naming them). Let us reframe our question: "Is it good to believe in a religion whose claims are *definitely* false on the grounds that it may or does bring hope or comfort?" We have now reached the essential issue involved in Part One.

Many religions of the world send out missionaries or their equivalent in an attempt to win converts to their particular doctrine. The members of that religion, who support the expenses of the missionary effort, feel that some benefit to both the "converted" and those who "convert" must accrue from this effort. Since many of the actual or potential convertees are already members of some *other* religion, the reason for attempting to convert them must be other than the mere fact that having *some* religion is a good thing. It must be felt by the convertors that their particular religion is somehow *better* than the one(s) the convertees presently hold. One factor in this could, of course, be the belief that the convertor's religion is true,

15

while the one presently held by the convertee is false. This points up the fact that what we are dealing with is a matter of degree, rather than a clear distinction between benefits on the one hand and no benefits on the other. It would seem that, in the minds of some people, *limited* benefits accrue to the believer in an untrue religion, while *greater* benefits accrue to those who believe in a true religion. The alleged benefits may be of the same type (e.g., hope and comfort), but the difference is in the *amount* of those benefits that different religions provide.

Let us now look at the two different aspects of the question. First, are there *any* benefits to a believer that are not obtained by a nonbeliever? Second, are those benefits greater for a believer in a true religion than for one whose religion is false? In order to examine these questions, we must make a few assumptions: first, we must assume that there is some way to quantify or at least measure benefits; second, it must be assumed that people prefer happiness over unhappiness; third, that the more happiness there is, the better things are for the human race as a whole; fourth, that we can know the falsity of at least *some* religions; and fifth, that knowledge is better than ignorance. This last assumption would have to be the case even if the knowledge occasionally led to *some* unhappiness.

Now let's see where all of these assumptions and questions take us. People want to be happy rather than unhappy (assumption 2). It provides for happiness if we know that we and our relatives will not cease to exist at death, but will live on in spirit form. To "know" something is, of course, not the same as to "believe" it; in order to know something, we must have *facts* and be aware of those facts, whereas to *believe* something we need only have *opinions*. Therefore, in order to *know* that our relatives survive death, we must have actual facts, not just wishes or hopes. Since no one can presently claim to have such facts, one cannot say that immortality is *known* to be true. Therefore, it cannot provide anyone with happiness to "know" that immortality is true, since no one does actually know this. Thus, all happiness that comes from the idea of immortality emanates from the *belief* that it is true. Since beliefs are not necessarily true (in fact, many are completely false), only those that *are* true can provide happiness. Since no one has demonstrably true beliefs about immortality, no one can rightly claim that their beliefs about the existence of immortality bring happiness.

This exact same argument form can be used with respect to religion rather than just one doctrine (immortality). It comes out that one's beliefs about religion cannot be rightfully claimed to bring happiness. It should be pointed out that this conclusion is reached in the same manner as above because knowledge of the truth of a religion cannot be shown. Of course, many people *believe* that their religions are true, but no one has the *facts* required to prove that a given religion is true. Therefore, the statement that belief in any religion brings happiness is not true *unless* one has knowledge that a specific religion is true. Since, at the present time, no one possesses such knowledge, no one can rightfully claim that some specific religion brings happiness. Of course, they may get a feeling of happiness, but it would not be correct to say that it came *from* the religion, but only that a belief in anything protective is comforting, including belief in a rabbit's foot.

The point of all this is to demonstrate that the "benefit" of religion, namely happiness, is not an *actual* benefit. In like manner, it can be shown that comfort is not really brought about by religion. We fool ourselves by getting the idea in our heads that because we *think* a process makes us happy, that therefore the process or system is good. As Theodore Roosevelt said, "In the long run, the most unpleasant truth is a safer companion than a pleasant falsehood."

Let's return now to our second question, which we have almost answered: "Are the benefits to those who believe in a *true* religion greater than the benefits to those who believe in a *false* religion?" As we have seen, the happiness or comfort that the believer purportedly receives comes not from the religion itself, but from the general feeling of comfort that emerges from belief in anything that promises to be protective. Since the actual religion is not the source of the comfort, it would make no difference if the religion were true or false with respect to the *amount* of happiness derived from the belief. There may be some connection between quantity of happiness received and the depth (or quantity) of belief, but there do not seem to be any careful studies on this subject, which is only tangential to our present discussion.

We can now examine the first question: whether there are *any* benefits accruing to a believer but not to the nonbeliever? In order to look at this question, we have to agree about what "benefit" means in *this* case. The word is usually defined as "something helpful, favorable or beneficial." Again, this does not really help us, because we do not know from who's perspective the judgment is being made. If an atheist were to do the judging, perhaps he would view any obstruction of clear, rational thinking as nonbeneficial. On the other hand, a religious person would view an increase in "faith" as beneficial *by definition*. We are in a quandry except if we leave open the whole question of whether anything the believer receives from religion that the nonbeliever does not, is to count as a *benefit*. Perhaps we can simply see what it is that the believer claims to receive from his or her belief and refrain from categorizing that something as a benefit or nonbenefit.

The first thing that the believer claims to receive from religion is "peace of mind." The very claim assumes that nonbelievers do *not* have peace of mind. This is patently false. Hundreds of nonbelievers have written or spoken publicly about their peace of mind. In fact, many contend that they never had peace of mind *until* they became nonbelievers. Of course, there are some nonbelievers who do not have peace of mind; then again, there are many *believers* who lack it as well. In fact, the large numbers of people who change from one religion to another are probably examples of believers without peace of mind. Hence, the statement that believers have peace of mind while nonbelievers do not is simply false.

Believers claim to have attained salvation while nonbelievers cannot be considered saved. Of course, no one *knows* that they really will have salvation. Such knowledge, if it can be had, is available only after one is dead, and then everything depends upon whether the believer's particular religion is true or not. We can safely label the claim to salvation as unsubstantiated.

The next thing claimed by believers is that they are more moral or righteous or charitable than those who do not believe. The facts say otherwise. Studies of prison populations have *invariably* shown that there are virtually no atheists in prisons. Since this claim would imply that atheists are more immoral, it would follow that there would be lots of atheists in prisons, since they must be committing a large share of the crimes. (We assume that atheists are not immune from being caught, tried, or convicted if they commit crimes.) No, the opposite seems to be true. Prisons are largely filled with believers in religion, people who were believers *before* they were confined, although some certainly were "saved" after they arrived at prison. Besides, personal knowledge of the fact that many of the greatest benefactors of mankind were admitted atheists gives the lie to any strict correlation between morality and religious belief. People like Thomas Edison, Andrew Carnegie, and Florence Nightingale were all atheists. The list could be greatly extended, and would include many of the greatest humanitarians ever known. Nearly everyone knows someone who is an atheist. Is that person immoral in his or her daily behavior? We need only locate one person who is both an atheist and moral to disprove the idea that atheists *have* to be immoral. However, I think the evidence is also overwhelming that, as a class, atheists are just as moral as believers (maybe even *more* so). They certainly give as much to charity and humanity. Even the atheist Soviet Union provides hospitals and care for its poor.

Another claim of the believer is that he has a "personal relationship" with God, which the nonbeliever does not have. While it is obvious that nonbelievers do not have such a "relationship," it is less obvious that the believer *does*. How can the believer document his position? Surely the believer may *feel* this way, but feelings do not count as facts. There seems to be no way to support this extraordinary claim, and, in fact, the entire basic claim that God exists cannot be proven. It would appear that there is no demonstrable truth to this claim, and it may even be hallucinatory in nature.

The benefits of religion, as claimed, are therefore rather nebulous. Of course, anyone who feels better as a result of his or her religious beliefs is certainly entitled to maintain them, as long as they do not hurt other people. The problem comes when an attempt is made to convert the nonreligious to religion. If untrue statements are made, then there is an objection on ethical grounds. One of these untrue statements (unless arguments, which have thus far escaped me, can be mustered in its support) is that real benefits accrue as a direct result of the religion in which one believes. The various aspects of this issue are discussed in the following selections.

Thoughts on Religion

"Diderot"

The name "Diderot" appears here in quotation marks because, although this piece is modelled upon Diderot's writings and attributed to him, the best modern scholarship indicates that it is *not* really his work. The late Professor Arthur M. Wilson, one of the world's leading authorities on Diderot, was of the opinion that the work started out as a faithful translation of Diderot's *Additions* to his *Philosophic Thoughts* (the *Additions* were published anonymously in 1770, having been written most probably in 1762). The "translator" of the present piece, however, soon started putting words into Diderot's mouth. In fact, he became more openly atheistic than Diderot himself ever was in his own writings.

There is no clue as to who actually wrote the present piece. It seems to have been first published by Richard Carlile in 1819. Many of Carlile's obscure works, seemingly first translated from the French, were supplied to him by his friend Julian Hibbert. Whether Hibbert is the one who took a piece actually written by Diderot and added to it in this supposed translation is unknown. The piece itself has been out of print for many years.

Doubts in religious matters, far from being blameable—far from being acts of impiety, ought to be regarded as praiseworthy, when they proceed from a man who humbly acknowledges his ignorance, and arise from the fear of offending God by the abuse of reason.

To admit any conformity between the reason of man, and the eternal reason of God, and to pretend that God demands the sacrifice of human

21

reason, is to maintain that God wills one thing, and intends another thing at the same time.

When God, of whom I hold my reason, demands of me to sacrifice it, he becomes a mere juggler that snatches from me what he pretended to give.

If I renounce my reason, I have no longer a guide—I must then blindly adopt a *secondary principle,* and the matter in question becomes a supposition.

If *reason* be a gift of Heaven, and we can say as much of *faith,* Heaven has certainly made us two presents not only incompatible, but in direct contradiction to each other. In order to solve the difficulty, we are compelled to say either that *faith* is a chimera, or that reason is useless.

Pascal, Nicole and others have said, that God will punish with eternal torments the faults of a guilty father upon all his innocent offspring; and that this is a proposition *superior* to reason, and not in *contradiction* to it; but what shall we propose as being contradictory to reason if such blasphemy as this is not so?

Bewildered in an immense forest during the night, and having only one small torch for my guide, a stranger approaches and thus addresses me:—*"Friend, blow out thy light, if thou wouldst make sure of the right path."* This stranger was a priest.

If my reason be the gift of Heaven, it is the voice of Heaven that speaks; shall I hearken to it?

Neither merit nor demerit is applicable to the judgment of our rational faculties, for all the submission and good-will imaginable could not assist the blind man in the perception of colors.

I am compelled to perceive evidence where it is, or the want of evidence where it is not, so long as I retain my senses; and if my judgment fail me, it becomes a *misfortune,* not a *sin.*

The Author of Nature would not reward me for having been a *wit,* surely, then, he will not *damn* me for having been a *fool.* Nay, more; he will not *damn* me even for being wicked. Is not my own conscience a sufficient punishment for me?

Every virtuous action is accompanied with an inward satisfaction; every criminal action with chagrin and remorse. The mind acknowledges without shame its repugnance to such, or such propositions, although there is neither virtue nor vice in the belief or disbelief of them.

If grace be necessary to belief, let us wait till that grace be sent us from above.

God surely will not punish us for the want of that which it has not pleased him to bestow upon us. You tell me to ask this grace in my prayer, but is not grace necessary to assist me in asking for *faith,* the want of which I cannot discover by the light of reason?

The true religion, interesting the whole human race at all times and in all situations, ought to be eternal, universal, and self-evident; whereas the religions pretended to be revealed having none of these characteristics, are consequently demonstrated to be false.

The miracles, of which only a few men are said to have been witnesses, are insufficient to prove the truth of a religion that ought to be believed by the whole world.

The pretended facts with which all revealed religion is supported are *ancient* and *wonderful;* that is to say, the most suspicious evidence possible, to prove things the most incredible; for to prove the truth of the Gospel by a miracle, is to prove an absurdity by a contradiction in nature.

Is it quite certain that the God of the Christians is the true God? It appears that the Devil is a much more powerful Being, seeing that the number of the damned is so much greater than that of the elect.

The Son of God died purposely to vanquish the Devil. In order to gain his point he was reduced to the necessity of dying, and yet the Devil has ever since had the ascendancy. How then are we benefitted by the death of the Son of God?

The God of the Christians, for an apple, punished all the human race and killed his own son. This only proves that God is a father who makes a great deal to do about his apples, and cares very little for his children.

A God that *killed God* to *appease God,* was an expressive phrase of La Hontan, a phrase of itself sufficient to destroy the Christian religion, a phrase that will still retain its absurdity, should one hundred folio volumes be written to prove it rational.

But what will God do to those who never heard of the death of his Son? or who, having heard of him, still remained unbelievers? Will he punish the deaf for not hearing? Will he torment the weak-headed for not understanding an inconceivable absurdity?

Why are the miracles of Jesus Christ true, and those of Esculapius, Pythagoras, and Apollonius, false?

All the Jews at Jerusalem who saw the great miracles of Jesus, were doubtless converted? By no means.—So far from having any belief in him, they put him to death. These Jews (whom a God himself came to convert) must have been a very stiff-necked race.—We have in every country seen the people drawn aside and deceived by a single false miracle, and yet all the true miracles of Jesus made very little impression on the minds of the Jews. The miracle of their incredulity is no doubt wonderful; however, our priests reply, that this obstinacy of the Jews had been predicted as a chastisement from Heaven. In that case why did God work so many miracles when the futility of them had been foreseen?

It is morally certain that Caesar existed. The existence of Jesus is as certain as the existence of Caesar;—it is thence inferred that the resurrection of Jesus is also certain, but the conclusion is false; the existence of Caesar was not miraculous, wherefore should the existence of Jesus be thought so?

The religion of Jesus, announced by ignorant fanatics (who were either easily deceived or easily deceived others) made the first Christians; the same religion now preached by learned men continues to make unbelievers.

You tell me that these ignorant Apostles suffered death to prove the truth of what they preached to mankind; instead of which they proved only their own enthusiasm, or the chastisement of the people on whom they practiced their hypocrisy. To suffer martyrdom in any cause proves nothing, except that our party is not the most powerful.

How did it happen that God permitted to be put to death those men that he sent purposely to convert the world? Would it not have been more in conformity with the divine attributes to change the hearts of the people?

As for the martyrs who suffered after the time of the Apostles, they were not witnesses of the miracles of Jesus; they died to maintain that those who had instructed them in the Christian religion, had neither deceived themselves nor wished to deceive others.

We attest what we have ourselves seen, or what we believe we have seen. When we attest what others have seen, we prove nothing, except that we are willing to believe them on their words. The whole fabric of Christianity is built on the authority of those who had formerly an interest in establishing it, and who now have an interest in maintaining it.

It is pretended, that submission to legislative authority forbids all examination and reasoning; but do not the interested Priests of all the religions on earth pretend to possess this authority? Does it not equally belong to the Bramins, the Talapoins, the Bonzes, the Molochs, as well as to the Ministers of Christianity?

It is the education of youth which makes a Christian believe in Christ, a Turk in Mahomet, and an Indian in the incarnations of the Vestnou. It is the education of youth which makes the Siamese believe the wonders that are told him about Sommonocodom.

Faith, in every country, is only a blind deference to the sentiments of the priests, who are always infallible where they are sufficiently powerful.

Our priests are unceasingly talking to us of the weakness and errors of the human mind; but is the mind of a priest more infallible than mine? Is his understanding less subject to error than that of an unbeliever? May not his passions and interests deceive him in the same way that others are deceived?

We no sooner refuse to believe on the bare word of a priest, than he endeavors to frighten us; but the terror he excites in us is not a convincing argument, neither can fear be a motive of credibility. *Believe, or you will be damned.* This is the strongest argument in Theology.

But is it certain that I shall be damned for not believing what appeared to me incredible? Divines have long been asked to reconcile the dogma of eternal punishment with that of infinite mercy; but this they will not meddle with; yet still they persist in representing our heavenly Father as a tyrant, to whom no father of a family would wish to have any resemblance.

Why would you punish a guilty wretch when no utility can arise from his punishment? What good results to mankind, or to the Deity himself, from the punishment of the millions of unfortunate beings who have already been damned?

The dogma of eternal punishment is the offspring of folly, of atrocity, and of blasphemy. If God will punish eternally, what proportion exists between the offense and the chastisement? If he punish for his own satisfaction, he becomes a monster of barbarity; if he punish to correct others, his rigor is useless for those who are not witnesses of it.

But further:—Why is this God so wrathful? Can man, either living or dead, tarnish his glory and disturb his repose and felicity? If God be offended at sin, it is because he *wills* to be offended. If God will eternally punish sin, it is because he wills that sin shall eternally be committed.

It is pretended that God will burn the wicked man (who can do nothing against him) in a fire that shall endure forever; yet should we not regard as culpable any father who should plan the easiest death imaginable for his son, though that son had compromised his honor, his fortune, or even his life?

God the Father judges mankind deserving of his eternal vengeance; God the Son judges them worthy of his infinite mercy; the Holy Ghost remains neutral. How can we reconcile this verbiage with the unity of the will of God?

All the evils that could possibly be committed would only merit an infinite punishment; yet, in order that we may always be terrified at the idea of Deity, the priests have made *man* sufficiently powerful to offend the Author of Nature to all eternity.

All the evil which man is capable of committing is not all the evil that possibly might be committed. How can a finite being, a worm of earth, offend the infinite being who created him, or disturb the powers which regulate the universe?

I should, without hesitation, believe any respectable individual who might bring me the intelligence of any army having obtained a victory over its opponent, etc.; but should the whole population of Paris assure me that a dead man rose from his grave, I would not believe a word of it. When we find that an historian has imposed upon us, or that a whole nation has been deceived, we must not take these for prodigies.

A single demonstration is more convincing than fifty unconnected facts. Pontiff of Mahomet!—cause the lame man to walk, the dumb to speak, the blind to see, or the dead to rise from their graves, and to thy great astonishment my faith shall not be shaken. Wouldst thou have me to become thy proselyte—lay aside these pranks and let us reason together. I have more dependance on my judgment than I have on my eyes.

How canst thou believe that God requires to be worshipped? Weak mortal! What need has the Deity of thy homage? Dost thou think that thou canst add any thing to his happiness or to his glory? Thou mayest honor thyself by raising thy thoughts to the Great Author of thy being, but thou canst do nothing for him, he is too much above thy insignificance. Always bear in mind, that if any kind of worship be more acceptable to him than the rest, it must be that which proceeds from an honest heart. What matter then in what manner thou expressest thy sentiments? Does he not read them in thy mind? What matters it in what garments, in what attitude, in what language thou addressest him in prayer? Is he like those kings of the earth who reject the petitions of their subjects, because they have been ignorant of, or disregarded some little formality? Pull not down the Almighty to thy own littleness, but believe that if one worship were more agreeable to him than another, he would have made it known to the whole world. Believe that he receives with the same goodness the wishes of the Mussulman, the Catholic, and the Indian; that he hears with the same kindness the prayers of the savage, who addresses him from the midst of a forest, as those of a Pontiff, who wears the tiara.

Nothing could be better adapted to overthrow morality and destroy it altogether, than to couple it with religion; neither could anything be more pernicious than to make men believe that they offended God when they injured themselves or their fellow-creatures; and hence arose the necessity of obtaining God's favor, without any regard to the duties they owe to their brethren.

Reason tells us that when we commit crimes, it is men, and not God, that we injure; and common sense tells us that we injure ourselves when we give way to disorderly passions. The Christian religion teaches us to imitate a God that is cruel, insiduous, jealous, and implacable in his wrath. Christians! with such a model before you, what will be your morality? Can the God of Moses, of Joshua, and of David, be the God of an honest man?

A religion is dangerous when it confounds our ideas of morality; a religion is false when it destroys the perfections of the Deity; a religion is detestable when it substitutes for its worship a vindictive demon instead of a beneficent God.

Christians! in obeying your gospels to the letter, you will be neither citizens, husbands, fathers, friends, nor faithful subjects. You will be pilgrims on earth—strangers in your own country—fierce enemies to yourselves—and your brethren, and your groans even will not leave you the hope of ever being happy.

Belief Not the Safe Side

Robert Taylor

The Reverend Robert Taylor, M.B., was one of the strangest converts to atheism in the history of the movement. He was a brilliant child who studied medicine, was licensed as a surgeon, and then decided that he wanted to be a clergyman rather than a physician. He was admitted to the University of Cambridge, where he showed himself to be an outstanding student, and received his bachelor's degree. Taylor was later ordained as an Anglican clergyman and licensed. At the age of thirty he accepted a position as curate of the town of Midhurst in 1814.

Reverend Taylor soon met a man at Midhurst who was eventually to become his one and only friend there. This was Henry Ayling, a wealthy man who had become an infidel through his extensive reading. Soon Taylor was engaged in lengthy discussion with Ayling and was making heavy use of his fine library. As a result, Taylor became a deist. For an ordained clergyman of this time, this was considered a serious crime. Taylor was eventually tricked by his bishop into relinquishing his clerical license, thus effectively ending his ministerial career.

The year 1824 found Robert Taylor in London at the start of a new phase of his career. Always a brilliant speaker, he had opened a public hall at which he lectured. At first, the authorities ignored him, even though many of his "sermons" were decidedly anti-Christian, but always scholarly. When the crowds began to grow appreciably, Taylor was arrested and charged with blasphemy. He defended himself clad in his full canonical robes, but was speedily convicted and sentenced to a year in jail. That year was one of the most productive of his life. Taylor wrote two books: *The Diegesis,* a history of early Christianity, and *The Syntagma,* a defense of the principles of his

Christian Evidence Society against the attack of a Christian clergyman. It seems that Taylor's society—not the one of the same name that now exists—was actually looking at the evidence for Christianity and found it wanting.

Upon his release from jail, Taylor and a friend, the radical atheist publisher Richard Carlile, set upon an "Infidel Mission" in northern England, challenging clergymen to debate. Again in London, Taylor opened a lecture hall called the Rotunda. There he gave lectures on the astronomical basis of the Christ myth. As crowds grew, Taylor was again arrested on a charge of blasphemy. This time he was convicted and sentenced to two years in prison with none of the privileges he had had the first time. He wrote nothing and was allowed no visitors. He emerged from confinement a broken and defeated man. Taylor left England and traveled to France, where he married a wealthy widow and retired from public life. He died in 1844.

The present selection is from one of Taylor's lectures at the Rotunda. It was initially published as a pamphlet, as were all of his weekly lectures, under the name of *The Devil's Pulpit*. The lecture was originally delivered on February 11, 1830, and first published as a collected work under the above title in 1831. The book of lectures was reprinted several times during the late nineteenth century, but has been out of print since the turn of the century. Many of Taylor's ideas about the astronomical basis of Christianity have been discarded, but his ideas about the dangers of belief sound as fresh today as they did 150 years ago.

"Ye blind guides, which strain at a gnat and swallow a camel."
—Matthew xxiii. 24.

The gentlemen who distribute religious tracts, the general body of dissenting preachers, and almost all persons engaged in the trade of religion, imagine themselves to have a mighty advantage against infidels, upon the strength of that last and reckless argument—that whether the Christian religion be true or false, there can be no *harm* in believing; and that belief is, at any rate, the safe side.

Now to say nothing of this old Popish argument, which a sensible man must see is the very essence of Popery, and would oblige us to believe all the absurdities and nonsense in the world, inasmuch as if there be no harm in believing, and there *be* some harm and danger in *not* believing, the more we believe, the better; and all the argument necessary for any religion whatever, would be, that it should frighten us out of our wits; the more terrible, the more true; and it would be our duty to become the converts of that religion, whatever it might be, whose priests could swear the loudest, and damn and curse the fiercest.

But I am *here,* to grapple with this Popery in disguise, this wolfish argument in sheepish clothing, upon scriptural ground, and on scriptural ground only; taking the scriptures of the Old and New Testament, for this argument's sake, to be of divine authority.

The question proposed is, "Whether is the believer or the unbeliever the more likely to be saved, taking the scriptures to be of divine authority?" And I stand here on this divine authority, to prove that the unbeliever is the more likely to be saved: that unbelief, and *not* belief, is the safe side; and that a man is more likely to be damned for believing the gospel, and *because* of his having believed it, than for rejecting and despising it, as I do.

I propose to sift this question, with more careful diligence, and to bring all its merits before you, with the utmost fairness, candor, and truth, taking words and meanings in their most ordinary acceptation, submitting the result to the judgments of your own mind, no judgment of mine withstanding. Let your good patience hear,—let such conviction as shall follow on your patient hearing, decide.

But, if such a patient hearing be more than good Christians be minded to give us, when thus I advance to meet them on their own ground, their impatience and intolerance itself will supply the evidence and demonstration of the fact, that, after *all,* they dare not stand to the text of their own book; that is not the Bible that they go by, nor God whom they regard: but that they want to be *God-a-mighties* themselves, and would have us take *their* words for God's word; you must read it as *they* read it, and understand it as they understand it! you must *"skip, and go on,"* just where a hard word comes in the way of the sense *they* choose to put upon't: you must believe the book contains what you see with your own eyes that it does *not* contain: you must shut your eyes, and not see what it *does* contain: or you'll be none the nearer the mark of *their* liking, though you should, "from the table of your memory," wipe away all trivial fond records,

All saws of books, all forms, all pressures past,
That youth and observation copied there.
And God's commandment, it alone should live
Within the book and volume of your brain,
Unmixed with baser matter.

And though you should be "a scholar, and a ripe and good one," with all advantages that education and learning can confer on man, as familiar with the text of the original Greek, as with your mother tongue; the most illiterate bungling ass, the smutched artificer, the dirty kern, the cobbler from his lapstone, the weaver from his loom, having once given his mind to religion, will expect that *your* understanding should submit to *his;* and that you should receive not merely the text he quotes, but whatever sense he chooses to understand, or to misunderstand, from it. So that the Sun itself is not more apparent in the Heavens, than is the fact, that religion is nothing more than the moody melancholy of an overbearing and tyrannical disposition; and your religious man, nothing more than an usurping, saucy knave, who wants to be your master.

> How calm and sweet the victories of life!
> How terrorless the triumph of the grave!
> How ludicrous the priest's dogmatic roar;
> The weight of his exterminating curse,
> How light! and his affected charity,
> To suit the pressure of the changing times,
> With palpable deceit! but for *thy* aid,
> Religion! but for thee, proflic fiend,
> That peoplest earth with demons, hell with men,
> And heaven with slaves!
>
> Shelley's *Queen Mab*

Hear the pulpit, Sirs! and their word of God, to be sure, it is all joy and peace in believing,—"mild, as blest voices, uttering praise,—soft, as the down upon the ring-dove's breast—sweet, as the south wind that breathes upon a bank of violets, stealing and giving odors." Hear *itself*, Sirs! the gospel itself; uncommented on by any gloss of mine, and marvel!

"The word of God is quick and powerful, and sharper than any two-edged sword, piercing even to the dividing asunder of soul and spirit, and of the joints and marrow" (Heb. iv. 12). What is hypocrisy? What is deceit? If greater hypocrisy and deceit can be, or be conceived, than that men should put heaven in their shop-windows, when hell is in the shop? That they should cry "peace! peace! when there is no peace;" and call their gospel "glad tidings of great joy," which, when we come to look into it, presents descriptions of grief, and woe, and pain, the bare imagination of which doth blanch the cheek of health to ashy paleness, and "makes the seated heart knock at the ribs against the use of nature."

> Regions of sorrow, doleful shades, where peace
> And rest can never dwell; hope never comes
> That comes to all; but torture without end,
> And pain of inextinguishable fire
> Still urges, and a fiery deluge, fed
> With ever-burning sulphur unconsumed.

And are THESE "glad tidings of great joy?" Is the liability which Christian men stand in, if the gospel be true, of being infinitely and eternally miserable, so tempting as to tempt a man to *wish* that it may be true; when that liability, if the gospel be true, and the scriptures, from Genesis to Revelations, be of divine authority, impends *more* over the believer than the unbeliever; and that the unbeliever is more likely to be saved in consequence of his unbelief, and by virtue of his unbelief; and the believer more likely to be lost and damned to all eternity, because he *did* believe, and in consequence of his having believed?

Taking the authority of scripture, for this argument's sake, to be decisive, I address the believer who would give himself airs of superiority, would chuckle in an imaginary safety in believing, and presume to threaten the unbeliever as being in a worse case, or more dangerous plight, than *he*. "Hast thou no fears for thy presumptuous self? when on the showing of thine *own* book, the safety (if safety there be) is *all* on the unbelieving side?" When for any one text that can be produced, seeming to hold out any advantage or safety in believing, we can produce *two,* in which the better hope is held out to the *unbeliever?* For only one apparent exhortation to believe, we can produce two *forbiddances* to believe, and many threatenings of God's vengeance *to,* and for the crime and folly of believing? To this proof I proceed by showing you:

1st. What the denunciations of God's vengeance are: with no comment of mine, but in the words of the text itself.

2d. That these dreadful denunciations are threatened to believers; and that they are *not* threatened to unbelievers: and

3d. That all possible advantages and safety, which believing could confer on any man, are likely, and *more* likely to be conferred on the unbeliever, than on the believer.

That the danger of the believer is so extreme, that no greater danger can possibly be.

1st. What are the denunciations of God's vengeance? "There are," (says the holy Revelation xiv. 10) "who shall drink of the wine of the wrath of God, which is poured out without mixture into the cup of his indignation, and shall be tormented with fire and brimstone, and the smoke of their torment ascendeth up for ever and ever; and they have no rest day nor night." There's "glad tidings of great joy" for you. The Christian may get over the terror of this denunciation by the selfish and ungenerous chuckle of his "Ah! well, these were very wicked people, and must have deserved their doom; it need not alarm us: it doesn't apply to us." But good-hearted men would rather say, "It *does* apply. We cannot be indifferent to the misery of our fellow creatures. The self-same Heaven that frowns on them, looks lowering upon us." And who were they? and what was *their* offense? Was it Atheism? was it Deism? was it Infidelity? No! it was for church and chapel-going; it was for adoring, believing and worshipping. They worshipped the beast: I know not what beast they worshipped; but I know that if you go into any of our churches and chapels at this day, you will find them worshipping *the Lamb;* and if worshipping a *lamb,* be not most suspiciously like worshipping a *beast,* you may keep the color in your cheeks, while mine are blanched with fear. The unbeliever only can be absolutely safe from this danger. He only who has no religion at all, is sure not to be of the wrong religion. He who worships neither God nor Devil, is sure not to mistake one of those gentlemen for the other.

But will it be pretended, that these are only metaphors of speech, that the thing said is not the thing that's *meant.* Why, then, they are very ugly metaphors. And what is saying that which you don't mean, and meaning the contrary to what you say, but LYING?

But if the Christian hath a right to say that there are some parts, and even *many* parts of Scripture, which are not to be taken as strictly and literally *true;* but which must be understood as *metaphors* and *allegories:* what right can he have to dispute *our* right to maintain, that the whole gospel story is a metaphor and an allegory from first to last; that there is not a word of truth in it: that it was not written to pass for truth; but only as a vehicle to convey moral instruction, after the well-known Oriental style; a fable with a moral to it: of which the duller wit of those Western nations forgot the moral, and ran away with the fable?

And what worse can become of the Infidel, who makes it the rule of his life "to hear and speak the plain and simple truth," than of the Christian, whose religion itself is a system of metaphors and allegories, of double meanings, of quirks and quiddities, in dread defiance of the text that warns him, that, "All liars shall have their part in the lake which burneth with fire and brimstone" (Rev. xxi. 8).

Is it a parable that a man may merely entertain his imagination withal, and think no more on it—though not a word be hinted about a parabolical signification, and the text stands in the mouth of him, who, we are told, was the truth itself? And *he* it is who brought life and immortality to light, that hath described in the 6th of Luke, such an immortality as that of one who was a sincere believer,—a man of Abraham, who took the Bible for the rule of his life; and was anxious to promote the salvation of his brethren, yet found for himself no savior, no salvation; but "In Hell he lifted up his eyes, being in torment, and saith; Father Abraham, have mercy on me, and send Lazarus, that he may dip the tip of his finger in water, and cool my tongue, for I am tormented in this flame." But that request was refused. "Then he said, I pray thee, therefore, Father, that thou wouldst send him to my father's house; for I have five brethren, that he may testify unto them, lest they also come to this place of torment." But that request was refused. There's "glad tidings of great joy" for you.

That the believer's danger of coming or going into that place of torment is so great, that greater cannot possibly be: and that his belief will stand him in no stead at all, but make his plight a thousand times worse than if he had not been a believer; and that unbelief is the safer side,—Christ himself being judge,—I quote no words but his to prove.

Is the believer concerned to save his soul, then shall he most assuredly be damned for being so concerned: for Christ hath said, "Whosoever will save his soul shall lose it" (Matthew xvi. 25).*

Is the believer a complete beggar? if he not be so,—if he hath a rag that he doth call his own, he will be damned to all eternity. For Christ hath said, "Whosoever he be of you who forsaketh not all that he hath, he cannot be my disciple" (Luke xvi. 33).

Is the believer a rich man? and dreams *he* of going to Heaven? "It is easier for a camel to go through the eye of a needle" (Matthew xix. 24). Is he a man at all, then he cannot be saved: for Christ hath said: "Thou believest that there is one God;" saith St. James, "Thou dost well, the devils also believe and tremble" (James ii. 19). And so much good, and no more, that comes to damned spirits in the flames of Hell, is all the good that ever did or can come of believing; "For though thou hast all faith, so that thou couldst remove mountains," saith St. Paul, "It should profit thee nothing" (1 Cor. xiii. 2).

Well, then! let the good Christian try what saying his prayers will do for him: *this* is the good that they'll do for him; and he hath Christ's own word to comfort him in't. "He shall receive the greater damnation" (Luke xx. 47).

Well, then, since believing will not save him, since faith will not save him, since prayer will not save him, but all, so positively makes things all the worse, and none the better, here's one other chance for him. Let him go and receive the Sacrament, the most comfortable Sacrament, you know, "of the body and blood of Christ;" remembering, as all good communicants should, "that he is not worthy so much as to gather up the crumbs that fall from that table." "Truth, Lord! But the dogs eat of the crumbs that fall from their master's table!" O what happy dogs. But let those dogs remember, that it is also *truth,* that "He that eateth and drinketh unworthily, eateth and drinketh damnation to himself" (1 Cor. xvi. 29). O what precious eating and drinking.

> My God! and is thy table spread;
> And doth thy cup with love o'erflow?
> Thither be all thy children led,
> And let them all thy sweetness know.

---

*It is to be regretted that Taylor has quoted this text, as his argument was all sufficient without it. The word ψυχή, here rendered *soul,* may also mean *life,* as in the common version.— *Publisher.*

That table is a snare, that cup is deadly poison, that bread shall send thy soul to hell.

Well, then, try again, believer: perhaps you had better join the Missionary Society, and subscribe to send these glad tidings of these blessed privileges, and this jolly eating and drinking to the Heathen.

Why, then, you have Christ's own assurance, that when you shall have made one proselyte, you shall have just done him the kindness of making him twofold more the child of Hell than yourself (Matthew xxiii. 15).

Is the believer liable to the ordinary gusts of passion, and in a passion shall he drop the hasty word "thou fool?" for that one word, "he shall be in danger of Hell-fire (Matthew v. 22).

Nay, Sirs, this isn't the worst of the believer's danger. Would he but keep his legs and arms together, and spare his own eyes and limbs, he doth by that very mercy to himself damn his eyes and limbs,—and hath Christ's assurance that it would have been profitable for him rather to have plucked out his eyes, and chopped off his limbs, and so to have wriggled and groped his way through the "straight gate and the narrow way that leadeth unto life," than having two eyes and two arms, or two legs, to be cast into Hell, into the fire that never shall be quenched, where their "worm dieth not, and the fire is not quenched" (Mark ix. 43).

Well, then! will the believer say,—what were all the miracles and prophecies of both the Old and the New Testament *for?*—those unquestionable miracles, and clearly accomplished prophecies, if it were not that men should believe? Why, absolutely, they were the very arguments appointed by God himself to show us that men should not believe; but that damnation should be their punishment if they did believe. "To the law and the testimony," Sirs! These are the very words: Of miracles, saith God's word, "They are the spirits of devils, that work miracles" (Revelation xvi. 14). And it is the Devil who "deceiveth them which dwell on the earth, by means of those miracles which he hath power to do" (Revelation xiii. 14). So much for miracles.

Is it on the score of prophets and of prophecies, then, that you will take believing to be the safe side? Then, "thus saith the Lord of Hosts, the God of Israel, the prophets prophesy falsely, and the priests bear rule by their means" (Jeremiah v. 31). "The prophet is a fool: the spiritual man is mad." (Hosea ix. 7). "Thus saith the Lord of Hosts, harken not unto the prophets" (Jeremiah xxiii. 16). "O, Israel, thy prophets are like the foxes of the desert" (Ezekiel xiii. 4). "They lie unto thee" (Jeremiah xiv. 14). "And they shall be tormented day and night for ever and ever" (Revelations xx. 10). "And the punishment of the prophet shall be even as the punishment of him that seeketh unto him" (Ezekiel xiv. 10).

Nay, more, *then,* it is, when God hath determined to damn men, that he, in every instance, causeth them to become believers, and to have faith in divine Revelation, in order that they may be damned. Believers, and none but believers, becoming liable to damnation; believers, and none but believers, being capable of committing that unpardonable sin against the Holy Ghost, which hath never forgiveness, neither in this world, nor in that which is to come. "Whereas, all other kinds of blasphemy shall be forgiven unto men, and all sorts of blasphemy wherewith soever they shall blaspheme." But there is no forgiveness for believers (Mark iii. 28). For it is written, "for this cause God shall send them strong delusion, that they should believe a lie: that they all might be damned" (2 Thesselonians ii. 11). If, then, the evidence of the Christian religion were as strong as you please, where would be your evidence to show that that evidence itself was not strong delusion? And if God doth send men strong delusion, I guess the delusion is likely to be strong enough.

So when it was determined by God that the wicked Ahab should perish, the means to bring him to destruction, both of body and soul, was to make him become a believer. I offer no comment of my own on words so sacred; but those are the words: "Hear thou, therefore, the word of the Lord. I saw the Lord sitting upon his throne, and all the hosts of Heaven standing by him on his right hand and on his left. And the Lord said, Who shall persuade Ahab that he may go up and fall at Ramoth Gilead? and one said on this manner, and another said on that manner. And there stood forth a spirit and stood before the Lord, and said—I will persuade him. And the Lord said unto him, Wherewith? And he said, I will go forth, and I will be a lying spirit in the mouth of all his prophets. And he said, thou shalt persuade him, and prevail also. Go forth and do so. Now, therefore, behold the Lord hath put a lying spirit in the mouth of all thy prophets" (1 Kings xxii. 22). There were 400 of 'em; they were "the goodly fellowship of the prophets" for you;

> All of them inspired by the spirit from on high,
> And all of them lying as fast as they could lie.

So much for getting on the safe side by believing. Had Ahab been an infidel, he would have saved his soul alive. As it was, we may address him in the words of St. Paul to just such another fool;—"King Ahab, believest thou the prophets? I know that thou believest; but not better than I know, that, for that very belief, fell slaughter on thy soul: and where thou soughtest to be saved by believing, it was by believing thou wert damned."

So when Elijah had succeeded in converting the 450 worshippers of Baal, who had been safe enough while they were Infidels, and they began crying "the Lord He is God, the Lord He is God:" the moment they got into the right faith, they found themselves in the wrong box; and the prophet, by the command of God, put a stop to their *Lord-Godding,* by cutting their throats for 'em. "Elijah brought them down to the brook of Kishon, and slew them there" (1 Kings xviii. 40). He brought them to the brook, ye know, for the convenience of baptizing and killing them at the same time. I suppose they were on the safe side of the brook. O, what a blessed thing, ye see, to be converted to the true faith.

Thus all the sins and crimes that have been committed in the world, and all God's judgments upon sin and sinners, have been the consequence of religion, and faith, and believing.

What was the first sin committed in the world? It was believing. Had our great mother Eve not been a believing, credulous fool, she would not have been in the transgression. Who was the first reverend divine that began preaching about God and immortality? It was the Devil. What was the first *lie* that was ever told, the very damning and damnable lie? It was the lie told to make folks believe that they would not be dead when they were dead; that they should not surely die, but that they should be as gods, and live in a future state of existence. When God himself hath declared, that there is no future state of existence: that "Dust thou art, and unto dust shalt thou return." Who is it, then, that prefers believing in the Devil rather than in God, but the believer. And from whom is the hope of a future state derived, but from the father of lies?—the Devil. But—

If, in defiance of so positive a declaration of Almighty God, men will have it that there is a future state of existence after death, who are they who shall sit down with Abraham, and Isaac, and Jacob, in the Kingdom of Heaven, but unbelievers; let 'em come "from the north, from the south, from the east, or from the west?" And who are they that shall be cast out, but believers, "the children of the kingdom"?

As St. Peter very charitably calls them, "cursed children" (2 Peter ii. 14). That is, I suppose, children with beards; children that never grew to sense enough to put away childish things, but did in gawky manhood, like newborn babes, desire the pure milk and lollipop of the gospel. "For such is the Kingdom of Heaven."

And who are they whom Christ will set upon his right hand, and to whom he will say, "Come, ye blessed of my Father," but unbelievers, who never troubled their minds about religion, and never darkened the doors of a gospel-shop? But who are they to whom he will say, "Depart, ye cursed, into everlasting fire, prepared for the devil and his angels," but believers, every one of them believers, chapel-going folks, Christ's blood-men, and incorrigible bigots, that had been bothering him all their days with their "Lord, Lord?" to come off at last with no better reward of their faith than that he will "protest unto them, I never knew ye."

One text there is, and only one, against ten thousand of a contrary significancy, which, being garbled and torn from its context seems, for a moment, to give the advantage to the believer: the celebrated sixteenth chapter of Mark, verse 16: "He that believeth, and is baptized, shall be saved; but he that believeth not, shall be damned." But little will this serve the deceitful hope of the Christian, for it is immediately added: "And these signs shall follow them that believe; in my name shall they cast out devils; they shall speak with new tongues; they shall take up serpents; and if they drink any deadly things, it shall not hurt them; they shall lay hands on the sick, and they shall recover." Can the Christian show these signs, or any of them? Will he dare to take up a serpent, or drink prussic acid? If he hesitate, he is not a believer, and his profession of belief is a falsehood. Let belief confer what privilege it may, he hath no part nor lot in the matter: the threat which he denounces against Infidels hangs over himself, and he hath no sign of salvation to show.

Believing the gospel, then, (or rather, I should say, *professing* to believe it, for I need not tell you that there's a great many more professing to believe, than believing), instead of making a man the more likely to be saved, doubles his danger of damnation, inasmuch as Christ hath said, that "the last state of that man shall be worse than the first" (Luke xi. 26). And his holy apostle, Peter, addeth, "It would have been better for them not to have known the way (2 Peter ii. 21) of righteousness." The sin of believing makes all other sins that a man can commit so much the more heinous and offensive in the sight of God, inasmuch as they are sins against light and knowledge: and "the servant who knew his Lord's will, and did it not, he shall be beaten with many stripes" (Luke xii. 47). While unbelief is not only innocent in itself, but so highly pleasing to Almighty God, that it is represented as the cause of his forgiveness of things which otherwise would not be forgiven. Thus St. Paul, who had been a blasphemer, a persecutor, an injurious, assures us that it was for this cause he obtained mercy, "because he did it ignorantly in unbelief" (1 Timothy i. 13). Had he been a believer, he would as surely have been damned as his name was Paul. And 'tis the gist of his whole argument, and the express words of the eleventh chapter of the Epistle to the Romans, that "God included them all in unbelief, that he might have mercy upon all." It is said of Abraham himself, that "he staggered not at the promises of God, through unbelief" (Romans iv. 20). It being nothing but belief that sets men staggering. And when the whole Jewish nation became unbelievers, God was so pleased with them for it, that he actually saved the whole Gentile world in compliment to them: they have been the most money-getting people ever since. And it is expressly declared, that the Gentiles obtained mercy through their unbelief (Romans xi. 30). Unbelief being the essential qualification and recommendation to God's mercy, not without good reason was it the pious father of the boy that had the Devil in him, when he had need of Christ's mercy, and knew that unbelief would be the best title to it, cried out and said with tears, "Lord, I believe, help thou mine unbelief" (Mark ix. 24).

While the apostles themselves, who were most immediately near and dear to Christ, no more believing the gospel than I do: and for all they have said and preached about it, they never believed it themselves, as Christ told 'em that they hadn't so much faith as a grain of mustard-seed. And the Evangelist, John, bears them record, to their immortal honor, that, "though Christ had done so many miracles among them, yet believed they not" (John xii. 37).

And the same divine authority assures us, that "neither did his brethren believe in him" (John vii. 5). Which, then, is "the safe side," Sirs, on the showing of the record itself? On the unbelieving side, the infidel stands in the glorious company of the apostles, in the immediate family of Christ, and hath no fear; while the believer doth as well, and no better than the devils in Hell, who believe and tremble. While the first believers of Christianity— the martyrs, as they would pretend to be, who are said to have sealed the truth with their blood, had the seal of God's providence upon them—that it was a lie that they sealed with their blood; for how could God's providence express his displeasure and indignation against believers more strongly than by bringing them to a bad end?

If there were in reason any danger of guilt in being an unbeliever, if it could be thought or feared for a moment that God would punish a man for being an Infidel; that is, for the mere error of his thought, if an error it be— the mere mistake of the mind, made by God himself liable to be mistaken; what chance, what hope, what dream of salvation, could exist for the believer? The chance of salvation is a chance not worth having; it is a madman's dream. It is a hope but as of a man who is to be hanged. It is a gallows hope: "For if the righteous scarcely be saved, where shall the ungodly and the sinner appear?"

But let not the sinner be cheated by the belief that belief will keep him safe from any denunciation threatened against unbelief. His very belief itself is *founded* upon unbelief. He cannot maintain his notion of being accountable to God, and that he shall exist in a future state, without flying in the face of his own Bible, making it a nose of wax, twisting it to his own conceit, taking the part he likes, and in the sense he likes it, but rejecting what likes not him. (Does the Infidel do more than this?) Does his brain-sick vanity lead him to think that he is of so much consequence, that his every thought, word and deed is registered in Heaven, and that an accusing angel flits up to Heaven's chancery to insult the majesty of God, with an account how a beggar's callet stole a cabbage-net?

And doth he not, by that very vanity, as much trample upon the word of God as ever did an Infidel, where that word hath said, "Is it any pleasure to the Almighty that thou art righteous? Or is it a gain to him that thou makes thy way perfect" (Job xxii. 3). "And if thou sinnest, what dost thou unto him? or, if thy transgressions be multiplied, what dost thou into him?" (Job xxxv. 6).

Dreams the cracked fool of his superiority to the brute creation, and that when he dies there shall be not as sheer and final an end of him as of them? And is he not himself an Infidel and an unbeliever in that very text of God's words, which saith, and which hath the testimony of his own reason, and of his own senses, and of all nature, and the experience of all time, and of all places, and of all men in all the world, in attestation of what it saith? "That which befalleth the sons of men, befalleth beasts; even one thing befalleth them. As the one dieth, so dieth the other: yea, they have all one breath; so that a man hath no pre-eminence about a beast: all go unto one place: all are of the dust: and all turn to dust again" (Ecclesiastes iii. 12).

Well, then, Sirs! What comes of their appeal to reason, as to belief being the safe side? What comes of their appeal to scripture, as to belief being the safe side? Their ground fails them on every side.

In what, then, originated the mighty hue and cry against unbelief, and the exceeding bitterness of the saints against the unbelievers? How comes the free exercise of our thoughts, which should be as free as air, and our free speech as free as our free thoughts, to be so grievous to the clergy, from the proud prelate who swells in the throne of a cathedral to the ragamuffin that sweeps the hayloft of God a'mighty's second wife, Mother Soapsuds, and her little Shiloh? It spoils their trade: it crosses the paths of their ambition.

Should men become unbelievers, and act and reason like men,

Othello's occupation's gone!

The craft, Sirs, the most gainful craft going—the craftiest of all crafts, would be in danger: the craft that makes men fools to make them slaves, and promises them a heaven of happiness to reconcile them to a world of misery. All the tricks of all the religion that ever was in the world, on the part of those who have not themselves been the dupes and tools of others, have never been aught else than a scheming, greedy, grasping at unrighteous gain, and a tyrannous usurpation of an undue influence over the minds that could be easily cajoled and terrified.

The whole argument, then, of terror and danger, which the priests denounce against unbelievers, is the danger and terror to themselves. Their "He that believeth not shall be damned," when interpreted to its real meaning, means no more than damn them that don't deal at our shop.

And, as you value real happiness, and solid, substantial peace of mind, don't go to their shops, avoid them as you would a pestilence. In infidelity, in unbelief (let me not be misunderstood), in that entire scorn, that total rejection, contempt and hatred of the gospel, which is my pride and boast to exhibit to the world, you will enjoy a reality of safety which the dupes of faith do not dream of. You will be safe from those imaginary terrors that alarm the guilty mind: you will be safe from those chimerical dreams of a kingdom of heaven, like unto a grain of mustard seed, that you must get through a needle's eye first,—the straight gate, the narrow way, of which you have to be sure the blessed assurance, that if you should seek to enter in you should not be able. You will be safe from those bad feelings and angry passions which you see dim the faces of religious people. You will be safe from that bad heart, and remorseless and vindictive temper, by which alone a man could bear to believe in such accursed trash as all false religion is. By rejecting religion altogether, you will save yourselves from that liability to madness, and that crackiness and confusion about the brains, which you see with your own eyes, that all religious people are so peculiarly subject to. I speak this upon my right to have an opinion upon this subject, as being, as I am, a member of the Royal College of Surgeons, and having made the structure and philosophy of the human brain matter of my particular study. I speak what I do know, and testify what I have seen. Religion is the poison of the brain: by rejecting religion altogether, you will be safe from all cares and anxieties, but for your well-being and well-doing in life; and in death, without a fear, without a doubt, without a wish, will resign your being into the hands of the good and gracious Father of us all. In a word, to be an Infidel is to be on the safe side; to be an Infidel is the highest style, the noblest privilege, this greatest happiness of man. Let me die the death of an Infidel, and let my last end be like this. And *down,* I say, DOWN WITH PRIESTCRAFT.

The Question of Method
as Affecting Religious Thought

Anonymous

This work, purportedly written by "A Clergyman of the Church of England," is truly anonymous. All attempts to identify the author have failed. This much is known: the work was published in 1873 by Thomas Scott, a British freethought publisher. Scott was responsible for the publication of about 150 pamphlets of varying lengths, all written from a freethought perspective. Almost all of Scott's publications were original, written specifically for him, and a few were first time English translations. Many of the publications were written by clergymen, both former and current, a number of whom were willing to have their names attached, though many were not. The present pamphlet was one of the latter. It has never before been reprinted, and was extremely difficult to find, since there are almost no extant sets of the Scott pamphlets in libraries.

Whence comes the possibility of that strange fact,—strange indeed, yet in the present day by no means unfrequent,—that men having like opportunities and abilities come to utterly diverse conclusions on religious subjects? You may note, say for example, two brothers, each possessed of unusual talents, starting from the same early training, each animated by a pure zeal for truth, one of whom, through whatever wanderings, holds fast at least by the great doctrines of Christianity, while the other leaves all orthodox belief far behind him. For—wonder at the fact if you will—we are constrained to admit that men do doubt and disbelieve every Christian dogma, who, whatever judgment may hereafter be passsed upon them, live, so far as human eye can see, not less pure or upright lives than the most strenuous upholders of the faith. How can these things be? How can two men, both sane and sound, affirm of the same fountain, the one that its waters are sweet, the other that they are bitter? Christianity is true or it is false. That is to say, those occurrences on which all orthodox bodies found their religion have historically happened or they have not. The issue is a simple one, and one might suppose that honest men who wished for nothing but the truth would have little difficulty in arriving at a similar conclusion one way or other. Yet we find that men apparently possessed of honesty, ability and learning, hold contrary opinions on the subject. The object of the present paper is to point out the broad beaten road which leads to orthodoxy, and also the narrow thorny path which ends in unbelief.

Now if in studying the same subject inquirers arrive at opposite conclusions, either they must start from different premises, or they must adopt a different method of inquiry. Obviously, starting from different premises is a fruitful source of difference in religious as in other matters. Thus in disputes between a Christian and an unbeliever the former will often base his arguments upon biblical texts, forgetting that the other will by no means accept them as conclusive. The one starts from the premise that the Bible affords an infallible source of information, the truth of which the other denies. Such an argument often ends in mere bitterness, as the parties do not see that there is no common ground between them on which the argument may rest. Or if they consent to go deeper, and discuss the proposition which to one side formed the premise of the previous argument, yet again they fail to find common ground, and therefore to appear reasonable to each other. Now the source of the difference must surely be this, that they approach the subject in a different spirit: each adopts a different method of inquiry. I believe the most common method used by the orthodox party is that of assuming some one point,—as the authority of the Church, or of the Bible—and then arguing from that. This method, however, labors under the disadvantage mentioned above. However satisfactory it may be to the individual who accepts it, it cannot enable him to convince unbelievers. Such a method may even to some extent be open to the charge brought against it by uncivil persons of being a *petitio principii.*

To those who endeavor to go to the root of the matter, there are, as far as I can see, but two methods which they can use as instruments of thought, between which they must take their choice. I shall call these *the emotional method* and *the critical method.*

These may be briefly characterized as follows:

The former method accepts an explanation simply as satisfactory to the mind: it does not seek to compare or test further: it rests on intimate conviction. The critical method, on the contrary, mistrusts every hypothesis until verified; if an explanation seems probable in itself, it is not allowed to rest there: it is brought face to face with other facts and theories, and questioned as to its agreement with them; it is, in short, tested in every conceivable way, and not accepted unless it can endure the trial. The critical method is based on verification.

I shall now endeavor to show that while the latter method has its value—perhaps is the only one of any value—in scientific inquiries, the emotional method alone can lead to orthodox results in religious investigations.

In ancient times the critical method was almost or quite unknown. Whatever men wished to explain, from the genesis of the earth and the human race to the derivation of a word, was explained out of hand, and evolved with child-like confidence out of the mind of the explainer. When Pindar told of the birth of Ajax (Aias), he derived the name from αἰετος (aietos) an eagle. It was enough for him that the first two letters corresponded in each word, and that the explanation seemed to him a probable one. When Eve bared her first-born she called him Cain, and said I have gotten (from the verb *kanah,* to get) a man. There was a sufficient resemblance between Kain and kanah; although, according to the critical method, Cain would seem to have been a smith (ֵ֑ן) by name, although not in trade, and Cain's sons were smiths. These two examples will suffice to show the principle on which names were anciently derived. But a similar method was employed in other and more important matters. In order to illustrate this, perhaps the reader will allow me to tell him a story out of Philo. An animal is placed on the list of those allowed to be eaten in Leviticus xi. 22, which our translators, for some mysterious reason, call "beetle," and which the Septuagint version as unaccountably renders ophiomachus, serpent-fighter. Now Philo had already proved to his satisfaction that the Serpent which tempted Eve was *pleasure.* Therefore the reason why this ophiomachus was recommended for the Jewish table was plain. "For," says he, "this ophiomachus seems to be nothing else than *temperance* symbolically, which wages endless war against intemperance and pleasure." I was charmed when I read this passage, for nothing could more evidently set forth the advantages of the emotional method. See how beautifully the old worthy works it out! The δφιομάχης, which he lit on in his Septuagint, fitted into the theory he was constructing, just like a long-sought, queer-cornered bit in a child's puzzle-map. Then what "uses," what edification, proceed from this interpretation? What earthly meaning could there be in bidding the Hebrews eat a particular sort of locust? But when you understand how the locust represents asceticism, what light and interest is shed on the Mosaic command! And to think that Philo and we should have lost all this had he only been cursed with the very smallest tincture of the critical method! Had he had any notion of verifying his facts, he would have compared the Septuagint with the Hebrew version, and thus have found that the name of the creature in the original langauge has nothing to do with serpents, but means simply *a leaper* (chargol), and so his theory would have fallen to pieces at once. Fortunately he was secure in the strength of his method; the inward satisfaction which he felt was ample proof of the correctness of his position; and as the Septuagint version suited him, why should he go further to seek another which might not suit so well? It would be easy to multiply instances of the use of the emotional method from the writings of authors of all ages; but I forbear to quote further from uninspired writers. To do so would seem to be the more unnecessary, inasmuch as this method, and no other, was employed by the writers of the Books contained in the New Testament.

If this be shown, it will be obvious that those who wish to hold to the faith which those holy men promulgated must walk in their steps and use their method. If we attempt to use the critical method in the exegesis of the Bible, we commence by placing ourselves at a point of view utterly different from that at which its authors contemplated their subject; and shall therefore understand it in a sense alien from theirs. It is by so doing that so many writers and others, whose learning and honesty of purpose are beyond all question, have changed that which Christians hold to be the Word of God into a collection of more or less curious myths. When the New Testament writers found a passage of the Hebrew Scriptures which seemed to them to bear upon the life of Christ, they assumed at once that it was in its origin prophetic of him. For example, Matthew remembers the words of Hosea, "Out of Egypt have I called my Son." The critical inquirer remembers that the prophet was alluding to the Exodus of Israel. To the Evangelist it is sufficient that these words, taken apart from their context, serve to illustrate his narrative. So little did the Evangelists and Apostles care for such accuracy as is required by the critical method, that their quotations from the older Scriptures are often distortions of the words and meaning of the originals, at least as these latter have come down to us. I am not now writing a treatise on prophecy, and it will be sufficient to request the reader who may doubt the assertion to compare the quotations in the New Testament with the prophecies themselves; he will often be able to detect the distortion, even if he has no knowledge of the original languages. I may observe here that what has been said holds true of the doctrine of Types. What critical inquirer could ever believe that the narratives of the brazen serpent, of David, Jonah, etc., have any reference to Christ? These stories are complete in themselves as they stand in the Old Testament, and do not require any further fulfillment. He alone who proceeds always on the emotional method can perceive that the fact that an older narrative may profitably be employed to illustrate the life of Christ, justifies the assumption that it was intended to do so. So impressed, however, were the Apostolic writers with the truth of this doctrine, that they seemed to have considered the Hebrew Scriptures as of little importance for any other purpose. Thus Paul cares only for the story of Isaac and Ishmael in so far as they typify the Christian and Jewish churches, and for that of the passage of the Red Sea as exemplifying the doctrine of Baptism. When he reads the words, "To Abraham and his seed were the promises made," he does not understand "seed" to refer to the descendants of the patriarch, as any critical student would, but he insists upon applying it to Christ. Indeed, Paul is perhaps the most consistent of all the New Testament writers in his exclusion of the critical spirit. So much so, that he rests entirely on his emotional convictions. He is far indeed from comparing critically the accounts of the Resurrection. He will not confer with flesh and blood. He rejects all knowledge of Christ "after the flesh;" his inner belief, apart from all comparison with the convictions of others, or verification from external facts, is sufficient for him.

It is impossible within the limits of the present paper to do more than illustrate the position here taken up by a few examples. But I feel no doubt that any candid person who will consider those here brought forward, and himself search the Scriptures for others, will be convinced that the writers of the books composing our Bible had not the very slightest idea of the critical method, and would, could they have understood it, have condemned it as unsuited to their purposes. If this be so, let those who would continue to think as the evangelists and prophets thought, beware how they tamper with a method so alien from their spirit.

At the risk of being tedious I must adduce another example of the danger of deserting the emotional method. Many such suggest themselves; indeed the adoption of the opposite method breaks up the Bible in all directions, and leaves, in place of one homogeneous infallible book, a collection of tales, most of them of little historical value. I cannot, however, go into this subject any further at present. The one instance which follows may be sufficient to serve as a caution to those who wish to stand in the paths of orthodoxy in these slippery days.

The apparent contradictions in the Gospel narratives have driven our orthodox commentators into great straits, except when they have got over a difficulty by omitting to notice it. They would, however, find no difficulty at all if they had sufficient faith in the emotional method, and forebore the attempt to wield the weapons of their adversaries.

They need not fear lest they should fail to be secure against doubts and disputations if they will be careful to avoid the critical method. When the critical inquirer compares the different narratives of the life of Christ, he finds, among other points of a similar nature, that Jesus is said to have ascended to heaven both from Bethany and also from a mountain in Galilee. According to Matthew,—who is so far confirmed by the narrative which closes the second Gospel as we have it,—the disciples met the risen Christ by appointment in Galilee. There Mark further informs us that the Ascension took place, they having first been charged to go at once (as it appears) and teach all nations. In Luke, on the contrary, the Eleven do not quit the immediate neighborhood of Jerusalem; nay, they are expressly charged not to do so until they should be "endued with power from on high." This account agrees with that given in Acts, while John does not mention the Ascension at all. Here we see plainly the effect of the comparing or critical method. To one who adopts it, it seems impossible that the disciples could both have remained at Jerusalem for a considerable time, and also during part of that very time have been in Galilee; nor less so that one and the same Ascension should have taken place at Bethany and on a far distant mountain. The emotionalist, on the other hand, feels no difficulty. To compare the different and differing accounts in a critical spirit would be foreign to his nature. Each several account satisfies and edifies him, and he cares for nothing more. Should such an one be pressed to the point by an unbeliever, he might reply that the sojourn of the disciples at Jerusalem is to be understood in a spiritual sense. They were commanded to tarry at Jerusalem, that is, not to break with the Jews and Jewish customs, until the descent of the Holy Ghost. For the double site assigned to the Ascension I have indeed no explanation to suggest; yet I am confident that the holy ingenuity of a second Philo—who would care nothing for historic truth and everything for spiritual edification—would explain this also as triumphantly as the first turned the leaping locust into a slayer of allegorical serpents.

If the reader has done me the honor to follow my arguments up to this point, it is ten chances to one that he feels somewhat disposed to quarrel with my position.

It is likely enough that he will ask whether the critical method be not that by which all scientific discoveries have been made, and all our knowledge of historic truth obtained; whether, if that be so, it be not the right method to use in that inquiry which is of all others most important; and whether in fact many eminent writers on religious subjects have not used that method and no other. To the last question I reply, that I am not acquainted with the works of any theologian who has successfully used the critical method and at the same time kept within the confines of orthodoxy; nor can I conceive it possible that there should be such. There are, indeed, orthodox writers who use with more or less success the critical method throughout the bulk of their work; but, so far as I know, they always start with one or more assumptions which are arrived at by the emotional, not the critical method. They assume the authority of the Bible or of the Church; the necessity of a Divine revelation, and of its miraculous character; the authenticity of the sacred writings on which they rely; and other such points. Having made these assumptions, or some of them, they may proceed to deduce their conclusions from them by the critical method. But the propositions on which their whole subsequent reasoning is based are assumed, not as critically demonstrated, but as appearing natural and necessary to the mind of the writer. The superstructure may be critical, but the foundation is emotional; and it is from the latter, not the former, that the entire work must take its distinguishing character.

With regard to the other question, viz., whether the critical method be not the better, and therefore the right one to employ, it should be considered that either method is an instrument for aiding us to attain certain ends. We must choose the one best fitted for our purpose. The critical method is an admirable instrument for enabling us to ascertain truth of fact. If we wish to acquaint ourselves with the probability of a reported occurrence having really taken place or otherwise, with no care whether we are led to the affirmative or the negative conclusion, the critical method will serve our turn. But—I am addressing myself to those who are predetermined to preserve their orthodox faith—is this desired? The critical method is very exacting. If we adopt it we must take nothing for granted: we must not say I will believe this because it satisfies my emotional needs; or because it is so conducive to public morality and the peace of the individual mind. This method binds us to the pursuit of truth pure and simple, uninfluenced by any preconceived wish as to the result. The emotional method, on the contrary, allows a man's feelings to determine his belief. If we adopt it we shall never need to trouble ourselves with disagreeable questions, such as, Do we know when and by whom the Gospels were written? Do they or do they not contain numerous contradictory statements? Are the accounts therein given of the doings and sayings of Christ in all cases to be relied upon as matters of historical certainty? and the like. These and many such beset the path of the critical inquirer like importunate beggars, who will not be shaken off until they have their answer. He whose first object is to continue steadfast in his religious belief should refuse altogether to enter upon such inquiries. To deal with them candidly implies a wish to know the truth rather than to continue orthodox; and such a wish, if acted on, is apt to be fatal to orthodoxy. The importance of inquiry after truth in religious matters has been much overstated. An orthodox believer should never inquire after truth; he should assume that he has it. The word *truth* is indeed occasionally used in the Bible, yet always in a sense widely different from that in which it is used by the modern critic. Thus the Apostle says: "We can do nothing against the truth, but for the truth;" but by *truth* he means his own system of religious belief, the truth of which he assumes, and which indeed is the only truth for which he cares. So, again, Christians are bidden "search the Scriptures." But it is implied, as I have attempted to show, that they are to use a method of search,—a mode of interpretation,— which certainly would not lead to such truth as is sought by the man of science or modern historian.

I say again, let your wish to know truth always stand second to your desire to continue orthodox; otherwise there is much danger that your truth will not be that of the Church or of the Bible. Should anyone say in reply to this: "What is orthodoxy to me? I desire to know whether or not the religion I have been taught to profess be really founded on fact. If it be so, it will stand the severest testing by the most rigorous method; if not, I will none of it:" to such an one the arguments used in this paper are not addressed. Let him go on his way, if he is sure he has strength to follow it out: taking however this warning with him. I have known those who have acted as he proposes to act; who, starting with a more or less orthodox belief, have insisted on subjecting it to the critical method without fear or favor. The consequence has been that they have found themselves in the end stripped of most of those garments with which their earliest instructors had invested their minds, and, in some cases, with their worldly prospects blasted. Let him then count the cost first, lest having begun he should not dare to finish.

I turn for a concluding word to those who prize their religious faith above all things: who know that it brings them peace, comfort, and worldly prosperity; and are not to be ousted from these solid advantages by a sneer about honesty. Let such be careful to abide by the emotional method, to take the satisfaction which religion and religious books bring to their minds as the surest—the only—basis of their belief. The men of science have with their critical method "turned the world upside down" as effectually as did the Apostles of old. Beware then how you allow yourselves to inquire on their method into the truth of sacred narratives. Consider that faith is not as robust as it was; it now needs hot-house treatment: it must be glazed, and warmed artificially, and kept from rude scientific contact. Guard it from critical thought as you do your exotic plants from frost. Consider, a few degrees of cold will consign it to a grave from which no coming spring can summon it to resurrection.

Pascal's Wager

Alfred W. Benn

Alfred William Benn was a prolific British historian who specialized in the history of ancient Greece. Benn was born in Ireland in 1843. He obtained his Bachelor of Arts degree at the University of London, and then left England for an extended period to live abroad. Most of his life was spent in Italy and Switzerland. Benn wrote many volumes on ancient Greek history and philosophy. At the same time, he was the author of *The History of English Rationalism in the Nineteenth Century* (2 volumes), a work that fills an essential gap in the literature. Perhaps this represented Benn's own philosophic position, since it is so far unrelated to his other writings. Additional clues can be found in his intellectual autobiography, *Revaluations: Historical and Ideal*. Benn died in Italy in 1916.

The present selection comes from *Revaluations*, which was published by Watts & Co. in London in 1909. The book has never been reissued.

A certain rustic moralist in Mr. Thomas Hardy's *Far from the Madding Crowd* gives his opinion about the relative chances of salvation contingent on attending church or chapel in the following homely but telling terms:—

"We know very well that if anybody goes to heaven they [chapel-folk] will. They've worked hard for it and they deserve to have it, such as 'tis. I'm not such a fool as to pretend that we who stick to the church have the same chance as they, because we know we have not. But I hate a feller who'll change his old ancient doctrine for the sake of getting to heaven."

So far the excellent Coggan, for such is the name of Mr. Hardy's pothouse philosopher. Whether churchmen or dissenters should be credited with the better chance of salvation is a deep question in which I do not propose to enter. The Conformist and the Nonconformist conscience may safely be left to take care of themselves. But the ingenuous confidences of this particular churchman suggest a problem of wider interest on which I propose to offer a few remarks. Is there any method of salvation that may be called distinctly mean? I believe there is at least one such, and I am sorry to say that it is a method recommended by no less an authority than Pascal.

What the French call *"le pari de Pascal"*—in English, Pascal's wager or bet—forms the theme of one of the most celebrated passages in his fragmentary defense of Christianity, published after his death and universally known as the *Pensées.* . . .

It runs as follows. Speaking by the light of nature, says Pascal, God, supposing him to exist, must be out of relation to ourselves. Being without parts or limits, he is infinitely incomprehensible. We can neither know what he is, nor even that he is. This admission goes beyond that form of modern Agnosticism according to which we can say with certainty that the Unknowable exists, but not what it is. And, of course, it goes very far beyond Herbert Spencer's affirmation of an Unknowable which is infinite, eternal, an energy, and the cause of all things. But we are not to take so skeptical a confession as defining Pascal's own position. Being a Christian, he has other sources of information than the light of nature. His supposed skeptic—who turns out to be a very real skeptic with a place in French literary history—has none. But the skeptic's ignorance cuts both ways. It leaves the nonexistence of God as uncertain as his existence. Reason supplies no means of choosing between the two alternative possibilities. Nevertheless, we are obliged to back one side or the other, to play at a game of hazard in which, at an infinite distance, heads or tails will turn up. "But," answers the skeptic, "I do not want to play at all; in such a doubtful case as what you describe prudence bids us abstain." To which Pascal replies: "You must bet; you are in for it; it does not depend on your will." For as his . . . editors put it, in an elucidatory addition to the text, "Not to bet is to bet for the nonexistence of God." . . .

Why must I bet? No reason whatever is given, but it needs only a very slight acquaintance with the dogmatic Christianity of Pascal's time to supply what he leaves unsaid. To be saved man must believe positively in the existence of God; to leave it an open question is to incur the same penalty as complete atheism—that is, eternal damnation.

Here we come at once on a flagrant self-contradiction, which, even if it stood alone, would leave the skeptic triumphant. Pascal began by saying that God, as infinite, is unrelated to us. But, if so, he can neither save nor damn us: our future fate has nothing to do with his existence or non-existence, still less with our opinion or absence of opinion on the subject.

I do not profess to know much about the turf; but I strongly suspect that anyone who had such loose notions as Pascal about the laws of betting, if he acted on them, would soon be cleared out of every penny he possessed—that is, supposing his ignorance to be real; while, if it were assumed for the purpose of eluding payment, he would before long find himself turned off every race-course in England.

However, we will let that pass. We will suppose that the words "out of relation" slipped in by an unfortunate oversight, and would have been deleted had the author lived to see his work through the press; noting, however, that they were allowed to stand. . . . Let it be granted as not impossible that the infinite Being, if he exist, is no other than the God of Catholicism. But there is a long way from possibility to certainty, and Pascal himself has warned us that the knowledge, if any, of God's existence is quite distinct from the knowledge of his attributes. Assuming there to be a God, that bare fact leaves us in absolute ignorance about his character. Now it might fairly be contended that the number of different characters which may possibly be ascribed to an infinite being is infinite, and even infinite in the second degree on account of the possible permutations and combinations of attributes. Accordingly, the conditions of the wager must be altered. Pascal has appealed to the light of reason, and to reason he must go. Apart from objective evidence, of which there is at present no question, the chances against his theology's being true are at least infinity to one.

It is, however, on the cards that Pascal, admitting so much, might still maintain that a man of sense was justified in staking his life on the existence of God. In order to make this clear we must examine the conditions of the wager.

"If you win," he tells us, "you win everything; if you lose, you lose nothing." In the more concrete language of religious belief, if there is a God and you have faith in his promises you gain everlasting felicity; if there is no God, death ends all. It is not precisely explained what is meant by staking your life; but, as Pascal is addressing himself to a careless worldling, he must be supposed to mean what such a person would call "life"—that is to say, an existence, of sensual and social enjoyment. The author of the *Thoughts* would not admit that the abandonment of such a life involved any real sacrifice; and so far the serious moralist of any religion or of no religion would not be disposed to quarrel with him. But in fact, as we shall see presently, there is much more involved—certainly more than the sage who finds life "very tolerable without its amusements" is prepared to give up.

Of course no Christian, and Pascal less than another, believes that eternal felicity can be won as the fruit of such a cold-blooded calculation, such brutal cynicism, to use M. Sully Prudhomme's blunt phrase, as would seem to be implied by the aleatory proceeding recommended. Simply as a bet it would, to the Searcher of all hearts, be no more than the celebrated short prayer, "O God, if there be a God, save my soul, if I have a soul!" In fact, it is only the first step towards acquiring a genuine conviction. And Pascal does not leave us in doubt about the second step. His skeptic is made to reply: "I fully acknowledge the force of your reasoning. But is there no way of seeing the faces of the cards?" "Yes, there are the Scriptures, *etc.*" "But what if I am so constituted that I cannot believe?" "Do what others in your position have done before. Act as if you believed; take holy water, attend Mass, *etc.* The natural effect of all that will be to make you believe, and to stupify you." "But that is just what I am afraid of." "Why so? What have you to lose?"

I do not think that such a method would commend itself to the ingenuous mind of Mr. Hardy's rustic. I fear Coggan would "hate a feller" who submitted to such a degradation "for the sake of getting to heaven." Even the editors were ashamed to print this precious advice, softening it down into a harmless recommendation to imitate the conduct of believers. Victor Cousin was the first to publish the words as they were originally written. That brilliant rhetorician was neither a deep nor a sincere thinker; but he still retained some respect for truth and reason. He asked, Was that, then, the last word of human wisdom, and can we only approach the supreme Intelligence by the sacrifice of our own? But nowadays, among orthodox Frenchmen, Victor Cousin would pass for a dangerous character—an "intellectual." . . .

Besides a natural if sinful objection to part with his reason, the skeptic has still a difficulty. The hope of salvation is all very well, but against the happiness it gives we have to set the fear of hell. To which Pascal replies, sensibly enough from his point of view: Which has more reason to fear it, he who remains in ignorance if there be a hell, with the certainty of being damned if there is one, or he who is certainly persuaded of its existence, with the hope of being saved if it does exist?

This is a very important passage. Both Ernest Havet, in his notes to the *Pensées,* and M. Sully Prudhomme, in his essay on the wager, have assumed, as not needing discussion, that backing the wrong side involves not only the loss of eternal felicity, but also the positive payment of an infinite penalty under the form of everlasting torment. A more recent critic, however, repudiates their interpretation. The eminent philosopher M. Lachelier . . . declares peremptorily that hell has no place in the wager. As the terms are first stated it certainly is not mentioned; but to insist on the omission seems more like a lawyer than a philosopher. And even from the strictly legal point of view M. Lachelier's contention seems unjustifiable. In drawing out the full significance of the wager we have a right to interpret its conditions in the light of its author's known and unconcealed opinions about the future fate of unbelievers. To say that I am obliged to bet must mean that my refusal would entail the same consequences as if I betted against God's existence and lost. And that must be more than the mere privation of eternal felicity, for so much the skeptic is already prepared to face with equanimity. Besides, when he asks to see the faces of the cards played Pascal refers him to Scripture for information; and we know that in the eyes of a seventeenth-century Catholic, Scripture consigns the infidel to eternal torment.

One is almost ashamed to labor so obvious a point. But it is a question of some interest why the chance of damnation is left to be inferred when it might have been made to figure with such tremendous effect in the wager as originally stated. I apprehend that the reason is one of simple politeness. Pascal was a gentleman; and the skeptic for whose benefit he started the whole idea of making the supreme verities a subject of betting was also a gentleman and a dear friend of his, the Chevalier de Méré, a man of the worl, and apparently, like others of the kind, a gamester. That is why Pascal addresses him in terms borrowed from the favorite amusement of his class; and that is also, I suggest, why he spares him words not suited to polite ears. Both, however, understand perfectly what the truth of the Catholic theory would imply. A losing bettor not only misses infinite happiness, but has to pay the stakes by suffering infinite misery. And with great tact the first reference to this unpleasant aspect of the wager is put into the mouth, not of the Christian advocate, but of the hesitating skeptic. Méré, not Pascal, is made responsible for introducing it into the discussion. To convince ourselves that the softening down of the risk incurred by infidelity is a mere concession to the rules of personal politeness, we need only turn to the passages where Pascal has to deal with mankind in general. Here the loss of felicity is not mentioned as a motive for belief. With his usual and incomparable splendor of rhetoric, he describes death as infallibly destined to place the impious and indifferent under the horrible necessity of submitting either to eternal annihilation or to eternal misery, without knowing which of these eternities has been prepared for them for ever. And this alternative, such as it is, must not be thought of as existing objectively in the nature of things, or rather in the unknown purposes of Providence, but subjectively in the reasonable apprehensions of the doubter.

Judged by Jesuit or modern Ultramontane standards, the author of the *Provinciales* and the *Pensées* may have been a heretic. But he was far too good a Catholic to entertain for a moment the idea that hell could mean annihilation. He speaks *ad hominem*. If you are right in your unbelief, you will cease to exist at death; if you are wrong, you will certainly be tormented for ever.

So much being established, let us return to the wager and its implications. It was presented under the form of an even chance, with nothing to lose (except one's reason) on the one event, and everything to gain on the other. One is struck by the suspicious resemblance to a plea sometimes advanced for trying a quack remedy. It may do good, and it can't do harm. Now, in the case of a drug about which we know nothing—for the modesty of that "may do good" is really a confession of complete ignorance—the possibility of harm is precisely measured by the possibility of benefit. For us the chances are equal, because neither event is anything more than a chance. And an attentive examination shows that Pascal's reasoning suffers from the same fatal flaw.

From respect for so great a name two enormous assumptions have been let pass. We withdrew our objection to the logical impossibility that a Being out of all relation to man can affect man's future fate. And we accepted as an even chance the infinitesimally small probability that an infinite personality, supposing it to exist, has exactly the character of the God in whom Jansenist Catholics believed. But our concessions must end here. What security has Méré that in accepting the wager he sacrifices no more than his reason and the healthy enjoyment of life? "You have," says his friend, "the word of God." Is that so certain? or is it a sufficient guarantee? It will not do to call the question blasphemous, for our moralist has imbued us with the idea that truth is a matter of geography, and we know what the Nicene Creed would be called across the Straits of Gibraltar.

Here we have the nemesis of agnosticism as a method of faith. A universal solvent is created and then poured into some consecrated chalice in the ingenuous expectation that the holy vessel will resist its corrosive action. In a series of brilliant aphorisms congealing the loose and lazy skepticisms of Montaigne into a hailstorm of diamond-pointed epigrams, Pascal had denounced the supposed eternal laws of human morality as a set of arbitrary expedients, varying from country to country, and merely intended to win respect for the authority of their princes. From such a discordant medley of customs no fixed moral standard or natural system of ethics can be elicited. Still less can our ideas of what is right and good be applied to the criticism of God's ways with man. Anterior to revelation we cannot predicate morality, more than any other attribute, of the infinite Being; nor can a self-revealing Deity be expected to act in conformity with human notions of right and wrong when those notions are not comfortable with one another.

Pascal accepts the consequences of his skeptical theology with cynical candor. "What," he exclaims, "can be more opposed to our wretched rules of justice than the eternal damnation of a child without any will of its own for a sin in which it seems to have had so little share that it was committed six thousand years before the said child came into existence?" In fact, moral distinctions are created by God; and "the sole reason why sins are sins is that they are contrary to his will." Were the whole human race to be eternally damned, God would stand acquitted of injustice.

Nevertheless, with an inconsistency not uncommon among skeptics, Pascal recognizes one kind of moral obligation as universally binding, so much so as even to impose itself on God in his relations to man. And that is the obligation of keeping a promise. It is mentioned quite naively as a self-evident truth, valid apparently on both sides of the Pyrenees. "There is a reciprocal duty between God and man . . . God is bound to fulfill his promises." If we have backed the winning card, the stakes will be honestly paid.

I know not what answer the Chevalier de Méré made to the aleatory apologetics of his illustrious friend; but his conversion was delayed so long as probably to have been effected by considerations of a different order. He might well have required a better security for the divine fidelity than Pascal's guarantee. It seems rather rash to infer that, because a gentleman keeps his word and pays his debts of honor, the Jansenist God will. A Being who is wholly unaccountable may mean something different from what he says, or the exact opposite, or nothing at all. An irresponsible despot is generally not less remarkable for perfidy than for cruelty. He who predestines little children to eternal damnation may quite possibly be reserving the Sisters . . . for the same fate. We were told that the whole human race might justly be sent to hell, and how do we know that the full divine right may not after all be exercised. . . .

What is more, Pascal's interpretation of Scripture goes to prove that deceit and treachery are among the revealed attributes of his God. A particularly nauseous quality of that personage is that, not content with exercising his undoubted privilege of damning human beings at sight, he tries to manufacture a colorable pretext for their condemnation by introducing difficulties into the Bible. "There is obscurity enough to blind the reprobate, and clearness enough to make them inexcusable." "Do you suppose that the prophecies quoted in the New Testament are mentioned to make you believe? No, it is to prevent you from believing." The whole Jewish people were purposely blinded to the real meaning of the Messianic prophecies in order that their rejection of Jesus Christ might render then unsuspected witnesses to the authenticity of the evidentiary documents committed to their charge. Had they accepted the gospel, it might have been said that they had forged the predictions by which its supernatural origin is attested, and of whose antiquity is the sole guarantee. . . .

Our only knowledge of God, our only proof that there is a God, comes through the Messianic prophecies of the Old Testament and their fulfillment in Jesus Christ. But it is of the very essence of these prophecies to be ambiguous and misleading. We asked to be shown the cards with which that awful game for our soul's salvation is being played "at an infinite distance," and our wish has been gratified: the cards are no other than the pages of Scripture. And now we learn that their color and value depend entirely on the inscrutable will of the dealer. He can call black red and a king a knave. He can change trumps at pleasure and count an ace as eleven points or as one. That is how his antitype, Napoleon, played chess, moving the pieces just as he liked, regardless of rules. Our Ariel-souled thinker constructs a God meaner if not more malignant than the Setebos of Caliban, in that wonderful study of

Robert Browning's which is also such a scathing satire on the creed of his youth. Granting that such a person exists, our conduct cannot be affected one way or the other by the fact. Being unable to take his word for anything, we are exactly in the same position as if he had never spoken. Perhaps after all he is less amenable to the charms of adulation and submission than his more abject adorers would have us believe. Our moral superiority over him may at last make its ascendancy felt. Possibly in that case his first impulse would be to wreak vengeance on the reptile souls who sought to stupefy their reason by the copious use of masses and holy water. Then we who never stooped to that degradation will intercede with the converted Moloch for the shivering wretches, who may escape with no worse penalty than transmigration into the bodies of apes.

Briefly, then, the existence of an infinite Being out of relation to ourselves cannot possibly influence our future fate. . . . Assuming such a deity to exist, the chances are precisely equal that he will or that he will not behave towards us in any particular manner. Therefore, so far as theology goes, Méré is rationally justified in adopting the line of conduct that seems most agreeable to his own desires. When the door of death opens it is even betting whether the lady or the tiger will receive him.

Metaphor apart, no revelation can be of any practical value unless it is assumed to come from a person whose word we can trust. But the veracity of God is only guaranteed by his general moral perfection, and such perfection can only be conceived as the consummation of human goodness. But goodness includes justice as known to us by earthly examples, and these, according to Pascal himself, forbid us to believe that innocent little children can merit eternal torments—or, we may add, that Méré could merit them for honestly using his reason to find out the truth, or even the judges of Galileo for suppressing it. In theology the method of Descartes is a surer guide than the method of Montaigne.

The idea of accepting Christianity (understood in an orthodox sense) as a probability which seems safer to believe than to disbelieve has been traced back to Arnobius, from whom Pascal is supposed to have derived it through Raymond Sebond, whose *Natural Theology* he had certainly read. But the after fortunes of the argument are more interesting than its origin. It had the singular good fortune to be taken up by Butler and made the very keynote of his *Analogy,* whence it passed to the leaders of the Tractarian Movement, betraying its inherent weakness by the conflicting interpretations respectively put on it by Newman and Keble.

I do not know whether Butler had or had not read Pascal; but his theory of probability as applied to the evidences of Christianity is a distinct improvement on the wager, in so far as it encourages instead of abolishing the use of reason. On the other hand, his appeal to the most degrading of all "pragmatic" motives is considerably more explicit, and will hardly be denied even by the most unscrupulous of apologists. After detailing the arguments for revealed religion based on the performance of miracles and the fulfillment of prophecy, he shows an uneasy consciousness of their insufficiency, but urges as a make-weight that "a mistake on the one side may be, in its consequences, much more dangerous than a mistake on the other." Butler alleges, it is true, that he gives this ominous warning, not to influence the judgment, but the practice, of his readers. The distinction, however, is not easy to grasp, nor is any attempt made to illustrate it. If his sole object was to strengthen the motives for virtuous action irrespective of creed, he ought to have made his meaning plainer. Many of the Deists would have agreed with him in recommending a high and pure standard of morality, while deprecating the attempt to compromise it by a reference to selfish hopes or fears. In any case, judgment and practice cannot be isolated from one another, nor made amenable to different orders of motives, least of all when we are discussing a creed most of whose advocates consider that a man is morally responsible for his belief. It is difficult not to think that Butler knew this, although he avoids committing himself to an open use of the argument *ad terrorem.* Nor will any reservation make his theoretical assumption anything but a gross fallacy. There is no safe side in religion, for there is no experience to show where safety lies. To seek safety may, for aught we know, be the most dangerous, as it is certainly the most pusillanimous, of choices.

In the controversy between theology and rationalism it requires a greater effort of abstraction than most minds are capable of to grasp this possibility, and to appreciate its bearing on the aleatory method of belief. And as between Roman Catholicism and the various Protestant sects all doubt would vanish. The superior safety of belonging to the Church which alone claimed to monopolize the means of salvation was constantly urged as a motive for submitting to its pretensions, and proved, in fact, a most efficacious method of proselytism. Henry of Navarre is said to have put the argument in a particularly pointed form. The Protestant divines whom he consulted on the subject reluctantly admitted that he might be saved if he became a Catholic. The Catholic divines told him without hesitation that he would certainly be damned if he remained a Protestant. He therefore chose that side which, by universal agreement, offered the best prospect of escaping from perdition. What the great King had offered, more than half in irony, as an excuse for his politic apostasy was accepted in deadly earnest by many persons of quality in England under Charles I as a reason for deserting the cause of the Reformation. Charles II's deathbed conversion was probably dictated by the same motive; and, if so, it offers a crowning example of the adroit opportunism by which his whole life was guided. In this as in other respects the ablest of all the Stuarts bore a close resemblance to his grandfather, the ablest of the Bourbons. When Butler wrote the danger from Rome had greatly diminished, but had not wholly disappeared, as we learn from Neal's *History of the Puritans* (1732) and Middleton's *Free Inquiry* (1747). It is therefore rather surprising that he did not observe what consequences might be drawn from an argument, perhaps derived from Pascal, in favor of Pascal's creed.

If English churchmen did not draw the logical consequences of their greatest champion's apologetic method, their escape is due not only to the happy inconsistency of the theological intellect, but also to the pervasive influence of eighteenth-century rationalism, extending as it did far beyond the small circle of avowed freethinkers. Whatever else Englishmen might believe, their own Deists and the Voltairean movement abroad gradually convinced them that Popery was a superstition too absurd for even a Frenchman to accept—destined to speedy extinction, Horace Walpole thought, if the ill-advised abrogation of our penal laws had not given it a new lease of life. It would have surprised the dilettante of Strawberry Hill to hear that his own experiments in Gothic architecture had rather more to do with the dreaded revival of medieval faith than the repeal of some obsolete statutes. Anyhow, by accident or otherwise, he proved a true prophet. Whether as grim wolf or good shepherd, two centuries after *Lycidas* Rome once more put in play the arts against which Milton had raised his warning voice. Or rather the natural magnetism exercised by the larger on the smaller body acted without the help of any direct proselytism on the part of Jesuits or others to disintegrate the Church of England and to draw its detached fragments into the central orb of Christendom. . . .

Cardinal Newman briefly refers to Butler's doctrine of probability as the guide of life as that whence his own theory of faith took its rise. Keble treats it at much greater length, and in particular connection with the issue on which he and his greater friend parted company in a very interesting but little read document, the preface to his *Sermons, Academical and Occasional,* published in 1847, soon after Newman's secession.

The principle in question is stated as follows: "In practical matters of eternal import, the safer way is always to be preferred, even though the excess of seeming evidence may tell in any degree on the opposite side. Thus, if one mode of acting imply that there is an eternity and another contradict it . . . the tremendous, overwhelming interest at stake ought to determine a man's conduct to the affirmative side. He should act, in spite of seeming evidence, as if eternity were true."

Keble had not the same lingering regard for truth as such that still distinguished Butler; and the context clearly shows that "acting" means not merely conformity to Christian ethics, but also that adhesion to the Catholic creed which, in the supposed circumstances, some, among whom the present writer is one, would call, in plain language, cowardly and deceitful.

Fortunately, or rather inevitably, systematized immortality is suicidal. . . . Keble very frankly admits that "the principles of Butler and Pascal" cannot be limited to "the controversy with unbelievers." And if personally he had been disposed so to limit them, Newman would not have allowed him to stop short. So he proceeds to state the argument for going over to Rome in terms which I shall not transcribe, as they are substantially identical with the Bourbon argument (white plume argument, let us call it) already quoted.

Keble's way of getting out of it is amazing, and practically amounts to an abandonment of the whole principle. It is that "the argument put in this form proves too much, for it would equally show that Puritanism or Mahometanism, or the ancient Donatism, or any other exclusive system, is the safer way." And he also goes on to remark, rather late in the day, that there seems to be something "cold and ungenerous" about the method—in short, what we call mean. Accordingly, it is to be reserved for the exclusive benefit of unbelievers, and not mentioned in controversies among Christians. But we have seen that as against unbelievers the probabilist method is quite invalid. When the factor of inscrutable and irresponsible omnipotence has been introduced into our calculations the adoption of one particular alternative becomes no more advisable than the adoption of another. Whatever creed we profess or reject, the chances of our being saved or lost remain precisely equal. For a Being who is morally capable of damning us at all is capable of damning us for taking him at his word. Nor has the orthodox believer any right to charge those who do advance such an argument with irreverence or flippancy. To the God whose existence he assumes their reasoning may appear perfectly reverent and serious.

Pascal's method was destined to one more singular development before it silently took its place among the obsolete weapons of religious controversy. With the collapse of the Tractarian Movement the rationalistic movement which it had temporarily arrested returned in a flood, and before many years had passed became predominant at Oxford, at least among her more serious and intellectual residents. To meet this new danger Mansel delivered his famous Bampton Lectures in 1858. He does not, I think, ever mention the argument *ad terrorem,* but he follows Pascal in denying that our moral distinctions are applicable to the proceedings of an infinite Being about whose real nature we are totally ignorant; and he follows Butler in contending that every other system is open to as many objections as Christianity, or rather as his own particular version of Christianity.

. . . But the most resounding stroke of all came from John Stuart Mill. . . . Convince me, says Mill, that the world is ruled by an infinite Being of whom I know nothing except that his proceedings are incompatible with the highest human morality, "and I will bear my fate as I may. But there is one thing he shall not do: he shall not compel me to worship him. I will call no being good who is not what I mean when I apply that epithet to my fellow creatures; and if such a being can sentence me to hell for not so calling him to hell I will go." . . .

It has been said by some who are in full sympathy with Mill's contention that the sentiment here expressed, however admirable, is irreconcilable with his utilitarian ethics. I am not so sure of that. The moral degradation of worshipping an omnipotent demon through eternity might conceivably be more painful than any punishment in the demon's power to inflict. Or, on finding himself defied, he might "tak' a thought and men' "—to the great increase of the general felicity. But there seems a sort of pedantry about such considerations. If the supreme ironies are partly serious, supreme seriousness may well be a little ironical. There is such a phrase as "I bet you all to nothing," and as the language of the gaming-table has once been introduced it may here be appropriately used as best describing Mill's position. There is no more than an infinitesimally small chance that Mansel's nonmoral theology may be true; but neither on that chance nor on any other will a high-principled human soul forfeit its self-respect.

My object has been to show that to incur either intellectual or moral degradation on a calculation of selfish interest would be not only mean, but unavailing. For with the limitation of our knowledge assumed by the theologians who appeal to such motives there is no safe side, the chances either way being precisely equal whatever attitude towards the hidden arbiter of our destiny we assume. It remains, then, that our conduct should be determined by considerations equally applicable whether the supernatural does or does not exist.

Part Two

The History of Christianity

Introduction

There are many thousands of histories of Christianity, but a large number are of little value because they rely upon hearsay, legend, myth, untested opinions, copying from earlier works that relied on poor sources, and quoting from the Bible as if it were an unimpeachable historical source. An objective historian realizes that not all sources are reliable. Part of his job is to evaluate the reliability of source material. An objective historian realizes that there was considerable forging of "official" church documents in the Middle Ages, this during a time when the church had complete control over learning and the dissemination of knowledge. A good historian also knows how to distinguish propaganda from objective sources, and appreciates the value of original source materials over less valuable secondhand reports. He can spot good eyewitness or firsthand testimony, and is well aware that many previous historians have a subjective "axe" to grind, which reduces their reliability. Such intellectual bias often incorporates selective use and/or quotation of sources, which ignores other equally important work. In light of the above, it can be confidently said that many (most?) of the histories of Christianity are not entirely trustworthy.

What should the reader do in a case like this? While there are no clear answers, some helpful guidelines can be suggested. Avoid any history of Christianity published by a religious or denominational publisher. Avoid histories written by clergy or professors at seminaries. Avoid the work of historians who are cited in fundamentalist publications. The religious right wing is notorious for citing only those works which agree with at least part (if not often most) of their conclusions, and for neglecting to mention the majority of historians who disagree with *all* of their conclusions. While some would insist that the work of non-Christian historians should also not be trusted, this is clearly silly. Must a writer on Islamic history be a Moslem? Would his membership in an Islamic sect make readers more or less suspicious of his conclusions?

The history of Christianity proper must really begin with the life and ministry of Jesus of Nazareth, called the Christ. Unfortunately, that is one of the major problems for a historical study of Christianity. Outside of the New Testament and its Apocrypha, there is no hard evidence that Jesus ever lived. This is not to say that he did *not* live, but the burden of proof is upon those who assert that he lived and was the Messiah; they must produce convincing proof that this was so. The problem of the historicity of Jesus is a very complex one, and is treated in some detail in the first *Anthology of Atheism and Rationalism,* along with a number of pertinent selections. The problem will not be introduced here, except in the form of a summary.

These are the principal arguments *against* the historicity of Jesus: (1) There is no real evidence outside of the New Testament that a man named Jesus ever lived. (2) None of Jesus' teachings, as given in the New Testament, is original, for many can be found in earlier sources. This assumes that we have an accurate record in the New Testament of the sayings *attributed* to Jesus. (3) The story of Jesus' trial and death do not correspond with the legal possibilities open at that time. The Romans did not have a capital offense of blasphemy, and the Jews had death by stoning as the punishment for that offense. (4) We do not have any eyewitness accounts, even in the New Testament, of the life of Jesus; furthermore, the accounts in the New Testament were written many years later, by unknown followers. Thus, we have *no* contemporary biographical record of Jesus in *any* source. (5) There is no necessity for a religion to have an actual historical founder, even if it claims to have had one. Hinduism, for example, has no historical founder. (6) The entire basic outline of Jesus' life—i.e., born of a virgin, sent by God, rejected by men, killed by his countrymen, and then resurrected— is found in nearly identical form in the myths of many countries, including some cultures much older than Christianity. This suggests some "mythologizing" of the facts, if there *are* facts. These facts, plus the idea that Christianity can be explained *without* a historical Jesus, have made the historicity issue one that just will not go away.

When we begin an investigation of the history of Christianity, one critical thought should be kept in mind. Christianity prides itself on being the *only* major religion that is based upon historical fact. Hinduism, for example, does not even claim that its gods actually existed, nor does it feel an obligation to show that they did. Christianity, on the other hand, claims that it is true *because* it is historical. Therefore, an investigation of the real history of Christianity will not only be an important undertaking, but it will be the very basis for deciding whether Christianity is *true.* If the historical evidence is not there to support such things as the birth, life, death, and resurrection of Jesus, Christianity becomes another false religion. The burden of proof is always upon the person who says that something is so, and if that proof cannot be produced, then the truth of what is said lacks support.

Let us also remember that the early history of Christianity is entirely the history of Catholicism; it had complete control and was the only type of Christianity for more the 1,500 years. To set the milieu of early Christianity, let us also remember that only a few people could read, there was no printing but only hand copying of manuscripts, and lying in the cause of advancing "the faith" was an accepted practice. In fact, St. Augustine found lying among the clergy so prevalent that he wrote two books (*De Mendacio* in 395 A.D. and *Contra Mendacium* in 420 A.D.), urging that it stop. Add to this the fact that the church controlled all of the copying of manuscripts in scriptoriums (which were staffed by monks) and one begins to see the magnitude of the problem. What controls were there upon monks who wanted to change a few sentences in a manuscript they were copying? Many works prior to 1400 were generated from a single manuscript copy.

Well, what about the New Testament? This is, of course, the major source for the life of Jesus and for the history of the very earliest period of Christianity. Surely no monk would tamper with the Bible itself. That *may* be true, but the problem comes earlier than this. We have no actual copy of the New Testament dated before the year 350 A.D. This is not to say that we lack knowledge of the text before that time. We do know that the four Gospels could not have been written before 55 A.D., starting with the book of Matthew and proceeding through the books of Mark and Luke to the book of John in about 100 A.D. Of course, we have none of those copies. We have only one Gospel dating back to 350 A.D. It is true, as some fundamentalists claim, that this is better documentation than for almost any other ancient book, but we are not asked to believe literally in the life-directing force of any other book. We are not asked to base our whole life upon the work of Aristotle or Plato. In addition, these thinkers do not claim to have performed miracles, been the "son of God" or the Messiah, to punish people with eternal torment for not accepting what has been written, or to be literally true. These extraordinary claims are made for the New Testament, at least by some Christians. As the philosopher David Hume said, extraordinary claims require an extraordinary amount of evidence to be offered if we are properly to believe them. Rather than offer an extraordinary amount of evidence for such extraordinary claims as the resurrection of Jesus from the dead, virtually *no* evidence is offered except a piece of undocumented hearsay called the Gospels.

What would qualify as adequate evidence for the truth of the Gospels? Of course, an appearance of Jesus in front of a crowd of nonbelievers, in which he performed extraordinary feats that could not be done except by supernatural intervention (such as violating the laws of physics and chemistry), would be a sort of "retroactive" proof. If the question is intended to ask what *past* evidence would be required, then the answer would be different. Acceptable evidence would include any manuscripts or documents actually written by eyewitnesses to the events and signed by them as accurate. Also acceptable would be any first person accounts by historians who were not Christians but who were contemporaneous with the events in the Gospels. We do have the works (or parts of the works) of many such historians. In addition, any verifiably authentic physical objects associated with the life of Jesus would count as evidence, although they would only show that he lived, not that he was really the Messiah. The Shroud of Turin, had it been authentic, would serve as acceptable evidence of Jesus' life and death.

Unfortunately for Christians, none of these types of evidence is available at present. Yes, there has been a lot of forging of documents that would have been acceptable, such as the supposed letter of Pontius Pilate to the Roman authorities telling about the trial and execution of Jesus. This, too, has been exposed as a Medieval forgery. There is, in fact, an entire book of forged documents purportedly written by eyewitnesses to Jesus' life. It is called *The Archko Volume* and has been reprinted many times since its first appearance in the 1880s. It is only one example among many of pious attempts by Christians to create de novo evidence to make up for the lack of historical support for their claims.

Christian efforts to document what it views as factual historical evidence have produced many hundreds of volumes under the general literary category of apologetics. To try to read some of these books as a non-Christian historian, is a very depressing process. The historical evidence simply does not exist, and most of the authors of these works are driven back to a reliance upon the words of the Bible, and, quite understandably, such question-begging tactics will not do. The Bible may be used as a secondary source, but, by itself, it is inadequate. There have also been many works attacking the Christian efforts to document their sources. Many have correctly perceived the weakness in the Christian case, but all suffer from the impossibility of proving a negative. Christianity cannot be shown to be untrue. One can only show that a given piece of evidence is inadequate, or that all the individual pieces (one at a time) are inadequate. Therefore, the case for Christianity is unproven and undocumented. The burden of proof, as always, is upon the person who says something is so (i.e., the Christian in this case). Believers have failed to carry that burden.

Josephus Forgedly Testifies of Jesus

Joseph Wheless

Joseph Wheless was born the son of a banker in Nashville, Tennessee, in 1868, and was educated in private schools. He read law in his uncle's law office, and was admitted to the Tennessee Bar in 1889. He practiced law in Nashville and in St. Louis, specializing in Latin American legal cases, and at one point represented American interests in Mexico. After moving to New York City, he continued his law practice, which was interrupted by service in the Judge Advocate corps of the Army in the First World War and in Army Intelligence in the Second World War. He spoke five modern languages fluently and also knew ancient Greek, Hebrew, and Latin.

Wheless was a freethinker and often served as the attorney for various atheist organizations, including the Freethinkers of America and the American Association for the Advancement of Atheism. He made a hobby of the study of Jewish and Christian origins, for which his knowledge of ancient languages proved a tremendous asset. Wheless was the author of *Is It God's Word?* (a study of the Bible) and *Forgery In Christianity*. He also authored several Big Blue Books for Haldeman-Julius. Wheless died in 1950.

The present selection comes from *Forgery In Christianity*, which was first published by Alfred A. Knopf in 1930. The book is now quite difficult to find in the original edition. The selection discusses the forgery of what is (or was) viewed as the best single piece of evidence for Jesus' existence outside the New Testament, namely, the mention of Jesus in the works of Josephus, the historian of the Jews, who wrote the work from which the passage comes in about 90 A.D.

So many confessed Christian forgeries in Pagan and Christian names having been wrought to testify to Jesus Christ, it was, "one naturally expects," says *CE.,** that a Jewish "writer so well informed as Josephus" must know and tell about Jesus; "one naturally expects, therefore, a notice about Jesus Christ in Josephus." And with pride it pursues: "Antiquities, VIII, iii, 3, *seems* to satisfy this expectation." It proceeds to quote the passage, which differeth only as one translation naturally differs from another, from that in the Whitson translation; so I follow *CE.* In Chapter iii Josephus treats of "Sedition of the Jews against Pontius Pilate"; in section 1 he relates the cause and the suppression of the mutiny, the ensigns of the army displaying the idolatrous Roman Eagle, brought into the Holy City; in section 2 he tells of the action of Pilate in bringing "a current of water to Jerusalem, and did it with the sacred money," thus again arousing a clash with the fanatics; "there were great numbers of them slain by this means." Passing for the moment the notorious section 3, Josephus the Jew begins section 4: "About the same time, also, *another sad calamity* put the Jews in disorder," which he proceeds to relate, ending the long chapter. Note that these section numbers were not put in by Josephus, but are modern editor's devices to facilitate citation, like the chapters and verses in the Bible. And now for the much-debated section, sandwiched, in a whole chapter on "Sedition of the Jews," between the accounts of two massacres of his countrymen and "another sad calamity"; and thus we read—note the *parentheses* of *CE.* (viii, 376):—

> "About this time," quotes *CE.,* "appeared Jesus, a wise man (if indeed it is right to call Him a man; for He was a worker of astonishing deeds, a teacher of such men as receive the truth with joy), and He drew to Himself many Jews (and many also of the Greeks. This was the Christ). And when Pilate, at the denunciation of those that are foremost among us, had condemned Him to the cross, those who had first loved Him did not abandon Him. (For He appeared to them alive on the third day, the holy prophets having foretold this and countless other marvels about Him.) The tribe of Christians named after Him did not cease to this day." (sec.3.)

About this time, *also* "another sad calamity [?] put the Jews into disorder," (sec. 4) continues Josephus. *CE.* devotes over three long columns to the task of trying to prove that this section 3, or at least "the portions *not in parenthesis,*"—is genuine, and was written, sometime before his death in 94 A.D., by the Jewish Pharisee, Josephus. "A testimony so important," well says *CE.,* "could not escape the critics,"—and it has not. We cannot follow the lengthy and labored arguments; the simple reading of the section,

---

CE. = Catholic Encyclopedia.

in its bizarre context, and a moment's reflection, condemn it as a pious Christian forgery. If the Pharisee Josephus wrote that paragraph, he must have believed that Jesus was the Prophesied Messiah of his people—*"This was the Christ,"* Josephus is made to aver; he must then needs have been of "the tribe of Christians named after Him." But whatever Josephus may have said about Jesus is, indeed, *not* "a testimony so important"—when we remember what he did aver that he saw with his own eyes: the pillar of salt into which Mrs. Lot was turned; and Eleazar the magician drawing the devil by a ring and Solomonic incantations, through the nose of one possessed, before Vespasian and all his army. If Josephus had written that he knew Jesus the Christ personally, and had personally seen him ascend into heaven through the roof of the room in Jerusalem (Mk. xvi, 19, 20), *or* from the open countryside by Bethany (Lk. xxiv, 50, 51), *or* "on the mount called Olivet" (Acts i, 9, 12),—we should remember that pillar of salt and that devil-doctor, and smile.

But, when and how did this famous passage get into *The Antiquities of the Jews?* it is pertinent to ask. The first mention ever made of this passage, and its text, are in the Church History of that "very dishonest writer," Bishop Eusebius, in the fourth century,—he who forged the Letters between Abgar and Jesus, falsely declaring that he had found the original documents in the official archives, whence he had copied and translated them into his Ecclesiastical History. *CE.* admits, and I have the *Contra Celsum* here before me,—that "the above cited passage *was not known to Origen and the earlier patristic writers,"*—though they copied from Josephus the forged tale of the Letter of Aristeas about the translating of the Septuagint; and "its very place in the Josephan text is uncertain, since Eusebius (Hist. Eccl., II, vi) must have *found* it before the notices concerning Pilate, while it now stands *after* them" (HE. I, ii, p. 63); and it makes the curious argument, which implies a confession: "But the spuriousness of the disputed Josephan passage does not imply the historian's ignorance of the facts connected with Jesus Christ"! For a wonder, that "a writer so well informed as Josephus" should not, perhaps, know by hearsay, sixty years after Jesus Christ, some of the remarkable things circulated about him in current country-side gossip— (if, indeed, it were then current). But the fact is, that with the exception of this one incongruous forged passage, section 3, the world-mongering Josephus makes not the slightest mention of his wonder-working fellow-countryman, Jesus the Christ,—though some score of other Joshuas, or Jesuses, are recorded by him, nor does he mention any of his transcendent wonders. But, as *CE.* and I were saying, none of the Fathers, before Eusebius (about 324), knew or could find a word in the works of Josephus, of this momentous "testimony to Jesus," over a century after Origen. That it *did not exist in the time of Origen* is explicit by his own words; he cites the supposed references by Josephus to John the Baptist and to James, and expressly says that Josephus *ought to have spoken of Jesus* instead of James; though Origen does not correctly describe the reference to James; and the James passage, if not that also about John, has a suspicious savor of interpolation.

For a clear understanding of this, I will quote the passage of Origen in his work against Celsus; it completely refutes the claim that Josephus wrote the disputed and forged section 3. Origen says:

> I would like to say to Celsus, who represents the Jew accepting John somehow as a Baptist, who baptized Jesus, that the existence of John the Baptist, baptizing for the remission of sins, is related by one who lived no great time after John and Jesus. For in the 18th book of his *Antiquities of the Jews,* Josephus bears witness to John as having been a Baptist, and as promising purification to those who underwent the rite. Now this writer, although *not believing in Jesus as the Christ,* in seeking after the cause of the fall of Jerusalem and the destruction of the temple [said that it was "to avenge James the Just"], whereas he *ought to have said* that the conspiracy against Jesus was the cause of these calamities befalling the people, since they put to death Christ, who was a prophet, says nevertheless—being, although against his will, not far from the truth—that these disasters happened to the Jews as a punishment for the death of James the Just, who was a brother of Jesus (called Christ),—the Jews having put him to death, although he was a man most distinguished for his justice. (Origen, *Contra Celsum,* I, xlvii; *ANF.* iv, 416)

Josephus is thus quoted as bearing witness to John the Baptist, *not* as the Heaven-sent "forerunner" of the Christ, but simply as a Jewish religious leader and baptizer on his own account; and not a word by Josephus about the Christ, in whom it is admitted that he did not believe as such, nor even mentions as the most illustrious of those baptized by John, to the wondrous accompaniment of a voice from Heaven and the Holy Ghost in dove-like descent upon his head as he came up from the water. But Origen, in his effort to get some Christian testimony from him, misquotes Josephus and makes him say that John was baptizing "for the remission of sins," whereas Josephus expressly says that the efficacy of John's baptism was *not* for remission of sin but for the purification of the body, as any washing would be. To vindicate Josephus against Origen, the former's words are quoted. Josephus records the defeat of Herod by Aretas, king of Arabia Petrea; and goes on to say:

> Now some of the Jews thought that the destruction of Herod's army came from God, and that very justly, as a punishment of what he did against John, that was called the Baptist; for Herod slew him, who was a good man, and commanded the Jews to exercise virtue, both as to righteousness toward one another, and piety toward God, and so to come to baptism; for that

the washing would be acceptable to him, if they made use of it, *not* in order to the putting away of some sins, but for the purification of the body; supposing still that the soul was thoroughly purified beforehand by righteousness. Now, when many others came in crowds about him, for they were greatly moved by hearing his words, Herod, who feared lest the great influence John had over the people might put it into his power and inclination to raise a rebellion, (for they seemed ready to do anything he should advise,) thought it best, by putting him to death, to prevent any mischief he might cause, and not bring himself into difficulties, by sparing a man who might make him repent of it when it should be too late. Accordingly, he was sent a prisoner, out of Herod's suspicious temper, to Macherus, the castle I before mentioned, and was *there* put to death. (Josephus, *Antiq. Jews,* Bk. XVIII, v, 2.)

Beginning in section 4 of the same Book, and at length in various chapters, Josephus goes into details regarding Salome; but never a word of the famous dance-act and of the head of John the Baptist being brought in on a charger to gratify her murderous whim; the historical reason for the murder of John was political, not amorous or jealous, as related by Gospel-truth.

Father Origen again falls into error in citing Josephus, this time in the dubious passage where Josephus, who does not believe in the Christ, yet gives him that title in speaking of the death of James. With typical clerical bent Father Origen imputes the fall of Jerusalem and the destruction of the temple to the sin of the Jews in crucifying the Christ; and says that Josephus, in seeking the cause of the disasters which befell the Holy City and people, attributes them to the killing of the Christ's brother. The Holy City and temple were destroyed in 70 A.D., which was well after the time of the supposititious James, as his demise is recorded in the suspected passage of Josephus. He relates the death of Festus, which was in 62 A.D., the appointment by Nero of Albinus as his successor, and the murder of James at the instigation of the high priest Ananus, before Albinus can arrive. This sentence is to be read in the text of Josephus:

Festus was now dead, and Albinus was but upon the road; so he (Ananus) assembled the sanhedrin of judges, and brought before them the brother of Jesus, who was called Christ, whose name was James, and some others; and when he had formulated an accusation against them as breakers of the law, he delivered them to be stoned. (Jos., *Antiq. Jews,* Bk. XX, ix, 1.)

Bishop Eusebius cannot pass over this chance to turn another Jewish testimony for his Christ; he says that "The wiser part of the Jews were of the opinion that this—(the killing of James)—was the cause of the immediate siege of Jerusalem. . . . Josephus also has not hesitated to superadd his testimony in his works. "These things," he says, "happened to the Jews to avenge James the Just, who was the brother of him that is called Christ,

and whom the Jews had slain, notwithstanding his preeminent justice."
(Euseb. *Hist. Eccles.* Bk. II, ch. 23.)

The reader may judge of the integrity of these pretended Jewish testimonies to the Baptist and to the brother of the Christ, both suspicious *per se,* and both falsely cited by Father Origen, who in all this could not find the famous section 3, first found a century later by Bishop Eusebius; and which Origen makes it positive Josephus had not written and could not have written. Is it a violent suspicion, and uncharitable, to suggest that the holy Bishop who forged the Letter of his Christ, and lied about finding it in the Edessa archives, really "found," in the sense of *invented,* or forged, the Josephus passages first heard of in his Church History?

But Bishop Eusebius, with a sort of "stop thief" forethought, himself imputes forgery to those who would question or discredit his own pious inventions, while with unctuous fervor of pretended truth he appeals to the wonderful "testimonies of Josephus," which he has just fabricated. After quoting and misquoting Josephus with respect to John the Baptist and Jesus Christ, he thus solemnly vouches for their false witness: "When such testimony as this is transmitted to us by an historian who sprung from the Hebrews themselves, both respecting John the Baptist and our Savior, what subterfuge can be left, to prevent those from being convicted destitute of all shame, who have forged the acts against them?" (Eusebius, *HE.* I, xi.) The Bishop justly pronounces his own condemnation. This, says Gibbon, "is an example of no vulgar forgery." (Chap. xvi.) In view of the convicting circumstances, and of his notoriously bad record, it is not uncharitable to impute this Josephus forgery to Bishop Eusebius.

When Were Our Gospels Written?

Charles Bradlaugh

Charles Bradlaugh has sometimes been called "the English Ingersoll." While there are elements of truth in this comparison, there are also great inaccuracies. Bradlaugh was a unique and colorful character who cannot be simply compared to Ingersoll.

Bradlaugh was born of working-class parents in a London suburb in 1833. After only a few years of formal education, he was dismissed from his Sunday School teaching post at age seventeen after he dared to question some inconsistencies in the Thirty-nine Articles of the Church of England (the creed of the Anglican denomination). The minster, Rev. Packer, denounced young Bradlaugh as an atheist (which he was not at that time). His family kicked him out of the house, and he was left to fend for himself. In between brief periods of employment at various menial jobs, Bradlaugh would wander over to Bonner's Fields, where the open-air orators mounted their soap-boxes. At first he tried to defend Christianity against the attacks of the freethought orators, but he soon found that he could no longer do so. It was not long before Bradlaugh was speaking for the freethought side.

After a period of military service with the Dragoon Guards in Ireland, Bradlaugh took a position as a law clerk, while reading law himself. In order to shield himself and his employer from unpleasantries, he adopted the name "Iconoclast" in all his freethought speaking and writing.

Bradlaugh had the natural physical gifts that made him an effective orator. He was tall, extremely strong, and had a powerful, booming voice. He also had a scholarly bent, which led him to master Hebrew and Arabic on his own, as well as to become extremely well versed in the writings of the major Christian theologians. The combination of his knowledge of the law and his logical mind made him a formidable opponent on the lecture platform and elsewhere.

During the period from 1860 to 1891, when he died from kidney failure, Bradlaugh was at the center of the British freethought movement. He was a tireless worker, lecturing, writing, editing journals, raising money, engaging in endless lawsuits, running for Parliament, and the like. His struggle to take his seat in Parliament after being duly elected, occupied five full years. The House of Commons had refused to administer the oath of office to him, a majority claiming that it would not be binding on the conscience of an atheist. From Bradlaugh's successful struggle to obtain his seat came the "Oaths Bill," which allows those to whom an oath is abhorrent, to make an affirmation both in court and upon election to office.

There are two major biographies of Charles Bradlaugh. The most recent, and in many ways the better, is *President Charles Bradlaugh, M.P.* by David Tribe (London: Elek, 1971). Also useful is *Charles Bradlaugh: A Record of His Life and Works, With an Account of His Parliamentary Struggle, Politics and Teachings,* by his daughter, Hypatia Bradlaugh Bonner and John M. Robertson (London: T. Fisher Unwin, 1895, 2 volumes).

The present essay, *When Were Our Gospels Written?* is one of the earliest pamphlets written by Bradlaugh. It was first published by Austin & Co., in London in 1867. A revised and slightly lengthened edition was published by the Freethought Publishing Company in London in 1881. In some respects, Bradlaugh's scholarship has been revised by later discoveries of New Testament manuscripts. In the main, however, what he says about the dates of the Gospels is still held by a majority of New Testament scholars. Of course, little of what he says is original to Bradlaugh; he was merely synthesizing and reporting the best scholarship of his day. The present essay has been out of print since the early 1890s.

The Religious Tract Society, some time since [1866], issued, prefaced with their high commendation, a translation of a pamphlet by Dr. Constantine Tischendorf, entitled "When were our Gospels Written?" In the introductory preface we are not unfairly told that "on the credibility of the four Gospels the whole of Christianity rests, as a building on its foundations." It is proposed in this brief essay to deal with the character of Dr. Tischendorf's advocacy, then to examine the genuineness of the four Gospels, as affirmed by the Religious Tract Society's pamphlet, and at the same time to ascertain, as far as is possible in the space, how far the Gospel narrative is credible.

The Religious Tract Society states that Dr. Tischendorf's *brochure* is a repetition of "arguments for the genuineness and authenticity of the four Gospels," which the erudite Doctor had previously published for the learned classes, "with explanations" now given in addition, to render the arguments "intelligible" to meaner capacities; and as the "Infidel" and "Deist" are especially referred to as likely to be overthrown by this pamphlet, we may presume that the society considers that in the 119 pages—which the translated essay occupies—they have presented the best paper that can be issued on their behalf for popular reading on this question. . . .

Dr. Tischendorf states that he has since 1839 devoted himself to the textual study of the New Testament, and it ought to be interesting to the orthodox to know that, as a result of twenty-seven years' labor, he now declares that "it has been placed beyond doubt that the original text . . . had in many places undergone such serious modifications of meaning as to leave us in painful uncertainty as to what the apostles had actually written," and that "the right course to take" "is to set aside the received text altogether and to construct a fresh text."

This is pleasant news for the true believer, promulgated by authority of the managers of the great Christian depot in Paternoster Row, from whence many scores of thousands of copies of this incorrect received text have nevertheless been issued without comment to the public, even since the society have published in English Dr. Tischendorf's declaration of its unreliable character.

With the modesty and honorable reticence peculiar to great men, Dr. Tischendorf records his successes in reading hitherto unreadable parchments, and we learn that he has received approval from "several learned bodies, and even from crowned heads," for his wonderful performances. As a consistent Christian, who knows that the "powers that be are ordained of God," our "critic without rival," for so he prints himself, regards the praise of crowned heads as higher in degree than that of learned bodies.

The Doctor discovered in 1844 the MS. on which he now relies to confute audacious Infidelity, in the Convent of St. Catherine at Sinai; he brought away a portion, and handed that portion, on his return, to the Saxon Government—they paying all expenses. The Doctor, however, did not then divulge where he had found the MS. It was for the advantage of humankind that the place should be known at once, for, at least, two reasons. First, because by aid of the remainder of this MS.—"the most precious Bible treasure in existence"—the faulty text of the New Testament was to be reconstructed; and the sooner the work was done the better for believers in Christianity. And, secondly, the whole story of the discovery might then have been more easily confirmed in every particular.

For fifteen years, at least, Dr. Tischendorf hid from the world the precise locality in which his treasure had been discovered. Nay, he was even fearful when he knew that other Christians were trying to find the true text, and he experienced "peculiar satisfaction" when he ascertained that his silence had misled some pious searchers after reliable copies of God's message to all humankind; although all this time he was well aware that our received copies of God's revelation had undergone "serious modifications" since the message had been delivered from the Holy Ghost by means of the Evangelists.

In 1853, "nine years after the original discovery," Dr. Tischendorf again visited the Sinai convent, but although he had "enjoined on the monks to take religious care" of the remains of which they, on the former occasion, would not yield up possession, he, on this second occasion, and apparently after careful search, discovered "eleven short lines,"which convinced him that the greater part of the MS. had been destroyed. He still, however, kept the place secret, although he had no longer any known reason for so doing; and, having obtained an advance of funds from the Russian Government, he, in 1859, tried a third time for his "pearl of St. Catherine," which, in 1853, he felt convinced had been destroyed, and as to which he had nevertheless, in the meantime, been troubled by fears that the good cause might be aided by some other than Dr. Tischendorf discovering and publishing the "priceless treasure," which, according to his previous statements, he must have felt convinced did no longer exist. On this third journey the Doctor discovered "the very fragments which, fifteen years before, he had taken out of the basket," and also other parts of the Old Testament, the New Testament complete, and, in addition, Barnabas and part of Hermas.". . .

"Christianity," writes Dr. Tischendorf, "does not, strictly speaking, rest on the moral teaching of Jesus;" "it rests on his person only." "If we are in error in believing in the person of Christ as taught in the Gospels, then the Church herself is in error, and must be given up as a deception." "All the world knows that our Gospels are nothing else than biographies of Christ." "We have no other source of information with respect to the life of Jesus." So that, according to the Religious Tract Society and its advocate, if the credibility of the Gospel biography be successfully impugned, then the foundations of Christianity are destroyed. It becomes, therefore, of the highest importance to show that the biography of Jesus, as given in the four Gospels, is absolutely incredible and self-contradictory.

It is alleged in the Society's preface that all the objections of infidelity have been hitherto unavailing. This is, however, not true. It is rather the fact that the advocates of Christianity when defeated on one point have shuffled to another, either quietly passing the topic without further debate, or loudly declaring that the point abandoned was really so utterly unimportant that it was extremely foolish in the assailant to regard it as worthy attack, and that, in any case, all the arguments had been repeatedly refuted by previous writers.

To the following objections to the Gospel narrative the writer refuses to accept as answer, that they have been previously discussed and disposed of.

The Gospels which are yet mentioned by the names popularly associated with each do not tell us the hour, or the day, or the month, or—save Luke—the year, in which Jesus was born. The only point on which the critical divines, who have preceded Dr. Tischendorf, generally agree is, that Jesus was not born on Christmas day. The Oxford Chronology, collated with a full score of recognized authorities, gives us a period of more than seven years within which to place the date. So confused is the story as to the time of the birth, that while Matthew would make Jesus born in the lifetime of Herod, Luke would fix the period of Jesus's birth as after Herod's death.

Christmas itself is a day surrounded with curious ceremonies of pagan origin, and in no way serving to fix the 25th December as the natal day. Yet the exact period at which Almighty God, as a baby boy, entered the world to redeem long-suffering humanity from the consequences of Adam's ancient sin, should be of some importance.

Nor is there any great certainty as to the place of birth of Christ. The Jews, apparently in the very presence of Jesus, reproached him that he ought to have been born at Bethlehem. Nathaniel regarded him as of Nazareth. Jesus never appears to have said to either, "I was born at Bethlehem." In Matthew ii., 6, we find a quotation from the prophet: "And thou Bethlehem, in the land of Judah, art not the least amongst the princes of Juda, for out of thee shall come a Governor that shall rule my people Israel." Matthew lays the scene of the birth in Bethlehem, and Luke adopts the same place, especially bringing the child to Bethlehem for that same purpose, and Matthew tells us it is done to fulfill a prophecy. Micah v., 2, the only place in which similar words occur, is not a prophecy referring to Jesus at all. The words are: "But thou Bethlehem Ephratah, though thou be little among the thousands of Judah, yet out of thee shall he come forth unto me that is to be ruler in Israel, whose goings forth have been from of old, from everlasting." This is not quoted correctly in Matthew, and can hardly be said by any straining of language to apply to Jesus. The credibility of a story on which Christianity rests is bolstered up by prophecy in default of contemporary corroboration. The difficulties are not lessened in tracing the parentage. In Matthew i., 17, it is stated that "the generations from Abraham to David are fourteen generations, and from David until the carrying away into Babylon are fourteen generations, and from the carrying away into Babylon unto Christ are fourteen generations." Why has Matthew made such a mistake in his computation of the genealogies—in the last division we have only thirteen names instead of fourteen, even including the name of Jesus? Is this one of the cases of "painful uncertainty" which has induced the Religious Tract Society and Dr. Tischendorf to wish to set aside the *textus receptus* altogether?

From David to Zorobabel there are in the Old Testament twenty generations; in Matthew, seventeen generations; and in Luke, twenty-three generations. In Matthew from David to Christ there are twenty-eight generations, and in Luke from David to Christ forty-three generations. Yet, according to the Religious Tract Society, it is on the credibility of these genealogies as part of the Gospel history that the foundation of Christianity rests. The genealogy in the first Gospel arriving at David traces to Jesus through Solomon; the third Gospel from David traces through Nathan. In Matthew the names from David are Solomon, Roboam, Abia, Asa, Josaphat, Joram, Ozias; and in the Old Testament we trace the same names from David to Ahaziah, whom I presume to be the same as Ozias. But in 2nd Chronicles xxii., 11, we find one Joash, who is not mentioned in Matthew at all. If the genealogy in Matthew is correct, why is the name not mentioned? Amaziah is mentioned in chap. xxiv., v. 27, and in chap. xxvi., v. 1, Uzziah, neither of whom are mentioned in Matthew, where Ozias is named as begetting Jotham, when in fact three generations of men have come in between. In Matthew and Luke, Zorobabel is represented as the son of Salathiel, while in 1 Chronicles iii., 17-19, Zerubbabel is stated to be the son of Pedaiah, the brother of Salathiel. Matthew says Abiud was the son of Zorobabel (chap. i, v. 13). Luke iii., 27, says Zorobabel's son was Rhesa. The Old Testament contradicts both, and gives Meshullam, and Hananiah, and Shelomith, their sister (1 Chronicles iii., 19), as the names of Zorobabel's children. Is this another piece of evidence in favor of Dr. Tischendorf's admirable doctrine, that it is necessary to reconstruct the text?

In the genealogies of Matthew and Luke there are only three names agreeing after that of David, viz., Salathiel, Zorobabel, and Joseph—all the rest are utterly different. The attempts at explanation which have been hitherto offered, in order to reconcile these genealogies, are scarcely creditable to the intellects of the Christian apologists. They allege that "Joseph, who by nature was the son of Jacob, in the account of the law was the son of Heli. For Heli and Jacob were brothers by the same mother, and Heli, who was the elder, dying without issue, Jacob, as the law directed, married his widow; in consequence of such marriage, his son Joseph was reputed in the law the son of Heli." This is pure invention to get over a difficulty—an invention not making the matter one whit more clear. For if you suppose that these two persons were brothers, then unless you invent a death of the mother's last husband and the widow's remarriage Jacob and Heli would be the sons of the same father, and the list of the ancestors should be identical in each genealogy. But to get over the difficulty the pious do this. They say, although brothers, they were only half-brothers; although sons of the same mother, they were not sons of the same father, but had different fathers. If so, how is it that Salathiel and Zorobabel occur as father and son in both genealogies? Another fashion of accounting for the contradiction is to give one as the genealogy of Joseph and the other as the genealogy of Mary. "Which?" "Luke," it is said. Why Luke? what are Luke's words? Luke speaks of Jesus being, "as was supposed the son of Joseph, which was the son of Heli." When Luke says Joseph, the son of Heli, did he mean Mary, the daughter of Heli?

Does the Gospel say one thing and mean another? because if that argument is worth anything, then in every case where a man has a theory which disagrees with the text, he may say the text means something else. If this argument be permitted we must abandon in Spiritual criticism the meaning which we should ordinarily intend to convey by any given word. If you believe Luke meant daughter, why does the same word mean son in every other case all through the remainder of the genealogy? And if the genealogy of Matthew be that of Joseph, and the genealogy of Luke be that of Mary, they ought not to have any point of agreement at all until brought to David. They, nevertheless, do agree and contradict each other in several places, destroying the probability of their being intended as distinct genealogies. There is some evidence that Luke does not give the genealogy of Mary in the Gospel itself. We are told that Joseph went to Bethlehem to be numbered because he was of the house of David: if it had been Mary it would have surely said so. As according to the Christian theory, Joseph was not the father of Jesus, it is not unfair to ask how it can be credible that Jesus' genealogy could be traced to David in any fashion through Joseph?

So far from Mary being clearly of the tribe of Judah (to which the genealogy relates) her cousinship to Elizabeth would make her rather appear to belong to the tribe of Levi.

To discuss the credibility of the miraculous conception and birth would be to insult the human understanding. The mythologies of Greece, Italy, and India, give many precedents of sons of Gods miraculously born. Italy, Greece, and India, must, however, yield the palm to Judea. The incarnate Chrishna must give way to the incarnate Christ. A miraculous birth would be scouted today as monstrous; antedate it 2,000 years and we worship it as miracle.

Matthew i., 22, 23, says: "Now all this was done, that it might be fulfilled which was spoken of the Lord by the prophet, saying, Behold, a virgin shall be with child, and shall bring forth a son, and they shall call his name Emmanuel, which being interpreted is, God with us." This is supposed to be a quotation from Isaiah vii., 14-16: "Therefore the Lord himself shall give you a sign; Behold a virgin shall conceive, and bear a son, and shall call his name Immanuel. Butter and honey shall he eat, that he may know to refuse the evil, and choose the good. For before the child shall know to refuse the evil and choose the good, the land that thou abhorrest shall be forsaken of both her kings."

But in this, as indeed in most other cases of inaccurate quotation, the very words are omitted which would show its utter inapplicability to Jesus. Even in those which are given, the agreement is not complete. Jesus was not called Emmanuel. And even if his mother Mary were a virgin, this does not help the identity, as the Hebrew word OLME in Isaiah, rendered "virgin" in our version, does not convey the notion of virginity, for which the proper word is BeThULE; OLME is used of a youthful spouse recently married. The allusion to the land being forsaken of both her kings, omitted in Matthew, shows how little the passage is prophetic of Jesus.

The story of the annunciation made to Joseph in one Gospel, to Mary in the other, is hardly credible on any explanation. If you assume the annunciations as made by a God of all-wise purpose, the purpose should, at least, have been to prevent doubt of Mary's chastity; but the annunciation is made to Joseph only after Mary is suspected by Joseph. Two annunciations are made, one of them in a dream to Joseph, when he is suspicious as to the state of his betrothed wife; the other made by the angel Gabriel (whoever that angel may be) to Mary herself, who apparently conceals the fact, and is content to be married, although with child not by her intended husband. The statement—that Mary being found with child by the Holy Ghost, her husband, not willing to make her a public example, was minded to put her away privily—is quite incredible. If Joseph found her with child *by the Holy Ghost,* how could he even think of making a public example of her shame when there was nothing of which she could be ashamed—nothing, if he believed in the Holy Ghost, of which he need have been ashamed himself, nothing which need have induced him to wish to put her away privily. It is clear—according to Matthew—that Mary was found with child, and that the Holy Ghost parentage was not even imagined by Joseph until after he had dreamed about the matter.

Although the birth of Jesus was specially announced by an angel, and although Mary sang a joyful song consequent on the annunciation, corroborated by her cousin's greeting, yet when Simeon speaks of the child, in terms less extraordinary, Joseph and Mary are surprised at it and do not understand it. Why were they surprised? Is it credible that so little regard was paid to the miraculous annunciation? Or is this another case of the "painful uncertainty" alluded to by Dr. Tischendorf?

Again, when Joseph and Mary found the child Jesus in the temple, and he says, "Wist ye not that I must be about my father's business?" they do not know what he means, so that either what the angel had said had been of little effect, or the annunciations did not occur at all. Can any reliance be placed on a narrative so contradictory? An angel was specially sent to acquaint a mother that her son about to be born is the Son of God, and yet that mother is astonished when her son says, "Wist ye not I must be about my father's business?"

The birth of Jesus was, according to Matthew, made publicly known by means of certain wise men. These men saw his star in the East, but it did not tell them much, for they were obliged to come and ask information from Herod the King. Is astrology credible? Herod inquired of the chief priests and scribes; and it is evident Jeremiah was right, if he said, "The prophets prophecy falsely and the priests bear rule by their means," for these chief priests misquoted to suit their purposes, and invented a false prophecy by omitting a few words from, and adding a few words to, a text until it suited their purpose. The star, after they knew where to go, and no longer required its aid, went before them, until it came and stood over where the young child was. The credibility of this will be better understood if the reader notice some star, and then see how many houses it will be over. Luke does not seem to have been aware of the star story, and he relates about an angel who tells some shepherds the good tidings, but this last-named adventure does not appear to have happened in the reign of Herod at all. Is it credible that Jesus was born twice? After the wise men had left Jesus, an angel warned Joseph to flee with him and Mary into Egypt, and Joseph did fly, and remained there with the young child and his mother until the death of Herod; and this, it is alleged, was done to fulfill a prophecy. On referring to Hosea xi., 1, we find the words have no reference whatever to Jesus, and that, therefore, either the tale of the flight is invented as a fulfillment of the prophecy, or the prophecy manufactured to support the tale of the flight. The Jesus of Luke never went into Egypt at all in his childhood. Directly after the birth of the child his parents instead of flying away because of persecution into Egypt, went peacefully up to Jerusalem to fulfill all things according to the law, returned thence to Nazareth, and apparently dwelt there, going up to Jerusalem ever year until Jesus was twelve years of age.

In Matthew ii., 15, we are told that Jesus remained in Egypt, "That it might be fulfilled which was spoken of the Lord by the prophet saying, Out of Egypt have I called my son." In Hosea ii., 1, we read, "When Israel was a child, then I loved him, and called my son out of Egypt." In no other prophet is there any similar text. This not only is not a prophecy of Jesus, but is, on the contrary, a reference to the Jewish Exodus from Egypt. Is the prophecy manufactured to give an air of credibility to the Gospel history, or how will the Religious Tract Society explain it? The Gospel writings betray either a want of good faith, or great incapacity on the part of their authors in the mode adopted of distorting quotations from the Old Testament?

When Jesus began to be about thirty years of age he was baptized by John in the river Jordan. John, who, according to Matthew, knew him, forbade him directly he saw him; but, according to the writer of the fourth Gospel, he knew him not, and had, therefore, no occasion to forbid him. God is an "invisible" "spirit," whom no man hath seen (John i., 18), or can see (Exodus xxxiii., 20); but the man John saw the spirit of God descending like a dove. God is everywhere, but at that time was in heaven, from whence he said, "This is my beloved son, in whom I am well pleased." Although John heard this from God's own mouth, he some time after sent two of his disciples to Jesus to inquire if he were really the Christ (Matthew xi., 2, 3). Yet it is upon the credibility of this story, says Dr. Tischendorf, that Christianity rests like a building on its foundations.

It is utterly impossible John could have known and not have known Jesus at the same time. And if, as the New Testament states, God is infinite and invisible, it is incredible that as Jesus stood in the river to be baptized, the Holy Ghost was seen as it descended on his head as a dove, and that God from heaven said, "This is my beloved son, in whom I am well pleased." Was the indivisible and invisible spirit of God separated in three distinct and two separately visible persons? How do the Religious Tract Society reconcile this with the Athanasian Creed?

The baptism narrative is rendered doubtful by the language used as to John, who baptized Jesus. It is said, "This is he that was spoken of by the prophet Esaias, saying, The voice of one crying in the wilderness, prepare ye the way of the Lord, make his paths straight." Isaiah xl., 1-5, is, "Comfort ye, comfort ye my people, saith your God. Speak ye comfortably to Jerusalem, and cry unto her that her warfare is accomplished, that her iniquity is pardoned; for she hath received of the Lord's hand double for all her sins. The voice of him that crieth in the wilderness, Prepare ye the way of the Lord, make straight in the desert a highway for our God. Every valley shall be exalted, and every mountain and hill shall be made low: and the crooked shall be made straight, and the rough places plain: and the glory of the Lord shall be revealed." These verses have not the most remote relation to John? And this manufacture of prophecies for the purpose of bolstering up a tale, serves to prove that the writer of the Gospel tries by these to impart an air of credibility to an otherwise incredible story.

Immediately after the baptism, Jesus is led up of the Spirit into the wilderness to be tempted by the Devil. There he fasts forty days and forty nights.

John says, in chapter i., 35, "Again, the next day after, John stood and two of his disciples; and looking upon Jesus as he walked, he said, behold the Lamb of God. And the two disciples heard him speak, and they followed Jesus." Then, at the 43rd verse, he says, "The day following Jesus would go forth into Galilee, and findeth Philip, and saith unto him, follow me." And in chapter ii., 1, he says, "And the third day there was a marriage in Cana of Galilee, and the mother of Jesus was there; and both Jesus was called and his disciples into the marriage." According to Matthew, there can be no doubt that immediately after the baptism Jesus went into the wilderness to be tempted of the Devil. And we are to believe that Jesus was tempted of the Devil and fasting in the wilderness, and at the same time feasting at a marriage in Cana of Galilee? Is it possible to believe that Jesus actually did fast forty days and forty nights? If Jesus did not fast in his capacity as man, in what capacity did he fast? And if Jesus fasted, being God, the fast would be a mockery; and the account that he became a hungered must be wrong. It is barely possible that in some very abnormal condition or cataleptic state, or state of trance, a man might exist, with very slight nourishment or without food, but that a man could walk about, speak, and act, and, doing this, live forty days and nights without food is simply an impossibility.

Is the story that the Devil tempted Jesus credible? If Jesus be God, can the Devil tempt God? A clergyman of the Church of England writing on this says: "That the Devil should appear personally to the Son of God is certainly not more wonderful than that he should, in a more remote age, have appeared among the sons of God, in the presence of God himself, to torment the righteous Job. But that Satan should carry Jesus bodily and literally through the air, first to the top of a high mountain, and then to the topmost pinnacle of the temple, is wholly inadmissable, it is an insult to our understanding, and an affront to our great creator and redeemer." Supposing, despite the monstrosity of such a supposition, an actual Devil—and this involves the dilemma that the Devil must either be God-created, or God's co-eternal rival; the first supposition being inconsistent with God's goodness, and the second being inconsistent with his power; but supposing such a Devil, is it credible that the Devil should tempt the Almighty maker of the universe with "all these will I give thee if thou wilt fall down and worship me?" . . . .

The account of the calling of Peter is replete with contradictions. According to Matthew, when Jesus first saw Peter, the latter was in a vessel fishing with his brother Andrew, casting a net into the sea of Galilee. Jesus walking by the sea said to them—"Follow me, and I will make you fishers of men." The two brothers did so, and they became Christ's disciples. When Jesus called Peter no one was with him but his brother Andrew. A little further on, the two sons of Zebedee were in a ship with their father mending nets, and these latter were separately called. From John, we learn that Andrew was originally a disciple of John the Baptist, and that when Andrew first saw Jesus, Peter was not present, but Andrew went and found Peter who, if fishing, must have been angling on land, telling him "we have found the Messiah," and that Andrew then brought Peter to Jesus, who said, "Thou art Simon, the son of Jonas; thou shalt be called Cephas." There is no mention in John of the sons of Zebedee being a little further on, or of any fishing in the sea of Galilee. This call is clearly on land. Luke's Gospel states that when the call took place, Jesus and Peter were both at sea. Jesus had been preaching to the people, who pressing upon him, he got into Simon's ship, from which he preached. After this he directed Simon to put out into the deep and let down the nets. Simon answered, "Master, we have toiled all night and taken nothing; nevertheless at thy word I will let down the net." No sooner was this done, than the net was filled to breaking, and Simon's partners, the two sons of Zebedee, came to help, when at the call of Jesus, they brought their ships to land, and followed him.

Is it credible that there were three separate calls, or that the Gospels being inspired, you could have three contradictory versions of the same event? Has the story been here "painfully modified," or how do Dr. Tischendorf and the Religous Tract Society clear up the matter? Is it credible that, as stated in Luke, Jesus had visited Simon's house, and cured Simon's wife's mother, before the call of Simon, but did not go to Simon's house for that purpose, until after the call of Simon, as related in Matthew? It is useless to reply that the date of Jesus' visit is utterly unimportant, when we are told that it is upon the credibility of the complete narrative that Christianity must rest. Each stone is important to the building, and it is not competent for the Christian advocate to regard as useless any word which the Holy Ghost has considered important enough to reveal.

Are the miracle stories credible? Every ancient nation has had its miracle workers, but modern science has relegated all miracle history to realms of fable, myth, illusion, delusion, or fraud. Can Christian miracles be made the exceptions? Is it likely that the nations amongst whom the dead were restored to life would have persistently ignored the author of such miracles? Were the miracles purposeless, or if intended to convince the Jews, was God unable to render his intentions effective? That five thousand persons should be fed with five loaves and two fishes, and that an apparent excess should remain beyond the original stock, is difficult to believe; but that shortly after this—Jesus having to again perform a similar miracle for four thousand persons—his own disciples should ignore his recent feat, and wonder from whence the food was to be derived, is certainly startlingly incredible. If this exhibition of incredulity were pardonable on the part of the twelve apostles, living witnesses of greater wonders, how much more pardonable the unbelief of the skeptic of today, which the Religious Tract Society seek to overcome by a faint echo of asserted events all contrary to probability, and with nineteen centuries intervening.

The casting out the devils presents phenomena requiring considerable credulity, especially the story of the devils and the swine. Today insanity is never referable to demoniacal possession, but eighteen hundred years ago the subject of lunacy had not been so patiently investigated as it has been since. That one man could now be tenanted by several devils is a proposition for which the maintainer would in the present generation incur almost universal contempt; yet the repudiation of its present possibility can hardly be consistent with implicit credence in its ancient history. That the devils and God should hold converse together, although not without parallel in the book of Job, is inconsistent with the theory of an infinitely good Deity; that the devils should address Jesus as son of the most high God, and beg to be allowed to enter a herd of swine, is at least ludicrous; yet all this helps to make up the narrative on which Dr. Tischendorf relies. That Jesus being God should pray to his Father that "the cup might pass" from him is so incredible that even the faithful ask us to regard it as mystery. That an angel from heaven could strengthen Jesus, the almighty God, is equally mysterious. That where Jesus had so prominently preached to thousands, the priests should need any one like Judas to betray the founder of Christianity with a kiss, is absurd; his escapade in flogging the dealers, his wonderful cures, and his raising Lazarus and Jairus's daughter should have secured him, if not the nation's love, faith, and admiration, at least a national reputation and notoriety. It is not credible if Judas betrayed Jesus by a kiss that the latter should have been arrested upon his own statement that he was Jesus. That Peter should have had so little faith as to deny his divine leader three times in a few hours is only reconcilable with the notion that he had remained unconvinced by his personal intercourse with the incarnate Deity. The mere blunders in the story of the denial sink into insignificance in face of this major difficulty. Whether the cock did or did not crow before the third denial, whether Peter was or was not in the same apartment with Jesus at the time of the last denial, are comparatively trifling questions, and the contradictions on which they are based may be the consequence of the errors which Dr. Tischendorf says have crept into the sacred writings.

Jesus said, "as Jonah was three days and three nights in the belly of the whale, so shall the son of man be three days and three nights in the heart of the earth." Jesus was crucified on Friday, was buried on Friday evening, and yet the first who went to the grave on the night of Saturday as it began to dawn towards Sunday, found the body of Jesus already gone. Did Jesus mean he should be three days and three nights in the grave? Is there any proof that his body remained in the grave for three hours? Who went first to the grave? was it Mary Magdalene alone, as in John, or two Maries as in Matthew, or the two Maries and Salome as in Mark, or the two Maries, Joanna, and several unnamed women as in Luke? To whom did Jesus first appear? Was it, as in Mark, to Mary Magdalene, or to two disciples going to Emmaus, as in Luke, or to the two Maries near the sepulchre, as in Matthew? Is the eating boiled fish and honeycomb by a dead God credible? Did Jesus ascend to heaven the very day of his resurrection, or did an interval of nearly six weeks intervene?

Is this history credible, contained as it is in four contradictory biographies, outside which biographies we have, as Dr. Tischendorf admits, "no other source of information with respect to the life of Jesus"? This history of an earth-born Deity, descended through a crime-tainted ancestry, and whose genealogical tree is traced through one who was not his father; this history of an infinite God nursed as a baby, growing through childhood to manhood like any frail specimen of humanity; this history, garnished with bedevilled men, enchanted fig tree, myriads of ghosts, and scores of miracles, and by such garnishment made more akin to an oriental romance than to a sober history; this picture of the infinite invisible spirit incarnate visible as man; immutability subject to human passions and infirmities; the creator come to die, yet wishing to escape the death which shall bring peace to his God-tormented creatures; God praying to himself and rejecting his own prayer; God betrayed by a divinely-appointed traitor; God the immortal dying, and in the agony of the death-throes—stronger than the strong man's will—crying with almost the last effort of his dying breath, that he being God, is God forsaken!

If all this be credible, what story is there any man need hesitate to believe?

Dr. Tischendorf asks how it has been possible to impugn the credibility of the four Gospels, and replies that this has been done by denying that the Gospels were written by the men whose names they bear. In the preceding pages it has been shown that the credibility of the Gospel narrative is impugned because it is uncorroborated by contemporary history, because it is self-contradictory, and because many of its incidents are *prima facie* most improbable, and some of them utterly impossible. Even English infidels are quite prepared to admit that the four Gospels may be quite anonymous; and yet, that their anonymous character need be of no weight as an argument against their truth. All that is urged on this head is that the advocates of the Gospel history have sought to endorse and give value to the otherwise unreliable narratives by a pretense that some of the Evangelists, at least, were eyewitnesses of the events they refer to. Dr. Tischendorf says: "The credibility of a writer clearly depends on the interval of time which lies between him and the events which he describes. The farther the narrator is removed from the facts which he lays before us the more his claims to credibility are reduced in value." Presuming truthfulness in intention for any writer, and his ability to comprehend the facts he is narrating, and his freedom from a prejudice which may distort the picture he intends to paint correctly with his pen: we might admit the correctness of the passage we have quoted; but can these always be presumed in the case of the authors of the Gospels? On the contrary, a presumption in an exactly opposite direction may be fairly raised from the fact that immediately after the Apostolic age the Christian world was flooded with forged testimonies in favor of the biography of Jesus, or in favor of his disciples. . . .

Eusebius, in his "Ecclesiastical History," admits the existence of many spurious gospels and epistles, and some writings put forward by him as genuine, such as the correspondence between Jesus and Agbaras, have since been rejected as fictitious. It is not an unfair presumption from this that many of the most early Christians considered the then existing testimonies insufficient to prove the history of Jesus, and good reason is certainly afforded for carefully examining the whole of the evidences they have bequeathed us.

On p. 48, Dr. Tischendorf quotes Ireneus, whose writings belong to the extreme end of the second century, as though that Bishop must be taken as vouching the four Gospels as we now have them. Yet, if the testimony of Ireneus be reliable ("Against Heresies," Book III., cap. i.) the Gospel attributed to Matthew was believed to have been composed in Hebrew, and Ireneus says that as the Jews desired a Messiah of the royal line of David, Matthew having the same desire to a yet greater degree, strove to give them full satisfaction. This may account for some of the genealogical curiosities to which we have drawn attention, but hardly renders Matthew's Gospel more reliable; and how can the suggestion that Matthew wrote in Hebrew prove that Matthew penned the first Gospel, which has only existed in Greek? Ireneus, too, flatly contradicts the Gospels by declaring that the ministry of Jesus extended over ten years and that Jesus lived to be fifty years of age ("Against Heresies," Book II., cap. 22).

If the statement of Ireneus ("Against Heresies," Book III., cap. 11) that the fourth Gospel was written to refute the errors of Cerinthus and Nicolaus, have any value, then the actual date of issue of the fourth Gospel will be considerably after the others. Dr. Tischendorf's statement that Polycarp has borne testimony to the Gospel of John is not even supported by the quotation on which he relies. All that is said in the passage quoted (Eusebius, "Ecc. Hist.," Book V., cap. 20) is that Ireneus when he was a child heard Polycarp repeat from memory the discourses of John and others concerning Jesus. If the Gospels had existed in the time of Polycarp it would have been at least as easy to have read them from the MS. as to repeat them from memory. Dr. Tischendorf might also have added that the letter to Florinus, whence he takes the passage on which he relies, exists only in the writings of Eusebius, to whom we are indebted for many pieces of Christian evidence since abandoned as forgeries. Dr. Tischendorf says: "Any testimony of Polycarp in favor of the Gospel refers us back to the Evangelist himself, for Polycarp, in speaking to Ireneus of this Gospel as the work of his master, St. John, must have learned from the lips of the apostle himself, whether he was its author or not." Now, what evidence is there that Polycarp ever said a single word as to the authorship of the fourth Gospel, or of any Gospel, or that he even said that John had penned a single word? In the Epistle to the Philippians (the only writing attributed to Polycarp for which any genuine character is even pretended), the Gospel of John is never mentioned, nor is there even a single passage in the Epistle which can be identified with any passage in the Gospel of John.

Surely, Dr. Tischendorf forgot, in the eager desire to make his witnesses bear good testimony, that the highest duty of an advocate is to make the truth clear, not to put forward a pleasantly colored falsehood to deceive the ignorant. It is not even true that Ireneus ever pretends that Polycarp in any way vouched our fourth Gospel as having been written by John, and yet Dr. Tischendorf had the cool audacity to say "there is nothing more damaging to the doubters of the authenticity of St. John's Gospel that this testimony of St. Polycarp." Do the Religious Tract Society regard English Infidels as so utterly ignorant that they thus intentionally seek to suggest a falsehood, or are the Council of the Religious Tract Society themselves unable to test the accuracy of the statements put forward on their behalf by the able decipherer of illegible parchments? It is too much to suspect the renowned Dr. Constantine Tischendorf of ignorance, yet even the coarse English skeptic regrets that the only other alternative will be to denounce him as a theological charlatan. . . .

Dr. Tischendorf's style is well exemplified by the positive manner in which he fixes the date A.D. 139 to the first apology of Justin, although a critic so "learned" as the unrivalled Dr. Tischendorf could not fail to be aware that more than one-writer has supported the view that the date of the first apology was not earlier than A.D. 145, and others have contended for A.D. 150. The Benedictine editors of Justin's works support the latter date. Dr. Kenn argues for A.D. 155-160. On page 63, the Religious Tract Society's champion appeals to the testimony of Justin Martyr, but in order not to shock the devout while convincing the profane, he omits to mention that more than half the writings once attributed to Justin Martyr are now abandoned, as either of doubtful character, or actual forgeries, and that Justin's value as a witness is considerably weakened by the fact that he quotes the acts of Pilate and the Sybilline Oracles as though they were reliable evidence, when in fact they are both admitted specimens of "a Christian forgery." But what does Justin testify as to the Gospels? Does he say that Matthew, Mark, Luke, and John were their writers? On the contrary, not only do the names of Matthew, Mark, Luke, and John never occur as Evangelists in the writings of Justin, but he actually mentions facts and sayings as to Jesus, which are not found in either of the four Gospels. The very words rendered Gospels only occur where they are strongly suspected to be interpolated, Justin usually speaking of some writings which he calls "memorials" or "memoirs of the Apostles."

Dr. Tischendorf urges that in the writings of Justin the Gospels are placed side by side with the prophets, and that "this undoubtedly places the Gospels in the list of canonical books." If this means that there is any statement in Justin capable of being so construed, then Dr. Tischendorf was untruthful. Justin does quote specifically the Sybilline oracles, but never Matthew, Mark, Luke, or John. He quotes statements as to Jesus, which may be found in the apocryphal Gospels, and which are not found in ours, so that if the evidence of Justin Martyr be taken, it certainly does not tend to prove, even in the smallest degree, that four Gospels were specially regarded with reverence in his day. The Rev. W. Sanday thinks that Justin did not assign an exclusive authority to our Gospels, and that he made use also of other documents no longer extant. ("Gospels in 2nd Century," p. 117.)

On p. 94 it is stated that "as early as the time of Justin the expression "the Evangel" was applied to the four Gospels." This statement by Dr. Tischendorf and its publication by the Religious Tract Society call for the strongest condemnation. Nowhere in the writings of Justin are the words "the Evangel" applied to the four Gospels.

Lardner only professes to discover two instances in which the word anglicized by Tischendorf as "Evangel," occurs; $\varepsilon\nu\alpha\gamma\gamma\varepsilon\lambda\iota\omega$ and $\varepsilon\nu\alpha\gamma\gamma\varepsilon\lambda\iota\alpha$, the second being expressly pointed out by Schleiermacher as an interpolation, and as an instance in which a marginal note has been incorporated with the text; nor would one occurrence of such a word prove that any book or books were so known by Justin, as the word is merely a compound of $\varepsilon\nu$ good and $\alpha\gamma\gamma\varepsilon\lambda\iota\alpha$ message; nor is there the slightest foundation for the statement that in the time of Justin the word was ever applied to designate the four Gospels now attributed to Matthew, Mark, Luke, and John.

Dr. Tischendorf (p. 46) admits that the "faith of the Church . . . would be seriously compromised" if we do not find references to the Gospels in writings between A.D. 100 and A.D. 150; and—while he does not directly assert—he insinuates that in such writings the Gospels were "treated with the greatest respect," or "even already treated as canonical and sacred writings;" and he distinctly affirms that the Gospels "did see the light" during the "Apostolic age," "and before the middle of the second century our Gospels were held in the highest respect by the Church," although for the affirmation, he neither has nor advances the shadow of evidence.

The phrases, "Apostolic age" and "Apostolic fathers" denote the first century of the Christian era, and those fathers who are supposed to have flourished during that period, and who are supposed to have seen or heard, or had the opportunity of seeing or hearing, either Jesus or some one or more of the twelve Apostles. Barnabas, Clement, Hermas, Ignatius, and Polycarp, are those whose names figure most familiarly in Christian evidences as Apostolic fathers. But the evidence from these Apostolic fathers is of a most unreliable character. Mosheim ("Ecclesiastical History," cent. 1, cap. 2, sec. 3, 17) says that "the Apostolic history is loaded with doubts, fables, and difficulties," and that not long after Christ's ascension several histories were current of his life and doctrines, full of "pious frauds and fabulous wonders." . . .

. . . To quote the inimitable style of Dr. Tischendorf, "while so much has been lost in the course of centuries by the tooth of time and the carelessness of ignorant monks, an invisible eye had watched over this treasure, and when it was on the point of perishing in the fire, the Lord had decreed its deliverance;" "while critics have generally been divided between assigning it to the first or second decade of the second century, the Sinaitic Bible, which has for the first time cleared up this question, has led us to throw its composition as far back as the last decade of the first century." A fine specimen of Christian evidence writing, cool assertion without a particle of proof and without the slightest reason given. . . .

There is an epistle attributed to Clement of Rome, which has been preserved in a single MS. only where it is coupled with another epistle rejected as spurious. Dr. Donaldson ("Ante-Nicene Fathers," vol. i., p. 3) declares that who the Clement was to whom these writings are ascribed cannot with absolute certainty be determined. Both epistles stand on equal authority; one is rejected by Christians, the other is received. In this epistle while there is a distinct reference to an Epistle by Paul to the Corinthians, there is no mention by name of the four Gospels, nor do any of the words attributed by Clement to Jesus agree for any complete quotation with anyone of the Gospels as we have them. The Rev. W. Sanday is frank enough to concede "that Clement is not quoting directly from our Gospels."

Is it probable that Clement would have mentioned a writing by Paul, and yet have entirely ignored the four Gospels, if he had known that they had then existed? And could they have easily existed in the Christian world in his day without his knowledge? If anyone takes cap. xxv. of this epistle and sees the phoenix given as a historic fact, and as evidence for the reality of the resurrection, he will be better able to appreciate the value of this so-called epistle of Clement.

The letters of Ignatius referred to by Dr. Tischendorf are regarded by Mosheim as laboring under many difficulties, and embarrassed with much obscurity. Even Lardner, doing his best for such evidences, says, that if we find matters in the Epistles inconsistent with the notion that Ignatius was the writer, it is better to regard such passages as interpolations, than to reject the Epistles entirely, especially in the *"scarcity"* of such testimonies.

There are fifteen epistles of which eight are undisputedly forgeries. Of the remaining seven there are two versions, a long and a short version, one of which must be corrupt, both of which may be. These seven epistles, however, are in no case to be accepted with certainty as those of Ignatius. Dr. Cureton contends that only three still shorter epistles are genuine ("Ante-Nicene Fathers," vol. i., pp. 137 to 143). The Rev. W. Sanday treats the three short ones as probably genuine, waiving the questions as to the others ("Gospels in Second Century," pp. 77, and see preface to sixth edition "Supernatural Religion"). Ignatius, however, even if he be the writer of the epistles attributed to him, never mentions either of the four Gospels. In the nineteenth chapter of the Epistles to the Ephesians, there is a statement made as to the birth and death of Jesus, not to be found in either Matthew, Mark, Luke, or John.

If the testimony of the Ignatian Epistles is reliable, then it vouches that in that early age there were actually Christians who denied the death of Jesus. A statement as to Mary in cap. xix of the Epistle to the Ephesians is not to be found in any portion of the Gospels. In his Epistle to the Trallians, Ignatius, attacking those who denied the real existence of Jesus, would have surely been glad to quote the evidence of eye witnesses like Matthew and John, if such evidence had existed in his day. In cap. viii of the Epistles to the Philadelphians, Ignatius says, "I have heard of some who say: Unless I find it in the archives I will not believe the Gospel. And when I said it is written, they answered that remains to be proved." This is the most distinct reference to any Christian writings, and how little does this support Dr. Tischendorf's position. From which of our four Gospels could Ignatius have taken the words, "I am not an incorporeal demon," which he puts into the mouth of Jesus in cap. iii., the epistle to the Smyrneans? Dr. Tischendorf does admit that the evidence of the Ignatian Epistles is not of decisive value; might he not go farther and say, that as proof of the four Gospels it is of no value at all? . . .

It is pleasant to find a grain of wheat in the bushel of Tischendorf chaff. On page 98, and following pages, the erudite author applies himself to get rid of the testimony of Papias, which was falsified and put forward by Paley as of great importance. Paley says the authority of Papias is complete; Tischendorf declares that Papias is in error. Paley says Papias was a hearer of John, Tischendorf says he was not. We leave the champions of two great Christian evidence-mongers to settle the matter as best they can. If, however, we are to accept Dr. Tischendorf's declaration that the testimony of Papias is worthless, we get rid of the chief link between Justin Martyr and the apostolic age. It pleases Dr. Tischendorf to damage Papias, because the father is silent as to the gospel of John; but the Religious Tract Society must not forget that in thus clearing away the second-hand evidence of Papias, they have cut away their only pretense for saying that any of the Gospels are mentioned by name within 150 years of the date claimed for the birth of Jesus. In referring to the lost work of Theophilus of Antioch, which Dr. Tischendorf tells us was a kind of harmony of the Gospels, in which the four narratives are molded and fused into one, the learned Doctor forgets to tell us that Jerome, when he quotes as giving some account of Theophilus, actually doubted whether the so-called commentary was really from the pen of that writer. Lardner says: "Whether these commentaries which St. Jerome quotes were realy composed by Theophilus may be doubted, since they were unknown to Eusebius, and were observed by Jerome to differ in style and expression from his other works. However, if they were not his, they were the work of some anonymous ancient." But if they were the work of an anonymous ancient after Eusebius, what becomes of Dr. Tischendorf's "as early as A.D. 170?"

Eusebius, who refers to Theophilus, and who speaks of his using the

Apocalypse, would have certainly gladly quoted the Bishop of Antioch's "Commentary on the Four Gospels," if it had existed in his day. Nor is it true that the references we have in Jerome to the work attributed to Theophilus, justify the description given by Dr. Tischendorf, or even the phrase of Jerome, *"qui quatuor Evangelistarum in unum opus dicta compingen."* Theophilus seems, so far as it is possible to judge, to have occupied himself not with a connected history of Jesus, or a continuous discourse as to his doctrines, but rather with mystical and allegorical elucidations of occasional passages, which ended, like many pious commentaries on the Old or New Testament, in leaving the point dealt with a little less clear with the Theophillian commentary than without it. Dr. Tischendorf says that Theodoret and Eusebius speak of Tatian in the same way—that is, as though he had, like his Syrian contemporary, composed a harmony of the four Gospels. This is also inaccurate. Eusebius talks of Tatianus "having found a certain body and collection of Gospels, I know not how," which collection Eusebius does not appear even to have ever seen; and so far from the phrase in Theodoret justifying Dr. Tischendorf's explanation, it would appear from Theodoret that Tatian's Diatessaron was, in fact, a sort of spurious gospel, "The Gospel of the Four" differing materially from our four Gospels of Matthew, Mark, Luke, and John. Neither Ireneus, Clement of Alexandria, or Jerome, who refer to other works of Tatian, make any mention of this. Dr. Tisenchdorf might have added that Diapente, or "the Gospel of the Five," has also been a title applied to this work of Tatian.

In the third chapter of his essay, Dr. Tischendorf refers to apocryphal writings "which bear on their front the names of Apostles" "used by obscure writers to palm off" their forgeries. Dr. Tischendorf says that these spurious books were composed "partly to embellish" scripture narratives, and "partly to support false doctrine;" and he states that in early times, the Church was not so well able to distinguish true gospels from false ones, and that consequently some of the apocryphal writings "were given a place they did not deserve." This statement of the inability of the Church to judge correctly, tells as much against the whole, as against any one or more of the early Christian writings, and as it may be as fatal to the now received gospels as to those now rejected, it deserves the most careful consideration. According to Dr. Tischendorf, Justin Martyr falls into the category of those of the Church who were "not so critical in distinguishing the true from the false;" for Justin, says Tischendorf, treats the Gospel of St. James and the Acts of Pilate, each as a fit source whence to derive materials for the life of Jesus, and therefore must have regarded the Gospel of St. James and the Acts of Pilate, as genuine and authentic writings; while Dr. Tischendorf, wiser, and a greater critic than Justin, condemns the Gospel of St. James as spurious, and calls the Acts of Pilate "a pious fraud;"

but if Dr. Tischendorf be correct in his statement that "Justin made use of this Gospel" and quotes the "Acts of Pontius Pilate," then, according to his own words, Justin did not know how to distinguish the true from the false, and the whole force of his evidence previously used by Dr. Tischendorf in aid of the four Gospels would have been seriously diminished, even if it had been true, which it is not, that Justin Martyr had borne any testimony on the subject.

Such, then, are the weapons, say the Religious Tract Society, by their champion, "which we employ against unbelieving criticism." And what are these weapons? We have shown in the preceding pages, the *suppressio veri* and the *suggestio falsi* are amongst the weapons used. The Religious Tract Society directors are parties to fabrication of evidence, and they permit a learned charlatan to forward the cause of Christ with craft and chicane. But even this is not enough; they need, according to their pamphlet, "a new weapon;" they want "to find out the very words the Apostles used." True believers have been in a state of delusion; they were credulous enough to fancy that the authorized version of the Scriptures tolerably faithfully represented God's revelation to humankind. But no, says Dr. Tischendorf, it has been so seriously modified in the copying and recopying that it ought to be set aside altogether, and a fresh text constructed. Glorious news this for the Bible Society. Listen to it, Exeter Hall! Glad tidings to be issued by the Paternoster Row saints! After spending hundreds of thousands of pounds in giving away Bibles to soldiers, in placing them in hotels and lodging-houses, and shipping them off to negroes and slaves, it appears that the wrong text has been sent through the world, the true version being all the time in a waste-paper heap at Mount Sinai, watched over by an "invisible eye." But, adds Dr. Tischendorf, "if you ask me whether any popular version contains the original text, my answer is Yes and No. I say Yes as far as concerns your soul's salvation." If these are enough for the soul's salvation, why try to improve the matter? If we really need the "full and clear light" of the Sinaitic Bible to show us "what is the Word written by God," then most certainly our present Bible is not believed by the Religious Tract Society to be the Word written by God. The Christian advocates are in this dilemma: either the received text is insufficient, or the proposed improvement is unnecessary. Dr. Tischendorf says that "The Gospels, like the only begotten of the Father, will endure as long as human nature itself," yet he says "there is a great diversity among the texts," and that the Gospel in use amongst the Ebionites and that used amongst the Nazarenes have been "disfigured here and there with certain arbitrary changes." He admits, moreover, that "in early times, when the Church was not so critical in distinguishing the true from the false," spurious Gospels obtained a credit which they did not deserve. And while arguing for the enduring character of the Gospel, he requests you to set aside the received text altogether, and to try to construct a new revelation by the aid of Dr. Tischendorf's patent Sinaitic invention.

We congratulate the Religious Tract Society upon their manifesto, and on the victory it secures them over German Rationalism and English infidelity. The Society's translator, in his introductory remarks, declares that "circumstantial evidence when complete, and when every link in the chain has been thoroughly tested, is as strong as direct testimony;" and, adds the Society's penman, "This is the kind of evidence which Dr. Tischendorf brings for the genuineness of our Gospels. It would be difficult to imagine a more inaccurate description of Dr. Tischendorf's work. Do we find the circumstantial evidence carefully tested in the Doctor's boasting and curious narrative of his journeys commenced on a pecuniary deficiency and culminating in much cash? Do we find it in Dr. Tischendorf's concealment for fifteen years of the place, watched over by an invisible eye, in which was hidden the greatest biblical treasure in the world? Is the circumstantial evidence shown in the sneers at Renan? or is each link in the chain tested by the strange jumbling together of names and conjectures in the first chapter? What tests are used in the cases of Valentinus and Basilides in the second chapter? How is the circumstantial testimony aided by the references in the third chapter to the Apocryphal Gospels? Is there a pretense even of critical testing in the chapter devoted to the apostolic fathers? All that Dr. Tischendorf has done is in effect to declare that our authorized version of the New Testament is so unreliable, that it ought to be got rid of altogether, and a new text constructed. And this declaration is circulated by the Religious Tract Society, which sends the sixpenny edition to the Gospel with one hand, and in the other the shilling Tischendorf pamphlet, declaring that many passages of the Religious Tract Society's New Testament have undergone such serious modifications of meaning as to leave us in painful uncertainty as to what was originally written.

The very latest contribution from orthodox sources to the study of the Gospels, as contained in the authorized version, is to be found in the very candid preface to the recently-issued revised version of the New Testament, where the ordinary Bible receives a condemnation of the most sweeping description. Here, on the high authority of the revisers, we are told that, with regard to the Greek text, the translators of the authorized version had for their guides "manuscripts of late date, few in number and used with little critical skill." For revisers add what freethinkers have long maintained, and have been denounced from pulpits for maintaining, viz., "that the commonly received next needed thorough revision," and, what is even more important, they candidly avow that "it is but recently that materials have been acquired for executing such a work with even approximate completeness." So that not only "God's Word" has admittedly for generations not been "God's Word" at all, but even now, and with materials not formerly known, it has only been revised with "approximate completeness," whatever those two words may mean. If they have any significance at all, they must convey the belief of the new and at present final revisers of the Gospel, that, even after all their toil, they are not quite sure that god's revelation is quite exactly rendered into English. So far as the ordinary authorized version of the New Testament goes—and it is this, the law-recognized, version which is still used in administering oaths—we are told that the old translators "used considerable freedom," and "studiously adopted a variety of expressions which would now be deemed hardly consistent with the requirements of faithful translation." This is a pleasant euphemism, but a real and direct charge of dishonest translation by the authorized translators. The new revisers add, with sadness, that "it cannot be doubted that they (the translaters of the authorized version) carried this liberty too far, and that the studied avoidance of uniformity in the rendering of the same words, even when occurring in the same context, is one of the blemishes of their work." These blemishes the new revisers think were increased by the fact that the translation of the authorized version of the New Testament was assigned to two separate companies, who never sat together, which "was beyond doubt the cause of many inconsistencies," and, although there was a final supervision, the new revisers add, most mournfully: "When it is remembered that the supervision was completed in nine months, we may wonder that the incongruities which remain are not more numerous."

Nor are the revisers by any means free from doubt and misgivings on their own work. They had the "laborious task" of "deciding between the rival claims of various readings which might properly affect the translation," and, as they tell us, "Textual criticism, as applied to the Greek New Testament, forms a special study of much intricacy and difficulty, and even now leaves room for considerable variety of opinion among competent critics." Next they say: "the frequent inconsistencies in the authorized version have caused us much embarrassment," and that there are "numerous passages in the authorized version in which . . . the studied variety adopted by the Translators of 1611 had produced a degree of inconsistency that cannot be reconciled with the principle of faithfulness." So little are the new revisers always certain as to what god means that they provide "alternative readings in difficult or debatable passages," and say "the notes of this last group are numerous and largely in excess of those which were admitted by our predecessors." And with reference to the pronouns and other words in italics we are told that "some of these cases . . . are of singular intricacy, and make it impossible to maintain rigid uniformity." The new revisers conclude by declaring that "through our manifold experience of its abounding difficulties we have felt more and more as we went onward that such a work can never be accomplished by organized efforts of scholarship and criticism unless assisted by divine help." Apparently the new revisers are conscious that they did not receive this divine help in their attempt at revision, for they go on: "We know full well that defects must have their place in a work so long and so arduous as this which has now come to an end. Blemishes and imperfections there are in the noble translation which we have been called upon to revise; blemishes and imperfections will assuredly be found in our own revision; ... we cannot forget how often we have failed in expressing some finer shade of meaning which we recognized in the original, how often idiom has stood in the way of a perfect rendering, and how often the attempt to preserve a familiar form of words, or even a familiar cadence, has only added another perplexity to those which have already beset us."

Parallels to the Teaching of Christ

Joseph McCabe

Joseph McCabe was a former Franciscan monk and priest ("Father Antony") who left the church. There are many of those, but what made McCabe unique, or at least unusual, was that he became a freethought lecturer and author par excellence. He authored approximately 200 books (plus about 100 Little Blue Books and 200 Big Blue Books for E. Haldeman-Julius.) McCabe claimed in his autobiography, *Eighty Years A Rebel,* that he had written more books than any living man at the time (1947). While it is difficult to verify this statement, he surely would be close to being the leader.

McCabe was born in Manchester, England, in 1867. After a Catholic education, he took his vows and eventually became a professor of philosophy at Catholic Louvain University in Belgium. In later years, McCabe was to discredit completely his Catholic education, claiming that he spent the rest of his life learning the truth about historical and religious matters about which he had been misinformed by his religiously biased teachers. McCabe *did* become an extremely learned man, writing and lecturing about many fields, including literature, geology, biology, history, sexology, psychology, philosophy, and theology. In most of his writings, his main aim was to tell the truth about whatever subject he was writing about, without accepting any distortions introduced by people with an axe to grind. He claimed that many books on the history of the Middle Ages had been colored by falsehoods introduced by clerical "scholars." During his rationalist phase, which ran from 1896 until his death in 1955, he earned his living entirely from speaking and writing. He was also responsible for about fifty translations, including the works of Ernst Haeckel, the founder of "monism." McCabe popularized evolution and simplified science for the masses.

For many years (until 1928), McCabe wrote largely for the British Rationalist

Press Association at the rate of two books a year. In 1928 he had a falling-out with the RPA. That was when E. Haldeman-Julius hired him to produce first Little Blue Books, then Big Blue Books upon demand. McCabe also wrote for many magazines including *The American Freeman* for Haldeman-Julius. McCabe had his own magazine entitled, appropriately enough, *The Joseph McCabe Magazine*. McCabe also edited *The Militant Atheist* for Haldeman-Julius.

McCabe married after leaving the priesthood and had several children. He wrote on a number of sexological topics in later life, and he was quick to point out that the Catholic church kept its clergy in ignorance and fear of sex. McCabe liked to point out the great harm that he saw Roman Catholicism doing in the world, but he was no mere anti-Catholic. He always tried to document his charges from his vast knowledge of many fields. Although Haldeman-Julius was a bit overblown in calling McCabe "the world's greatest scholar," there is no question that McCabe usually knew what he was talking about. He spent the rest of his life, until his death in 1955, writing for Haldeman-Julius and the RPA, with whom he was reconciled.

There is no biography of McCabe, although Haldeman-Julius did publish his autobiography. The influence of McCabe was diffuse, because he spread his writings over such a vast area. It can be said, however, that he must have helped in the enlightenment of millions of his readers in all walks of life.

The present selection is from *The Sources of the Morality of the Gospels*, published in 1914 by Watts & Company in London. The table makes up the section of the book from page 210 to 296. It is somewhat abridged in our reprinting, the first since the original 1914 edition went out of print before 1920.

[*Editor's Note:* The present selection consists of a part of a very lengthy table from McCabe's book. The table has been edited down so that it includes only the more famous New Testament verses. It should be understood that 1) if a verse is not listed in the present selection, it does not mean that it was not in the original McCabe chapter or that no parallels exist, and 2) McCabe was of the opinion that there was *nothing* of substance in the Gospels that did not have a precursor in the work of the Talmud, the Old Testament or Greek and Roman works. Obviously, not all verses can be included in this table. Some parallels may not be as good as others, but in many cases the similarity is striking.]

Parallels to the Teaching of Christ

THE GOSPELS	THE OLD TESTAMENT
Blessed are the poor in spirit; for theirs is the kingdom of heaven.	I dwell in the high and holy place . . . to revive the spirit of the humble.—*Is.*, lvii, 15.
	He that is of a lowly spirit shall obtain honor.—*Prov.* xxix, 23.
	Walk humbly with thy God.—*Micah,* vi, 8.

.   .   .

Blessed are the meek; for they shall inherit the earth.	The meek shall inherit the earth.—*Ps.* xxxvii, 11.
	The Lord lifteth up the meek.—*Ps.* cxlvii, 6.
	The meek shall increase their joy in the Lord.—*Is.,* xxix, 19.

.   .   .

Blessed are the merciful; for they shall obtain mercy.	He that followeth after righteousness and mercy, findeth life, righteousness, and honor.—*Prov.,* xxi, 21.
	Blessed is he that considereth the poor: the Lord will deliver him in time of trouble.—*Ps.,* xli, 1.

Blessed are the pure in heart; for they shall see God.	Who shall ascend into the hill of the Lord? . . . He that hath clean hands and a pure heart.—*Ps.* xxiv, 3-4.
	There is no price worthy of a continent soul.—*Ecclus.,* xxvi, 15.

THE TALMUD

The Law is not with the proud, but with the contrite of spirit.—*Tanchuma,* 84, 4.

We find the Law only in men of lowly spirit.—*Taanit,* 7, 1.

Whenever there is question in the Bible of the greatness of God, his love of the humble is recorded.—*Megillah,* 31.

. . .

When a man hath acquired meekness, then will he also acquire wealth, honor, and wisdom [R. Johanan].—*Midrash Jalkut Mishle,* 22.

He who offereth humility to God hath as much merit as if he had offered all the victims in the world.—*Sotah,* 8.

. . .

He who showeth mercy to his fellow creatures shall receive mercy from the Lord.—*Sabbath,* 151, 2.

The mark of Israel is the practice of mercy.—*Jebamot,* 79.

We must not kill even the smallest worm without need.—*Jalkut Tillim,* 1.

The school of Schammai says: Not only the open sin, but an unclean thought, maketh a man answerable to God.—*Baba mezia,* 44, 1.

The sinful mind is worse than the sin.—*Joma,* 28.

GREEK AND ROMAN

What disease shall we say that the rich man suffereth from but spiritual poverty?—PLUTARCH, *On Covetousness,* iv.

Any person may live happy in poverty, but few in wealth and power.—EPICTETUS, *Fragments,* cxxviii.

. . .

I will be meek and yielding to my enemies.—SENECA, *On the Happy Life,* xx, 5.

A calm and meek and humane temper is not more pleasant to those with whom we live than to him who possesseth it.—PLUTARCH, *On Restraining Anger,* xvi.

. . .

It is the mark of a generous and lofty mind to give aid, to do service.—SENECA, *On Benefits,* iii, 15.

Forgiveness is better than punishment: for the one is a proof of a gentle, the other of a savage, nature.—EPICTETUS, *Fragments,* lxiii.

Those who have been pre-eminent for holiness of life are released from this earthly prison, and go to their pure home, which is above.—PLATO, *Phaedo,* 114.

The refined and pure soul, imitator of God, raising itself above human things, placing nothing of itself outside itself.—SENECA, *Letter* cxxiv, 23.

THE GOSPELS

Blessed are the peacemakers; for they shall be called the children of God.

Think not that I came to destroy the law, or the prophets; I am not come to destroy, but to fulfill. For verily I say unto you, Till heaven and earth pass, one jot or one tittle shall in no wise pass from the law till all be fulfilled.

Ye have heard that it was said by them of old time: Thou shalt not commit adultery. But I say unto you, That whosoever looketh on a woman to lust after her hath committed adultery with her already in his heart.

THE OLD TESTAMENT

Seek peace and pursue it: the eyes of the Lord are upon the righteous.—*Ps.,* xxxiv, 14.

Nation shall not lift up sword against nation, neither shall they learn war any more; but they shall sit every man under his vine and under his fig-tree.—*Micah,* iv, 3.

The mountains shall depart, and the hills be removed; but my kindness shall not depart from thee, neither shall my covenant of peace be removed.—*Is.,* liv, 10.

He that keepeth the commandment keepeth his own soul; but he that despiseth his ways shall die.—*Prov.,* xix, 16.

Thou shalt not covet thy neighbor's wife.—*Exodus,* xx, 17.

Lust not after her beauty in thine heart.—*Prov.,* vi, 25.

I made a covenant with mine eyes; why then should I think upon a maid?—*Job,* xxxi, 1.

THE TALMUD

Love peace, and seek it at any price [Hillel].—*Pirke Abot,* 1, 12.

He who establisheth peace in his house is rewarded by God as if he had established peace in all Israel.—*Abot of R. Nathan,* 28.

He who maketh peace between neighbors will not only have eternal life, but even in this life good fruit will not be wanting to him.—*Peah,* 1, 1.

. . .

Not a letter of the Law will ever be destroyed.—*Cosri,* 1, 83.

Heaven and earth shall pass, but not the word of God.—*Bereshit rabba,* 10, 1.

Deuteronomy once cast itself before the throne of God, and complained: O Lord of the world, thou hast written thy law in me, and if the least in it be changed, the whole must fall. Yet, behold, King Solomon seeketh to extirpate the letter jod . . . And the Lord answered and said: Solomon and thousands of his like shall pass away, but thou shalt abide for ever.—[Jerusalem Talmud] *Sanhedrim,* 20, 3.

. . .

Whosoever regardeth even the little finger of a woman hath already sinned in his heart.—*Berachot,* 24, 1.

Whosoever looketh with lust on a woman's heel sins no less than if he had dishonored her.—[Jerus. Talmud] *Challah,* 58, 3.

GREEK AND ROMAN

A wise and good person neither quarreleth with any man, nor, as far as is possible, suffereth another to do so. The life of Socrates giveth us an example of this, as of other things; since he did not only avoid quarrelling himself, but did not even suffer others to quarrel.—EPICTETUS, *Discourses,* iv, 5.

If you always remember that God standeth by as a witness of whatever you do, either in soul or body, you will never err.—EPICTETUS, *Fragments,* cxv.

They who are bidden to suffer what timid mortals dread do but say: We seemed to God worthy that in us He should try how much human nature can endure.—SENECA, *On Providence,* iv, 8.

Our souls are connected and intimately joined to God. . . . Must he not be sensible of every movement of them?—EPICTETUS, *Discourses,* i, 14.

It is the intention, not the outward act, which makes the wickedness.—SENECA, *On the Happy Life,* xvi.

THE GOSPELS	THE OLD TESTAMENT
	Gaze not on a maid. . . . Turn away thine eye from a comely woman, and gaze not on another's beauty.—*Ecclus.,* ix, 5, 8.
	Look not upon every body in regard of beauty, and sit not in the midst of women.—*Ecclus.,* xlii, 12.
And if thy right eye offend thee, pluck it out and cast it from thee; for it is profitable for thee that one of thy members should perish, and not that thy whole body should be cast into hell. And if thy right hand offend thee, cut it off and cast it from thee; for it is profitable to thee that one of thy members should perish, and not that thy whole body should be cast into hell.	
It hath been said, Whosoever shall put away his wife, let him give her a writing of divorcement; but I say unto you, That whosoever shall put away his wife, saving for the cause of fornication, causeth her to commit adultery; and whosoever shall marry her that is divorced committeth adultery.[1]	Let none deal treacherously against the wife of his youth, for the Lord, the God of Israel, saith that he hateth putting away.—*Mal.,* ii. 15-16.

[1]Mark and Luke omit the exception in case of fornication, and make Jesus absolutely forbid divorce. The confusion which this has caused among theologians is merely an echo of the controversies of the ancient rabbis. Some,

THE TALMUD

A man must not look upon a beautiful woman, though she be not married; nor upon a married woman, though she be ugly.—*Abodah zarah,* 20, 1.

The Rabbis teach: Whosoever giveth money from his hand into the hand of a woman, that he may thus have occasion to regard her, is in danger of hell.—*Berachot,* 61, 1.

[In the *Midrash Jalkut,* section Vayecki, No. 16, at v. 48 *Genesis,* it is said that a rabbi burned his eye out when the devil tempted him in the form of a beautiful woman.] It is better for me to be burned by fire in this world, since that is light compared with the eternal fire. [Jerus. Talmud.]—*Jalkut Rubeni,* 65, 1.

It were better for the evil-minded to have been born blind.—*Tanchuma,* 71, 4.

A man shall not put away his wife unless it be for adultery.—*Gittin,* 90.

Whosoever shall put away his wife is hated of God. [R. Johanan and others.]—*Gittin,* 90, 2.

R. Eliezer said: Whosoever shall put away his first wife, over him the altar sheddeth tears.—*Sabbath* [ii, 60, Rod.].

If a man putteth his wife away with his left hand, let him take her back with the right.—*Sotah,* 46, 1.

GREEK AND ROMAN

Live as if God beheld thee.—SENECA. *Letter* x.

If a man lie with his own wife, imagining her another, he is an adulterer.—SENECA, *On Constancy,* vii, 4.

Is it for one paltry leg, wretch, that thou dost accuse the universe? Canst thou not forego that, in consideration of the whole? Canst thou not gladly yield it to Him who gave it?—EPICTETUS, i, 49.

The wise man counteth as temporary and uncertain, not only chattels and possessions and dignities, but even his body and eyes and hands, and whatever maketh life pleasant; and he liveth as one who hath received on trust, and is ever ready to restore cheerfully.—SENECA, *Of Tranquillity of Mind,* xi.

[Divorce was permitted by every Roman and Greek, so that one must not look in them for parallels to this reactionary tendency of later Jews. On chastity itself the pagan moralists insisted sternly.]

It is infamous for a man to exact chastity of his wife and corrupt the wives of others.—SENECA, *Letter* xciv, 26.

THE GOSPELS

like the famous R. Akiba, allowed divorce on slight grounds; some only for adultery; and some forbade it altogether.

Again, ye have heard that it hath been said by them of old time, Thou shalt not forswear thyself, but shalt perform unto the Lord thine oaths: but I say unto you, Swear not at all; neither by heaven, for it is God's throne; nor by the earth, for it is his footstool; neither by Jerusalem, for it is the city of the great King. Neither shalt thou swear by thy head, because thou canst not make one hair white or black. But let your communication be: Yea, yea; Nay, nay: for whatever is more than these cometh of evil.

THE OLD TESTAMENT

Thou shalt not take the name of the Lord thy God in vain.—*Ex.,* xx, 7.

When a man voweth a vow unto the Lord, or sweareth an oath to bind his soul with a bond, he shall not break his word.—*Numbers,* xxx, 2.

The heaven is my throne and the earth is my footstool.—*Is.,* lxvi, 1.

He that sweareth and nameth God continually shall not be cleansed from sin.—*Ecclus.,* xxiii, 10.

All things come alike to all . . . he that sweareth, as he that feareth an oath.—*Eccles.,* ix, 2.

Accustom not thy mouth to an oath, and be not accustomed to the naming of the Holy One. A man of many oaths shall be filled with iniquity, and the scourge shall not depart from his house.—*Ecclus.,* xxiii, 9-11.

THE TALMUD

Only when ye hold your women in honor will ye be rich.—*Baba mezia,* 59.

The altar sheddeth bitter tears over the man who treats his wife badly.—*Gittin,* 9.

Many readers of the Talmud have never sworn.—*Ketuboth,* 76.

[There were no civic or official oaths of any kind in ancient Judea.]

R. Jona saith that even an oath to confirm the truth hath evil consequences.—*Schebuot,* 39.

He who is given to oaths will end in perjury.—*Nedarim,* 20.

Like unto a king that hath made himself a throne, and maketh for himself a footstool.—*Midrash Gen. rabba,* 1.

Thou canst not make one hair black or white.—*Sepher Rasiel Haggadol,* 10, 2.

If all the men in the world were to unite in trying to make a raven's wing white, it would be of no avail.—*Vajikra rabba,* 19, 162.

The Yea of the godly is Yea, and his Nay is Nay.—*Ruth rabba,* 3, 18.

He who maketh a vow is, even if he keep it, an offender.—*Nedarim,* 22.

R. Nathan says: He who maketh a vow hath raised an heathen altar and sacrificed thereon.—*Jebamoth,* 109, 2.

GREEK AND ROMAN

Be neither a man of many words, nor busy about too many things . . . having need neither of oath nor of any man's testimony.— M. AURELIUS, iii, 5.

Avoid taking oaths, if possible, altogether; at any rate, as far as thou art able.—EPICTETUS, *Enchiridion,* xxxiii.

We need not raise our hands to heaven, nor beseech the keeper to admit us to the ear of the image, as though thus we might be better heard; God is near thee, is with thee, is within thee.—SENECA, *Letter* xli, 1.

Be mostly silent, or speak merely what is needful, and in few words.—EPICTETUS, *Enchiridion,* xxxiii.

THE GOSPELS

Ye have heard that it hath been said, An eye for an eye, and a tooth for a tooth; but I say unto you that ye resist not evil; but whosoever shall smite thee on thy right cheek, turn to him the other also. And if any man will sue thee at the law, and take away thy coat, let him have thy cloke also. And whosoever shall compel thee to go a mile, go with him twain.

THE OLD TESTAMENT

Thou shalt not take vengeance.—*Levit.,* xix, 18.

I gave my back to the smiters, and my cheeks to them that plucked off the hair.—*Is.,* 1, 6.

Let him give his cheek to him that smiteth him.—*Lament.,* iii, 30.

He that taketh vengeance shall find vengeance from the Lord.—*Ecclus.,* xxviii, 1.

Say not, I will do so to him as he hath done to me: I will render to the man according to his work.—*Prov.,* xxiv, 29.

Give to him that asketh thee, and from him that would borrow of thee turn not thou away.

Thou shalt not harden thine heart nor shut thine hand from thy poor brother. . . . Thou shalt open thine hand wide.—*Deut.,* xv, 7-11

The wicked borroweth and payeth not again, but the righteous dealeth graciously and giveth.—*Ps.,* xxxvii, 21.

Turn not away thine eye from one that asketh of thee.—*Ecclus.,* iv, 5.

THE TALMUD

They who bear injury without requiting it, who hear themselves slandered and reply not . . . it is of these the prophet speaketh when he saith: The friends of God will shine one day like the sun.—*Yoma,* 23, 1.

Love the man who punisheth thee.—*Derech Eretz,* 9.

If any demand thy ass, give him also the saddle.—*Baba kamma,* 92, 2.

[The above is described as a "proverb of the people."]

If thy friend call thee an ass, put on the yoke.—*Baba kamma,* 87.

If any man say to thee, kill this man or I will kill thee: thou must incur death rather than inflict it.—*Sanhedrim,* 74.

He doeth most worthily who giveth double the alms asked of him.—*Sabbath,* 36, 1.

Do works of mercy, that God may be merciful to you.—*Bereshit rabba,* 33, 32, 1.

GREEK AND ROMAN

When Cato was struck on the mouth, he was not angry, and sought no vengeance; he denied the deed.—SENECA, *On Constancy,* xiv, 3.

The best way of avenging thyself is not to become like the wrongdoer.—M. AURELIUS, vi, 6.

Never mind if someone doth despise thee as a fool, and insult thee, if he hath a mind; let him strike thee, by Zeus, and do thou be of good cheer, and do not mind the insulting blow, for thou wilt never come to any harm in the practice of virtue.—PLATO, *Gorgias,* 527.

There is this fine circumstance connected with the character of a Cynic that he must be beaten like an ass, and yet, when beaten, must love those who beat him, as the father, as the brother of all.—EPICTETUS, *Discourses,* ii, 12.

I found my lamp was stolen. I considered that he who took it away did nothing unaccountable.—EPICTETUS, i, 64.

All liberality is prompt, and it is the character of him who giveth freely to give quickly.—SENECA, *On Benefits,* ii, 5.

Nothing is nobler than magnanimity, meekness, and philanthropy.—EPICTETUS, *Fragments,* xlvi.

THE GOSPELS

And when thou prayest, thou shalt not be as the hypocrites are; for they love to pray standing in the synagogues and in the corners of the streets, that they may be seen of man. Verily, I say unto you, They have their reward.

But thou, when thou prayest, enter into thy closet, and when thou hast shut the door, pray to thy Father, which is in secret; and thy father which seeth in secret shall reward thee openly. But when ye pray, use not vain repetitions, as the heathen do; for they think that they shall be heard for their much speaking. Be not ye there for like unto them; for your Father knoweth what things ye have need of before ye ask him.

THE OLD TESTAMENT

Rend your heart, and not your garments.—*Joel,* ii, 13.

When ye spread forth your hands, I will hide mine eyes from you: yea, when ye make many prayers I will not hear.—*Is., i,* 15.

Pride is hateful before the Lord and before men.—*Ecclus.,* x, 7.

He went in therefore, and shut the door upon them twain, and prayed unto the Lord.—*2 Kings,* iv, 33.

Can any hide himself in secret places that I shall not see him? saith the Lord.—*Ezech.,* xxiii, 23.

God is in heaven, and thou upon earth; therefore, let thy words be few.—*Eccles.,* v, 2.

He knoweth not that the eyes of the Lord are ten thousand times brighter than the sun, beholding all the ways of men, and looking into secret places.—*Ecclus.,* xxiii, 19.

THE TALMUD

It would not befit that lowliness of mind which prayer should inspire to stand on a lofty place and pray.— *Berachot,* 10, 2.

Who are they that will not behold the face of God? First hypocrites, then liars.—*Sotah,* 42.

Pray with bent head, conscious before whom ye stand.—*Berachot,* 30, 2.

Let our humility and good deeds plead before thee [prayer of R. Johanan].—*Berachot,* 16, 2.

The just of earlier days gave an hour to recollection before prayer.—*Berachot,* 30, 2.

God is nigh only to those who seek him in truth.—*Berachot,* 31.

When ye pray, remember whom ye are addressing [R. Eleazar].—*Berachot,* 28, 2.

When thou prayest to God, let thy words be few.—*Berachot,* 61, 1.

Better is a short prayer with devotion than a long prayer without fervor.—*Menachoth,* 110.

Pray not unless thou be in a holy and devout mood.—*Erubin,* 65.

God knows man's thoughts before they are conceived.—*Baba mezia,* 58, 2.

GREEK AND ROMAN

We prefer to invoke the Gods, to whom we make fitting supplication, silently and in our hearts.— SENECA, *On Benefits,* ii, 1.

Wait not for applauses, and shouts, and praises, in order to do good.—EPICTETUS, *Fragments,* lxxxiii.

Make thyself worthy of the help of the divinity.—M. AURELIUS, xii, 14.

When thou hast shut thy doors and darkened thy room, remember never to say that thou art alone. God is within, and thy genius is within; and what need have they of light to see what thou art doing?— EPICTETUS, *Discourses,* i, 54.

God seeth the minds of all men bared of the material vesture.—M. AURELIUS, xii, 2.

On all occasions call on the Gods, and perplex not thyself about the length of time in which thou shalt do this.—M. AURELIUS, vi, 23.

THE GOSPELS	THE OLD TESTAMENT
After this manner therefore pray ye: Our Father which art in Heaven, hallowed be thy name. Thy kingdom come. Thy will be done in earth as it is in heaven.	Thou, O Lord, art our Father.—*Is.*, lxiii, 16. Like as a father pitieth his children, so the Lord pitieth them that fear him.—*Ps.* ciii, 13. Our God is in the heavens; he hath done whatsoever he hath pleased.—*Ps.*, cxv, 3.
Give us this day our daily bread.	Feed me with food convenient [properly apportioned] for me.—*Prov.*, xxx, 8.
And forgive us our debts, as we forgive our debtors.	Forgive thy neighbor the hurt that he hath done thee, and then thy sins shall be pardoned when thou prayest.—*Ecclus.*, xxviii, 2.
And lead us not into temptation; but deliver us from evil: For thine is the kingdom, and the power, and the glory for ever. Amen.[1]	Thine, O Lord, is the greatness, and the power, and the glory.—1 *Chron.*, xxix, 11.

[1] The "Lord's Prayer" is much shorter in *Luke*, and is unknown in *Mark*. It is commonly regarded by theologians as a composition not due to Jesus.

THE TALMUD

On whom do we rely? On our Father who is in heaven.—*Sotah,* 9, 15.

["Our Father in heaven" is a common phrase in old Jewish prayers.]

Magnified and sanctified be his great name in the world which he hath created according to his will. May he establish his kingdom. . . . [Opening of the ancient Kaddish prayer.]

What is a short prayer? R. Eliezer said: Thy will be done in heaven, and peace to those who fear thee on earth.—*Berachot,* 29, 2.

Blessed be God every day for the daily bread he gives us [Hillel].— *Jom Tob,* 16, 1.

Whosoever is ready to forgive shall have his sins forgiven.— *Megillah,* 28.

Lead me neither into sin nor into temptation.—*Berachot,* 16, 2.

Never should a man bring himself into temptation, as David did.—*Sanhedrim,* 107, 1.

Praised be the name of the glory of thy kingdom for ever [close of public prayers in the temple].— (Jerus. Talmud) *Berachot,* 13, 3.

GREEK AND ROMAN

We ought not to pray at all, or we ought to pray in this simple and noble fashion.—M. AURELIUS, v, 7.

Wilt thou not feel thyself to be ennobled on knowing thyself to be the son of God?—EPICTETUS, *Discourses,* i, 2.

Have no will but the will of God, and who shall restrain thee?— EPICTETUS, *Discourses,* i, 17.

Hast thou often seen a beggar who did not live to old age—nay, to extreme old age?—EPICTETUS, *Discourses,* iii, 26.

If ye go forth, returning evil for evil and injury for injury . . . we shall be angry with you while you live, and our friends, the laws in the world below, will receive you as an enemy.—PLATO, *Crito,* 54.

Virtue cometh to the virtuous by the gift of God.—PLATO, *Meno,* 100.

Since I am a reasonable creature, it is my duty to praise God . . . nor will I ever desert this post so long as it is permitted me.— EPICTETUS, *Discourses,* i, 16.

THE GOSPELS

For if ye forgive men their trespasses, your heavenly Father will also forgive you; but if ye forgive not men their trespasses, neither will your Father forgive your trespasses.

Moreover, when ye fast, be not as the hypocrites, of a sad countenance; for they disfigure their faces, that they may appear unto men to fast. Verily, I say unto you, they have their reward. But thou, when thou fastest, anoint thy head and wash thy face; that thou appear not unto men to fast, but unto thy Father which is in secret, and thy Father, which seeth in secret, shall reward thee openly.

Lay not up for yourselves treasures upon earth, where moth and rust doth corrupt, and where thieves break through and steal; but lay up for yourselves treasures in heaven, where neither moth nor rust doth corrupt, and where thieves do not break through nor steal; for where your treasure is, there will your heart be also.

THE OLD TESTAMENT

Man cherisheth anger against man, and doth he seek healing from the Lord? Upon a man like himself he hath no mercy, and doth he make supplication for his own sins?—*Ecclus.*, xxviii, 3.

Behold ye fast for strife and debate, and to smite with the fist of wickedness.—*Is.*, xxxviii, 4.

The works of all flesh are before him, and it is not possible to be hid from his eyes.—*Ecclus.*, xxxix, 19.

Labor not to be rich ... for riches certainly make themselves wings; they fly away as an eagle towards heaven.—*Prov.*, xxiii, 4.

Bestow thy treasure according to the commandments of the Most High, and it shall profit thee more than gold.—*Ecclus.*, xxix, 11.

THE TALMUD

So long as thou thyself art compassionate, God will show thee mercy; but if thou hast no mercy, God will have none for thee [Gamaliel ii].—*Sabbath,* 130.

Who are they that will not behold the face of God? First, hypocrites.—*Sotah,* 42.

[In J. Hagigah, 77, 4, there is a story in which a pious Jew sees a Jewess in hell. "And he said to those (who were about): Why is she here? And they said to him: This woman fasted and made it known to others." The hero of the story lived before Christ.]

Let a man not lower himself with fasting.—*Taanit,* 22, 2.

It is not the sackcloth and the fasting which bring rain, but repentance and good works.—*Taanit,* 16.

They took their pleasure in gathering earthly riches, but I seek heavenly goods. . . . My forefathers gathered in a place where the hand of man could steal, but I put my treasures in a place where none can enter. . . . My forefathers heaped up riches which brought them no profit, but I seek what brings salvation.—*Baba bathra,* 11, 1.

I will teach my son only the Law, for we are nourished by its

GREEK AND ROMAN

It is the part of a great mind to despise injury.—SENECA, *On Anger,* ii, 32.

When Diogenes was asked, How shall I avenge myself on my enemy? he said, By living virtuously and honestly.—PLUTARCH, *On the Usefulness of Enemies,* iii.

Many people shed tears only in order that they may show them.—SENECA, *On Tranquillity,* 15.

Vain is the greatness of pride, and it bringeth into contempt even things of high esteem.—SENECA, *On Benefits,* ii, 13.

When thou hast learned to nourish thy body frugally, pride not thyself upon it; nor, if thou dost drink water, say upon every occasion: I drink water.—EPICTETUS, *Enchiridion,* xlvii.

The reality, and not the appearance, of virtue is to be followed above all things, as well in public as in private life.—PLATO, *Gorgias,* 527.

Know that thief and robber cannot reach the things that are properly thy own.—EPICTETUS, *Discourses,* i, 18.

What tyrant, what robber, what thief, or what court can be formidable to those who count the body and its possessions as nothing?—EPICTETUS, *Discourses,* i, 35.

The sum of our happiness must not be placed in the flesh: the goods which reason affordeth are true,

THE GOSPELS	THE OLD TESTAMENT

. . .

No man can serve two masters; for either he will hate the one, and love the other; or else he will hold to the one and despise the other. Ye cannot serve God and Mammon.

Give me neither poverty nor riches . . . lest I be full and deny thee.—*Prov.,* xxx, 8-9.

He that loveth gold shall not be justified: and he that followeth corruption shall have enough thereof.—*Ecclus.,* xxxi, 5.

Therefore I say unto you Take no thought for your life, what ye shall eat or what ye shall drink; nor yet for your body, what ye shall put on. Is not the life more than meat, and the body than raiment?

They that seek the Lord shall not want any good thing.—*Ps.,* xxxiv, 10.

Cast thy burden upon the Lord, and he shall sustain thee.—*Ps.,* lv, 22.

A covetous man's eye is not satisfied with his portion; and wicked injustice drieth up his soul.—*Ecclus.,* xiv, 9.

Behold the fowls of the air: for they sow not, neither do they reap, nor gather into barns; yet your heavenly Father feedeth them. Are ye not much better than they?

Who provideth for the raven his food?—*Job,* xxxviii, 41.

He giveth food to all flesh; for his mercy endureth for ever.—*Ps.,* cxxxvi, 25.

THE TALMUD

fruits in this world, and the capital is saved for the world to come.—*Kiddushin*, 82.

My forefathers served Mammon, but my mind is set upon the treasures of the soul. . . . My fathers sought the things of this world, but I seek a heavenly reward.—*Baba bathra*, 11, 1.

He who created the day found also the food thereof; wherefore he who, having sufficient food for the day, says, What shall I eat tomorrow? is one of the men of little faith [R. Eliezer].—*Mechilta to Exod.*, 16, 4.

Hast thou ever seen a bird, or a beast of the forest, that must obtain its food by work? God feeds them, and they strive not to secure their nourishment.—*Kiddushin*, 4.

GREEK AND ROMAN

solid, and eternal; they cannot die nor be diminished.—SENECA, *Letter* lxxiv, 16.

The perfect man, full of divine and human virtues, can lose nothing: his goods are guarded by solid and unshakable walls.—SENECA, *On Constancy*, vi, 8.

Where our interest is, there too is our piety directed.—EPICTETUS, *Enchiridion*, xxxi.

. . .

If thou findest in human life anything better than justice, truth . . . turn to it with all thy soul. . . . If nothing appears to be better than the deity which is planted in thee, give place to nothing else.—M. AURELIUS, iii, 6.

I do nothing but go about persuading you all, old and young alike, not to take thought for your persons or your properties, but first and chiefly to care about the greatest improvement of the soul.—PLATO, *Apology*, 30.

Make not an idol of thy clothes, and thou wilt not be enraged with the thief.—EPICTETUS, *Discourses*, i, 64.

Despise the flesh as if thou wert now dying.—M. AURELIUS, ii, 2.

Must a philosopher be more helpless and anxious than the brute-beasts? each of which is self-sufficient, and wants neither proper food, nor any suitable and natural

THE GOSPELS	THE OLD TESTAMENT
Which of you by taking thought can add one cubit to his stature? And why take ye thought for raiment? Consider the lilies of the field, how they grow; they toil not, neither do they spin; and yet I say unto you, That even Solomon in all his glory was not arrayed like one of these.	Thou openest thy hand and satisfiest the desire of every living thing.—*Ps.*, cxlv, 16. Who maketh the grass to grow upon the mountains. He giveth to the beast his food, and to the young ravens which cry.—*Ps.*, cxlvii, 8-9.

.   .   .

Judge not, that ye be not judged. For with what judgment ye judge, ye shall be judged; and with what measure ye mete, it shall be measured to you again. And why beholdest thou the mote that is in thy brother's eye, but considerest not the beam that is in thine own eye? Or how wilt thou say to thy brother, Let me pull out the mote out of thine eye, and, behold, a beam is in thine own eye? Thou hypocrite, first cast out the beam out of thine own eye, and then shalt thou see clearly to cast out the mote out of thy brother's eye.	Thou shalt in any wise rebuke thy neighbor, and not suffer sin upon him.—*Levit.*, xix, 17. There is a reproof that is not comely; and there is a man that keepeth silence, and he is wise.—*Ecclus.*, xx, 1. Judge of thy neighbor by thyself: and be discreet in every point.—*Ecclus.*, xxx, 15.

.   .   .

THE TALMUD

Hast thou ever seen a lion bearing a burden, or a stag gathering the summer's fruits, or a wolf buying oil? . . . And shall I, who have been created to serve my Creator, be more anxious about my food? (Jerusalem Talmud.)

God's providence reaches all creatures: from the horns of the unicorn to the eggs of the lice.—*Sabbath,* 107, 2.

.   .   .

Judge every one as favorably as ye can.—*Pirke Abot,* i, 6.

Judge not thy neighbor until thou hast stood in his place [Hillel].—*Pirke Abot,* 2, 4.

With the measure with which a man measureth shall it be meted unto him.—*Sotah,* 8, 2.

The fault from which thou art not free blame thou not in another.—*Baba mezia,* 59, 2.

R. Johanan said: There was a time when to him who said, Remove the toothpick from thy tooth, a man used to say, Do thou remove the beam from thine own eye.—*Baba bathra,* 15, 2.

GREEK AND ROMAN

provision.—EPICTETUS, *Discourses,* i, 35.

Any one thing in creation is sufficient to demonstrate a Providence to a humble and grateful mind.—EPICTETUS, *Discourses,* i, 16.

It is a mark of want of intellect to spend much time in things relating to the body.—EPICTETUS, *Enchiridion,* xli.

When thou art offended with any man's transgression, presently reflect upon thyself, and consider what thou thyself art guilty of in the same kind.—M. AURELIUS, x, 30.

Take care that thou be far removed from the things thou findest fault with in another.—PLUTARCH, *On the Use of Enemies,* iv.

Whenever Plato was among evil-doers, he was wont to ask himself: Do I myself perchance have the same vice?—PLUTARCH, *On the Usefulness of Enemies,* iv.

Thou wilt commit the fewest faults in judging if thou art faultless in thy own life.—EPICTETUS, *Fragments,* lvii.

If we would be righteous judges, let us first persuade ourselves that none of us is blameless.—SENECA, *On Anger,* ii, 28.

THE GOSPELS

Ask, and it shall be given unto you; seek, and ye shall find; knock, and it shall be opened unto you; for every one that asketh receiveth; and he that seeketh findeth; and to him that knocketh it shall be opened. Or what man is there of you, whom if his son ask bread, will he give him a stone? Or, if he ask a fish, will he give him a serpent? If ye, then, being evil, know how to give good gifts unto your children, how much more shall your Father which is in heaven give good things to them that ask him?

Therefore all things whatsoever ye would that men should do to you, do ye even so to them; for this is the law and the prophets.

Enter ye in at the strait gate; for wide is the gate, and broad is the way, that leadeth to destruction, and many there be which go in thereat. Because strait is the gate, and narrow is the way which leadeth unto life, and few there be that find it.

THE OLD TESTAMENT

I love them that love me; and those that seek me early shall find me.—*Prov.*, viii, 17.

Then shall ye call upon me; and ye shall go and pray unto me, and I will hearken unto you. And ye shall seek me, and find me, when ye shall search for me with all your heart. And I will be found of you, saith the Lord.—*Jer.*, xxix, 12-14.

Who did call upon him, and he did despise him?—*Ecclus.*, ii, 10.

Thou shalt love thy neighbor as thyself.—*Levit.*, xix, 18.

What thou thyself hatest, do to no man.—*Tobit*, iv, 15.

The way of sinners is made smooth with stones, and at the last end thereof is the pit of Hades.—*Ecclus.*, xxi, 10.

The righteous live for ever, and in the Lord is their reward.—*Wisdom*, v, 15.

THE TALMUD

The doors of prayer are never closed.—*Sotah*, 49.

Adam prayed to the Lord, and rain fertilized the earth. From this we see that the prayer of the just is heard by God.—*Chulin*, 60, 1.

And Hillel said: What thou dost not like, do thou not to thy neighbor. That is the whole law; all the rest is explanation.—*Sabbath*, 31, 1.

If thou wouldst not have another take away what is thine, take not thou what belongs to thy neighbor [R. Akiba].—*Abot of R. Nathan*.

Penance and good works are a shield against evil chances.—*Pirke Abot*, 4, 13.

The number of those who have a claim to felicity is very small.—*Sukkah*, 145, 2.

GREEK AND ROMAN

God hath not merely provided for our needs; we are loved even to delight.—SENECA, *On Benefits*, iv, 5.

Doing this, and living after this manner, we shall receive our reward from the Gods and those who are above us.—PLATO, *Laws*, iv, 718.

The Gods, like good parents who smile at their ill-natured children, cease not to heap benefits even on them who doubt the existence of their benefactors, but scatter their favors with equal hand among all nations.—SENECA, *On Benefits*, vii, 31.

If thou wouldst be well spoken of, learn to speak well of others.—EPICTETUS, *Enchiridion*, vi.

What thou avoidest suffering thyself, seek not to impose on others.—EPICTETUS, *Fragments*, xxxviii.

[When Kung-fu-tse was asked for a general rule of behavior, he replied in a word which means literally "as heart," or "Have a heart in common with your neighbor." His counsel was not negative, as is often said.

Wherefore I say, let a man be of good cheer about his soul, who, having cast away the pleasures and ornaments of the body . . . has arrayed the soul, not in some foreign attire, but in her own proper jewels, temperance and justice and courage and nobility and truth—in these adorned, she is ready to go on her

THE GOSPELS

THE OLD TESTAMENT

Beware of false prophets, which come to you in sheep's clothing, but inwardly they are ravening wolves. Ye shall know them by their fruits. Do men gather grapes of thorns, or figs of thistles? Even so every good tree bringeth forth good fruit; but a corrupt tree bringeth forth evil fruit. Every tree that bringeth not forth good fruit is hewn down, and cast into the fire. Wherefore by their fruits ye shall know them.[1]

[1]These and the following are obviously not words of Jesus; they are related to the later dissensions among his followers.

Not every one that saith unto me, Lord, Lord, shall enter into the kingdom of heaven; but he that doeth the will of my Father which is in heaven. Many will say unto me in that day, Lord, Lord, have we not prophesied in thy name? and in thy name have cast out devils? and in thy name done many wonderful works? And then will I profess unto them, I never knew you; depart from me, ye that work iniquity.

Therefore whoever heareth these sayings of mine, and doeth them, I will liken him unto a wise man, which built his house upon a rock; and the rain descended, and the floods came, and the winds blew,

Thou shalt not hearken unto the words of that prophet.—*Deut.,* xiii, 3.

Hearken not unto the words of the prophets that prophesy unto you.—*Jerem.,* xxiii, 16.

Therefore I will judge you. O house of Israel, everyone according to his ways.—*Ezech.,* xviii, 30.

Let us destroy the tree with the fruit thereof.—*Jerem.,* xi, 19.

If the ungodly put forth boughs, and flourish for a season . . . their fruit shall be useless, never ripe to eat, and fit for nothing.—*Wisdom,* iv, 45.

Trust ye not in lying words, saying, The temple of the Lord, the temple of the Lord. But if ye thoroughly amend your ways and your doings . . . then will I cause you to dwell in this place.—*Jerem.,* vii, 4-5.

Then shall they call upon me, but I will not answer; they shall seek me early, but I will not answer.—*Prov.,* i, 28.

Depart from me, all ye workers of iniquity.—*Ps.,* vi, 8.

Timber girt and bound into a building shall not be loosened with shaking: so a heart established in due season on well-advised counsel shall not be afraid. A heart settled upon a thoughtful understanding is

THE TALMUD

GREEK AND ROMAN

journey to the world below.—PLATO, *Phaedo,* 115.

Even from the stalk ye know what fruit the gourd will bear.—*Berachot,* 48, 1.

The world is judged with goodness, and each is dealt with according to his works.—*Pirke Abot,* 3, 19.

If the companion be corrupt, he who converses with him will be corrupted likewise.—EPICTETUS, *Enchiridion,* xxxiii.

Virtue looketh with unfaltering eyes on the torments that are prepared for her: she betrayeth no change of countenance whether fortune offer prosperity or adversity.—SENECA, *On Constancy,* v., 5.

It is not fine words, but good deeds, that avail—*Pirke Abot,* 1, 17.

The unholy do only waste their much service upon the Gods.—PLATO, *Laws,* iv, 717.

R. Elisha ben Abiya said: To whom shall I liken a man whose deeds are good, and who is zealous for the Law? To a man who, in building a house, putteth stone below and brick above, so that when

The good man will stand firm, and bear, not only patiently but gladly, whatever happens; he will know that every adversity is a law of nature; and, just as the good soldier bears wounds and counts his

THE GOSPELS	THE OLD TESTAMENT
and beat upon that house; and it fell not; for it was founded upon a rock. And everyone that heareth these sayings of mine, and doeth them not, shall be likened unto a foolish man, which built his house upon the sand; and the rain descended, and the floods came, and the winds blew, and beat upon that house; and it fell; and great was the fall of it.	as ornament of plaster on a polished wall.—*Ecclus.*, xxii, 16-18. Through wisdom is a house builded; and by understanding it is established.—*Prov.*, xxiv, 3.

.   .   .

I am come to set a man at variance against his father, and the daughter against her mother, and the daughter-in-law against her mother-in-law. And a man's foes shall be they of his own household. He that loveth father and mother more than me is not worthy of me: and he that loveth son or daughter more than me is not worthy of me. And he that taketh not his cross, and followeth after me, is not worthy of me. He that findeth his life shall lose it; and he that loseth his life, for my sake, shall find it.	For the son dishonoreth the father, the daughter riseth up against her mother, the daughter-in-law against her mother-in-law; a man's enemies are those of his own house.—*Micah*, vii, 6. My friends scorn me.—*Job*, xvi, 20. My son, if thou comest to serve the Lord, prepare thy soul for temptation.—*Ecclus.*, ii, 1. He that serveth God according to his good pleasure shall be accepted.—*Ecclus.*, xxxv, 16.

THE TALMUD

the flood cometh it is not shaken. And to whom shall I liken a man whose deeds are not good, yet he is zealous for the law? To a man who putteth brick below and stone above; and, when but a little water cometh, it beareth it away.—*Abot of R. Nathan,* 24.

R. Elazar ben Azarjah said: To what shall I liken the man whose wisdom is greater than his deeds? To a tree whose branches are many and roots few; and the wind cometh, and teareth it up, and casteth it on its face.... But to what shall I liken him whose deeds are greater than his wisdom? To a tree whose branches are few and roots many, so that even if all the winds in the world come and rage against it, they cannot move it from its position.—*Pirke Abot,* 3, 18.

Shortly before the coming of the Messiah, the son will rise against the father, and the daughter against the mother, and the daughter-in-law against the mother-in-law. Each will find enemies in those of his own house. In those days men will trust none but God.—*Sotah,* 49, 2.

What shall a man do to live? He shall die. What shall a man do to die? He shall live.—*Taanit,* 32, 32.

GREEK AND ROMAN

scars, and even in death loves the emperor for whom he falls, he will ever bear in mind that old precept: Follow God.—SENECA, *On the Happy Life,* xv, 5.

It is the part of a great man to conquer the calamities and terrors of morals.—SENECA, *On Providence,* iv, 1.

He that lifteth himself above great adversity, and beareth the evils which crush others, is consecrated by his sufferings.—SENECA, *To Helvia,* xiii, 6.

I am a sort of gad-fly, given to the State by God [Socrates].—PLATO, *Apology,* 30.

No man seemeth to me to have a higher regard for virtue, none to be more devoted to it, than he who hath forfeited the repute of a good man in order to save his conscience.—SENECA, *Letter,* lxxxi, 20.

May not he who is truly a man cease to care about living a certain time? ... He leaveth all that with God.—PLATO, *Gorgias,* 512.

Conscience giveth joy, even when it is oppressed.—SENECA, *On Benefits,* iv, 21.

THE GOSPELS

He that receiveth you receiveth me, and he that receiveth me receiveth him that sent me. He that receiveth a prophet in the name of a prophet shall receive a prophet's reward; and he that receiveth a righteous man in the name of a righteous man shall receive a righteous man's reward. And whosoever shall give to drink unto one of these little ones a cup of cold water only in the name of a disciple, verily I say unto you, he shall in no wise lose his reward.

The blind receive their sight, and the lame walk, the lepers are cleansed, and the deaf hear, the dead are raised up, and the poor have the Gospel preached to them. And blessed is he whosoever shall not be offended in me.

.   .   .

Then shall the righteous shine forth as the sun in the kingdom of their Father.

Not that which goeth into the mouth defileth a man, but that which cometh out of the mouth, this defileth a man. . . . For out of the

THE OLD TESTAMENT

Thou renderest to every man according to his work.—*Ps.,* lxii, 12.

And she went and did according to the saying of Elijah . . . and the barrel of meal wasted not, neither did the cruse of oil fail, according to the word of the Lord, which he spake by Elijah.—1 *Kings,* xvii, 15-16.

Whoso stoppeth his ears at the cry of the poor, he also shall cry himself, but shall not be heard.—*Prov.,* xxi, 13.

Do good to one that is lowly.—*Ecclus.,* xii, 5.

Then the eyes of the blind shall be opened, and the ears of the deaf shall be unstopped. Then shall the lame man leap as an hart, and the tongue of the dumb sing.—*Is.,* xxv, 5-6.

And they that be wise shall shine as the brightness of the firmament, and they that turn many to righteousness as the stars for ever and ever.—*Daniel,* xii, 3.

Excellent speech becometh not a fool: much less do lying lips a prince.—*Prov.,* xvii, 7.

THE TALMUD

If ye give ear to my angel, it is as if ye hearkened unto me.—*Schemoth rabba,* 32.

He who feedeth one learned in divine things will be blessed by God and man.—*Sohar to Gen.,* 129, 512.

He who taketh his neighbor into his house hath the same reward as if the Schechina [divine spirit] itself entered his house.—*Shir hashirim rabba,* 13, 3.

What God will do in the days of the Messiah he has already shown in the days of his prophets. God saith: In the days of the Messiah I will cause the blind to see.—*Vajikra rabba,* 27, 171, 2.

The land in which the dead arise is the land in which the kingdom of the Messiah will open.—*Bereshit rabba,* 72, 3.

They who are persecuted and hate not . . . are the elect of God, of whom it is written: They shine with the splendor of the sun.—*Sabbath,* 88, 2.

Keep thy mouth from sin, and thy body from wrong, and God will be with thee [R. Meir].—*Berachot,* 17, 1.

GREEK AND ROMAN

The rites of hospitality are taught by Heaven.—PLATO, *Laws,* iv, 718.

The stranger who cometh from abroad shall be received in a friendly spirit . . . showing respect to Zeus, the god of hospitality.—PLATO, *Laws,* xii, 953.

What sort of a man is he who giveth the name of brother to his friend and will not walk the same way with him?—PLUTARCH, *On Fraternal Love,* iii.

The wise man will stretch out his hand to the shipwrecked, and will give hospitality to the exile and alms to the needy.—SENECA, *On Clemency,* vi.

Consider that thou dost not thrive merely by the food in thy stomach, but by the elevation of thy soul. For the former is evacuated,

THE GOSPELS	THE OLD TESTAMENT
heart proceed evil thoughts, murders, adulteries, fornications, thefts, false witness, blasphemies; these are the things which defile a man: but to eat with unwashen hands defileth not a man.	For the imagination of man's heart is evil from his youth.—*Genesis,* viii, 21.
	A fool's mouth is his destruction, and his lips are the snare of his soul.—*Prov.,* xviii, 7.
	The heart of fools is in their mouth; but the mouth of wise men is their heart.—*Ecclus.,* xxi, 26.
If any man will come after me, let him deny himself, and take up his cross, and follow me.	My son, if thou comest to serve the Lord, prepare thy soul for temptation.—*Ecclus.,* ii, 1.
For what is a man profited, if he shall gain the whole world, and lose his own soul? or what shall a man give in exchange for his soul? For the Son of man shall come in the glory of his Father, with his angels; and then he shall reward every man according to his works.	What profit hath a man of all his labor which he taketh under the sun?—*Eccles.,* i, 3.
	For the redemption of their soul is precious, and it ceaseth for ever.—*Ps.,* xlix, 8.
	For the work of a man shall he render unto him, and cause every man to find according to his ways.—*Job,* xxxiv, 11.
Verily, I say unto you, Except ye be converted, and become as little children, ye shall not enter into the kingdom of heaven. Whosoever therefore shall humble himself as this little child, the same is greatest in the kingdom of heaven. And whoso shall receive one such little	My soul is even as a weaned child.—Ps., cxxxi, 2.
	They that fear the Lord will prepare their hearts, and humble their souls in his sight.—*Ecclus.,* ii, 17.
	He that loveth pureness of

THE TALMUD

God gave man his spirit in a state of perfect purity, and it is man's duty to restore it in the condition in which he received it.—*Sabbath,* 152, 2.

Penance and good works are a shield against evil chances.—*Pirke Abot,* 4, 13.

Weigh the hurt that cometh to thee of the transgression of a divine command against the reward that is promised thee for fulfilling it, and the gold of sin against the punishment that awaiteth the sinner.—*Pirke Abot,* 2, 1.

Each is dealt with according to his works.—*Pirke Abot,* 3, 19.

A man converted is like a new-born child.—*Jebamoth,* 62, 2.

A young man deserves praise when he becomes like the children.—*Tanchuma,* 36, 4.

Whosoever humbleth himself in this life for love of the Law, the

GREEK AND ROMAN

and carried off altogether; but the latter, though the soul is parted, remains uncorrupted through all things.—EPICTETUS, *Fragments,* xxvi.

Nothing is more unhappy than the man who hath never known adversity.—SENECA, *On Providence,* iii, 3.

We have to struggle against this flesh with all our minds.—SENECA, *To Marcia,* xxiv, 5.

In this present life I reckon that we make the nearest approach to knowledge when we have the least possible intercourse or communion with the body . . . but keep ourselves pure until the hour when God himself is pleased to release us.—PLATO, *Phaedo,* 67.

Never value anything as profitable to thyself which shall compel thee to break thy promise, to lose thy self-respect, to suspect, to curse, to act the hypocrite.—M. AURELIUS, iii, 8.

The soul doth not apprehend God unless it be pure and holy.—SENECA, *Letter* lxxxvii, 21.

Simple and modest is the work of philosophy. Draw me not aside to insolence and pride.—M. AURELIUS, ix, 28.

THE GOSPELS

child in my name receiveth me. But whoso shall offend one of these little ones which believe in me, it were better for him that a millstone were hanged about his neck, and that he were drowned in the depth of the sea. Woe unto the world because of offenses! For it must needs be that offenses come, but woe to that man by whom the offense cometh. ... Take heed that ye despise not one of these little ones; for I say unto you, that in heaven their angels do always behold the face of my Father which is in heaven. For the Son of Man is come to save that which was lost.[1]

[1]The references to the children's "belief," to scandals, etc., show that the writer   in part, at least   takes the word "children" in the not uncommon Jewish sense of converts. Whether the writer of the Gospel started from some literal reference of Jesus to children must remain open.

THE OLD TESTAMENT

heart, for the grace of his lips the king shall be his friend.—*Prov., xxii, 11.*

Incorruption bringeth near to God.—*Wisdom, vi, 19.*

The turning away of the simple shall slay them.—Prov., i, 32.

Do good to one that is lowly.—Ecclus., xii, 5.

Be not ashamed to instruct the unwise and foolish.—*Ecclus.,* xlii, 8.

.   .   .

Verily, I say unto you, That a rich man shall hardly enter into the kingdom of heaven. And again I say unto you, It is easier for a camel to go through the eye of a needle, than for a rich man to enter into the kingdom of God. Everyone that hath forsaken homes, or brethren, or sisters, or father, or mother, or wife, or children, or lands, for my name's sake, shall receive an hundredfold, and shall inherit everlasting life. But many that are first shall be last: and the last shall be first.

Blessed is the rich that is found without blemish, and hath not gone after gold. Who is he? and we will call him blessed: for wonderful things hath he done among his people—*Ecclus.,* xxxi, 8-9.

Who said unto his father, and to his mother, I have not seen him: neither did he acknowledge his brethren, nor knew his own children. . . . Bless, Lord, his substance, and accept the work of his hands.—*Deut.,* xxxiii, 9, 11.

THE TALMUD

same will be reckoned among the great in the kingdom of heaven.—*Baba mezia,* 84, 2.

If thou hast learned much, make not a boast thereof.—*Sanhedrim,* 93.

Whosoever leadeth his fellow man into sin doth worse than if he took away his life.—*Tanchuma,* 74, 1.

The proud man loseth his wisdom if he be wise.—*Pesachim,* 66.

Holiness leads to humility; humility to the fear of God.—*Abodah zarah,* 20.

Abai said: Ten thousand just are daily rejoiced with the sight of God in heaven.—*Sukkah,* 45, 2.

Whosoever giveth alms for the glory of heaven shall have his gift sown by God in the garden of Eden, where it will bear fruit a thousand-fold.—*Jalkut Rubeni,* 165, 3.

Art thou from Pombeditha, where they can drive an elephant through the eye of a needle?—*Baba mezia,* 38, 2.

[The above was a proverbial Jewish saying for an impossibility. Similarly, "sell all thou hast" is a common rabbinical expression for

GREEK AND ROMAN

Keep thyself simple, good, pure, serious, free from affectation, a friend of justice, a worshipper of the Gods, kind, affectionate, strenuous in all proper acts.—M. AURELIUS, vi, 30.

Who is there whom bright and agreeable children do not attract to play, and creep, and prattle with them?—EPICTETUS, *Discourses,* i, 216.

A sensible legislator will rather exhort the elders to reverence the younger, and above all to take heed that no young man sees or hears one of themselves doing or saying anything disgraceful.—PLATO, *Laws,* v, 729.

Souls find their way easiest to the Gods when they have been withdrawn early from the society of men, for they are the least soiled.—SENECA, *To Marcia,* xxiii.

The Gods are not fastidious: they lend a hand to the man who would rise.—SENECA, *Letter* lxxiii, 15.

.   .   .

Very rich and very good at the same time a man cannot be.—PLATO, *Laws,* v, 742.

It is a great thing not to be corrupted by the nearness of wealth: great is the man who is poor amid wealth.—SENECA, *Letter xx,* 10.

Riches are not among the number of things which are good. . . . It is difficult therefore for a rich person to be modest, or for a modest person to be rich.—EPICTETUS,

THE GOSPELS	THE OLD TESTAMENT
	Before destruction the heart of man is haughty, and before honor is humility.—*Prov.*, xviii, 12.

.   .   .

Thou shalt love the Lord they God with all thy heart, and with all thy soul, and with all thy mind. This is the first and great commandment. And the second is like unto it: Thou shalt love thy neighbor as thyself. On these two commandments hang all the law and the prophets.	Thou shalt love the Lord thy God with all thine heart, and with all thy soul, and with all thy might.—*Deut.*, vi, 5. Thou shalt love thy neighbor as thyself.—*Levit.*, xix, 18.

.   .   .

Then shall the king say unto them on his right hand, Come, ye blessed of my Father, inherit the kingdom prepared for you from the foundation of the world: for I was an hungered, and ye gave me meat: I was thirsty, and ye gave me drink: I was a stranger, and ye took me in: naked, and ye clothed me: I was sick, and ye visited me: I was in	Is not this the fast that I have chosen? . . . Is it not to deal thy bread to the hungry, and that thou bring the poor that are cast out to thy house? when thou seest the naked that thou cover him; and that thou hide not thyself from thine own flesh?—*Is.*, lviii, 6-7. But if a man be just, and do that which is lawful and right . . .

THE TALMUD

"make every effort."]

Joseph, son of Joshua, fell into a state of ecstasy during an illness. When his father asked him what he saw he said: A world upside down: they who are more highly esteemed here are below, and the lower are above. Verily, said the old man, thou hast seen in thy mind a rational world.—*Baba bathra,* 10, 3.

He who doth not observe the commandments in this world solely out of fear and love of God will have no reward in the life to come—*Sotah,* 36.

Grieve not, my son, we have yet another pardon for sin: that is, to do good and to love your neighbor.—*Abot of R. Nathan,* 4.

A Roman general asked R. Akiba: If your God loveth the poor, why doth he not feed them? He answered and said: In order that we may escape Gehenna.—*Baba bathra,* 10, 1.

Whosoever giveth drink and food to the wise and their disciples will receive a great reward from God.—*Bamidbar rabba,* 4, 191, 1.

GREEK AND ROMAN

Fragments, xviii.

Wealth is dangerous to the foolish, since vice groweth with wealth.—EPICTETUS, *Fragments,* xciv.

If such a thing as wife or child be granted thee, there is no objection: but if the Captain calls, run to the ship, and never look behind.—EPICTETUS, *Enchiridion,* vii.

No one who is a lover of money, a lover of pleasure, or a lover of glory, is likewise a lover of mankind.—EPICTETUS, *Fragments,* x.

What is sufficient? Why what else than to venerate the Gods and bless them, and to do good unto men.—M. AURELIUS, v, 33.

Reverence the Gods, and help men. Short is life.—M. AURELIUS, vi, 30.

Think of God oftener than thou breathest.—EPICTETUS, *Fragments,* cxiv.

Thou must live for another, if thou wouldst live for thyself.—SENECA, *Letter xlviii,* 2.

How a man ought to order what relateth to his descendants, his kindred, his friends, and his fellow-citizens, and the rights of hospitality taught by Heaven . . . these things the laws will accomplish . . . and will thus render the State, if the Gods cooperate with us, prosperous and happy.—PLATO, *Laws,* iv, 718.

THE GOSPELS

prison, and ye came unto me. Then shall the righteous answer him, saying, Lord, when saw we thee an hungered and fed thee? or thirsty, and gave thee drink? When saw we thee a stranger, and took thee in? or naked, and clothed thee? Or when saw we thee sick, or in prison, and came unto thee? And the king shall answer and say unto them, Verily, I say unto you, Inasmuch as ye have done it unto one of the least of these my brethren, ye have done it unto me. Then shall he say also unto them on his left hand, Depart from me, ye cursed, into everlasting fire, prepared for the devil and his angels; for I was an hungered, and ye gave me no meat: I was thirsty, and ye gave me no drink: I was a stranger, and ye took me not in: naked, and ye clothed me not: sick and in prison, and ye visited me not. Then shall they also answer him, saying, Lord, when saw we thee an hungered, or athirst, or a stranger, or naked, or sick, or in prison, and did not minister unto thee? Then shall he answer them, saying, Verily I say unto you, Inasmuch as ye did it not to one of the least of these, ye did it not to me. And these shall go away into everlasting punishment; but the righteous into life eternal.

THE OLD TESTAMENT

hath given his bread to the hungry, and hath covered the naked with a garment . . . he shall surely live.—*Ezek.*, xviii, 5, 16.

Give thy bread to the hungry, and of thy garments to them that are naked.—*Tobit*, v, 16.

Be not slow to visit a sick man.—*Ecclus.*, vii, 34.

He that hath pity upon the poor lendeth unto the Lord: and that which he hath given will he pay him again.—*Prov.*, xix, 17.

When the poor and needy seek water, and there is none, and their tongue faileth for thirst, I, the Lord, will hear them.—*Is.*, xli, 17.

Depart from me, all ye workers of iniquity: for the Lord hath heard the voice of my weeping.—*Ps.*, vi, 8.

Shall not he render to every man according to his work?—*Prov.*, xxiv, 12.

Whoso mocketh the poor reproacheth his Maker: and he that is glad at calamities shall not be unpunished.—*Prov.*, xvii, 5.

He that despiseth his neighbor, sinneth: but he that hath mercy on the poor, happy is he.—*Prov.*, xiv, 21.

He that giveth unto the poor shall not lack; but he that hideth his eyes shall have many a curse.—*Prov.*, xxviii, 27.

The ungodly shall go from a curse into perdition.—*Ecclus.*, xli, 10.

THE TALMUD

God clotheth the naked . . . follow thou his example: God visiteth the sick . . . so do thou visit the sick: God comforteth those who mourn . . . so do thou comfort those who mourn.—*Sotah,* 14, 1.

We must feed and clothe even the poor of the heathen, and visit their sick.—*Gittin,* 61.

Whosoever giveth hospitality with generosity will be rewarded with Paradise.—*Jalkut Rubeni,* 42, 2.

Sin-offerings can, says R. Johanan ben Zakkai, cleanse only the sins of Israel: good deeds make amends even for the heathen.—*Baba bathra,* 10, 3.

So hospitable and charitable was Job that he had four doors made to his house, on the east, west, north, and south, so that a man coming from any of these directions would not need to search for the entrance of the house, but would find an inviting door from whichever side he arrived.—*Abot of R. Nathan,* 7.

Do works of mercy, that God may be merciful to you.—*Bereshit rabba,* 33, 32, 1.

GREEK AND ROMAN

The stranger who cometh from abroad shall be received in a friendly spirit . . . he shall depart, as a friend taking leave of friends, and be honored by them with gifts and suitable tributes of respect. These are the customs according to which our city should receive all strangers of either sex . . . showing respect to Zeus, the God of hospitality.— PLATO, *Laws,* xii, 953.

All good men will show mercy and humanity.—SENECA, *On Clemency,* v.

The immortal Gods love us, and—which is the greatest honor we could have—have placed us next to themselves.—SENECA, *On Benefits,* ii, 29.

Man is formed by nature to acts of benevolence.—M. AURELIUS, ix, 42.

THE GOSPELS

Her sins, which are many, are forgiven: for she loved much: but to whom little is forgiven, the same loveth little.

The Spirit of the Lord is upon me, because he hath appointed me to preach the gospel to the poor: he hath sent me to heal the broken-hearted, to preach deliverance to the captives, and recovering of sight to the blind, to set at liberty them that are bruised, to preach the acceptable year of the Lord.

Woe unto you that are rich! for ye have received your consolation. Woe unto you that are full! for ye shall hunger. Woe unto you that laugh now! for ye shall mourn and weep. Woe unto you when all men shall speak well of you! for so did their fathers to the false prophets.

No man, having put his hand to the plough, and looking back, is fit for the kingdom of God.

THE OLD TESTAMENT

Love coverth all sins.—*Prov.,* x, 19.

Thou lovest all things that are, and abhorrest none of the things which thou didst make.—*Wisdom,* xi, 24.

The Lord is full of compassion and mercy, and he forgiveth sins.—*Ecclus.,* ii, 11.

The Spirit of the Lord God is upon me: because the Lord hath anointed me to preach good tidings unto the meek: he hath sent me to bind up the broken-hearted, to proclaim liberty to the captives, and the opening of the prison to them that are bound: to proclaim the acceptable year of the Lord . . . to comfort all that mourn.—*Is.,* lxi, 1-2.

Woe to them that are at ease in Zion.—*Amos,* vi, 1.

Behold, my servants shall eat, but ye shall be hungry: behold, my servants shall drink, but ye shall be thirsty: behold, my servants shall rejoice, but ye shall be ashamed: behold, my servants shall sing for joy of heart, but ye shall cry for sorrow of heart, and shall howl for vexation of spirit.—*Is.,* lxv, 13.

Blessed is he that waiteth, and cometh to the thousand, three thousand and five and thirty days.—*Daniel,* xii, 12.

THE TALMUD	GREEK AND ROMAN

THE TALMUD

A disciple learned from R. Johanan: Every one that busies himself with the study of the law or with deeds of love . . . hath all his sins forgiven.—*Berachot,* 5 a.

GREEK AND ROMAN

The evil are won by persistent goodness.—SENECA, *On Benefits,* vii, 31.

Love is a mighty god, wonderful among gods and men . . . the source of the greatest benefits to us.—PLATO, *Symposium,* 178.

The wise man will give hospitality to the exile and alms to the needy; he will restore children to their weeping mothers, loose the chains of the captive, release the gladiator from his bondage, and even bury the body of the criminal.—SENECA, *On Clemency,* vi.

The sincerest reverer of heaven is he that eateth the labor of his own hands.—*Berachot,* 8.

The world was made only for Ahab ben Omri [rich] and Rabbi Chanina ben Dosa [poor]: for Ahab ben Omri this world, and for Rabbi Chanina ben Dosa the world to come.—*Berachot,* 61, 2.

Avarice is the worst pest of the human race.—SENECA, *To Helvia,* xiii, 2.

Let parents bequeath to their children, not a heap of riches, but the spirit of reverence.—PLATO, *Laws,* v, 729.

Fix thy desire or aversion on . . . health, power, honors, thy country, friends, and children . . . and thou wilt be unfortunate. But fix them on Zeus, on the Gods . . . and how canst thou be any longer unprosperous?—EPICTETUS, *Discourses,* ii, 17.

R. Simon said: Whosoever on the way reflecteth on parts of the Law and suddenly casteth his eyes on other things . . . acteth not

When a man hath found the chief good, he should take up his abode with it during the remainder of his life.—PLATO, *Laws,* v., 728.

THE GOSPELS	THE OLD TESTAMENT
Take heed and beware of covetousness: for a man's life consisteth not in the abundance of the things which he possesseth.	Gold hath been the ruin of man, and their destruction was present.—*Ecclus.*, xxxi, 6.

.   .   .

Father, forgive them, for they know not what they do.	Let them curse, but bless thou.—*Ps.*, cix, 28.

THE TALMUD

otherwise than if he had drawn evil on himself.—*Pirke Abot,* 3, 7.

He who chooseth the reading of the Scriptures for his chief business shall see his goods increase.—*Abodah Zarah,* 19, 2.

.   .   .

Love him that punisheth thee.—*Derech Eretz,* 9.

As the Lord is merciful and forgiving . . . be thou likewise.— *Sotah,* 13.

GREEK AND ROMAN

Go on thy way, and finish that which is set before thee.—M. AURELIUS, vi, 26.

Covetousness is the root of all evil—SENECA, *On Clemency,* i.

It were better to die of hunger, exempt from grief or fear, than to live in affluence with perturbation.—EPICTETUS, *Enchiridion,* xii.

I am not angry with my condemners, or with my accusers; they have done me no harm, although they did not mean to do me any good; and for this I may gently blame them [Socrates to his judges].—PLATO, *Apology,* 41.

Extract from a Reply
to the Bishop of Llandaff

Thomas Paine

Thomas Paine is perhaps the best known of the authors in this book, yet he is also one of the most misunderstood. His writings were largely political, but his one work written specifically to counter atheism *(The Age of Reason)* has caused Paine to be called an atheist. In reality Paine was a deist, but his work has been so influential in its effect upon orthodox readers that it must be represented in an anthology of this sort.

Paine was born at Thetford, England, in 1737. He had a meager formal education and then began work at the age of thirteen as a corset maker. He changed jobs frequently, finally becoming an excise tax collector. He was not happy or successful at any of these occupations.

In 1772 Paine met Benjamin Franklin in London. Franklin advised him to go to America and gave him a letter of introduction. Paine arrived in Philadelphia in 1774. His first position was as an editor of *The Pennsylvania Magazine.* Paine also wrote a number of articles under pseudonyms. His first book was *Common Sense* (1776), which vigorously argued for independence for the Colonies. The book was a best seller by the standards of the day and aroused popular support for the Declaration of Independence issued later that year.

During the Revolutionary War, Paine served as an aide to Gen. Nathanael Greene. He also wrote sixteen papers, each called "Crisis." The first of these opens with the well-known line, "These are the times that try men's souls." George Washington had this pamphlet read aloud to all the troops at Valley Forge to raise their morale.

Later in the war, Paine became secretary to the Committee for Foreign Affairs. He was forced to resign following a dispute and then became clerk of the General Assembly of Pennsylvania. When the war was over, Paine found that he was broke. His writings had sold hundreds of thousands of copies, but he had refused any royalty from them. He pleaded with Congress for financial assistance. Pennsylvania gave him some money, and New York State gave him a farm at New Rochelle. There Paine invented an iron bridge, and in 1787 he went to Europe to promote his bridge.

While he was in Europe, the French Revolution began. Paine wrote *Rights of Man* (1791) in an attempt to encourage the French in their revolution. Paine was elected a member of the French National Convention and went to France. There he advocated banishing, but not executing, King Louis XVI. This stand got him in trouble with the revolutionaries, and he was imprisoned from December 1793 to November 1794. While he was in prison, the first part of *The Age of Reason* was published (1794), with the second part published in 1796. This book gave Paine a reputation as an infidel, which far over- shadowed any recognition he had obtained for his contribution to liberty for the Colonies. He became a social outcast and lived in poverty in New York City and in New Rochelle. When he died in 1809, he was buried on his farm in New Rochelle. Ten years later, William Cobbett dug up his bones and took them to England. Cobbett's plan was to give Paine a funeral worthy of his contribution; however, things did not go well. Today Paine's bones remain lost somewhere in England. It is only in this century that Paine's great contribution has been recognized, and he has been restored to a place of honor in American history.

There have been a large number of biographies of Paine (no complete bibliography of his writings exists, however). The early biographies were rather superficial or openly hostile. The first thorough work is Moncure Conway's *The Life of Thomas Paine* (1896). It is, however, very uncritical. Recently three biographies of Paine have been published [A. Williamson's *Thomas Paine: His Life, Work and Times* (1973), S. Edwards' *Rebel* (1974), and David F. Hawke's *Paine* (1974)]. Of these Hawke's is the best.

The present selection was one of the few times Paine replied to his critics. Of all the books written in opposition to his *The Age of Reason*, Paine replied to only that of Richard Watson, the Bishop of Llandaff. It was possibly a part of what was eventually intended to be Part 3 of *The Age of Reason*. Part 3 was never published during Paine's lifetime, but the present essay was first made public in the magazine *The Theophilanthropist* in 1810. Also first published there was the selection included in my first *Anthology*. Again, *that* selection may have been a part of what Paine intended to be Part 3 of *The Age of Reason*. The present selection has appeared in a few editions of *The Age of Reason* and *The Theological Works of Thomas Paine*, as published in the last century. It has been out of print for many years.

GENESIS

The bishop says, "the oldest book in the world is Genesis." This is mere assertion; he offers no proof of it, and I go to controvert it, and to show that the book of Job, which is not a Hebrew book, but is a book of the Gentiles, translated into Hebrew, is much older than the book of Genesis.

The book of Genesis means the book of Generations; to which are prefixed two chapters, the first and second, which contain two different cosmogonies, that is, two different accounts of the creation of the world, written by different persons.

The first cosmogony begins at the first verse of the first chapter, and ends at the end of the third verse of the second chapter; for the adverbial conjunction *thus,* with which the second chapter begins, shows those three verses to belong to the first chapter. The second cosmogony begins at the fourth verse of the second chapter, and ends with that chapter.

In the first cosmogony the name of God is used, without any epithet joined to it, and is repeated thirty-five times. In the second cosmogony it is always the Lord God, which is repeated eleven times. These two different styles of expression show these two chapters to be the work of two different persons, and the contradictions they contain show they cannot be the work of one and the same person, as I have already shown.

The third chapter, in which the style of Lord God is continued in every instance, except in the supposed conversation between the woman and the serpent (for in every place in that chapter where the writer speaks, it is always the Lord God) shows this chapter to belong to the second cosmogony.

This chapter gives an account of what is called the fall of man, which is no other than a fable borrowed from, and constructed upon the religion of Zoroaster, or the Persians, or the annual progress of the sun through the twelve signs of the Zodiac. It is the *fall of the year,* the approach and *evil* of winter, announced by the ascension of the autumnal constellation of the *serpent* of the Zodiac, and not the moral *fall of man* that is the key of the allegory, and of the fable in Genesis borrowed from it.

The fall of man in Genesis, is said to have been produced by eating a certain fruit, generally taken to be an apple. The fall of the year is the season for the gathering and eating the new apples of that year. The allegory, therefore, holds with respect to the fruit, which it would not have done had it been an early summer fruit. It holds also with respect to place. The tree is said to have been placed in the *midst* of the garden. But why in the midst of the garden more than in any other place? The situation of the allegory gives the answer to this question, which is, that the fall of the year, when apples and other autumnal fruits are ripe, and when days and nights are of equal length, is the mid-season between summer and winter.

It holds also with respect to clothing and the temperature of the air.

It is said in Genesis, chap. iii. ver. 21, *"Unto Adam and his wife did the Lord God make coats of skins and clothed them."* But why are coats of skins mentioned? This cannot be understood as referring to any thing of the nature of *moral evil.* The solution of the allegory gives again the answer to this question, which is, that the *evil of winter,* which follows the fall of the year, fabulously called in Genesis the *fall of man,* makes warm clothing necessary.

. . . At present, I shall confine myself to the comparative antiquity of the books of Genesis and Job, taking, at the same time, whatever I may find in my way with respect to the fabulousness of the book of Genesis; for if what is called the fall of man, in Genesis, be fabulous or allegorical, that which is called the redemption, in the New Testament, cannot be a fact. It is morally impossible, and impossible also in the nature of things, that *moral good* can redeem *physical evil.* I return to the bishop.

If Genesis be, as the bishop asserts, the oldest book in the world, and consequently, the oldest and first written book of the Bible, and if the extraordinary things related in it, such as the creation of the world in six days, the tree of life, and of good and evil, the story of Eve and the talking serpent, the fall of man and his being turned out of Paradise, were facts, or even believed by the Jews to be facts, they would be referred to as fundamental matters, and that very frequently, in the books of the Bible that were written by various authors afterwards; whereas, there is not a book, chapter, or verse of the Bible, from the time Moses is said to have written the book of Genesis, to the book of Malachi, the last book in the Bible, including a space of more than a thousand years, in which there is any mention made of these things, or any of them, nor are they so much as alluded to. How will the bishop solve this difficulty, which stands as a circumstantial contradiction to his assertion?

There are but two ways of solving it.

First, that the book of Genesis is not an ancient book; that it has been written by some (now) unknown person, after the return of the Jews from the Babylonian captivity, about a thousand years after the time that Moses is said to have lived, and put as a preface or introduction to the other books, when they were formed into a canon in the time of the second temple, and, therefore, not having existed before that time, none of these things mentioned in it could be referred to in those books.

Secondly, that admitting Genesis to have been written by Moses, the Jews did not believe the things stated in it to be true, and, therefore as they could not refer to them as facts, they would not refer to them as fables. The first of these solutions goes against the antiquity of the book, and the second against its authenticity, and the bishop may take which he pleases.

But, be the author of Genesis whoever he may, there is abundant evidence o show, as well from the early Christian writers, as from the Jews themselves, that the things stated in that book were not believed to be facts. Why they have been believed as facts since that time, when better and fuller knowledge existed on the case, than is known now, can be accounted for only on the imposition of priestcraft.

Augustine, one of the early champions of the Christian church, acknowledges in his *City of God,* that the adventure of Eve and the serpent, and the account of Paradise, were generally considered as fiction or allegory. He regards them as allegory himself, without attempting to give any explanation, but he supposes that a better explanation might be found than those that had been offered.

Origen, another early champion of the church, says, "What man of good sense can ever persuade himself that there were a first, a second, and a third day, and that each of these days had a night when there were yet neither sun, moon, nor stars. What man can be stupid enough to believe that God, acting the part of a gardener, had planted a garden in the east, that the tree of life was a real tree, and that its fruit had the virtue of making those who eat of it live for ever?"

Maimonides, one of the most learned and celebrated of the Jewish Rabbins, who lived in the eleventh century (about seven or eight hundred years ago) and to whom the bishop refers in his answer to me, is very explicit, in his book, entitled *More Nevochim,* upon the nonreality of the things stated in the account of the Creation in the book of Genesis.

"We ought not (says he) to understand, nor to take according to the letter, that which is written in the book of the Creation, nor to have the same ideas of it with common men; otherwise, our ancient sages would not have recommended, with so much care, to conceal the sense of it, and not to raise the allegorical veil which envelopes the truths it contains. The book of Genesis, taken according to the letter, gives the most absurd and the most extravagant ideas of the Divinity. Whoever shall find out the sense of it, ought to restrain himself from divulging it. It is a maxim which all our sages repeat, and above all with respect to the work of six days. It may happen that some one, with the aid he may borrow from others, may hit upon the meaning of it. In that case he ought to impose silence upon himself; or if he speak of it, he ought to speak obscurely, and in an enigmatical manner, as I do myself, leaving the rest to be found out by those who can understand."

This is, certainly a very extraordinary declaration of Maimonides, taking all the parts of it.

First, he declares, that the account of the Creation in the book of Genesis is not a fact; that to believe it to be a fact, gives the most absurd and the most extravagant ideas of the Divinity.

Second, that it is an allegory.

Thirdly, that the allegory has a concealed secret.

Fourthly, that whoever can find the secret ought not to tell it.

It is this last part that is the most extraordinary. Why all this care of the Jewish Rabbins, to prevent what they call the concealed meaning, or the secret, from being known, and, if known, to prevent any of their people from telling it? It certainly must be something which the Jewish nation are afraid or ashamed the world should know. It must be something personal to them as a people, and not a secret of a divine nature, which the more it is known, the more it increases the glory of the Creator, and the gratitude and happiness of man. It is not God's secret, but their own, they are keeping. I go to unveil the secret.

The case is, the Jews have stolen their cosmogony, that is, their account of the Creation, from the cosmogony of the Persians, contained in the book of Zoroaster, the Persian lawgiver, and brought it with them when they returned from captivity by the benevolence of Cyrus, King of Persia; for it is evident from the silence of all the books of the Bible upon the subject of the Creation, that the Jews had no cosmogony before that time. If they had a cosmogony from the time of Moses, some of their judges who governed during more than four hundred years, or of their kings, the Davids and Solomons of their day, who governed nearly five hundred years, or of their prophets and psalmists, who lived in the meantime, would have mentioned it. It would, either as fact or fable, have been the grandest of all subjects for a psalm. It would have suited to a tittle the ranting, poetical genius of Isaiah, or served as a cordial to the gloomy Jeremiah. But not one word nor even a whisper, does any of the Bible authors give upon the subject.

To conceal the theft, the Rabbins of the second temple have published Genesis as a book of Moses, and have enjoined secrecy to all their people, who, by travelling, or otherwise, might happen to discover from whence the cosmogony was borrowed, not to tell it. The evidence of circumstances is often unanswerable, and there is no other than this which I have given, that goes to the whole of the case, and this does.

Diogenes Laertius, an ancient and respectable author whom the Bishop, in his answer to me, quotes on another occasion, has a passage that corresponds with the solution here given. In speaking of the religion of the Persians, as promulgated by their priests or magi, he says, the Jewish Rabbins were the successors of their doctrine. Having thus spoken on the plagiarism, and on the nonreality of the book of Genesis, I will give some additional evidence that Moses is not the author of that book.

Eben-Ezra, a celebrated Jewish author, who lived about seven hundred years ago, and whom the bishop allows to have been a man of great erudition, has made a great many observations, too numerous to be repeated here, to show that Moses was not, and could not be, the author of the book of Genesis, nor any of the five books that bear his name.

Spinoza, another learned Jew, who lived about a hundred and thirty years ago, recites, in his treatise on the ceremonies of the Jews, ancient and modern, the observations of Eben-Ezra, to which he adds many others, to show that Moses is not the author of these books. He also says, and shows his reasons for saying it, that the Bible did not exist as a book, till the time of the Maccabees, which was more than a hundred years after the return of the Jews from the Babylonian captivity.

In the second part of the *Age of Reason,* I have, among other things, referred to nine verses in the 36th chapter of Genesis, beginning at the 31st verse, "These are the kings that reigned in Edom, before there reigned any king over the children of Israel," which is impossible could have been written by Moses, or in the time of Moses, and could not have been written until after the Jew[ish] kings began to reign in Israel, which was not till several hundred years after the time of Moses.

The bishop allows this, and says "I think you say true." But he then quibbles, and says, that a small addition to a book does not destroy either the genuineness or authenticity of the whole book. This is priestcraft. These verses do not stand in the book as an addition to it, but as making a part of the whole book, and which it is impossible that Moses could write. The bishop would reject the antiquity of any other book if it could be proved from the words of the book itself that a part of it could not have been written till several hundred years after the reputed author of it was dead. He would call such a book a forgery. I am authorized, therefore, to call the book of Genesis a forgery.

Combining, then, all the foregoing circumstances together respecting the antiquity and authenticity of the book of Genesis, a conclusion will naturally follow therefrom; those circumstances are,

First, that certain parts of the book cannot possibly have been written by Moses, and that the other parts carry no evidence of having been written by him.

Secondly, the universal silence of all the following books of the Bible, for about a thousand years, upon the extraordinary things spoken of in Genesis, such as the creation of the world in six days—the garden of Eden—the tree of knowledge—the tree of life—the story of Eve and the serpent—the fall of man, and his being turned out of this fine garden, together with Noah's flood, and the tower of Babel.

Thirdly, the silence of all the books of the Bible upon even the name of Moses, from the book of Joshua until the second book of Kings, which was not written till after the captivity, for it gives an account of the captivity, a period of about a thousand years. Strange that a man who is proclaimed as the historian of the Creation, the privy-counsellor and confident of the Almighty—the legislator of the Jewish nation, and the founder of its religion; strange, I say, that even the name of such a man should not find a place in their books for a thousand years, if they knew or believed any thing about him, or the books he is said to have written.

Fourthly, the opinion of some of the most celebrated of the Jewish commentators, that Moses is not the author of the book of Genesis, founded on the reasons given for that opinion.

Fifthly, the opinion of the early Christian writers, and of the great champion of Jewish literature, Maimonides, that the book of Genesis is not a book of facts.

Sixthly, the silence imposed by all the Jewish Rabbins, and by Maimonides himself, upon the Jewish nation, not to speak of any thing they may happen to know, or discover, respecting the cosmogony (or creation of the world) in the book of Genesis.

From these circumstances the following conclusions offer—

First, that the book of Genesis is not a book of facts.

Secondly, that as no mention is made throughout the Bible of any of the extraordinary things related in Genesis, that it has not been written till after the other books were written, and put as a preface to the Bible. Every one knows that a preface to a book, though it stands first, is the last written.

Thirdly, that the silence imposed by all the Jewish Rabbins, and by Maimonides upon the Jewish nation, to keep silence upon every thing related in their cosmogony, evinces a secret, they are not willing should be known. The secret, therefore, explains itself to be, that when the Jews were in captivity in Babylon and Persia, they became acquainted with the cosmogony of the Persians, as registered in the Zend-Avesta, of Zoroaster, the Persian lawgiver, which, after their return from captivity, they manufactured and modelled as their own, and ante-dated it by giving to it the name of Moses. The case admits of no other explanation. From all which it appears that the book of Genesis, instead of being the *oldest book in the world,* as the bishop calls it, has been the last written book of the Bible, and that the cosmogony it contains, has been manufactured.

ON THE NAMES IN THE BOOK OF GENESIS

Every thing in Genesis serves as evidence or symptom, that the book has been composed in some late period of the Jewish nation. Even the names mentioned in it serve to this purpose.

Nothing is more common or more natural, than to name the children of succeeding generations, after the names of those who had been celebrated in some former generation. This holds good with respect to all the people, and all the histories we know of, and it does not hold good with the Bible. There must be some cause for this.

This book of Genesis tells us of a man whom it calls Adam, and of his sons Abel and Seth; of Enoch who lived 365 years, (it is exactly the number of days in a year), and that then God took him up. It has the appearance of being taken from some allegory of the Gentiles on the commencement and termination of the year by the progress of the sun through the twelve signs of the Zodiac, on which the allegorical religion of the Gentiles was founded.

It tells us of Methusaleh who lived 969 years, and of a long train of other names in the fifth chapter. It then passes on to a man whom it calls Noah, and his sons, Shem, Ham, and Japhet: then to Lot, Abraham, Isaac, and Jacob, and his sons, with which the book of Genesis finishes.

All these, according to the account given in that book, were the most extraordinary and celebrated of men. They were, moreover, heads of families. Adam was the father of the world. Enoch, for his righteousness, was taken up to heaven. Methuselah lived to almost a thousand years. He was the son of Enoch, the man of 365, the number of days in a year. It has the appearance of being the continuation of an Allegory on the 365 days of a year, and its abundant productions. Noah was selected from all the world to be preserved when it was drowned, and became the second father of the world. Abraham was the father of the faithful multitude. Isaac and Jacob were the inheritors of his fame, and the last was the father of the twelve tribes.

Now, if these very wonderful men and their names, and the book that records them, had been known by the Jews, before the Babylonian captivity, those names would have been as common among the Jews before that period as they have been since. We now hear of thousands of Abrahams, Isaacs, and Jacobs among the Jews, but there were none of that name before the Babylonian captivity. The Bible does not mention one, though from the time that Abraham is said to have lived, to the time of the Babylonian captivity, is about 1400 years.

How is it to be accounted for, that there have been so many thousands, and perhaps hundreds of thousands of Jews of the names of Abraham, Isaac, and Jacob since that period, and not one before? It can be accounted for but one way, which is that before the Babylonian captivity, the Jews had no such books as Genesis, nor knew any thing of the names and persons it mentions, nor of the things it relates, and that the stories in it have been manufactured since that time. From the Arabic name *Ibrahim* (which is the manner the Turks write that name to this day) the Jews have most probably manufactured their Abraham.

I will advance my observations a point further, and speak of the names of *Moses* and *Aaron,* mentioned for the first time in the books of Exodus. There are now, and have continued to be from the time of the Babylonian captivity, or soon after it, thousands of Jews of the names of *Moses* and *Aaron,* and we read not of any of that name before that time. The Bible does not mention one. The direct inference from this is, that the Jews knew of no such book as Exodus, before the Babylonian captivity. In fact, that it did not exist before that time, and that it is only since the book has been invented, that the names of *Moses* and *Aaron* have been common among the Jews.

It is applicable to the purpose, to observe, that the picturesque work, called *Mosaic-work,* spelled the same as you would say the *Mosaic* account of the creation, is not derived from the word *Moses* but from *Muses,* (the *Muses,*) because of the variegated and picturesque pavement in the temples dedicated to the *Muses.* This carries a strong implication that the name *Moses* is drawn from the same source, and that he is not a real but an allegorical person, as Maimonides describes what is called the *Mosaic* account of the creation to be.

I will go a point still further. The Jews now know the book of Genesis, and the names of all the persons mentioned in the first *ten chapters* of that book, from Adam to Noah: yet we do not hear (I speak for myself) of any Jew of the present day, of the name of Adam, Abel, Seth, Enoch, Methusaleh, Noah, Shem, Ham, or Japhet, (names mentioned in the first ten chapters,) though these were, according to the account in that book, the most extraordinary of all the names that make up the catalogue of the Jewish chronology.

The names the Jews now adopt, are those that are mentioned in Genesis after the tenth chapter, as Abraham, Isaac, Jacob, etc. How then does it happen, that they do not adopt the names found in the first ten chapters? Here is evidently a line of division drawn between the first ten chapters of Genesis, and the remaining chapters, with respect to the adoption of names. There must be some cause for this, and I go to offer a solution of the problem.

The reader will recollect the quotation I have already made from the Jewish Rabbin, Maimonides, wherein he says, "We ought not to understand nor to take according to the letter that which is written in the book of Creation. It is a maxim (says he) which all our sages repeat *above all,* with respect to the work of six days."

The qualifying expression *above all,* implies there are other parts of the book, though not so important, that ought not to be understood or taken according to the letter, and as the Jews do not adopt the names mentioned in the first ten chapters, it appears evident those chapters are included in the injunction not to take them in a literal sense, or according to the letter; from which it follows, that the persons or characters mentioned in the first ten chapters, as Adam, Abel, Seth, Enoch, Methuselah, and so on to Noah, are not real but fictitious or allegorical persons, and, therefore, the Jews do not adopt their names into their families. If they affixed the same idea of reality to them as they do to those that follow after the tenth chapter, the names of Adam, Abel, Seth, etc. would be as common among the Jews of the present day, as are those of Abraham, Isaac, Jacob, Moses and Aaron.

In the superstition they have been in, scarcely a Jew[ish] family would have been without an *Enoch,* as a presage of his going to heaven as ambassador for the whole family. Every mother who wished that the *days* of her son *might be long in the land* would call him *Methuselah;* and all the Jews that might have to traverse the ocean would be named Noah, as a charm against shipwreck and drowning.

This is domestic evidence against the book of Genesis, which joined to the several kinds of evidence before recited, shows the book of Genesis not to be older than the Babylonian captivity, and to be fictitious. I proceed to fix the character and antiquity of the book of Job.

JOB

The book of Job has not the least appearance of being a book of the Jews, and though printed among the books of the Bible, does not belong to it. There is no reference in it to any Jewish law or ceremony. On the contrary, all the internal evidence it contains shows it to be a book of the Gentiles, either of Persia or Chaldea.

The name of Job does not appear to be a Jewish name. There is no Jew of that name in any of the books of the Bible, neither is there now that I ever heard of. The country where Job is said or supposed to have lived, or rather where the scene of the drama is laid, is called Uz, and there was no place of that name ever belonging to the Jews. If Uz is the same as Ur, it was in Chaldea, or the country of the Gentiles.

The Jews can give no account how they came by this book, nor who was the author, nor the time when it was written. Origen, in his work against Celsus, (in the first ages of the Christian church), says, *that the Book of Job is older than Moses.* Eben-Ezra, the Jewish commentator, whom (as I have before said) the bishop allows to have been a man of great erudition, and who certainly understood his own language, says, that the book of Job has been translated from another language into Hebrew. Spinoza, another Jewish commentator of great learning, confirms the opinion of Eben-Ezra, and says moreover, *"Je crois que Job etait Gentil;"** I believe that Job was a Gentile.

The bishop, (in his answer to me) says, "that the structure of the whole book of Job, in whatever light of history or drama it be considered, is founded on the belief that prevailed with the Persians and Chaldeans, and other Gentile nations, of a good and an evil spirit."

In speaking of the good and evil spirit of the Persians, the bishop writes them *Arimanius* and *Oromasdes.* I will not dispute about the orthography,

---

*Spinoza on the ceremonies of the Jews, page 296, published in French at Amsterdam, 1678.

because I know that translated names are differently spelled in different languages. But he has nevertheless made a capital error. He has put the Devil first; for Arimanius, or, as it is more generally written, *Ahriman,* is the *evil spirit,* and *Oromasdes* or *Ormusd* the good spirit. He has made the same mistake in the same paragraph, in speaking of the good and evil spirit of the ancient Egyptians *Osiris* and *Typho,* he puts Typho before Osiris. The error is just the same as if the bishop in writing about the Christian religion, or in preaching a sermon, were to say the *Devil* and *God.* A priest ought to know his own trade better. We agree, however, about the structure of the book of Job, that it is Gentile. I have said in the second part of the *Age of Reason,* and given my reasons for it, that *the drama of it is not Hebrew.*

From the testimonies I have cited, that of Origen, who, about fourteen hundred years ago, said that the book of Job was more ancient than Moses, that of Eben-Ezra, who, in his commentary on Job, says, it has been translated from another language (and consequently from a Gentile language) into Hebrew; that of Spinoza, who not only says the same thing, but that the author of it was a Gentile; and that of the bishop, who says that the structure of the whole book is Gentile. It follows then in the first place, that the book of Job is not a book of the Jews originally.

Then, in order to determine to what people or nation any book of religion belongs, we must compare it with the leading dogmas or precepts of that people or nation; and therefore, upon the bishop's own construction, the book of Job belongs either to the ancient Persians, the Chaldeans, or the Egyptians; because the structure of it is consistant with the dogma they held, that of a good and evil spirit, called in Job, *God* and *Satan,* existing as distinct and separate beings, and it is not consistent with any dogma of the Jews.

The belief of a good and an evil spirit, existing as distinct and separate beings, is not a dogma to be found in any of the books of the Bible. It is not till we come to the New Testament that we hear of any such dogma. There the person called the Son of God, holds conversation with Satan on a mountain, as familiarly as is represented in the drama of Job. Consequently the bishop cannot say, in this respect, that the New Testament is founded upon the Old. According to the Old, the God of the Jews was the God of every thing. All good and evil came from him. According to Exodus, it was God, and not the Devil, that hardened Pharaoh's heart. According to the book of Samuel, it was an evil spirit from God that troubled Saul. And Ezekiel makes God to say, in speaking of the Jews, *"I gave them the statutes that were not good, and judgments by which they should not live."* The Bible describes the God of Abraham, Isaac, and Jacob in such a contradictory manner, and under such a two-fold character, there would be no knowing when he was in earnest and when in irony; when to believe, and when not. As to the precepts, principles, and maxims, in the book of Job, they show that the people, abusively called the heathen in the books of the Jews, had the most sublime ideas of the Creator, and the most exalted devotional morality. It was the Jews who dishonored God. It was the Gentiles who glorified him. As to the fabulous personifications introduced by the Greek and Latin poets, it was a corruption of the ancient religion of the Gentiles, which consisted in the adoration of a first cause of the works of the creation, in which the sun was the great visible agent.

It appears to have been a religion of gratitude and adoration, and not of prayer and discontented solicitation. In Job we find adoration and submission, but not prayer. Even the ten commandments enjoin not prayer. Prayer has been added to devotion, by the church of Rome, as the instrument of fees and perquisites. All prayers by the priests of the Christian church, whether public or private, must be paid for. It may be right, individually, to pray for virtues, or mental instruction, but not for things. It is an attempt to dictate to the Almighty in the government of the world. But to return to the book of Job.

As the book of Job decides itself to be a book of the Gentiles, the next thing is to find out to what particular nation it belongs, and lastly, what is its antiquity.

As a composition, it is sublime, beautiful, and scientific: full of sentiment, and abounding in grand metaphorical description. As a drama, it is regular. The dramatis personae, the persons performing the several parts, are regularly introduced, and speak without interruption or confusion. The scene, as I have before said, is laid in the country of the Gentiles, and the unities, though not always necessary in a drama, are observed here as strictly as the subject would admit.

In the last act, where the Almighty is introduced as speaking from the whirlwind, to decide the controversy between Job and his friends, it is an idea as grand as poetical imagination can conceive. What follows of Job's future prosperity does not belong to it as a drama. It is an epilogue of the writer, as the first verses of the first chapter, which gave an account of Job, his country and his riches, are the prologue.

The book carries the appearance of being the work of some of the Persian Magi, not only because the structure of it corresponds to the dogmas of the religion of those people, as founded by Zoroaster, but from the astronomical references in it to the constellations of the zodiac and other objects in the heavens, of which the sun, in their religion called Mithra, was the chief. Job, in describing the power of God, (Job ix. v. 27,) says, "Who commandeth the sun, and it riseth not, and sealeth up the stars—who alone spreadeth out the heavens, and treadeth upon the waves of the sea—who maketh Arcturus, Orion, and Pleiades, and the chambers of the south." All this astronomical allusion is consistent with the religion of the Persians.

Establishing then the book of Job, as the work of some of the Persian, or Eastern Magi, the case naturally follows, that when the Jews returned from captivity, by the permission of Cyrus, king of Persia, they brought this book with them: had it translated into Hebrew, and put into their scriptural canons, which were not formed till after their return. This will account for the name of Job being mentioned in Ezekiel, *(Ezekiel, chap. xiv. v. 14,)* who was one of the captives, and also for its not being mentioned in any book said or supposed to have been written before the captivity. . . .

The following is a disconnected part of the same work, and is now (1824) first published.

.   .   .

FUTURE STATE

The idea of a Future state was a universal idea to all nations except the Jews. At the time and long before Jesus Christ and the men called his disciples were born, it had been sublimely treated of by Cicero in his book on old age, by Plato, Socrates, Xenophon, and other of the ancient theologists, whom the abusive Christian church calls heathen. Xenophon represents the elder Cyrus speaking after this manner:

"Think not, my dearest children, that when I depart from you, I shall be no more: but remember that my soul, even while I lived among you, was invisible to you; yet by my actions you were sensible it existed in this body. Believe it therefore existing still, though it be still unseen. How quickly would the honors of illustrious men perish after death, if their souls performed nothing to preserve their fame? For my own part, I could never think that the soul, while in a mortal body, lives, but when departed from it dies; or that its consciousness is lost, when it is discharged out of an unconscious habitation. But when it is freed from all corporeal alliance, it is then that it truly exists."

Since, then, the idea of a future existence was universal, it may be asked, what new doctrine does the New Testament contain? I answer, that of corrupting the theory of the ancient theologists, by annexing to it the heavy and gloomy doctrine of the resurrection of the body.

As to the resurrection of the body, whether the same body or another, it is a miserable conceit, fit only to be preached to man as an animal. It is not worthy to be called doctrine.—Such an idea never entered the brain of any visionary but those of the Christian church;—yet it is in this that the novelty of the New Testament consists. All the other matters serve but as props to this, and those props are most wretchedly put together.

MIRACLES

The Christian church is full of miracles. In one of the churches of Brabant, they show a number of cannon balls, which, they say, the virgin Mary in some former war, caught in her muslin *apron* as they came roaring out of the cannon's mouth, to prevent their hurting the *saints* of her favorite army. She does no such feats now-a-days. Perhaps the reason is, that the infidels have taken away her muslin apron. They show also, between Montmatre and the village of St. Dennis, several places where they say St. Dennis stopped with his head in his hands after it had been cut off at Montmatre. The Protestants will call those things lies; and where is the proof that all the other things called miracles are not as great lies as those.

[There appears to be an omission here in the copy.]

Christ, say those Cabalists, came in the *fullness of time*. And pray what is the fullness of time? The words admit of no idea. They are perfectly Cabalistical. Time is a word invented to describe to our conception a greater or less portion of eternity. It may be a minute, a portion of eternity measured by the vibration of a pendulum of a certain length;—it may be a day, a year, a hundred, or a thousand years, or any other quantity. Those portions are only greater or less comparatively.

The word fullness applies not to any of them. The idea of fullness of time cannot be conceived. A woman with child and ready for delivery, as Mary was when Christ was born, may be said to have gone her full time; but it is the woman that is full, not time.

It may also be said figuratively, in certain cases, that the times are full of events; but time itself is incapable of being full of itself. Ye hypocrites! learn to speak intelligible language.

It happened to be a time of peace when they say Christ was born; and what then? There had been many such intervals: and have been many such since. Time was no fuller in any of them than in the other. If he were he would be fuller now than he ever was before. If he was full then he must be bursting now. But peace or war have relation to circumstances, and not to time; and those Cabalists would be at as much loss to make out any meaning of fullness of circumstances, as to fullness of time; and if they could, it would be fatal; for fullness of circumstances would mean, when there are no more circumstances to happen; and fullness of time when there is no more time to follow.

Christ, therefore, like every other person, was neither in the fullness of one nor the other.

But though we cannot conceive the idea of fullness of time, because we cannot have conception of a time when there shall be no time; nor of fullness of circumstances, because we cannot conceive a state of existence to be without circumstances; we can often see, after a thing is past, if any circumstance, necessary to give the utmost activity and success to that thing, was wanting at the time that thing took place. If such a circumstance was wanting, we may be certain that the thing which took place, was not a thing of God's ordaining; whose work is always perfect, and his means perfect means. They tell us that Christ was the Son of God; in that case, he would have known every thing; and he came upon earth to make known the will of God to man throughout the whole earth. If this had been true, Christ would have known and would have been furnished with all the possible means of doing it; and would have instructed mankind, or at least his Apostles, in the use of such of the means as they could use themselves to facilitate the accomplishment of the mission; consequently he would have instructed them in the art of printing, for the press is the tongue of the world; and without which, his or their preaching was less than a whistle compared to thunder. Since, then, he did not do this, he had not the means necessary to the mission; and consequently had not the mission.

They tell us in the book of Acts, chap. 2, a very stupid story of the Apostles' having the gift of tongues; and *cloven tongues of fire* descended and sat upon each of them. Perhaps it was this story of cloven tongues that gave rise to the notion of slitting Jackdaws tongues to make them talk. Be that however as it may, the gift of tongues, even if it were true, would be but of little use without the art of printing. I can sit in my chamber, as I do while writing this, and by the aid of printing, can send the thoughts I am writing through the greatest part of Europe, to the East Indies, and over all North America, in a few months. Jesus Christ and his Apostles could not do this. They had not the means, and the want of means detects the pretended mission.

There are three modes of communication. Speaking, writing and printing. The first is exceedingly limited. A man's voice can be heard but a few yards of distance: and his person can be but in one place.

Writing is much more extensive; but the thing written cannot be multiplied but at great expense, and the multiplication will be slow and incorrect. Were there no other means of circulating what priests call the word of God (the Old and New Testament) than by writing copies, those copies could not be purchased at less than forty pounds sterling each; consequently but few people could purchase them, while the writers could scarcely obtain a livelihood by it. But the art of printing changes all the cases, and opens a scene as vast as the world. It gives to man a sort of divine attribute. It gives to him mental omnipresence. He can be every where and at the same instant; for wherever he is read he is mentally there.

The case applies not only against the pretending mission of Christ and his Apostles, but against every thing that priests call the word of God, and against all those who pretend to deliver it; for had God ever delivered any verbal word, he would have taught the means of communicating it. The one without the other is inconsistent with the wisdom we conceive of the Creator.

The third chapter of Genesis, verse 21, tells us that *God made coats of skins and clothed* Adam and Eve. It was infinitely more important that man should be taught the art of printing than that Adam should be taught to make a pair of leather breeches, or his wife a petticoat.

There is another matter, equally striking and important, that connects itself with those observations against this pretended word of God, this manufactured book, called *Revealed Religion.*

We know that whatever is of God's doing is unalterable by man beyond the laws which the Creator has ordained. We cannot make a tree grow with the root in the air and the fruit in the ground: we cannot make iron into gold nor gold into iron; we cannot make rays of light shine forth rays of darkness, nor darkness shine forth light. If there were such a thing, as a word of God, it would possess the same properties which all his other works do. It would resist destructive alteration. But we see that the book which they call the word of God has not this property. That book says, Genesis chap. 1, verse 27, *"So God created man in his own image;"* but the printer can make it say, *So man created God in his own image.* The words are passive to every transposition of them, or can be annihilated and others put in their places. This is not the case with any thing that is of God's doing; and, therefore, this book, called the word of God, tried by the same universal rule which every other of God's works within our reach can be tried by, proves itself to be a forgery.

The bishop says, that *"miracles are a proper proof of a divine mission."* Admitted. But we know that men, and especially priests, can tell lies and call them miracles. It is therefore necessary, that the thing called a miracle be proved to be true, and also to be miraculous; before it can be admitted as proof of the thing called revelation.

The bishop must be a bad logician not to know that one doubtful thing cannot be admitted as proof that another doubtful thing is true. It would be like attempting to prove a liar not to be a liar, by the evidence of another, who is as great a liar as himself.

Though Jesus Christ, by being ignorant of the art of printing, shows he had not the means necessary to a divine mission, and consequently had no such mission; it does not follow that if he had known that art, the divinity of what they call his mission would be proved thereby, any more than it proved the divinity of the man who invented printing. Something therefore beyond printing, even if he had known it, was necessary *as a miracle,* to have proved that what he delivered was the word of God; and this was that the book in which that word should be contained, which is now called the Old and New Testament, should possess the miraculous property, distinct from all human books, of resisting alteration. This would be not only a miracle, but an ever existing and universal miracle; whereas, those which they tell us of, even if they had been true, were momentary and local; they would leave no trace behind, after the lapse of a few years, of having ever existed; but this would prove, in all ages and in all places, the book to be divine and not human; as effectually, and as conveniently, as aquafortis proves gold to be gold by not being capable of acting upon it; and detects all other metals and all counterfeit composition, by dissolving them. Since then the only miracle capable of every proof is wanting, and which every thing that is of a divine origin possesses; all the tales of miracles with which the Old and New Testament are filled, are fit only for imposters to preach and fools to believe.

Part Three

Atheist and Rationalist Poetry

Introduction

Atheist and rationalist poems are elusive. It would seem that there should be such things, but consulting any number of anthologies will rarely turn one up. Of course, there are a *few* well-known atheist poems. *The Rubaiyat of Omar Khayyam* (especially in the Edward FitzGerald translation) is probably the most famous. There is also the verse translation of Lucretius' *On the Nature of Things,* which must be considered a poem in this form. The only other widely known poem of this genre is *Invictus* by William Ernest Henley, especially its last two lines:

> I am the master of my Fate:
> I am the captain of my soul.

The present collection's contents will surprise many atheists and also many lovers of poetry. I have managed to uncover atheist or rationalist poetry by some very famous and first-rate poets. It is not a group of selections that any but the most thorough investigator or devotee of poetry will have read before. Nevertheless, it includes some very fine verse. Among the poets whose verse I (at least) consider atheistic or rationalistic are: Shelley, Byron, Keats, Browning, Kipling, Hardy, Sandberg, Dryden, Swinburne, and Masters. Although some people who are most particularly known for their religious heterodoxy (e.g., Thomas Paine and Robert G. Ingersoll) also wrote verse, it does not seem to me to be very good. I thought it best to let professional poets, a portion of whose works are atheistic in their themes, represent the best of atheist poetry.

This section will depart slightly from my previous format of providing an introductory essay followed by a biographical sketch of each of the authors. Because some of the selections are very short, it seemed best to incorporate the short author biographies into the introductory sketch. The bibliographical information about the particular poems did not seem especially important, and is usually very difficult to trace, since a single poem may have first appeared in a magazine or in an anthology, where it is concealed. In addition, many of these poems were composed long before they were ever published. Sometimes publication occurred only after the author's death.

JAMES THOMSON (1834-1882)

Many poetry experts have considered James Thomson's *City of Dreadful Night* to be the finest atheist poem in the English language, though his works in general are not well known. Since it is so very long only two representative selections are included here. The poem is quite fine technically, but I disagree that it is the best poetic *statement* of atheist philosophy available in English. I am not sure what my candidate would be, but I think there are better and *shorter* poems to be found, though perhaps no other work displays such technical qualities.

James Thomson was born in Glasgow, Scotland, in 1834. His mother had been very religious and had indoctrinated him with her ideas. His childhood was both uneventful and happy, at least until his father had a stroke and became physically and mentally incapacitated. Thomson was orphaned soon thereafter and went to live in a children's asylum. He was happy there as well, although uncertain of his future. It was suggested by the staff that he become an army schoolmaster, and although he was not excited by the idea, that is exactly what he became.

One of Thomson's postings was to Ballincollig, Ireland, and there he met the atheist Charles Bradlaugh (whose work appears in Parts 2 and 5 of the present volume). Their friendship lasted for more than twenty years and greatly influenced Thomson. His friendship with Bradlaugh was to begin a personal review of his religious ideas, which ended in Thomson's conversion to atheism. His army career ended abruptly after eight years, when Thomson was discharged, ostensibly for having taken a dip in a lake where swimming was prohibited. The more likely reason was that he suffered from alcoholism, a disease that was to wreck the rest of his life.

Thomson went to London, looked up Bradlaugh, and moved in with him and his family. They shared a home for four years. During that time, Thomson worked as a writer and editor, often on magazines that Bradlaugh edited. Many of his poems and prose pieces were first published in the freethought press through the assistance of Bradlaugh. Throughout this period, Thomson would disappear for periods of several days on drunken sprees. All attempts to help him with his drinking problem were to no avail, although it does seem to have been intermittent. For example, when Thomson went to the state of Colorado as an agent for the mining interests of a

London company, and later when he spent time in Spain as a reporter covering the Spanish Civil War, he seems to have been largely sober. Financial problems haunted him throughout his life, and he did not seem to be able to improve his lot in life, no matter how hard he tried.

Thomson continued to live in a series of furnished rooms after moving out of Bradlaugh's house in 1866. Nearly ten years later, in 1875, he had a serious quarrel with Bradlaugh, after which they never spoke again. Although Thomson's mood was increasingly despondent, he continued writing both prose and poetry. The first collected edition of his poems was published in 1880 and received mixed reviews. Two other collections, one each of poetry and prose, were also published before he died from complications of alcoholism in 1882. He had reached the grand old age of forty-eight.

The City of Dreadful Night was first published in four installments in Bradlaugh's magazine *The National Reformer* in 1874. It was subsequently republished in Thomson's first book of poems, *The City of Dreadful Night and Other Poems,* in 1880. It again appeared in his *Poetical Works of James Thomson,* published posthumously in 1895. The work is occasionally found in anthologies of minor Victorian poets but not commonly included in anthologies. Although very fine in its technical construction, often rising to the lyrical, it is quite long (more than 1,100 lines), dreadfully pessimistic and depressing. Nevertheless, it should not be taken as the typical attitude of the atheist. Most atheists, if not the vast majority, are cheerful and optimistic, in direct contrast to the attitude of Thomson, who seems to have had a very difficult and bitter life.

VOLTAIRINE DE CLEYRE (1866-1912)

Voltairine de Cleyre, a leading American anarchist and freethinker, actively pursued the dual careers of writing and lecturing. Born in Michigan, from the age of twelve, she was raised by her freethinking father. Finally the combined weight of poor local schools and family problems forced him to enroll Voltairine in a Catholic parochial school in nearby Canada, where he hoped she would get a better education. Although she initially hated the school, it was not long before she became acclimated: soon Voltairine emerged as an outstanding student. At the age of seventeen she left school and supported herself by giving piano lessons and by teaching French.

The execution of the Haymarket anarchists shocked de Cleyre, and she was eventually converted to anarchism. Soon Voltairine was writing for anarchist as well as freethought publications. She was an excellent public speaker and a poetess of some note. Residing primarily in Philadelphia, and always living in poverty, she taught English to immigrants and gave piano lessons. Voltairine died in 1912 and was buried in Chicago.

The Freethinker's Plea was written in Michigan in 1887, appeared in freethought and anarchist press publications several times, and first appeared in book form in the 1914 edition of *Selected Works of Voltairine de Cleyre*. It has not been reprinted since that time.

EDGAR LEE MASTERS (1869-1950)

Though famous as the author of the *Spoon River Anthology*, it is not so widely known that Edgar Lee Masters was a freethinker, the son of a freethinker, or that he wrote an important freethought poem. Masters was born in Garnett, Kansas, in 1869. His father had gone there to establish a law practice, but was unsuccessful. Shortly thereafter, the Masters family returned to Illinois, where Edgar Lee was raised. After school Lee (as he was then called) worked for a newspaper and was eventually persuaded by his father to study law in preparation for joining his practice. In those days, one apprenticed to an attorney and "read law." Masters did, and was admitted to the Illinois Bar in 1891. He tried to become a journalist in Chicago, but was unable to find a job. After spending a short time as a bill collector, Masters opened a law office. In 1903 he joined Clarence Darrow's law firm.

While practicing law, Edgar Lee Masters was also writing essays and poems. Although several volumes of his essays and many of his poems were published, he remained virtually unknown until 1914, when a St. Louis newspaper published 244 of his epigrams in free verse, under a pseudonym. After his authorship was revealed, the Macmillan company published the series of poems as *The Spoon River Anthology* in 1915. These frank and irreverent vignettes of people who supposedly lived in the Illinois town of "Spoon River," a fictitious composite place, became quite popular. After 1923, Masters moved to New York City, where he continued to turn out volumes of verse, and later several novels, none of which was as popular as his original collection of poems. He also wrote an autobiography entitled *Across Spoon River* (1936). He died in 1950.

The selection presented here comes from a book published by a tiny New York publisher in a 1933 limited edition. It was largely paid for by people who had subscribed in advance. The poem "Serpent in the Wilderness," which is the title poem, is one of six in the volume. It seems never to have been reprinted in book form, although Joseph Lewis did reprint it in his magazine *The Freethinker* in 1944.

SAMUEL PORTER PUTNAM (1838-1896)

Primarily known as an atheist or freethought lecturer and writer, Samuel Porter Putnam went to Dartmouth College, served in the Union Army during the Civil War, and then went to a theological seminary. After ordination, he preached in Illinois, later became a Unitarian, and eventually a freethinker. At that point he gave up all connection with Christianity. He worked in the New York Customs House until he decided to devote himself entirely to freethought work. Putnam became an editor of several freethought magazines, and an inveterate traveler and lecturer for the movement. By his own estimate, he traveled over 100,000 miles delivering lectures before the airplane or the automobile was invented. His most important book, *Four Hundred Years of Freethought,* was a massive history of the freethought movement. He did have a book of verse published, as well as several other books. "Why Don't He Lend a Hand?" was the title poem of Putnam's booklet of verse published about 1890. He died under mysterious circumstances in Boston; it appears that he was overcome by gas from a faulty lighting fixture.

PERCY BYSSHE SHELLEY (1792-1822)

Shelley needs little introduction. His fame as a poet is immense, despite his short life. What is less well known about him is that he was an outspoken atheist. Expelled from Oxford University for a pamphlet he published called *The Necessity of Atheism,* he never ceased to allow his views on religion to influence his poetry. Perhaps the sharpest reminder of this is the fact that his poem *Queen Mab* was banned and its several publishers prosecuted because the accompanying notes reveal Shelley's atheism. Part of the poem itself is also atheistic. *Queen Mab* was first published in 1813; several parts of this book-length poem are included here.

ARTHUR HUGH CLOUGH (1819-1861)

Born in Liverpool, Clough went to Oxford University, eventually becoming an instructor there. His feeling on religious questions finally led to his resignation, after which he headed a school in London. Upon leaving the school, he journeyed to Cambridge, Massachusetts, where he tutored and did some translating. Returning to England, Clough became an examiner in the Education Office. Some years later, while in Florence, Italy, working on some poems, he died. The work of Clough is marked by skepticism and doubt on religious issues. The selections reprinted here represent Clough at his skeptical peak.

ROBERT BROWNING (1812-1889)

Browning is known both for his poetry and for his relationship with Elizabeth Barrett. Much of his poetry has nothing to do with religion or atheism, but there are a few exceptions. One is *The Confessional*, which was written in Spain in 1845.

ALGERNON CHARLES SWINBURNE (1837-1909)

Swinburne was born in London, but spent most of his early life on the Isle of Wight. He attended Oxford University, and became a disciple of Rossetti. He published a number of volumes of verse that were acclaimed for their style but often criticized for containing radical ideas. *Songs Before Sunrise* was published in 1871. It contains the "Hymn to Man," from which I have excerpted the powerful final sections. The oft-quoted last line "Glory to Man in the highest! for Man is the master of things " is one of the strongest statements of the humanist position found in English literature. "Before a Crucifix" was published in Swinburne's *Collected Works;* however, I cannot trace where it first appeared (if elsewhere) or even when it was written.

JOHN DRYDEN (1631-1700)

Playwright and poet, Dryden was born in Northamptonshire, England. His career as a dramatist began when he attended Cambridge University; it occupied him exclusively for almost fifteen years. Thereafter poetry became his life's work. When James II ascended the throne, Dryden refused to take the Anglican oath, which resulted in the loss of many of his civil rights. He supported himself by his pen. The poem "Priestcraft" was a part of the volume entitled *Absolom and Achitophel,* published in 1681, a work often considered to be his finest book of verse. "Reason" is from his *Religio Laici,* which purports to be the work of a half-skeptical Anglican clergyman.

THOMAS HARDY (1840-1928)

Though trained as an architect, Hardy is best known as a novelist, with his most famous novels being *Tess of the D'Urbervilles, Far From the Madding Crowd, Return of the Native,* and *Jude the Obscure.* Hardy's verse was largely published late in his life. "God's Funeral" was written about 1910, but first published in the magazine *Fortnightly Review* in 1912.

W. J. LINTON (1812-1898)

Linton was primarily known as a wood engraver. He was British by birth, but came to the United States in 1867, settling in New Haven, Connecticut. While in England, Linton was associated with the Chartist movement, and was a friend of many of the British freethinkers of the pre-1870 period, such as the Holyoakes and James Watson. His wife, E. Lynn Linton, was a novelist. He authored a biography of Thomas Paine and several books on wood engraving. "Heaven on Earth" was one of his few published poems.

WILLIAM PLATT BALL (1844-1917)

A British author of freethought articles and pamphlets, Ball was the co-author, with G. W. Foote, of *The Bible Handbook,* one of the most popular of freethought Bible references. He also published one volume of verse. The poem "An Atheist's Thoughts," set forth below, was published in *The Freethinker* (London).

EURIPIDES (480 B.C.-406 B.C.)

This now famous poet of Greek tragedy abandoned painting for poetry and play writing. Many of the manuscripts we have of his plays are from the twelfth century and thereafter, so we do not know how accurate they are. Euripides may have been concerned with shaking the people's faith in the pagan deities. Thus the poem "There Are No Gods" may have been intended toward that end.

JOHN KEATS (1795-1821)

Keats was not particularly well educated in any formal sense, but he was an avid reader. His first book of verse, published while he was in his early twenties, was not well received. His second, however, was *Endymion* (1818), now viewed as a stunning achievement. The last volume in his all too brief life was *Lamia, Isabella and Other Poems* (1820), another masterpiece. The poem "Sonnet Written in Disgust of Vulgar Superstition" was written in 1816, and first appeared in the Aldine edition of his *Works* in 1876, entitled "Written on a Summer Evening."

ALFRED EDWARD HOUSMAN (1859-1936)

A. E. Housman is best known for his first collection of poems, published as *A Shropshire Lad.* The poetry is rather pessimistic, and it is only by his technical skill that Housman avoided repelling many readers. After twenty-six years passed, he published a second volume of verse, entitled *Last Poems.* After his death, a third volume, entitled *More Poems,* was published. The poem "The Carpenter's Son," although written much earlier, was first published in *Last Poems* (1922).

WILLIAM F. DENTON (1823-1883)

Born in England, he moved to the United States in 1848. Denton was a geologist and lecturer, in addition to being a poet. Among his travels were extended trips to Australia and New Guinea, where he eventually died of a tropical fever. Denton's publications include two books of verse, *Poems for Reformers* and *Radical Rhymes.* The two poems offered here, "The Freeman's Revolution" and "The Devil Is Dead!" are from *Radical Rhymes* (1879).

WILLIAM ERNEST HENLEY (1849-1903)

As a British poet who wrote only a small body of poems, Henley spent most of his career as a journalist. His few slim volumes of poems include "Invictus," probably his best known work, first published in *Echoes* in 1888. This is, in my opinion, the best known atheist poem in English. The poem itself was written in 1875.

CARL SANDBURG (1878-1967)

Renowned for his biographies of Abraham Lincoln, Sandburg is also remembered for a number of short poems. His work entitled "Manufactured Gods" is certainly not a popular one. It was first published in *The Smoke and Steel* in 1918.

GEORGE GORDON NOEL, LORD BYRON (1788-1824)

Born in London, Byron was raised in Scotland. He attended Cambridge University, where he was known for his hellraising. Byron's first book of verse is notable only for the distinction often given it as the worst first book of verse by a major poet. A long trip through Greece seems to have helped him, and his next book, *Childe Harold,* appearing in 1812, was widely acclaimed. Byron became the darling of society, noted for his many liaisons with women. Eventually scandal forced him to leave England. The remainder of his writing was therefore done abroad. After his death from a fever, his reputation began to decline in England, although it has recovered somewhat. His piece entitled "Prometheus" was written in 1816.

RUDYARD KIPLING (1865-1936)

Born in Bombay, India, the son of an Englishman, Kipling is noted for his prose, but he did write a considerable body of poetry as well. A world traveler, many of his tales are set in exotic locations. His best known works, the *Jungle Books* and *The Just So Stories,* were the products of one of the few times in his life when Kipling settled down in one place. In this case it was at Brattleboro, Vermont, where these works were written for his two children. The poem "Evarra and His Gods" was first published in book form in the American edition of *Departmental Ditties, Barrack Room Ballads, and Other Verses* in 1890. It had appeared in the *Scots Observer* magazine for October 4, 1890.

LAWRENCE FERLINGHETTI (1920-   )

Ferlinghetti is the most contemporary poet whose work is represented in these selections. It is not yet possible to tell how time will treat his poetry, but "Poem #5" from *A Coney Island of the Mind* is such a wonderful example of a satirical atheist poem that there was no way it could be omitted. Ferlinghetti's *Coney Island* was first published in 1958. His other works include *Pictures of the Gone World* and the novel *She.*

GRANVILLE LOWTHER (1848-1933)

An American editor and sometime college administrator, Lowther was also a minister and the author of *The Encyclopedia of Practical Horticulture.* The poem "The Agnostic" seems to have been published only in a magazine, but I have not been able to discover its source or the date of publication.

WHEATON HALE BREWER

This mysterious amateur poet seems to have left no permanent record of his existence in any of the biographical sources found in even the largest libraries. His poem "Lyrics of a Lost Soul" also seems to have had an ephemeral publication in a journal and has left no other trace.

City of Dreadful Night

James Thomson

VIII

While I still lingered on that river-walk,
    And watched the tide as black as our black doom,
I heard another couple join in talk,
    And saw them to the left hand in the the gloom
Seated against an elm bole on the ground,
Their eyes intent upon the stream profound.

"I never knew another man on earth
    But had some joy and solace in his life,
    Some chance of triumph in the dreadful strife:
My doom has been unmitigated dearth."

"We gaze upon the river, and we note
The various vessels large and small that float,
Ignoring every wrecked and sunken boat."

"And yet I asked no splendid dower, no spoil
    Of sway or fame or rank or even wealth;
    But homely love with common food and health,
And nightly sleep to balance daily toil."

"This all-too-humble soul would arrogate
Unto itself some signalising hate
From the supreme indifference of Fate!"

"Who is most wretched in this dolorous place?
    I think myself; yet I would rather be
    My miserable self than He, than He
Who formed such creatures to His own disgrace.

"The vilest thing must be less vile than Thou
    From whom it had its being, God and Lord!
    Creator of all woe and sin! abhorred,
Malignant and implacable! I vow

"That not for all thy power furled and unfurled,
    For all the temples to Thy glory built,
    Would I assume the ignominious guilt
Of having made such men in such a world."

"As if a Being, God or Fiend, could reign,
    At once so wicked, foolish, and insane,
    As to produce men whom He might refrain:

"The world rolls round for ever like a mill;
    It grinds out death and life and good and ill;
    It has no purpose, heart or mind or will.

"While air of Space and Time's full river flow
    The mill must blindly whirl unresting so:
    It may be wearing out, but who can know?

"Man might know one thing were his sight less dim;
    That it whirls not to suit his petty whim,
    That it is quite indifferent to him.

"Nay, does it treat him harshly as he saith?
    It grinds him some slow years of bitter breath,
    Then grinds him back into eternal death."

XIV

Large glooms were gathered in the mighty fane,
    With tinted moongleams slanting here and there;
And all was hush: no swelling organ-strain,
    No chant, no voice or murmuring of prayer;

No priests came forth, no tinkling censers fumed,
And the high altar space was unillumed.

Around the pillars and against the walls
    Learned men and shadows; other seemed to brood
Bent or recumbent in secluded stalls.
    Perchance they were not a great multitude
Save in that city of so lonely streets
Where one may count up every face he meets.

All patiently awaited the event
    Without a stir or sound, as if no less
Self-occupied, doomstricken, while attent.
    And then we heard a voice of solemn stress
From the dark pulpit, and our gaze there met
Two eyes which burned as never eyes burned yet:

Two steadfast and intolerable eyes
    Burning beneath a broad and rugged brow;
The head behind it of enormous size.
    And as black fir-groves in a large wind bow,
Our rooted congregation, gloom-arrayed,
By that great sad voice deep and full were swayed:—

O melancholy Brothers, dark, dark, dark!
O battling in black floods; without an ark!
    O spectral wanderers of unholy Night!
My soul hath bled for you these sunless years,
With bitter blood-drops running down like tears:
    Oh, dark, dark, dark, withdrawn from joy and light!

My heart is sick with anguish for your bale;
Your woe hath been my anguish; yea, I quail
    And perish in your perishing unblest.
And I have searched the highths and depths, the scope
Of all our universe, with desperate hope
    To find some solace for your wild unrest.

And now at last authentic word I bring,
Witnessed by every dead and living thing;
    Good tidings of great joy for you, for all:
There is no God; no Fiend with names divine
Made us and tortures us; if we must pine,
    It is to satiate no Being's gall.

It was the dark delusion of a dream,
That living Person conscious and supreme,
    Whom we must curse for cursing us with life;
Whom we must curse because the life He gave
Could not be buried in the quiet grave,
    Could not be killed by poison or by knife.

This little life is all we must endure,
The grave's most holy peace is ever sure,
    We fall asleep and never wake again;
Nothing is of us but the mouldering flesh,
Whose elements dissolve and merge afresh
    In earth, air, water, plants, and other men.

We finish thus; and all our wretched race
Shall finish with its cycle, and give place
    To other beings, with their own time-doom:
Infinite eons ere our kind began;
Infinite eons after the last man
    Has joined the mammoth in earth's tomb and womb.

We bow down to the universal laws,
Which never had for man a special clause
    Of cruelty or kindness, love or hate:
If toads and vultures are obscene to sight,
If tigers burn with beauty and with might,
    Is it by favor or by wrath of fate?

All substance lives and struggles evermore
Through countless shapes continually at war,
    By countless interactions interknit:
If one is born a certain day on earth,
All times and forces tended to that birth,
    Not all the world could change or hinder it.

I find no hint throughout the Universe
Of good or ill, of blessing or of curse;
    I find alone Necessity Supreme;
With infinite Mystery, abysmal, dark,
Unlighted ever by the faintest spark
    For us the flitting shadows of a dream.

O Brothers of sad lives! they are so brief;
A few short years must bring us all relief:
    Can we not bear these years of laboring breath?
But if you would not this poor life fulfil,
Lo, you are free to end it when you will,
    Without the fear of waking after death.—

The organ-like vibrations of his voice
    Thrilled through the vaulted aisles and died away;
The yearning of the tones which bade rejoice
    Was sad and tender as a requiem lay:
Our shadowy congregation rested still
As brooding on that "End it when you will."

Queen Mab

Percy Bysshe Shelley

.　.　.

Now, to the scene I shew, in silence turn,
And read the blood-stained charter of all woe,
Which Nature soon, with re-creating hand,
Will blot in mercy from the book of earth.
How bold the flight of passion's wandering wing,
How swift the step of reason's firmer tread,
How calm and sweet the victories of life,
How terrorless the triumph of the grave!
How powerless were the mightiest monarch's arm,
Vain his loud threat, and impotent his frown!
How ludicrous the priest's dogmatic roar!
The weight of his exterminating curse,
How light! and his affected charity,
To suit the pressure of the changing times,
What palpable deceit!—but for thy aid,
Religion! but for thee, prolific fiend,
Who peoplest earth with demons, hell with men,
And heaven with slaves!

Thou taintest all thou look'st upon!—the stars,
Which on thy cradle beamed so brightly sweet,
Were gods to the distempered playfulness
Of thy untutored infancy: the trees,
The grass, the clouds, the mountains, and the sea,

All living things that walk, swim, creep, or fly,
Were gods: the sun had homage, and the moon
Her worshippers, Then thou becamest, a boy,
More daring in thy frenzies: every shape,
Monstrous or vast, or beautifully wild,
Which, from sensation's relics fancy culis;
The spirits of the air, the shuddering ghost,
The genii of the element, the powers
That give a shape to Nature's varied works,
Had life and place in the corrupt belief
Of thy blind heart: yet still thy youthful hands
Were pure of human blood. Then manhood gave
Its strength and ardor to thy frenzied brain;
Thine eager gaze scanned the stupendous scene
Whose wonders mocked the knowledge of thy pride:
There everlasting and unchanging laws
Reproached thine ignorance. Awhile thou stoodst
Baffled and gloomy; then thou didst sum up
The elements of all that thou didst know;
The changing seasons, winter's leafless reign,
The budding of the heaven-breathing trees,
The eternal orbs that beautify the night,
The sun-rise, and the setting of the moon,
Earthquakes and wars, and poisons and disease,
And all their causes, to an abstract point,
Converging, thou didst bend, and called it—God!
The self-sufficing, the omnipotent,
The merciful, and the avenging God!
Who, prototype of human misrule, sits
High in heaven's realm, upon a golden throne,
Even like an earthly king; and whose dread work,
Hell, gapes for ever for the unhappy slaves
Of fate, whom he created, in his sport,
To triumph in their torments when they fell!
Earth heard the name; earth trembled, as the smoke
Of his revenge ascended up to heaven,
Blotting the constellations; and the cries
Of millions, butchered in sweet confidence
And unsuspecting peace, even when the bonds
Of safety were confirmed by wordy oaths
Sworn in his dreadful name, rung through the land;
Whilst innocent babes writhed on thy stubborn spear,
And thou didst laugh to hear the mother's shriek

Of maniac gladness, as the sacred steel
Felt cold in her torn entrails!

Religion! thou wert then in manhood's prime:
But age crept on: one God would not suffice,
For senile puerility; thou framedst
A tale to suit thy dotage, and to glut
Thy misery-thirsting soul, that the mad fiend
Thy wickedness had pictured, might afford
A plea for sating the unnatural thirst
For murder, rapine, violence, and crime,
That still consumed thy being, even when
Thou heardst the step of fate;—that flames might light
Thy funeral scene, and the shrill horreut shrieks
Of parents dying on the pile that burned
To light their children to thy paths, the roar
Of the encircling flames, the exulting cries
Of thine apostles, loud commingling there,
        Might sate thine hungry ear
        Even on the bed of death!
But now contempt is mocking thy grey hairs;
Thou art descending to the darksome grave,
Unhonored and unpitied, but by those
Whose pride is passing by like thine, and sheds
Like thine, a glare that fades before the sun
Of truth, and shines but in the dreadful night,
That long has lowered above the ruined world.

                .   .   .

        O Spirit! through the sense
By which thy inner nature was apprised
    Of outward shews, vague dreams have rolled,
    And varied reminiscences have waked
        Tablets that never fade;
    All things have been imprinted there,
    The stars, the sea, the earth, the sky,
    Even the unshapeless lineaments
        Of wild and fleeting visions
            Have left a record there
            To testify of earth.

These are my empire, for to me is given
The wonders of the human world to keep,
And fancy's thin creations to endow
With manner, being, and reality;
Therefore a wondrous phantom, from the dream
Of human error's dense and purblind faith,
I will evoke, to meet thy questioning.
      Ahasuras, rise!

      A strange and woe-worn wight
     Arose beside the battlement,
      And stood unmoving there.
His inessential figure cast no shade
     Upon the golden floor;
His port and mien bore mark of many years,
And chronicles of untold ancientness
Were legible within his beamless eye:

. . .

Is there a God?—aye, an almighty God,
And vengeful as almighty! Once his voice
Was heard on earth; earth shuddered at the sound;
The fiery-visaged firmament expressed
Abhorrence, and the grave of nature yawned
To swallow all the dauntless and the good
That dared to hurl defiance at his throne,
Girt as it was with power. None but slaves
Survived,—cold-blooded slaves, who did the work
Of tyrannous omnipotence; whose souls
No honest indignation ever urged
To elevated daring, to one deed
Which gross and sensual self did not pollute.
These slaves built temples for the omnipotent fiend,
Gorgeous and vast: the costly altars smoked
With human blood, and hideous peans rung
Through all the long-drawn aisles. A murderer heard
His voice in Egypt, one whose gifts and arts
Had raised him to his eminence in power,
Accomplice of omnipotence in crime,
And confident of the all-knowing one.
      These were Jehovah's words.

. . .

Why Don't He Lend a Hand?

Samuel P. Putnam

You say there is a God
   Above the boundless sky,
A wise and wondrous deity
   Whose strength none can defy.
You say that he is seated
   Upon a throne most grand,
Millions of angels at his beck—
   Why don't he lend a hand?

See how the earth is groaning,
   What countless tears are shed,
See how the plague stalks forward
   And brave and sweet lie dead.
Homes burn and hearts are breaking,
   Grim murder stains the land;
You say he is omnipotent—
   Why don't he lend a hand?

Behold, injustice conquers;
   Pain curses every hour;
The good and true and beautiful
   Are trampled like the flower.
You say he is our father,
   That what he wills doth stand;
If he is thus almighty
   Why don't he lend a hand?

What is this monarch doing
    Upon his golden throne,
To right the wrong stupendous,
    Give joy instead of moan?
With his resistless majesty,
    Each force at his command,
Each law his own creation—
    Why don't he lend a hand?

Alas! I fear he's sleeping,
    Or is himself a dream,
A bubble on thought's ocean,
    Our fancy's fading gleam.
We look in vain to find him
    Upon his throne so grand,
Then turn your vision earthward—
    'Tis we must lend a hand.

'Tis we must grasp the lightning,
    And plow the rugged soil;
'Tis we must beat back suffering,
    And plague and murder foil;
'Tis we must build the paradise
    And bravely right the wrong;
The god above us faileth,
    The god *within* is strong.

The Freethinker's Plea

Voltairine de Cleyre

Grand eye of Liberty, light up my page!
Like promised morning after night of age
Thy dawning youth breaks in the distant east!
Thy cloudy robes like silken curtains creased
And swung in folds are floating fair and free!
The shadows of the cycles turn and flee;
The budding stars, bright minds that gemmed the night,
Are bursting into broad, bright-petaled light!
Sweet Liberty, how pure thy very breath!
How dear in life, how doubly dear in death!

The stinging thorn lies hid beside the rose;
The bud is blighted ere its leave unclose;
So pleasure born of Hope may oft-time yield
A stinging smart of thorns, a barren field!
But let it be: the buds will bloom again,
The fields will freshen in the summer rain;
And never storm scowls dark but still, somewhere,
A bow is bending in the upper air.
Then learn the law if thou wouldst live aright;
And know no unseen power, no hand of might,
Can set aside the law which wheels the stars;
No incompleteness its perfection mars;
The buds will wake in season, and the rain
Will fall when clouds hang heavy, and again
The snows will tremble when the winter's breath

Congeals the cloud-tears, as the touch of Death
Congeals the last drop on the sufferer's cheek.
Thus do all Nature's tongues in chorus speak:
"Think not, O man, that thou canst e'er escape
One jot of Justice's law, nor turn thy fate
By yielding sacrifice to the Unseen!"
Purged by thyself alone canst thou be clean.
One guide to happiness thou mayst learn:
Love toward the world begets love in return.
And if to others you the measure mete
Of love, be sure your harvest will be sweet;
But if ye sow broadcast the seed of hate,
Ye'll reap again, albeit ye reap it late.
Then let your life-work swell the great flood-tide
Of love towards all the world; the world is wide,
The sea of life is broad; its waves stretch far;
No range, no barrier, its sweep may bar;
The world is filled, is trodden down with pain;
The sea of life is gathered up of rain,—
A throat, a bed, a sink, for human tears,
A burial of hopes, a miasm of fears!
But see! the sun of love shines softly out,
Flinging its golden fingers all about,
Pressing its lips in loving, soft caress,
Upon the world's pale cheek; the pain grows less,
The tears are dried upon the quivering lashes,
An answering sunbeam 'neath the white lids flashes!

Ah, slaves that suffer in your self-forged chains,
Praying your Christ to touch and heal your pains,
Tear off your shackling irons, unbind your eyes,
Seize the grand hopes that burn along the skies!
Worship not God in temples built of gloom;
Far sweeter incense is the flower-bloom
Than all the fires that Sacrifice may light;
And grander is the star-dome gleaming bright
With glowing worlds, than all your altar lamps
Pale flickering in your clammy, vaulted damps;
And richer is the broad, full, fair sun sheen,
Dripping its orient light in streams between
The fretted shafting of the forest trees,
Throwing its golden kisses to the breeze,
Lifting the grasses with its finger-tips,

And pressing the young blossoms with warm lips,
Show'ring its glory over plain and hill,
Wreathing the storm and dancing in the rill;
Far richer in wild freedom falling there,
Shaking the tresses of its yellow hair,
Than all subdued within the dim half-light
Of stained glass windows, drooping into night.
Oh, grander far the massive mountain walls
Which bound the vista of the forest halls,
Than all the sculptured forms which guard the piles
That arch your tall, dim, gray, cathedral aisles!
And gladder is the carol of a bird
Than all the anthems that were ever heard
To steal in somber chanting from the tone
Of master voices praising the Unknown.
In the great wild, where foot of man ne'er trod,
There we find Nature's church and Nature's God!
Here there are no fetters! though is free as air;
Its flight may spread far as its wings may dare;
And through it all one voice cries, "God is love,
And love is God!" Around, within, above,
Behold the working of the perfect law,—
The law immutable in which no flaw
Exists, and from which no appeal is made;
Ev'n as the sunlight chases far the shade
And shadows chase the light in turn again,
So every life is fraught with joy and pain;
The sea of life is dimpled o'er with smiles,
The sun of love the cloud of woe beguiles,
And turns its heavy brow to forehead fair,
Framed in the glory of its sun-gilt hair.
Be thine the warming touch, the kiss of love;
Vainly ye seek for comfort from above,
Vainly ye pray the Gods to ease your pain;
The heavy words fall back on you again!
Vainly ye cry for Christ to smooth your way;
The thorns sting sharper while ye kneeling pray!
Vainly ye look upon the world of woe,
And cry, "O God, avert the bitter blow!"
Ye cannot turn the lightning from its track,
Nor call one single little instant back;
The law swerves not, and with unerring aim
The shaft of justice falls; he bears the blame

Who violates the rule: do well your task,
For justice overtakes you all at last.
. Vainly ye patient ones await reward,
Trusting th' Almighty's angel to record
Each bitter tear, each disappointed sigh;
Reward descends not, gifted from on high,
But is the outgrowth of the eternal law:
As from the earth the toiling seed-germs draw
The food which gives them life and strength to bear
The storms and suns which sweep the upper air,
So ye must draw from out the pregnant earth
The metal true wherewith to build your worth;
So shall ye brave the howling of the blast,
And smile triumphant o'er the storm at last.
Nor dream these trials are without their use;
Between your joys and griefs ye cannot choose,
And say your life with either is complete:
Ever the bitter mingles with the sweet.
The dews must press the petals down at night,
If in the dawning they would glisten bright;
If sunbeams needs must ripen out the grain
Not less the early blades must woo the rain:
If now your eyes be wet with weary tears,
Ye'll gather them as gems in after years;
And if the rains now sodden down your path,
Ye'll reap rich harvest in the aftermath.

Ye idle mourners, crying in your grief,
The souls ye weep have found the long relief:
Why grieve for those who fold their hands in peace?
Their sore-tried hearts have found a glad release;
Their spirits sink into the solemn sea!
Mourn ye the prisoner from his chains let free?
Nay, ope your ears unto the living cry
That pleads for living comfort! Hark, the sigh
Of million heartaches rising in your ears!
Kiss back the living woes, the living tears!
Go down into the felon's gloomy cell;
Send there the ray of love: as tree-buds swell
When spring's warm breath bids the cold winter cease,
So will his heart swell with the hope of peace,
Be filled with love, for love is Nature's God;
The God which trembles in the tender sod,

The God which tints the sunset, lights the dew,
Sprinkles with stars the firmament's broad blue,
And draws all hearts together in a free
Wide sweep of love, broad as the ether-sea.
No other law or guidance do we need;
The world's our church, to do good is our creed.

The Confessional

Robert Browning

It is a lie—their priests, their pope,
Their saints, their . . . . all they fear or hope
Are lies; and lies—there! through my door
And ceiling, there! and walls and floor,
There, lies—they lie, shall still be hurled,
Till, spite of them, I reach the world.

You think priests just and holy men!
Before they put me in this den,
I was a human creature too,
With flesh and blood like one of you.
A girl that laughed in Beauty's pride,
Like lilies in your world outside.

I had a lover—shame avaunt!
This poor, wrenched body, grim and gaunt,
Was kissed all over till it burned,
By lips the truest, love e'er turned
His heart's own tint: one night they kissed
My soul into a burning mist.

So, next day when the accustomed train
Of things grew round my sense again,
"That is a sin," I said—and slow,
With downcast eyes, to church I go,
And passed to the confession chair,
And tell the old, mild father there.

But when I falter Beltran's name,
"Ha?" quoth the father; "much I blame
The sin; yet wherefore idly grieve?
Despair not; strenuously retrieve!
Nay, I will turn this love of thine
To lawful love—almost divine.

"For he is young and led astray,
This Beltran—and he schemes, men say,
To change the laws of Church and State;
So, thine shall be an angel's fate,
Who, ere the thunder breaks, shall roll
Its cloud away and save his soul.

"For when he lies upon thy breast,
Thou may'st demand, and be possessed
Of all his plans, and next day steal
To me, and all these plans reveal,
That I and every priest, to purge
His soul, may fast and use the scourge."

That father's beard was long and white.
With love and truth his brow was bright;
I went back, all on fire with joy,
And that same evening bade the boy
Tell me, as lovers should, heart-free,
Something to prove his love to me.

He told me what he would not tell
For hope of heaven or fear of hell:
And I lay listening in such pride,
And, soon as he had left my side,
Tripped to the church by morning light,
To save his soul in his despite.

I told the father all his schemes,
Who were his comrades, what their dreams;
"And now make haste," I said "to pray
The one spot from his soul away.
To-night he comes, but not the same
Will look!"—At night he never came.

Nor next night; on the afternoon
I went forth with a strength new-born,
The church was empty; something drew
My steps into the street; I knew
It led me to the market place—
Where, lo—on high—the father's face!

That horrible black scaffold drest—
The stapled block . . . . God sink the rest!
That head strapped back, that blinding vest,
Those knotted hands and naked breast—
Till near one busy hangman pressed—
And—on the neck those arms caressed. . . . .

No part in aught they hope or fear!
No heaven with them, no hell;—and here,

No earth—not so much space as pens
My body in their worst of dens—
But shall bear God and man my cry—
Lies—lies, again—and still, they lie!

There is No God

Arthur Hugh Clough

"There is no God," the wicked saith,
　　"And truly it's a blessing,
For what he might have done with us
　　It's better only guessing."

"There is no God," a youngster thinks
　　"Or really, if there may be,
He surely didn't mean a man
　　Always to be a baby."

"There is no God, or if there is,"
　　The tradesman thinks, "'twere funny
If he should take it ill in me
　　To make a little money."

"Whether there be," the rich man says,
　　"It matters very little,
For I and mine, thank somebody,
　　Are not in want of victual."

Some others, also, to themselves
　　Who scarce so much as doubt it,
Think there is none, when they are well,
　　And do not think about it.

But country folks who live beneath
  The shadow of the steeple;
The parson and the parson's wife,
  And mostly married people;

Youths green and happy in first love,
  So thankful for illusion;
And men caught out in what the world
  Calls guilt, in first confusion;

And almost everyone when age,
  Disease, or sorrows strike him,
Inclines to think there is a God,
  Or something very like him.

The Latest Decalogue

Arthur Hugh Clough

Thou shalt have one God only; who
Would be at the expense of two?
No graven images may be
Worshipped—except the currency.
Swear not at all—for, thy curse
Thine enemy is none the worse.
At Church on Sunday to attend
Wilt serve to keep the world thy friend.
Honor thy parents—that is, all
From whom advancement may befall.
Thou shalt not kill—but need'st not strive
Officiously to keep alive.
Do not adultery commit;
Advantage rarely comes of it.
Thou shalt not steal—an empty feat
When 'tis so lucrative to cheat.
Bear not false witness; let the lie
Have time on its own wings to fly.
Thou shalt not covet; but tradition
Approves all forms of competition.

Heaven on Earth

W. J. Linton

When kings are forgotten and priests are no more,
When royal and righteous mean truth at the core,
When work stands for worship, and worship is worth,
The kingdom of heaven will come on the earth.

When valor is noble, when toil is secure,
When hope may be cheerful, and sacrifice sure,
When service shrinks not from its glorious girth,
The kingdom of heaven will come on the earth.

When honor means duty, when duty is known,
When faith dwells no more in her closet alone,
When conscience to consequent action gives birth,
The kingdom of heaven will come on the earth.

When love liketh wisdom, and worshippeth right,
When peace kisseth him who has fought the good fight,
When virtue is mother of beauty and worth,
The kingdom of heaven will come on the earth.

The Serpent in the Wilderness

Edgar Lee Masters

XIV

Jesus predicted that the world would come to an end
Before the generation which he addressed had passed away.
And many believed this would happen,
And looked to see the sky cast its stars as a fig tree casts its fruit;
And to see the sun darkened, and the moon failing of its light,
And the powers of heaven shaken, and Jesus descending
In clouds with great power and glory, attended by angels.
Whereupon the dead would come from their graves,
And the good would be caught up into heaven,
And the evil cast into the bottomless pit prepared for the devil
    and his angels.
Nearly all of the words of Jesus were founded upon fear;
And these prophecies of Jesus filled the world with terror,
And even at last shook the iron heart of Rome.
And for long centuries
After the generation which Jesus said would see the end
    of the world
Had passed away, still the fear that Jesus had instilled stayed
    alive,
And has not died to this day, and is used everywhere wherewith
    to recruit churches,
And to get money for popes, cardinals, priests, and for preachers
Of the Baptist, Methodist, Presbyterian, Campbellite, and other
    denominations,

Who live in ease off the money gathered by fear,
While scarcely any of them are enlightened or worth anything
    to civilization.
And it will be some centuries before it becomes an accepted
    understanding
That Jesus had no mind capable of doing good for the world,
While possessing power to put Socrates and men like him aside
So that they could do little for the world.
That this has been so and is yet so is just as mysterious
As the so-called problem of evil can be to any mind.
For no one can explain why Athens, which was indeed a city
    set upon a hill,
Did not last forever for the benefit of all climes and peoples;
And why Jerusalem, a village of demons and camel's dung,
Became the shrine of the world
Whereto men still make pilgrimages to see the place where
    Jesus died for men,
While few are interested in the jail where Socrates gave up his life
Rather than surrender his freedom to think.

Robert G. Ingersoll

Edgar Lee Masters

To the lovers of Liberty everywhere,
But chiefly to the youth of America
Who did not know Robert G. Ingersoll,
Remember that he helped to make you free!
He was a leader in a war of guns for freedom,
But a general in the war of ideas for freedom!
He braved the misunderstanding of friends,
He faced the enmity of the powerful small of soul,
And the insidious power of the churches;
He put aside worldly honors,
And the sovereignty of place,
He stripped off the armor of institutional friendships
To dedicate his soul
To the terrible deities of Truth and Beauty!
And he went down into age and into the shadow
With love of men for a staff,
And the light of his soul for a light—
And with these alone!
O you martyrs trading martyrdom for heaven,
And self-denial for eternal riches,
How does your work and your death compare
With a man's for whom the weal of the race,
And the cause of humanity here and now were enough
To give life meaning and death as well?—
I have not seen such faith in Israel!

Before a Crucifix

Algernon Charles Swinburne

O hidden face of man, whereover
    The years have woven a viewless veil,
If thou wast verily man's lover,
    What did thy love or blood avail?
Thy blood the priests make poison of,
And in gold shekels coin thy love.

So when our souls look back to thee
    They sicken, seeing against thy side,
Too foul to speak of or to see,
    The leprous likeness of a bride,
Whose kissing lips through his lips grown
Leave their God rotten to the bone.

When we would see thee man, and know
    What heart thou hadst toward men indeed,
Lo, thy blood-blackened altars; lo,
    The lips of priests that pray and feed
While their own hell's worm curls and licks
The poison of the crucifix.

Thou badst let children come to thee;
    What children now but curses come?
What manhood in that God can be
    Who sees their worship, and is dumb?
No soul that lived, loved, wrought, and died
Is this their carrion crucified.

Nay, if their God and thou be one,
    If thou and this thing be the same,
Thou shouldst not look upon the sun;
    The sun grows haggard at thy name.
Come down, be done with, cease, give o'er,
Hide thyself, strive not, be no more.

Hymn to Man

Algernon Charles Swinburne

The bow of your godhead is broken, the arm of your conquest is stayed;
Though ye call down God to bear token, for fear of you none is afraid.
Will ye turn back times, and the courses of stars, and the season of souls?
Shall God's breath dry up the sources that feed time full as it rolls?
Nay, cry on him then till he show you a sign, till he lift up a rod;
Hath he made not the nations to know him of old if indeed he be God?
Is no heat of him left in the ashes of thousands burnt up for his sake?
Can prayer not rekindle the flashes that shone in his face from the stake?
Cry aloud; for your God is a God and a Savior; cry, make yourselves lean;
Is he drunk or asleep, that the rod of his wrath is unfelt and unseen?
Is the fire of his old loving-kindness gone out, that his pyres are acold?
Hath he gazed on himself unto blindness, who made men blind to behold?
Cry out, for his kingdom is shaken; cry out, for the people blaspheme;
Cry aloud till his godhead awaken; what doth he to sleep and to dream?
Cry, cut yourselves, gash you with knives and with scourges,
    heap on to you dust;
Is his life but as other gods' lives? is not this the Lord God of your trust?
Is not this the great God of your sires, that with souls and
    with bodies was fed,
And the world was on flame with his fires? O fools, he was God,
    and is dead.
He will hear not again the strong crying of earth in his ears as before,
And the fume of his multitudes dying shall flatter his nostrils no more.
By the spirit he ruled as his slave is he slain who was mighty to slay,
And the stone that is sealed on his grave he shall rise not and
    roll not away.

Yea, weep to him, lift up your hands; be your eyes as a fountain of tears;
Where he stood there is nothing that stands; if he call,
    there is no man that hears.
He hath doffed his king's raiment of lies now the wane of his
    kingdom is come;
Ears hath he, and hears not; and eyes, and he sees not; and mouth,
    and is dumb.
His red king's raiment is ripped from him naked, his staff broken down;
And the signs of his empire are stripped from him shuddering;
    and where is his crown?
And in vain by the wellsprings refrozen ye cry for the warmth of his sun—
O God, the Lord God of thy chosen, thy will in thy kingdom be done.
Kingdom and will hath he none in him left him, nor warmth in his breath;
Till his corpse be cast out of the sun will ye know not the truth of
    his death?
Surely, ye say, he is strong, though the times be against him and men;
Yet a little, ye say, and how long, till he come to show judgment again?
Shall God then die as the beasts die? who is it hath broken his rod?
O God, Lord God of thy priests, rise up now and show thyself God.
They cry out, thine elect, thine aspirants to heavenward,
    whose faith is as flame;
O thou the Lord God of our tyrants, they call thee, their God,
    by thy name.
By thy name that in hell-fire was written, and burned at
    the point of thy sword,
Thou art smitten, thou God, thou art smitten, thy death is upon thee,
    O Lord.
And the love-song of earth as thou diest resounds through
    the wind of her wings—
Glory to Man in the highest! for Man is the master of things.

Priestcraft

John Dryden

For priests of all religions are the same
Of whatsoe'er descent their Godhead be.
Stock, Stone or other homely pedigree,
In his defense his servants are as bold,
As if he had been born of beaten gold . . .
For 'twas their duty, all the learned think
T'espouse his cause by whom they eat and drink.

The Egyptian rites the Jebusites embraced
Where Gods were recommended by their taste.
Such sav'ry Deities must needs be good
As serv'd at once for worship and for food.
By force they could not introduce these Gods,
For Ten to One in former days was odds.
So Fraud was used (the sacrificer's trade).
Fools are more hard to conquer than persuade.

Reason

John Dryden

Dim as the borrow'd beams of moon and stars
To lonely, weary, wandering travelers,
Is Reason to the soul; and as on high
Those rolling fires discover but the sky,
Not light us here; so Reason's glimmering ray
Was lent, not to assure our doubtful way
But guide us upward to a better day,
And as those nightly tapers disappear,
When day's bright lord ascends our hemisphere;
So pale grows Reason at Religion's sight;
So dies, and so dissolves, in supernatural light.

God's Funeral

Thomas Hardy

I

I saw a slowly stepping train—
Lined on the brows, scoop-eyed, and bent and hoar—
Following in files across a twilit plain
A strange and mystic form the foremost bore.

II

And by contagious throbs of thought
Or latent knowledge that within me lay
And had already stirred me, I was wrought
To consciousness of sorrow even as they.

III

The forborne shape, to my blurred eyes,
At first seemed man-like, and anon to change
To an amorphous cloud of marvellous size,
At times endowed with wings of glorious range.

IV

And this phantasmal variousness
Ever possessed it as they drew along:
Yet throughout all it symboled none the less
Potency vast and loving-kindness strong.

V

Almost before I knew I bent
Towards the moving columns without a word;
They growing in bulk and numbers as they went,
Struck out sick thoughts that could be overheard:—

VI

"O man-projected Figure, of late
Imaged as we, thy knell who shall survive?
Whence came it we were tempted to create
One whom we can no longer keep alive?

VII

"Framing him jealous, fierce at first,
We gave him justice as the ages rolled,
Will to bless those by circumstance accursed,
And long-suffering, and mercies manifold.

VIII

"And, tricked by our own early dream
And need of solace we grew self-deceived,
Our making soon our maker we did deem,
And what we had imagined we believed.

IX

"Till, in Time's stayless stealthy swing,
Uncompromising rude reality
Mangled the monarch of our fashioning,
Who quavered, sank; and now has ceased to be.

X

"So, toward our myth's oblivion,
Darkling and languid-lipped, we creep and grope
Sadlier than those who wept in Babylon,
Whose Zion was a still abiding hope.

XI

"How sweet it was in years far hied
To start the wheels of day with trustful prayer
To lie down liegely at the eventide
And feel a blessed assurance He was there!

XII

"And who or what shall fill his place?
Whither will wanderers turn distracted eyes
For some fixed star to stimulate their pace
Towards the goal of their enterprise?"

XIII

Some in the background then I saw,
Sweet women, youths, men, all incredulous
Who chimed: "This is a counterfeit of straw,
This requiem mockery! Still he lives to us!"

XIV

I could not buoy their faith: and yet
Many I had known; with all I sympathized,
And though struck speechless, I did not forget
That what was mourned for, I, too, long had prized.

XV

Still, how to bear such loss I deemed
The insistent question for each animate mind,
And gazing, to my growing sight there seemed
A pale yet positive gleam low down behind.

XVI

Whereof, to lift the general night,
A certain few who stood aloof had said
"See you upon the horizon that small light—
Swelling somewhat?" Each mourner shook his head.

XVII

And they composed a crowd of whom
Some were right good, and many nigh the best . . .
Thus dazed and puzzled 'twixt the gleam and gloom
Mechanically, I followed with the rest.

An Atheist's Thoughts

William Platt Ball

'Tis easy, when the many cheer and rulers bless,
To serve a faith that some revere and all profess—
To cringe to cruel deeds, to laud the rich and strong,
To guard and honor throned fraud and wrong.

But when fair Truth would save a world despite its frowns,
Its poison'd javelins at her hurl'd, its thorny crowns,
Its onslaught as on leprous Crime from some foul den,
While Falsehood's mask seems truth sublime to men:

Then is the time for loyal hearts to dare true deeds,
To be such men and act such parts as shame the creeds.
Then should we fight for truth, for worth; and, strong of heart,
In this the noblest war on earth take part.

While Christian poison's vaunted still Earth's panacea,
While saints deluded strive to kill each new idea,
And seek by monstrous myths to climb to paradise,
Yet brand plain truth and duty crime or vice:

Arise! Unsheathe the sword of light; plain truth avow;
Against Religion's hordes unite: the time is now.
Ever she bars man's onward way, the tyrant's friend;
Her power to curse and rob and slay must end.

Mother of mischief, source of woe and fellest rage,
Of living truth the deadliest foe in every age,
Still her will fears and hopes delude: many she binds,
Enslaving, as her spell-bound brood, men's minds.

Strike hard for souls in prison pent; dare all her spite.
Until her giant force is spent, still smite and smite.
Spare not her frauds—God, priest, or pope—till thought be free;
Until their real, if humbled, hope, men see.

On earth's most precious triumphs bent, of moral might.
Smite prejudice with argument, smite wrong with right.
But brave men will not fear to fall in fiercer strife
If need be; they will give their all—their life.

Thus shall we speed each righteous cause, thus help earth's throngs
To sweep away oppressive laws and cruel wrongs.
Man's war for men must never cease while one remains
To lift to light, or to release from chains.

Arm'd Science aids the war we wage; she fills our ranks.
Stoutly her legion'd facts engage the foe's turn'd flanks.
Earth's hope, man's moral sense, takes form more firm each hour,
Wakes from deception, and grows warm with power.

Dark Superstition's phantoms one by one shall pass away,
The lamp of Truth, a glowing sun, spread endless day.
Slave of that lamp, not of the creeds, Nature's caress
Our all-compelling pray'r of deeds must bless;

Till, harvested the fields hard won, due virtues met,
On happy realms of men the sun shall never set—
On men no longer fiercely blind, but wiser grown,
With war and want and all their kind unknown.

For sage and hero shall not cease to lead our race
Forth from its brutish miseries and all that's base:
And man shall learn his onward way, nor turn aside,
But law well-fathomed shall obey as guide.

Be this a dream or what it may, come hope or fear,
Some simple duties of to-day at least are clear.
An inward impulse sure and strong demands that we
From tyranny and fraud and wrong be free.

Evolving law, stern lord of earth, compels our fight;
His sons must follow foremost worth, must love the right,
Sowing the fields, for time's increase, with their best deeds,
Of joy deep-rooted and of peace sure seeds.

So may we work in Love's own might, so build and sow
That household joys and all delight may surely grow,
And spread afar one wide domain of glowing life,
Whose toil is sweet, since purged of pain and strife.

Thus earth shall breathe an atmosphere of hope and love,
The splendor of a due career each soul shall prove.
We, for these ends so fair, so vast, on Truth rely;
Misleading phantoms of the past must die.

Emotion waste on air we shun, vain love recall;
E'en could God be, he needeth none; man needs it all.
Reverence for Man, care for His fate well cherish'd, then
Lives all that's truly good and great in men.

We will not, cannot, help grand lies to keep us slaves
To ignorance and to mysteries that ignorance craves.
Ever would we, though earth's long youth aid the one plan
Of changing man to truth, not truth to man.

Nor need high thought and pure fare worse for Ficton's fall;
Wonder itself, the Universe, enfolds us all;
Heav'n's starry radiance sublime shines as it shone;
Eternities of teeming time roll on.

Nor Nature's broad magnificence, sea, sky, and field,
Nor Art's heart-music sweet, shall hence less rapture yield:
Nor childhood's charm, nor friendship's grasp, shall e'er grow old,
Or mother's kiss, or lovers' clasp, grow cold.

Life's course, life's joys, remain the same, but conscience, freed
From prison chains, can teach true fame, true thought, true deed.
And when life fades and joy and strife, can he repent
Who looks back on an honest life well spent?

The war of progress and good sense for ever glows
With feeling far, far more intense than "pleasure" knows;
And Thought's resolve and patient care and earnest gaze
Shall well replace the beggar's pray'r and praise.

We are no lawless mutineers. We smile at those
Who in their foolish hates and fears deem us their foes,
Nay, could pure Truth and Justice be a god most real,
To such in reverence deep would we appeal.

But since there is no living God, then Man, alone,
Set free to shape his fate, must plod towards the throne
Of ideal Good on earth by ways that earnest wills
Shall find or make through each rough maze of ills.

The passing losses of to-day we do not scorn;
But be they bitter as they may they must be borne.
Old thoughts die hard. They linger still. Their influence blinds,
Till new thoughts grow and form and fill new minds.

On conquering Fate by valiant skill, man is resolv'd;
And step by step the means, the will, shall be evolv'd.
We are content to pioneer for paths ahead
Where shadow-smitten men yet fear to tread.

To win true hearts, Omnipotence should show on earth
Not blood-stained skill, but innocence, not might, but worth.
In vain invent your guiltless God and blame the laws
He never by his slightest nod bids pause.

Oh, who that had almighty power could hear earth's cry
Of pain and wrong yet hour by hour stand idly by?
Oh, such a God, of whom men dream, should first atone
Not for men's sins but sin supreme, his own.

Are men rank cowards, to be shock'd that some should dare
To judge Omnipotence, lest mock'd by semblance fair?
A just and wise Omnipotence, if such could be,
Would smile well pleased such honest sense to see.

And could almighty Love make hell? But nay, his own
Revolt from half the tale they tell but have outgrown.
The pleasant only they would fain find true at last,
Yet wish the crowd to dread hell's pain aghast.

O brave and true, whom cruel foes have made to feel
Fast bleeding wounds and savage blows that yet shall heal,
Suffer and fight, till shameful wrong shall hide its head,
Till, pierced with earnest pen and tongue, 'tis dead.

Fight on by precious truth impell'd where war resounds,
Fighting with mighty passion held in wisdom's bounds:
Resolute beyond all words for man's great gain,
Your deeds are true, your words as swords not vain.

Love shall be yours, and peace that comes to eyes that see
The promised land of happy homes of souls set free,
Whose joy shall soothe your grief to rest and nerve your will
Your heart with music of the blest shall thrill.

The Freeman's Resolution

William F. Denton

I will not bow to a titled knave,
    Nor crouch to a lordly priest:
A martyr's torments I'd rather brave,
    Than be of my manhood fleeced.

I'll bend my knee to no fancied god,
    I'll fear no ghost so wan,
Erect and free I'll stand on the sod,
    And act as becomes a man.

I'll pin my faith to no bigot's sleeve;
    I'll swallow no griping creed;
I'll ask my Reason what to believe,
    And ever her answer heed.

I'll hide no truth in a coward heart,
    The world would be blest to know;
My boldest thought as it wills impart,
    Nor check the mind's onward flow.

I'll love the true, I will do the right,
    Ruled only by Reason's sway,
Let all do so; and the world's dark night
    Will melt into rosy day.

The Devil Is Dead!

William F. Denton

Sigh priests, cry aloud, hang your pulpits with black;
Let sorrow bow down every head,
The good friend who bore all your sins on his back—
Your best friend, the Devil, is dead!

Your church is a corpse, you are guarding its tomb,
The soul of your system has fled.
The dead-knell is tolling your terrible doom;
It tells us the Devil is dead.

'Twas knowledge gave Satan a terrible blow;
Poor fellow! He took to his bed.
Alas! Idle priests, that such things should be so—
Your master, the Devil, is dead.

You're bid to the funeral, ministers all;
We've dug the old gentleman's bed:
Your black coats will make a most excellent pall,
To cover your friend who is dead.

Aye! Lower him mournfully into the grave,
Let showers of teardrops be shed;
Your business is gone; there are no souls to save—
Their tempter, the Devil, is dead.

Woe comes upon woe: you can ne'er get your dues—
Hell's open—the damned souls have fled:
They took to their heels when they heard the good news;
Their jailer, the Devil, is dead.

Your preachings henceforth will be needed no more;
Revivals are knocked on the head;
The orthodox vessel lies stranded on shore;
Her captain, the Devil, is dead.

There Are No Gods

Euripides

Doth some one say that there be gods above?
There are not; no, there are not. Let no fool,
Led by the old false fable, thus deceive you.
Look at the facts themselves, yielding my words
No undue credence: for I say that kings
Kill, rob, break oaths, lay cities waste by fraud,
And doing thus are happier than those
Who live calm pious lives day after day.
How many little States that serve the gods
Are subject to the godless but more strong,
Made slaves by might of a superior army!
And you, if any ceased from work and prayed
To gods, nor gathered in his livelihood,
Would learn gods are not. All Divinity
Is built up from our good and evil luck.

Translated by J. A. Symonds

The Carpenter's Son

Alfred Edward Housman

Here the hangman stops his cart;
Now the best of friends must part,
Fare you well, for ill fare I:
Live, lads, and I will die.

Oh, at home had I but stayed
'Prenticed to my father's trade,
Had I stuck to plane and adze,
I had not been lost, my lads.

Then I might have built perhaps
Gallows-trees for other chaps,
Never dangled on my own,
Had I but left ill alone.

Now, you see, they hang me high,
And the people passing by
Stop to shake their fists and curse;
So 'tis come from ill to worse.

Here hang I, and right and left
Two poor fellows hang for theft;
All the same's the luck we prove,
Though the midmost hangs for love.

Comrades all, that stand and gaze,
Walk henceforth in other ways;
See my neck and save your own;
Comrades all, leave ill alone.

Make some day a decent end,
Shrewder fellows than your friend.
Fare you well, for ill fare I:
Live, lads, and I will die.

Sonnet Written in Disgust of Vulgar Superstition

John Keats

The church bells toll a melancholy round,
    Calling the people to some other prayers,
    Some other gloominess, more dreadful cares,
More hearkening to the sermon's horrid sound.
Surely the mind of man is closely bound
    In some black spell; seeing that each one tears
    Himself from fireside joys, and Lydian airs,
And converse high of these with glory crown'd.
Still, still they toll, and I should feel a damp,—
    A chill as from a tomb, did I not know
That they are dying like an outburnt lamp;
    That 'tis their sighing, wailing ere they go
    Into oblivion;—that fresh flowers will grow,
And many glories of immortal stamp.

Manufactured Gods

Carl Sandburg

They put up big wooden gods.
Then they burned the big wooden gods
And put up brass gods and
Changing their minds suddenly
Knocked down the brass gods and put up
A dough-face god with gold ear-rings.
The poor mutts, the pathetic slant heads,
They didn't know a little tin god
Is as good as anything in the line of gods,
Nor how a little tin god answers prayer
And makes rain and brings luck
The same as a big wooden god or a brass
Or dough-face god with golden ear-rings.

Invictus

William Ernest Henley

Out of the night that covers me,
　　Black as the Pit from pole to pole,
I thank whatever gods may be
　　For my unconquerable soul.

In the fell clutch of circumstance
　　I have not winced nor cried aloud.
Under the bludgeonings of chance
　　My head is bloody, but unbowed.

Beyond this place of wrath and tears
　　Looms but the horror of the shade,
And yet the menace of the years
　　Finds, and shall find me, unafraid.

It matters not how strait the gate,
　　How charged with punishments the scroll,
I am the master of my fate:
　　I am the captain of my soul.

Prometheus

George Gordon Noel
Lord Byron

Titan! to whose immortal eyes
    The sufferings of mortality,
    Seen in their sad reality,
Were not as things that gods despise;
What was thy pity's recompense?
A silent suffering, and intense;
The rock, the vulture, and the chain,
All that the proud can feel of pain,
The agony they do not show,
The suffocating sense of woe,
    Which speaks but in its loneliness,
And then is jealous lest the sky
Should have a listener, nor will sigh
    Until its voice is echoless.

Titan! to thee the strife was given
    Between the suffering and the will,
    Which torture where they cannot kill;
And the inexorable Heaven,
And the deaf tyranny of Fate,
The ruling principle of Hate,
Which for its pleasure doth create
The things it may annihilate,
Refused thee even the boon to die:
The wretched gift Eternity

Was thine—and thou hast borne it well.
All that the Thunderer wrung from thee
Was but the menace which flung back
On him the torments of thy rack;
The fate thou didst so well foresee,
But would not to appease him tell;
And in thy Silence was his Sentence,
And in his Soul a vain repentance,
And evil dread so ill dissembled,
That in his hand the lightnings trembled.

Thy Godlike crime was to be kind,
      To render with thy precepts less
      The sum·of human wretchedness,
And strengthen Man with his own mind;
But baffled as thou wert from high,
Still in thy patient energy,
In the endurance, and repulse
      Of thine impenetrable Spirit,
Which Earth and Heaven could not convulse,
      A mighty lesson we inherit:
Thou art a symbol and a sign
      To Mortals of their fate and force;
Like thee, Man is in part divine,
      A troubled stream from a pure source;
And Man in portions can foresee
His own funereal destiny;
His wretchedness, and his resistance,
And his sad unallied existence:
To which his Spirit may oppose
Itself—an equal to all woes,
      And a firm will, and a deep sense,
Which even in torture can descry
      Its own concentered recompense,
Triumphant where it dares defy,
And making Death a Victory.

Evarra and His Gods

Rudyard Kipling

Read here,
This is the story of Evarra—man—
Maker of Gods in lands beyond the sea.
 Because the city gave him of her gold,
 Because the caravans brought turquoises,
 Because his life was sheltered by the King,
 So that no man should maim him, none should steal,
 Or break his rest with babble in the streets
 When he was weary after toil, he made
 An image of his God in gold and pearl,
 With turquoise diadem and human eyes,
 A wonder in the sunshine, known afar
 And worshiped by the King; but, drunk with pride,
 Because the city bowed to him for God,
 He wrote above the shrine: *"Thus Gods are made,*
 And whoso makes them otherwise shall die."
 And all the city praised him. . . . Then he died.

Read here the story of Evarra—man—
Maker of Gods in lands beyond the sea.
 Because his city had no wealth to give,
 Because the caravans were spoiled afar,
 Because his life was threatened by the King,
 So that all men despised him in the streets,
 He hacked the living rock, with sweat and tears,
 And reared a God against the morning-gold,

A terror in the sunshine, seen afar,
And worshiped by the King; but, drunk with pride,
Because the city fawned to bring him back,
He carved upon the plinth: *"Thus Gods are made,*
And whoso makes them otherwise shall die."
And all the people praised him. . . . Then he died.

Read here the story of Evarra—man—
Maker of Gods in lands beyond the sea.
Because he lived among a simple folk,
Because his village was between the hills,
Because he smeared his cheeks with blood of ewes,
He cut an idol from a fallen pine,
Smeared blood upon its cheeks, and wedged a shell
Above its brows for eyes, and gave it hair
Of trailing moss, and plaited straw for crown.
And all the village praised him for his craft,
And brought him butter, honey, milk, and curds.
Wherefore, because the shoutings drove him mad,
He scratched upon that log: *"Thus Gods are made,*
And whoso makes them otherwise shall die."
And all the people praised him. . . . Then he died.

Read here the story of Evarra—man—
Maker of Gods in lands beyond the sea.
Because his God decreed one clot of blood
Should swerve one hair's-breadth from the pulse's path,
And chafe his brain, Evarra mowed alone,
Rag-wrapped, among the cattle in the fields,
Counting his fingers, jesting with the trees,
And mocking at the mist, until his God
Drove him to labor. Out of dung and horns
Dropped in the mire he made a monstrous God,
Abhorrent, shapeless, crowned with plantain tufts,
And when the cattle lowed at twilight time,
He dreamed it was the clamor of lost crowds,
And howled among the beasts: *"Thus Gods are made,*
And whoso makes them otherwise shall die."
Thereat the cattle bellowed. . . . and he died.

Yet at the last he came to Paradise,
And found his own four Gods, and that he wrote;
And marveled, being very near to God,

What oaf on earth had made his toil God's law,
Till God said, mocking: "Mock not. These be thine."
Then cried Evarra: "I have sinned!"—Not so.

If thou hadst written otherwise, thy Gods
Had rested in the mountain and the mine,
And I were poorer by four wondrous Gods,
And thy more wondrous law, Evarra. Thine,
Servant of shouting crowds and lowing kine."
Thereat with laughing mouth, but tear-wet eyes,
Evarra cast his Gods from Paradise.

This is the story of Evarra—man—
Maker of Gods in lands beyond the sea.

A Coney Island of the Mind

Lawrence Ferlinghetti

.   .   .

Sometime during eternity
                     some guys show up
and one of them
        who shows up real late
               is a kind of carpenter
    from some square-type place
            like Galilee
    and he starts wailing
           and claiming he is hep
     to who made heaven
         and earth
            and that the cat
     who really laid it on us
       is his Dad

And moreover
  he adds
     It's all writ down
          on some scroll-type parchments
   which some henchmen
        leave lying around the Dead Sea somewheres
    a long time ago
        and which you won't even find
for a coupla thousand years or so
        or at least for

nineteen hundred and fortyseven
                    of them
            to be exact
                    and even then
        nobody really believes them
                            or me
                                for that matter

        You're hot
                    they tell him

        And they cool him

        They stretch him on the Tree to cool

            And everybody after that
                            is always making models
                    of this Tree
                            with Him hung up
    and always crooning His name
                            and calling Him to come down
                    and sit in
                            on their combo
            as if he is *the* king cat
                            who's got to blow
        or they can't make it

        Only he don't come down
                        from His tree

    Him just hang there
                    on His Tree
                            looking real Petered out
                    and real cool
                            and also
            according to a roundup
                            of late world news
        from the usual unreliable sources
                            real dead

Lyrics of a Lost Soul

Wheaton Hale Brewer

Why do I blindly worship at the shrine
    My fathers slowly built from nothingness?
Why hail the unknown, calling it divine;
    And cringing, urge the infinite to bless?
Why, when I see the bleeding sun descend,
    Should I be filled with awe and holy dread;
And humbly pray that some unseen defend
    Me through the night? Why should I bow my head
        And seek a benediction from this air,
        Reasoning a God in nature, everywhere?

I cannot! Let me burst apart the thongs
    That tie my intellect to this dread God!
I will go forth, aloof from servile throngs
    And watch their feeble grovelings on the sod.
If God is in me, surely then I am
    Equal and free and fellow with the Lord!
Behold, I take my rapt gaze from the sky
    To find on earth that beauty and accord
        That is the incense-peace of heaven: the rest
        Of the once-ransomed on the Savior's breast!

They tell me I must still have faith, have faith,
    Have faith in what, and whom and where, I say!
I know from whence I am: and no pale wraith
    Hides in my blood and bone till judgment day.

The universe still stretches on and on:
    And matter, now unfettered, in due time
Elsewhere will build up others such as we:
    Elsewhere the cities will pour forth their grime
        And these new beings will, as ages creep,
        Fear the great dark, and evolution's sweep.

There is no heaven, no hell, no dim hereafter?
    Shall I be I for my short span of years?
Then must I pass with only echoing laughter
    To mark my passage—or the sob of tears?
But neither matter to the scheme of things;
    And yet, there still is something lasting left.
Though nothing marks dead beggars from dead kings,
    This world of value is not all bereft.
        Perchance beyond the men that live today,
        A mightier race on earth shall hold its sway.

Yes; there shall be at last a world of peace,
    Where men are brother; open-hearted, strong,
And proud to give; where living shall release
    To brighter pathways those who have so long
Only existed. If I live not then,
    At least the thought is goodly recompense
For all my struggles in this world of men
    To make respect mean more than reverence;
        That my descendants may participate
        In full enjoyment of a better state.

So I shall seek salvation for my life
    Building my future in the men to come,
Enjoying all the vigor of keen strife
    And casting from me filth and froth and scum.
The sun shall shine for me each day, a light
    To brighten the long avenue that leads
Into the future. Low and faint, and slight
    As insect whispers heard across the meads
        Calls opportunity to my deaf ear.
        I must live greatly; greatly I shall hear.

And as men hear the clarion call that tells
    The eternal worth of minutes unto man,
They shall behold the happiness that swells
    From bud to blossom in life's little span.
So shall the need for useless faith lie dead.
    Thus men may know themselves as gods again.
And knowing this, may move with lifted head
    Clear eyes, clean limbed, able to serve or reign.
        Kings among men, and men among the kings,
        Masters of petty, servants of great things.

Outside the window is a greening tree;
    Beyond, a church, moss-covered, and cold stone.
Tell me: is that still church more true to me
    Than life earth-sprung, by nature daily blown
With the fresh winds of morning, rigorous
    And keen? No! From all time this tree has sprung.
Worlds have died for its being. Vigorous
    It stands, each year more nobly, widely flung.
        Hark! I am such as you, three; let us raise
        Together, while we live, the good world's praise.

The Agnostic

Granville Lowther

"I know not whence I came,
  I know not whither I go;"
But I am here on this little sphere
  With longings to learn and grow.

My path through the ages past
  May have been through clay and clod;
And I do not know if the way I go
  Leads back to the dust, or to God.

The forces of Nature fight
  And science seems so austere
That I wonder at last when the wars are past,
  Will good in it all appear?

I read and reason and wait,
  And think and ponder and prove
But I do not foresee an eternity
  Of personal pain or love.

I know not the "Great World Ground"
  I know not the "Great First Cause"
But I know loss and gain, and pleasure and pain
  Resulting from governing laws.

I know not of heaven or Hell
   Where all earth's inhabitants go;
But I know as we give surely receive
   And reap whatsoever we sow.

The Dying Atheist

Anonymous

Now closed around the deepening shades of death
    And life with all its glory fades away,
Ere long those lips will yield the expiring breath,
    And this worn frame be given to decay.

Such is the lot of everything that lives,
    From humble worm to intellectual man;
Thus fades the flower that freshening fragrance gives,
    Thus all things end even as all things began.

'Tis folly to ignore the many links
    Which bind all creatures in one vast embrace,
Yet human pride in righteous horror shrinks
    From owning kindred with the lower race.

But as from germs doth spring all life around,
    So man from nobler germs his being draws,
With all his genius—all his thoughts profound,
    He yet must yield himself to Nature's laws.

Like frailest form of life that crawls the earth,
    Man in his majesty must bow to fate,
And 'neath that ground which giveth all things birth,
    Return at last to his primordial state.

So must I die, and so be laid at rest,
      Inanimate as though I'd ne'er had been
No more entranced by joy, by care oppressed,
      A withered mass, uncomely to be seen.

But yet I'm troubled by no christian fears,
      No lurid glow of hell lights up my path,
I shed no craven penitential tears,
      Nor cry for succor from almighty wrath.

No blood-polluted god awaits my soul,
      I would not have a god appeased by blood;
What though dark seas of death before me roll,
      Can I not brave the depths of Jordan's flood?

Away, false fears, ye spectres of the mind,
      Creations of the artful priests of yore,
Religion's quicksands I have left behind,
      To plant my footsteps on truth's rocky shore.

And as I gaze upon the sea of life,
      And see Death's valley far below me lie;
I feel assured I leave this worldly strife,
      To rest in peace beneath that changeful sky.

The good I've wrought, perchance, may not bring forth,
      Till 'mongst the living I've long ceased to be,
Then let mankind judge my humble worth,
      And o'er my failings pass in charity.

And you my faithful friends I leave behind,
      To perfect all which I have tried to do;
Raise up the weak, instruct the darkened mind,
      Make gladness for the many—not the few.

Thus will I pass away, content in peace,
      Knowing my trust is placed in worthy hands;
In patient labor you should never cease
      To spread your light abroad to distant lands.

Now I must slumber, I am old and gray,
      And fain would leave this scene of all my woe;
My one regret, that when I'm passed away,
      Still struggling multitudes must come and go.

Strange darkness falls across my feeble eyes,
    And short and rapid comes and goes my breath;
And now doth fade from view those azure skies,
    Good-bye to all, I yield myself to death.

Behold he sleeps,—raise up his hoary head,
    How calm and grave his last departing hours,
E'er many days we'll lay him with the dead,
    And say farewell, and strew his grave with flowers.

Part Four

Immortality/Life After Death

Introduction

Man has yearned for immortality since he first comprehended the idea of death. People have always feared death and, indeed, a good case can be made for the idea that the origin of religion itself was largely in response to an attempt to overcome this fear. Most religions have some position on the survival of death, with the most frequent solution being a way by which to overcome physical death. Usually, it is only the believers in the particular religion who will survive death. All others will die.

The doctrine of a future life is usually made a part of the particular religion and is documented by alleged revelation from its god or founder. Rarely is any other proof offered. The trouble with this state of affairs is that it requires an act of "faith" in order to accept the deity or prophet in the first place (since no conclusive proof is offered), and then a further act of faith is needed to believe that this deity or prophet gave the particular revelation that there was an afterlife. Nonmembers of the religious group often find these acts of faith difficult to accept. Freethinkers find them ludicrous attempts at proof, which fail completely.

Of course, it could be argued that even if the revelation route does not seem well documented, there is another "proof" for life after death, namely, the idea that without the promise of immortality, life would lack all meaning and the foundation of ethical obligation would be undermined. This is a curious argument. It is difficult to argue with much force that a claim lacking evidentiary support *must* be true for otherwise things will be in a sorry state. Perhaps they either *are* in a sorry state, or perhaps they can still function *without* the thing that is supposedly necessary. It appears that an adequate justification for ethical behavior can be produced without postulating an afterlife.

There are, in addition to the religious tradition touched upon briefly above, five other areas of evidence that pertain to efforts at establishing the existence of life after death. These areas are: 1) the existence of ghosts,

2) the evidence for past lives obtained through hypnotic regression, 3) the evidence of reincarnation, 4) the evidence from physical or mental mediums, and 5) the evidence from near-death experiences. These will be examined in turn.

Ghosts

The first evidence offered in support of an afterlife is the existence of ghosts. True, if there really are ghosts, or visible manifestations of a part (the "soul"?) of a now-dead person, this would indeed be strong evidence for the existence of an afterlife. While there are many people who claim to have seen a "ghost," upon closer scrutiny, it often turns out that something was either heard, seen, or felt, but the characterization of that something as a *ghost* is not merited by the facts. Hearing footsteps and creaking doors or experiencing cold drafts and the like may be puzzling, but they are not tantamount to seeing the identifiable form of a deceased person.

Next we come to the matter of "hard" evidence. There are many purported photographs of ghosts. Confining ourselves only to those showing forms recognizable as human, there is only one conclusion that can be reached by the evidence: there has been a considerable amount of deception with regard to the photographs. *All* such photographs have been shown to be double exposures, paste-ups, or other manipulations of the photographic process. Yes, there are photographs that show light "blobs," streaks, or cloudy areas on the film, some of which may not be attributable to deliberate manipulation. However, this does not shed much light on the evidence for actual ghosts. A streak or blob is not evidence of anything except light reaching the lens. Other physical evidence of ghosts is quite skimpy. There are a few objects supposedly thrown by ghostlike beings, but unless their actual flight was witnessed, these objects do not differ from other objects of the same kind that were *not* thrown. There are the mysterious objects supposedly "apported." This subject is covered more thoroughly below under the heading of mediums, but it can be briefly summarized: the unusual things are not the objects themselves (most are quite ordinary), but rather the fact that they are out of place. For example, a rose suddenly appears in a sealed room, when the room supposedly contained no rose earlier. The problem, then, becomes one of finding out if there was a natural way in which the rose (or other object) could have been introduced into the room. Professional conjurors have been of great assistance in this matter, usually finding a way in which the "apport" could have been introduced through trickery.

Reincarnation and Past Lives

The evidence from reincarnation would indeed be a strong indication that there was an afterlife *if* there were good evidence for reincarnation in the first place. One kind of evidence often used in reincarnation studies is xenoglossia. This is the ability to speak a foreign language to which one has never before been exposed in *this* life. The idea, of course, is that the language must have been learned in a previous life. A careful study of the actual words spoken by xenoglossics, done by an expert in linguistics, has shown that the responses given are rudimentary. They do not indicate a thorough knowledge of the languages in question (in this instance Swedish and German). The real ability to speak a language fluently without prior exposure would indeed be *strong* evidence of reincarnation (or something similar). There do not seem to be any cases of people who can speak languages that are now dead (e.g., ancient Egyptian dialects, Latin, Mayan, and the like), and there is little reason to conclude that there should not be people who were reincarnated from these cultures.

With regard to the other evidence for reincarnation, its worth seems to rest entirely upon the opinion of the researcher. For example, Ian Stevenson, one of the foremost reincarnation investigators, admits that his evidence is entirely anecdotal. He does, however, have quite a bit of such evidence. In science, even the social sciences, anecdotal evidence is of very low value. It has a use, and that use is usually to give experimenters clues about how to design a study that will incorporate the proper questions and controls. There do not seem to be such studies in the field of reincarnation. There is a group of hypnosis studies in which individuals are regressed backward, supposedly past the point of birth and into a previous life. The problem with hypnosis studies is that the subjects are very anxious to please the hypnotist. That desire to please may take the form of using one's imagination or memory to construct completely fanciful "past lives." When the data about such characters, who supposedly lived in a certain place at a certain time, are checked, one almost always comes up with nothing. Of course, we do not have good records about the lives of less well-known persons. In England, however, there are good municipal records, but still no confirmations. The results of regression to "past lives" remains very questionable.

Mediums

Physical or mental mediums are not very popular today, but in the period from about 1880 to 1930, they were very much in vogue. Many of these mediums were "physical" in the sense that they claimed to be able to produce physical manifestations of the "spirits" who lived beyond the grave. Among this physical evidence were small things belonging to the deceased, ectoplasm (a white, moist, stringy substance that exuded from an orifice of the medium's body), and "apports," which were physical objects transported into a sealed room by "spiritual" means. While apports do not necessarily constitute evidence for the existence of life after death, even if there really were some supernatural force involved (highly unlikely, as many mediums have been caught smuggling items into the room), the production of physical objects belonging to the deceased *may* have some relevance. It does seem strange that a "spirit" would happen to need his watch in the afterlife, but many mediums have produced the pocket watch of a dead person as "evidence" that they were in contact with his spirit. Again, ectoplasm, which has often been identified as cheesecloth when closely examined, does not seem to be relevant with regard to evidence for survival of death, no matter what the ectoplasm turns out to be.

Mental mediums produce the voice or thoughts of a deceased person, at least according to *their* claims. In a number of cases, information not otherwise known outside the immediate family has been revealed by a medium, purportedly giving "proof" that the information came from the dead relative. Such claims have been significantly undermined with the discovery of large files of personal information in the offices of various spiritualist organizations. Looking in the purses or wallets of subjects is also reported. Even more damning is the fact that most "spirits" seem to have forgotten any of the foreign languages they knew. The famous escape artist Houdini was very suspicious when the "spirit" of his mother was unable to converse with him in Yiddish, the language she normally used with him. Mediumship is so fraught with demonstrated fraud that *any* so-called evidence from this area must be viewed with extreme skepticism.

Near-Death Experiences (NDEs)

The near-death experience (NDE) has recently been offered as evidence for survival of death. Several things must be understood before we can examine whether NDEs do indeed offer any evidence for survival. First, it must be recognized that the old standard of death as the cessation of heartbeat and breathing has been ruled insufficient and in many states has been legally replaced or augmented by the cessation of electrical activity in the brain (brain death) as the criterion of death. With that in mind, an examination of the evidence shows that *no* person whose brain activity has ceased for more than a few seconds has ever come back to life. This means that no one who was actually dead has come back to tell us what death is like. The term *near*-death experience recognizes this fact. What can a person who is one foot from the edge of a thousand-foot precipice tell us about the experience of falling off the precipice? Not much. That is probably a good way of looking at what NDEs can tell us about the experience of death. Again, this implies nothing at all about whether any useful information can be obtained regarding what happens *after* death. There is an additional problem: the receptor organ that is gathering the impressions of what is happening is virtually nonfunctional. Remember that the person having an NDE is probably not breathing and the heart has stopped pumping blood to the brain. As a result, the brain is being starved of both oxygen and glucose, two necessary nutrients if it is to continue functioning. Any visual images obtained by the brain in its nonfunctional condition (toxic substances like carbon dioxide and wastes are also accumulating), must be viewed as possibly pathologically induced. We know that the presence of too much carbon dioxide can induce hallucinations. In addition, the types of images seen during an NDE appear to be culturally determined. People in India see images related to the Hindu idea of an afterlife, while Western NDEs are marked by Judeo-Christian images.

The out-of-body experience (OBE), which often marks an NDE, can also be viewed as being of some relevance to the question of survival. It does seem strange, however, that the majority of OBEs are *not* associated with NDEs, but rather occur near the time when a person is falling asleep. Exactly how the brain functions at this "hypnogogic" time is not well understood, but more study may explain the OBE without tying it to the presence of a "soul" or "astral body."

At this point, we should address a few things that seem to be evidence *against* immortality. Perhaps the strongest single piece of evidence against immortality is that *all* people seem to die, their physical remains are disposed of in some acceptable manner, and they never reappear. In short, the evidence militates against the *fact* of survival, no matter how comforting a *belief* in it may be. Then there is the problem of whether a discarnate (without a body) "spirit" can meaningfully exist. By meaningfully, I have in mind both a logically non-self-contradictory existence, and as one from which any information can pass to a living human being. It would seem that the second statement is false. Receiving or sending meaningful information requires sense organs, and a spirit (which has no physical body) cannot have sense organs. Even "ESP" requires sense organs, although perhaps different ones than those we normally utilize.

The question of whether it is self-contradictory to exist and yet be without a body is a difficult one; philosophers have argued it for centuries. Unanimity of opinion does not exist, but it seems as if the burden of proof rests squarely on the shoulders of the person who asserts that it *is* possible for a "personality" or spirit to exist without a physical body. Many philosophers recognize that the concept of "personality" or identity depends upon the presence of a physical body. If a "spirit" is to have any meaningful communication with a living human being (and many ghost reports involve no such communication), then it would seem necessary to have a physical body (or at least a head and neck, with lungs); otherwise, no sounds could be made, no language used, and no response heard. It will not do to say that this could be done by ESP or telepathy, as both of these would seem to require *some* sort of sense organs.

Perhaps the next strongest piece of evidence against the existence of an afterlife is that when cases of supposed information from the "next world" come to those in this world, either through mediums, automatic writing, messages, or what have you, they invariably contain no solid information that only the deceased could have known. Why not? Surely *something* is known only to those who have died, and surely they must be able to reveal *something* about their surroundings.

This brief review of the evidence for immortality has not attempted anything like thorough coverage. Rather, a short and admittedly superficial review has been made of some of the major pieces of evidence claimed as support for an afterlife. None has been found very convincing. Even the writings that comprise the Bible are not very specific about what the activities of those who survive death, outside of Hell, will be like. Although these writings carry very little weight for an unbeliever, even they fail to provide any real evidence for survival. We are left, as a result of all this, more with hope for the survival of death than with any hard evidence. Aspects of this dilemma are discussed in the various selections that comprise this section.

Life, Death and Immortality

Annie Besant

Like the proverbial cat, Annie Besant really did have nine lives. In fact, her most definitive biographer, Arthur Nethercot, titled the two-volume biography of her life *The First Five Lives of Annie Besant* and *The Last Four Lives of Annie Besant.* The first five lives are really the only ones that need concern us here, because the last four lives were intimately involved with the Theophist movement.

Nethercot calls Annie Besant's first five lives "The Christian Mother," "The Atheist Mother," "The Martyr of Science," "The Socialist Labor Agitator,"and "The Chela of the Mahatmas." These titles will help guide us through the career of this remarkable woman.

Annie Wood was born in London in 1847. In 1867 she married Frank Besant, an Anglican clergyman who was the brother of writer Walter Besant. She settled down to what promised to be the uneventful life of the wife of an English country parson. What a surprise it must have been when six years and two children later, she left him to become an atheist lecturer and associate of Charles Bradlaugh. Her religious belief dissipated after reading and listening to the discussions of people who were friendly with Charles Voysey, a heretical clergyman of the period. Soon she was writing anonymous pamphlets for the freethought publisher Thomas Scott. It was only a matter of time before she was lecturing in public. After hearing Charles Bradlaugh lecture, and after talking with him, Annie Besant was given a job writing for his publication, *The National Reformer.* She then became a lecturer for Bradlaugh's National Secular Society. She was a naturally gifted speaker. Her partnership with Bradlaugh grew, and soon the two became the acknowledged leaders of British freethought.

Annie Besant continued to author a large number of pamphlets and several books, including her autobiography. She debated with a number of clergymen. Because of her atheism, she lost a court battle to her husband for custody of their children. In 1877 she and Bradlaugh successfully defended themselves against charges of publishing an obscene work: they had reprinted an early birth control book by Charles Knowlton.

In the 1880s Annie Besant showed interest in socialism and became friends with George Bernard Shaw and other Fabian socialists. In 1889 she announced that she was now a Theosophist, a situation which came about after she had been asked to review a book, entitled *The Secret Doctrine*, by Helena Blavatsky, the founder of Theosophy. The book impressed her very much and she went to see the author. The magnetic Mrs. Blavatsky must have captivated her, for she suddenly joined the Theosophists, gradually severing all ties with Bradlaugh by 1891, after which Annie Besant remained a Theosophist until her death in 1933. She led the movement for many years after the death of Mrs. Blavatsky.

The present selection was first published as a pamphlet by the Freethought Publishing Company of London in 1886. It has not been republished till now.

Of all the questions which, throughout the centuries, have escaped from the lips of man, there is none which has been asked with such persistence, none which has possessed interest more perennial, than "Whence do I come? Whither shall I go?" Man's origin, man's hereafter, have ever been of intensest interest to man. When Paulinus stood before Eadwine of Northumbria and preached the faith of Christ, it is said that an aged ealderman of Eadwine's court cried out: "As a swallow's flight across a lighted hall, so seems the life of man. The swallow flieth in at one door, tarrieth awhile in the light, and thereafter flieth out again into the darkness. So for a moment is the life of man in our sight, but of what it was before and what it shall be after we know nought. If the message of the stranger tell of this, let us hear it." As the flight of the swallow, from darkness to darkness, man's life has been in the past. Out of the darkness of the womb, into the darkness of the grave, man passes across his narrow strip of life. Two vast eternities stretch ocean-like on either side of the island of individual existence, and through the darkness that enshrouds them no human eye, it has been thought, could ever pierce. On this mystery religions have claimed to cast light, but the darkness has only been as a screen, on which the magic-lantern of faith has thrown strange figures, fanciful resemblances of human life on earth. In later time the true light of science has rippled over the space where darkness had reigned, and human life is seen to be no isolated phenomenon, but a part of one great cycle, wherein that which we call death is as natural as that which we call life.

The answers of the various religions of the world are all of the nature of guesses, and are unsupported by proven fact. Hinduism says that all life is an emanation from the divine existence; the creative power is ever emitting, ever reabsorbing, individual lives; it alone IS; all else is *maya,* illusion. Hence the reverence shown to all living things by the Brahmin; he will not slay the lowest creature, since it shares with him the divine essence, and all the forms with which the deity clothes itself are to him sacred.

Buddhism sees life as a state of unrest, each individual life passing through a circle of changes so long as it continues imperfect; the life rises through stage after stage, or if unworthy in one stage it is degraded to a lower for its next probation; at length, becoming perfect, it passes into Nirvana, is absorbed into the All. To escape from life's unrest, from the circle of existence, is the aim of the Buddhist philosopher; the unruffled serenity of unconsciousness is his goal; the loss of the One in the All is the hope on which his world-weary eyes are fixed.

These mystic Oriental religions are profoundly Pantheistic; one life pulsing through all living things; one existence bodying itself forth in all individual existences; such is the common ground of those mighty religions which number among their adherents the vast majority of human kind. And in this magnificent conception they are in accord with modern science; the philosopher and the poet, with the far-reaching glance of genius, caught sight of that unity of all things, "the One in the Many" of Plato, a belief which is the glory of modern science to have placed upon the future foundation of ascertained fact. . . .

. . . Life is not a contrast to non-living nature, but a further development. The more knowledge advances the more plainly is it shown that there are physical and chemical processes upon which life depends. Heat is produced by combustion in the organism, as it is in the fire; starch is converted into sugar there, as it is in the chemical laboratory; urea, which is so constant a product of the body's chemistry, can be formed artificially by the chemist; and the process of excitation in a nerve, on the closure of a constant stream, appears to be analogous to the process of electrolysis, in which hydrogen is given off at the negative pole. The peculiarity of life is the complexity of combination in so small a space, the intimate operation of many simultaneously acting forces in the microcosm of the organic cell."

It is perhaps a little difficult for the nonchemical reader to appreciate the extreme difference of results that may flow from mere rearrangement of the atoms forming a substance. Even in the case of a single element, we may have very different bodies consisting of it alone, different because of some differences of combination of its atoms; thus a lump of the element carbon may be lampblack, or graphite, or diamond, according to whether it is amorphous (without form, *i.e.* noncrystalline), or is a rhombohedral or an octohedral crystal. Yet a nonchemist would scarcely identify the carbon which sparkles on his finger in a diamond, with that in the pencil with which he writes, or that which floats down on his paper from a smoky chimney. . . .

We may borrow an illustration from another science to show how result depends upon arrangement of matter. Everyone knows the exquisite irridescence of mother-of-pearl, the tender delicate hues which melt into each other, glowing with soft radiance. How different is the dull dead surface of a piece of wax. Yet take that dull black wax and mold it so closely to the surface of the mother-of-pearl that it shall take every delicate marking of the shell, and when you raise it the seven-hued glory shall smile at you from the erstwhile colorless surface. For though it be to the naked eye imperceptible, all the surface of the mother-of-pearl is in delicate ridges and furrows, like the surface of a newly ploughed field; and when the waves of light come dashing up against the ridged surface they are broken like the waves on a shingly shore, and are flung backwards, so that they cross each other and the on-coming waves; and as every ray of white light is made up of waves of seven colors, and these waves differ in length each from the others, the fairy ridges fling them backward separately and each ray reaches the eye by itself; so that the color of the mother-of-pearl is really the spray of the lightwaves, and comes from arrangement of matter once again. Give the dull black wax the same ridges and furrows, and its glory shall differ in nothing from that of the beautiful shell.

To apply our illustration: as the color belongs to one arrangement of matter and the dead surface to another, so life belongs to some arrangements of matter, and is their resultant, while the resultant of other arrangements is death.

Once grasp this view of life, and the question "Where does the life go to at death?" becomes meaningless. A result "goes" nowhere when its cause is no longer present; it simple ceases. Raise a gas to incandescence, and the result is light; shut the gas off, and the light goes out; it does not go somewhere else, and continue as light in some other sphere; you have removed the cause, and the effect ceases. When the combinations and disassociations of compounds in the body cease to go on within certain limits, life ceases, and other phenomena set in which we class together as death.

Further, the degree of life varies with the complexity of the combination and the coordination of many diverse organs. The life of the vegetable differs in much from the life of the animal, when we compare together the complex organisms of the vegetable and animal kingdoms. The simple organisms of each are almost indistinguishable, and the simplest organisms which exist form the common stem of the two diverging branches of living things. The life of the single cell consists in very limited activities; how far it is "conscious" who shall say? the organism moves, feeds, and reproduces itself; it has no sense, no nerves, no muscles, no digestive or respiratory or circulatory system; yet it lives. Stage by stage the simple is succeeded by the complex; cells unite to form tissues, first of similar cells; then differences arise in the cells from differences of external conditions; pressure, contact, action of heat and light, all help to modify the various cells, and differentiated tissues are gradually formed. These differentiated tissues perform different works, and the activities of the body increase—the life increases. Yet another complexity arises; these differentiating tissues become coordinated in their growth; integration proceeds step by step with differentiation; until, in the most highly evolved organism, we have the greatest complex of activities working in perfect harmony, and the totality of these forms the life of the human being. He shares "life" with the amoeba, but what definition can adequately include the twain?

If life be thus analyzed, what is to be said of death? Death is rearrangement; it is the disassociation of the compounds whose resultant was life; the breaking up of the complex organic products, and their gradual revolution into the simpler inorganic forms; until the living body, with its compounds of wonderful variety and intricacy, is resolved through stage after stage of ever-increasing simplicity into those ultimate fates of all living things, carbon dioxide, water, and ammonia; and then these recommence the upward building once more.

Nor are the changes we call death simultaneous over the whole body; the body does not die at once; it dies gradually, tissue after tissue. The muscles die when their semi-fluid substance begins to coagulate, and the *rigor mortis* sets in; the glandular tissues die later, and they work (and are therefore living), as every nurse knows, for some little time after "death"; hair and nails grow in similar fashion; the brain is sometimes dead ere the body is regarded as a corpse. It is the death of the heart and lungs only that is recognized as "death"; when the pulse ceases, and then the mirror held to the lips is not dulled by a breath, then the bystanders say: "He is gone." And in this there is some truth, since with the ceasing of the circulation and with the non-supply of oxygen to the tissues chemical changes must set in in them all, which tend to disintegration. And though some few tissues may for a brief while continue to live, yet their life must needs be very limited; the nervous system cannot work without the gaseous and solid materials brought to it by the blood, and when the nervous stimulus is withdrawn life must cease, even in the lowest tissues. But it is interesting to note that the tissues in which life persists the longest are those whose cells most resemble the lower cellular forms of living things. Retaining more independence, they do not at once die with the death of the higher tissues.

It is obvious that if the reasoning applied to life and death in the preceding pages be accepted, the word "immortality" is not predicable of any of the material arrangements there spoken of. Nor, indeed, do the believers in immortality now claim it for what they call the "perishable body". It is true that in the Apostles' Creed, accepted by the whole Catholic Church, Christians constantly repeat their belief in "the resurrection of the body," as well as in "the life everlasting." It is true that in the Visitation of the Sick, in the authorized Book of Common Prayer, the priest is directed to examine the sick person as to his belief, and to ask: "Dost thou believe in . . . the resurrection of the flesh; and everlasting life after death?" And to this the sick person answers: "All this I stedfastly believe." But it is very generally understood that these words must be taken in a nonnatural sense, and that while they may have, and indeed did, represent the belief of the very ignorant primitive Christians, they are absolutely meaningless at the present day. Knowing, as we now do, what becomes of "the body," "the flesh"; knowing that it passes through various stages of "decay," that is, of disassociation and recombination into simpler and simpler forms, until water, ammonia, and carbon dioxide are all that remains; knowing that many of the intermediate products have been taken up by the roots of plants, and have been broken up and recombined in the wonderful chemical laboratory of the vegetable cells, and that these ultimate products will have the same fate; knowing that many of the vegetables thus built up have supplied food to animals—is not the churchyard a favorite pasture-ground for sheep in many country districts?—and that these animals have in their turn formed food for man, and have thus built the materials of past generations into the living tissues of the present: knowing all this, how can the Christian say with full faith: "I believe in the resurrection of the flesh"?

.   .   .

The later Jews and the Egyptians—from both of which nations Christianity took much of its creed—were firm believers in the absolute resurrection of the body. The curious vision of the valley of dry bones, narrated in Ezekiel xxxvii., may be taken as a partial rehearsal of the expected resurrection drama. And the Jews held the curious fancy that one very hard bone in the human skeleton—named from this belief the *os sacrum,* or holy bone— never suffered decay, but remained as a nucleus for the resurrection body; which would be formed therefrom, I presume, as Eve was formed from out a rib. The Egyptians did not trust to a single bone; they preferred to ensure the continuance of the whole body. Hence their custom of embalming the dead, so that the spirit on the resurrection morning might not fail of lodgment in its own dwelling-place. And I cannot help thinking that if there is really to be a resurrection of the flesh, the Egyptians were far more rational than modern-day Christians. For under the present plan, we use up our ancestors' bodies for the building of our own frames, as countrymen use the stones from ruined castles to make walls for their fields; and it will be no more possible for everyone to reclaim the materials which erstwhile formed his body, than it would be to build up both castle and walls at the same moment out of the same stones.

Apart, however, from any of these fables of the resurrection of the flesh, there exists a widespread belief in the prolongation of the individual consciousness after death. Man is regarded as consisting of two things, a body and a spirit; the body is considered to be dead *per se,* and the spirit is the living agent which animates the body, inhabiting it and using it as an instrument, as a man goes into an animal in a pantomime, and gives to the inanimate piece of mechanism the gestures of the living creature. It is this spirit for which immortality is now alone claimed by the educated; it is this which "leaves the body" at death, and which, "freed from the burden of the flesh," continues to exist while its former body decays, and will, it is alleged, continue to exist for ever.

Now to this claim it might be sufficient to say, "Not proven"; for the duty of proving an allegation lies on the person who makes it, not on the one who declines to accept it without some demonstration being brought forward in its support. . . .

Let us see how far mental activity, which is the supposed domain of the "spirit," is dependent on the bodily organization. When the babe is born, it shows no sign of mind. For a brief space hunger and repletion, cold and warmth, are its only sensations. Slowly the specialized senses begin to function; still more slowly muscular movements, at first aimless and reflex, become coordinated and consciously directed. There is no sign here of an intelligent spirit controlling a mechanism; there is every sign of a learning and developing intelligence, developing *pari passu* with the organism of which it is a function. As the body grows the mind grows with it, and the childish mind of the child develops into the hasty, quickly-judging, half-informed, unbalanced youthful mind of the youth; with maturity of years comes maturity of mind, and body and mind are vigorous in their prime; as old age comes on, and the bodily functions decay, the mind decays also, until age passes into senility, and body and mind sink into second childhood. Has the immortal spirit decayed with the organization, or is it dwelling in sorrow bound in its "house of clay"? If this be so, the spirit must be unconscious, or else separate from the very individual whose essence it is supposed to be; for the old man does not suffer when his mind is senile, but is contented as a little child. And not only is this constant simultaneous growth and decay of body and mind to be observed, but we know that mental functions are disordered and suspended by various physical conditions. Alcohol, many drugs, fever, disorder the mind; a blow on the cranium suspends its functions, and the "spirit" returns with the surgeon's trepanning. Does the "spirit" take part in dreams? Is it absent from the idiot, from the lunatic? Is it guilty of manslaughter when the madman murders, or does it helplessly watch its own instrument performing actions at which it shudders? If it can only work here through an organism, is its nature changed in its independent life, severed from all with which it was identified? Can it, in its "disembodied state," have anything in common with its past?

Professor Clifford, in his essay on the "Unseen Universe," criticizes the notion of a supposed ether which prepares for the life immortal.

Far greater, indeed, is the work which the second ether has to perform: nothing less than the fashioning of a "spiritual body." While our consciousness proceeds *pari passu* with molecular disturbance in our brains, this molecular disturbance agitates the first ether, which transfers a part of its energy to the second. Thus is gradually elaborated an organism in that second or unseen universe, with whose motions our consciousness is as much connected as it is with our material bodies. When the marvellous structure of the brain decays, and it can no more receive or send messages, then the spiritual body is replete with energy, and starts off through the unseen, taking consciousness with it, but leaving its molecules behind. Having grown with the growth of our mortal frame, and preserving in its structure a record of all that has befallen us, it becomes an organ of memory, linking the future with the past, and securing a personal immortality. Can another body, then, avail to stay the hand of death, and shall man by a second nervous system escape scot free from the ruin of the first? We think not. The laws connecting consciousness with changes in the brain are very definite and precise, and their necessary consequences are not to be evaded by any such means. Consciousness is a complex thing made up of elements, a stream of feelings. The action of the brain is also a complex thing made up of elements, a stream of nerve-messages. For every feeling of consciousness there is at the same time a nerve-message in the brain. This correspondence of feeling to nerve-message does not depend on the feeling being part of a consciousness, and the nerve-message part of the action of a brain. How do we know this? Because the nervous system of animals grows more and more simple as we go down the scale, and yet there is no break that we can point to and say, "above this there is consciousness or something like it; below there is nothing like it." Even to those nerve-messages which do not form part of the continuous action of our brains, there must be simultaneous feelings which do not form part of our consciousness. Here, then, is a law which is true throughout the animal kingdom; nerve-message exists at the same time with feeling. Consciousness is not a simple thing, but a complex; it is the combination of feelings into a stream. It exists at the same time with the combination of nerve-messages into a stream. If individual feeling always goes with stream of nerve-messages, does it not follow that when the stream of nerve-messages is broken up, the stream of feelings will be broken up also, will no longer form a consciousness? does it not follow that when the messages themselves are broken up, the individual feelings will be resolved into still simpler elements? The force of this evidence is not to be weakened by any number of spiritual bodies. Inexorable facts connect our consciousness with this body that we know; and that not merely as a whole, but the parts of it are connected severally with parts of our brain-action. If there is any similar connection with a spiritual body, it only follows that the spiritual body must die at the same time with the natural one. Consider a mountain rill. It runs down in the sunshine, and its water evaporates; yet it is fed by thousands of tiny tributaries, and the stream flows on. The water may be changed again and again, yet there still is the same stream. It widens over plains, or is prisoned and fouled by towns; always the same stream; but at last

> "even the weariest river
> Winds somewhere safe to sea!"

When that happens, no drop of water is lost, but the stream is dead.

Life Without Immortality

Corliss Lamont

[Henry] Corliss Lamont was born in New Jersey in 1902. His mother was a Corliss family member, and his father was from the long line of Scotch Lamonts who emigrated to the United States in the 1700s. His father, Thomas Lamont, had made a fortune in the banking world and eventually served as chairman of the board of J. P. Morgan and Company. Young Corliss (as he was always called) attended Harvard University as his father had, then took his Ph.D. in philosophy at Columbia University in 1932. He served as instructor in philosophy at Columbia and later taught at The New School for Social Research.

The subject of Corliss Lamont's dissertation was the idea of immortality, and during the writing of it, he shifted from being a believer in immortality to being a strong disbeliever. That dissertation was revised and later issued as *The Illusion of Immortality* in 1935. It has gone through several editions. Along with the increased disbelief in immortality, Lamont found himself increasingly becoming a political and religious radical. He describes himself as eventually embracing Socialism. During the era of Senator Joseph McCarthy in the 1950s, Lamont was called upon to testify at the Army McCarthy hearings of the House Committee on UnAmerican Activities about whether he had had any help from "Communists" in the writing of his book *The Peoples of the Soviet Union*. Lamont refused to testify on First Amendment grounds, and filed suit challenging the legality of the whole McCarthy Committee. He was vindicated in Federal Appeals Court, and all contempt charges were dismissed. He also challenged the right of the Post Office to censor his mail (again, he won) and the right of the CIA to open his personal mail (he won again).

Lamont has been one of the foremost authors of books on humanism, and supporters of humanist causes. His *Humanism as a Philosophy* (later retitled *The Philosophy of Humanism*) is a standard introduction to the field.

The present selection is an edited version of "Life Without Immorality," chapter 7 of his *The Illusion of Immortality*. Although this book is not difficult to obtain, like many of the other sources in this volume, it is the best extant work critical of the idea of immortality, so it belongs in any collection of the best writing on the subject.

---

1. An Affirmative Philosophy

Assuming that immortality is an illusion, what then? What effect does or ought this knowledge have on the living of our lives? It was no less a person than Ralph Waldo Emerson who said: "No sooner do we try to get rid of the idea of immortality than pessimism raises its head. . . . Human griefs seem little worth assuaging; human happiness too paltry (at the best) to be worth increasing. The whole moral world is reduced to a point. Good and evil, right and wrong, become infinitesimal, ephemeral matters. The affections die away—die of their own conscious feebleness and uselessness. A moral paralysis creeps over us."[1] In an Easter Day address, to take a typical contemporary statement, Bishop Manning warned that loss of faith in the life to come robs men "of their hope and vision and joy in life here and now" and "makes this life inexplicable and futile and unmeaning to them."[2] Now all of us know plenty of persons living today who, rejecting belief in or skeptical of immortality, show no signs of moral paralysis, decay of the affections, loss of happiness, or feelings of futility. Indeed, perhaps the best way to answer such assertions as the above is not to argue, but simply to point.

First of all, I would point to that considerable number of the great and the good of the past who, disbelieving in personal survival, yet led most fruitful and vital careers. Among the ancient Greeks are the famous philosophers, Democritus, Aristotle, and Epicurus; and the two notable physicians, Galen and Hippocrates. Among the ancient Romans are Lucretius and Marcus Aurelius, Julius Caesar and Pliny the Elder, Ovid and Horace. The foremost Arabian philosopher, Averröes, one of the outstanding intellects of the Middle Ages, denies the immortality of the individual human personality, as does his school in general. Passing to modern philosophy, we find upholding this same conclusion such illustrious minds as Benedict Spinoza, David Hume, Baron d'Holbach, Ludwig Feuerbach, Auguste Comte, Karl Marx, Friedrich Nietzsche, Ernst Haeckel, Herbert Spencer, and Bernard Bosanquet. Men of action with such varying backgrounds and careers as Vladimir I. Lenin, Jawaharlal Nehru, Sun Yat-sen, Vilhjalmur Stefansson, Robert Ingersoll and

Clarence Darrow unite in treating the idea of a future life as a total illusion. The American inventor, Thomas A. Edison; the botanist, Luther Burbank; the biologist and Nobel Prize winner, Hermann J. Muller; the chemist and Nobel Prize winner, Linus Pauling; the psychologist, G. Stanley Hall; and the founder of psychoanalysis, Sigmund Freud, agree that there is no after-existence.

The three most eminent of twentieth-century American philosophers, Morris R. Cohen, John Dewey, and George Santayana, are convinced that this life is all. Following suit are outstanding Humanists or naturalists such as Professors Abraham Edel of the College of the City of New York, Sidney Hook of New York University, Horace M. Kallen of the New School, Roy Wood Sellars, formerly of the University of Michigan; and Joseph L. Blau, John H. Randall, Jr., and Herbert W. Schneider of Columbia University. Benedetto Croce and Giovanni Gentile, the leading philosophers of modern Italy, reject the idea of a future life. In England Bertrand Russell, Julian Huxley, and Sir Arthur Keith, Bernard Shaw, H. G. Wells and Harold J. Laski, have taken the same stand. And Albert Einstein asserts that he cannot believe "the individual survives the death of his body, although feeble souls harbor such thoughts through fear or ridiculous egotism."[3] This roll of distinguished believers in personal immortality—and there are many others—in and of itself refutes such statements as those of Emerson and Manning.

Other figures of great note can be listed as regarding the idea of immortality with varying degrees of doubt. The Chinese sage, Confucius, would only say: "While you do not know life, what can you know about death?"[4] Buddha, founder of one of the world's leading religions, leaves undetermined whether the goal of Nirvana implies extinction or consciousness for the personality.[5] Other agnostics on the question of immortality have been Cicero, the Roman orator; John Stuart Mill, the English utilitarian; G. F. Hegel, the German idealist; William James, the American pragmatist; Thomas H. Huxley, the well-known biologist; Charles W. Eliot, renowned President of Harvard University; and Robert Louis Stevenson, the author, who talks about "this fairy tale of an eternal tea party."[6] Of course, skeptics concerning immortality, even if they do not reach the stage of downright denial of an after-life, do not use the idea of survival as an inspiration to action or as a motive for morality. Hence our roll of doubters, like that of the definite disbelievers, makes the dire lamentations of the immortalists seem more than a trifle extravagant.

In 1914, Professor Leuba conducted a statistical inquiry among distinguished American scientists that supports these considerations. He found that a large proportion of them either disbelieved in or doubted the existence of a future life.[7] Out of one thousand scientists responding to the questionnaire only 50.6 percent, a fraction over half, expressed belief in immortality. Among the more eminent of these men the percentage of believers was 36.9 percent while among the less eminent it was 59.3 percent, thus showing that the greater the scientist, the greater the likelihood of lack of faith in immortality. Further inquiry brought out that the highest proportion of skeptics and disbelievers were among the biologists, sociologists and psychologists, the last-named group taking the lead here with a figure of 81.2 percent. Professor Leuba explains this fact on the ground that these classes of scientists more than any others recognize the ruling presence of law in organic and psychical life. This harmonizes with our own opinion that biology, psychology and their associated sciences provide the most convincing evidence against the idea of personal survival. Professor Leuba repeated his study in 1933 and reported that a considerably higher proportion of scientists disbelieved in or doubted immortality than in 1914.[8]

There are illustrious people as well as individuals who have gotten along very well without belief in immortality. The Old Testament Hebrews had a highly developed moral code that depended not in the slightest on the belief in gloomy and ethically neutral Sheol. The same statement holds true in regard to the Homeric Greeks and their dismal Hades. The Athenian Greeks at the very height of their civilization in the fifth century B.C., one of the greatest creative periods in the history of man, were not influenced to a decisive extent by the notion of life beyond the grave. While the Athenians frequently discussed the theme of immortality, their general attitude is reflected in the great Funeral Oration of Pericles as reported by the historian Thucydides.

In this address there is no suggestion of personal continuance after death or of preoccupation with the idea. Pericles is clear that the lustre the Athenian dead have achieved is a this-worldly, humanistic one. They sacrificed themselves "to the commonwealth and received, each for his own memory, praise that will never die, and with it the grandest of all sepulchres, not that in which their mortal bones are laid, but a home in the minds of men, where their glory remains fresh to stir to speech or action as the occasion comes by. For the whole earth is the supulchre of famous men, and their story is not graven only on stone over their native earth, but lives far away, without visible symbol, woven into the stuff of other men's lives."[9]

In later centuries, during the decline of Greece, the Epicureans, who commanded the allegiance of a great many intelligent men, made the denial of an after-existence a cardinal doctrine of their philosophy. And though there was some disagreement on the matter among the Stoics, they formulated and followed their sublime and heroic way of life with little or no reference to the conception of a hereafter. Throughout the history of Europe, especially during the Renaissance and modern times, large numbers of persons have not included faith in a beyond as a part of their philosophies, as the Church itself has indicated in many a resounding blast. And of course in India, so far as this worldly-conduct is connected with belief in an after-existence, it is in the main with a conception far removed from the Christian doctrine of a worthwhile personal survival.

In the world at present, we find in Soviet Russia the leaders of the nation and a majority of the people possessed of a positive disbelief not only in immortality, but in God as well. Yet in the Soviet Union we have witnessed since the Communist Revolution of 1917 an impressive outpouring of constructive labor and energy during both war and peace. Other peoples may dislike the ethical standards which the Russians have established and the goals for which they are striving, but it is irrefutable that these Russians have had the strength and initiative to build a new form of society which constitutes a challenge to the rest of mankind in such important fields as economics, education, health and science. Likewise other countries where the Communists have won control, such as Czechoslovakia, Yugoslavia, and China with its close to 650,000,000 inhabitants, are now actively following a Marxist philosophy which specifically repudiates any idea of a hereafter and at the same time encourages vigorous effort and hard work.

Only, then, by shutting one's eyes to much of the past and much of the present can one possibly maintain that belief in immortality is necessary for the good life, the spiritual life, the intellectual life, the happy life, the strenuous life or the useful life. "It may indeed be said that no man of any depth of soul has made his prolonged existence the touchstone of his enthusiasms. . . . What a despicable creature must a man be, and how sunk below the level of the most barbaric virtue, if he cannot bear to live for his children, for his art, or for country!"[10] Or for humanity as a whole, I may add. What Pomponazzi stated back in the sixteenth century, when discussing the matter of recompense in heaven, always has been and always will be true, namely, that it is more virtuous to act ethically without hope of reward than with such hope.

In effect, the immortalists build up their case for the moral need of a future life by belittling the intelligence and decency of ordinary men, in short, by libeling the human race, including themselves. For there are precious few of them who, if they were deprived of their faith in immortality, would thereupon give up the moral habits of a lifetime and cease to be good citizens, kind fathers and devoted shepherds of their flocks. And it is positively indecent to claim that men will act decently only if they are guaranteed the *pourboire,* as Schopenhauer called it, of *post-mortem* existence. Nor is it possible to believe that the great religious heroes of the immortalists, from Jesus to Phillips Brooks, would have been small and selfish men had they been convinced that death meant the end.

It was not a religious leader, however, but a noted agnostic, Thomas Huxley, who gave the classic expression of protest against the shallow philosophy of the professional immortalists. In a famous letter to the author, Charles Kingsley, Huxley writes concerning his son's funeral: "As I stood beside the coffin of my little son the other day, with my mind bent on anything but disputation, the officiating minister read, as a part of his duty, the words, 'If the dead rise not again, let us eat and drink, for tomorrow we die.' I cannot tell you how inexpressibly they shocked me. . . . I could have laughed with scorn. What! because I am face to face with irreparable loss, because I have given back to the source from whence it came the cause of a great happiness, still retaining through all my life the blessings which have sprung and will spring from that cause, I am to renounce my manhood, and, howling, grovel in bestiality? Why, the very apes know better, and if you shoot their young, the poor brutes grieve their grief out and do not immediately seek distraction in a gorge."[11]

It is my conviction that the frank recognition of human mortality, far from undermining morals and stopping progress, will, other things being equal, do exactly the opposite. People will then realize that here and now, if ever, they must develop their possibilities, win happiness for themselves and others, take their stand and do their part in the enterprises that seem highest. They will understand as never before the reality of quickly-passing time and the serious duty of making the most of it. It will be an excellent thing for everyone to know that there is no heaven of angelic alchemy that can transmute a copper life to gold. The compensatory aspects of belief in immortality will no longer dull the nerve of effort. Furthermore, to confront with simple and unfailing courage the stern fact that death means death is in itself an ethical achievement of deep significance and one that strongly sustains the moral obligation of men to seek and accept the truth wherever it may lead.

The Reverend Kirsopp Lake, for many years Professor of Ecclesiastical History at Harvard University, has unequivocally asserted that the growing disbelief in personal survival is a social gain, having "raised rather than lowered the standard of life. The pursuit of individual Immortality consumed a lamentable amount of energy in past generations. To attain salvation was thought to be the object of existence. . . . Men went on year after year thinking of nothing so much as how to save their own souls. . . . In general there was produced a type of selfishness all the more repulsive because it was sanctified. In place of a quest for Immortality there is today among the most active and virile of our contemporaries a new attitude towards life; for they have almost suddenly ceased thinking about their own Immortality and regard their work as more important than their own souls. . . . The object of their work is in their minds the improvement of the world in which our children are to live. It is an unselfish object, and the pursuit of a better world for another generation to inherit has become the surrogate for the hope of a better world above for ourselves to enjoy."[12]

In striving for that better world upon this earth, would not men fight harder, for example, against war and the menace of war, if they were convinced that the millions who die in international conflict forever lose their right to live? We see the other side of the coin when the belief in immortality is utilized as an apology for war. Thus *The New York Times* of September 11, 1950, at the height of the Korean War, reported as follows on a Sunday sermon by Monsignor William T. Greene of the Catholic Church:

"Sorrowing parents whose sons have been drafted for combat duty were told yesterday in St. Patrick's Cathedral that death in battle was part of God's plan for populating the 'kingdom of heaven.'" And in England in 1954 the Archbishop of Canterbury, the highest church dignitary in the land, expressed the opinion that "the hydrogen bomb is not the greatest danger of our time. After all, the most it could do would be to transfer vast numbers of human beings from this world to another and more vital one into which they would some day go anyhow."[13] Such statements made in all seriousness demonstrate how religious faith in an after-life may weaken the struggle for world peace.

Expressing the military viewpoint is the comment on an earlier edition of this book [*The Illusion of Immortality*] by a former captain in the United States Army and a graduate of West Point. He wrote me that if a commander in the armed forces looks upon death as "a mere episode in an individual's life, about as important as graduation from grade-school, then whatever natural gift of sangfroid he may have is given an immense reinforcement. . . . It means that, without in any way needing to steel himself to a hard, pitiless inhumanity that will both warp him and insensibly vitiate his purpose, he can yet view the carnage incidental to battle and not be perturbed at it in any way, knowing that, whatever it looks like, even so far as the precious individuals themselves are concerned, it is hardly more important than if his men had nose-bleeds, or thumbs sawed off while guiding logs through a gang-saw."

As I pointed out in chapter 5, it is possible to give up entirely belief in immortality and still retain faith in some kind of God. In modern times, especially, many thoughtful persons, of diverse philosphical and religious allegiances, have taken this position. All this, however, is not to say that for those who have been taught for long years to rely on the assurance of a beyond, sudden loss of that illusion may not constitute a great shock and for some even lead to spiritual disintegration. The crumbling of a cornerstone in one's philosophy is a serious matter. But such crumblings do not usually occur abruptly; the process is gradual, giving time for a new and different principle of action to take the place of the old. No single idea, such as that of immortality, is in my opinion all-important; what is of supreme importance is an inclusive and integrated philosophy of life, one that places the individual in a definite relationship to both society and Nature. This is what men need; this is what other ways of life—Stoicism, Epicureanism, Confucianism, Buddhism—have given. Today in the modern world we have available purely secular philosophies more appropriate for the modern scene. And these make no point of relying on the promise of immortality, or specifically deny that promise altogether.

What these modern ways of life have in common is a devotion to the this-worldly welfare of men. The most enlightened of them, such as Humanism,[14] Materialism[15] and Naturalism,[16] set up the happiness, freedom and progress of all humanity as their supreme goal. This ultimate loyalty to the ultimate interests of all mankind, including one's own finest possibilities, is, I would suggest, a thing high enough and broad enough for any man to integrate his life around. As an incentive to the good life it is far more effective and noble than reliance on individual immortality and the philosophy that goes with it. Philosophies and religions of egoism and wish-fulfillment are pardonable and perhaps necessary in the childhood of the race; but mankind is growing up at last and can well afford to leave behind the attachments and symbols of immaturity. We would do well to heed the counsel of the poet Don Marquis:

> Give up the dream that Love may trick the fates
> To live again somewhere beyond the gleam
> Of dying stars, or shatter the strong gates
> Some god has builded high: give up the dream.
> Flame were not flame unless it met the dark—
> The beauty of our doomed, bewildered loves
> Dwells in the transcience of the moving spark
> Which pricks oblivion's blackness as it moves;
> A few more heartbeats and our hearts shall lie
> Dusty and done with raptures and with rhyme:
> Let us not babble of eternity
> Who stand upon this little edge of time!
> Even old godheads sink in space and drown,
> Their arks like the foundered galleons sucked down.[17]

No matter how important or irreplaceable a man may seem to himself or others, the world will get along without him, as it did before his birth. And it might help to instill a proper humility and sense of proportion if everyone would reflect that when he dies, there will remain on earth at least 2,800,000,000 human beings to carry on. That the descendants of our present two and four-fifths billion inhabitants may at the end of two hundred million or a billion or a trillion years find this earth unlivable, owing to the sun's becoming too hot or too cold, should not greatly agitate us. Even the absolute certainty of that eventuality a trifling million years from now would not seem very terrible. In his some 500,000 years of existence the species man has made a considerable number of notable achievements, none of which would be less notable if the world one day ended.

The most significant of these achievements have come to pass only in the last few thousand years, since the invention of what is known as science, which, in its modern and most successful form, has been on the scene for only a few hundred years. So in a million more years man's accomplishments might well exceed the most sanguine expectations and the most ambitious dreams. In that time he might discover, for instance, how to bring about the mutation which would result in a new species, Superman. It is conceivable that either man or Superman might, through science and particularly through nuclear power, gain such control over the mechanisms of this whirling planet, the solar system and the sources of energy and heat that extinction of life on this earth could be postponed indefinitely.

Today, especially since the successful launching of earth satellites, we can envision the possibility of human migration by means of atomic-propelled rocket ships to some other planet in our solar system, or beyond, where life could flourish. It seems likely that in this universe of infinite space and time many other planetary systems have come into being. In his book *Of Stars and Men,* Professor Shapely offers the opinion that scattered throughout the unending array of galaxies with their more than 100 quintillion stars, there are certainly 100 million planetary systems, and probably far more, in which some degree of organic evolution has taken place.[18] If this is true, then without much doubt living forms at least as highly developed as man already exist in other parts of the cosmos.

It is quite conceivable that science should some day be able to preserve indefinitely the vitality of human organisms and thereby bring about a species of immortality for human personalities. Of course, no matter what strides are made in medicine and its associated sciences, human beings will always be subject to fatal accidents. But with this qualification it is conceivable that men might ultimately learn how not to die. Romantic and attractive, however, as this possibility may seem at first glance, it would not be without its drawbacks. If practically nobody departed this earth through death, there would arise a population problem far more critical than any with which the world has ever been confronted. And even as things are, the spectacle of old and stubborn men in high places has caused wits to suggest the motto, "While there's death, there's hope!"

Santayana adds another most relevant consideration when he observes: "Not a single man or woman has ever existed whom I should wish to engage to play forever, rather than fill my theater from age to age with fresh faces, and new accents of nature. Continual perfection would be my ideal, not individual perpetuity."[19] Thus, while it may well be desirable, and some day possible, to extend the normal span of human life to a hundred years or more, the preservation of individual lives interminably would be of doubtful value.

The progressive lengthening of the life-span through the elimination of the causes of premature death is a rational and humane idea. If 90 percent of the people in every country lived to a good old age, the larger part of the unhappiness caused by death would disappear. The way to meet the challenge of premature death is not to promise men consolation in a life beyond, but to abolish so far as possible this type of death entirely. Writes one father who lost a most promising boy at the age of fifteen through a blister infection that at first seemed trivial: "Bacteria—the lowest order of life—had brought this tragedy. The lowest has triumphed over the highest! Here was a boy in perfect physical condition, vibrant with health, energetic and athletic—a boy with a superior mind and high ideals, wholesome, affectionate, fastidious, tenderly considerate of others. and here, attacking him, were these bacteria, having neither mental nor moral qualities.[20] This statement is only too true; but it does not call either for flight to a supernatural realm of compensation or for bitter pessimism and resignation. What it calls for, in addition to great fortitude on the part of the parents, is a more strenuous and effective campaign against bacteria and all the other brute, amoral forces which are able to snuff out so abruptly the life of man.

It remains to be said, however, that in the shock of personal loss we are frequently fair neither to life nor to death. The tragedy of some fine character's dying in youth or in the prime of life sometimes seems so great that it overshadows the consideration that, after all, this person did live happily and usefully for a number of years. We allow a fateful and unhappy conclusion to cast a gloom over all that has gone before. But unless we accept the perverse philosophy that a value can be a value only if it lasts forever, this procedure is not justified. Life can be very short, but at the same time it can be very sweet. The old Greek saying, "Whom the gods love die young," is not without wisdom. The fifteen-year-old boy mentioned above enjoyed his life to the utmost while it lasted and contributed a high and joyous quality to the life of others. Death could not alter this fact; for however death may affect the future, it cannot touch the past.

Most parents would prefer the experience and pleasure of having had healthy and happy children, no matter at what early age they perished, to having had no children whatsoever. What Plutarch wrote to his wife after the death of their little daughter is as pertinent today as in the first century A.D. "Let us call to mind," he said, "the years before our little child was born. We are now in the same condition as then, except that the time she was with us is to be counted as an added blessing. Let us not ungratefully accuse Fortune of what was given us, because we could not also have all that we desired. What we had, and while we had it, was good, though now we have it no longer."[21]

2. *The Meaning of Death*

In justice to death it must be stated that the fate of those who die, whether early or late, is not really very dire. For if we are right in calling immortality an illusion, the dead have no consciousness that they are missing life or that the living are missing them. They cannot grieve over being parted from those whom they love. After life's fitful fever they sleep well; nothing can touch them further, not even dreams. The grave, as Job said, is a place where the wicked cease from troubling and the weary are at rest. Those who have passed on prematurely or in any other way can experience no sting, no sorrow, no disappointment, no remorse, no anything. As Epicurus pithily summed up the matter three hundred years before the birth of Christ: "When we are, death is not; and when death is, we are not."[22] Only if there is a future life need we worry about the dead or need the dead worry about themselves. Only immortality can disturb their eternal peace.

If death is the end, we can feel sorry for ourselves that we have lost a dear friend and for our country or humanity in general that it has lost a man of distinguished abilities; but we cannot rationally feel sorry for the departed person himself, since he is nonexistent and can know neither sorrow nor gladness. We cannot be sorry for him as dead, but only for him as dying and as dying unwillingly, conscious that he was leaving this life prematurely with much of his rightful human experience being denied him. We can continue to regret that he as a living person was not able to go on enjoying the goods of existence; we can wish intensely that he were alive again so that he could share our pleasure in this or that. But it is unreasonable to transfer these wishes and regrets to the departed *as dead,* because as dead he is as completely insensible to all such things as any piece of earth or non-living matter. He is just exactly as nonexistent as he was before birth and conception.

It is the living, not the dead, who suffer when death has done its work. The dead can no longer suffer; and we may properly praise death when it puts an end to extreme physical pain or distressing mental decay. Without pretending that the dead can in any sense enjoy their release from the vicissitudes of life, we can be glad that a deceased person is no longer subject to the trials and tribulations which may have afflicted him. And it is surely legitimate to use euphemisms like *sleep* and *rest* in reference to the departed. The familiar expression, "May he rest in peace" (*Requiescat in pace* is the traditional Latin), is a poetic sentiment that can be used without any connotation of supernaturalism.

It is, however, misleading to talk of death as a "reward," since a true reward like a true punishment entails conscious experience of the fact. To him, then, who sacrifices his life for some ideal and goes forever into the blank silences of oblivion, death is hardly a reward. While some men surrender up their lives on behalf of their fellows feeling sure of attaining eternal bliss thereby, there are many others who do so in the full knowledge that death means their absolute end. No higher type of morality exists than to make one's death count in this fashion. There may come a time in the career of any man when to die will prove more effective for his central purposes than to live; when through his death what he stands for will become more clear and convincing than in any other way. The great unyielding martyrs of the past, men like Socrates and Jesus, have established this point beyond cavil. And many lesser persons—the unnumbered, unsung heroes of history and everyday existence—have likewise demonstrated their contempt for death in the name of life or of love or of some other supreme commitment.

It has usually been assumed that death as such is a very great evil and the worst enemy of man. Now certain specific ways in which death has manifested itself throughout human history, constantly striking down individuals and indeed multitudes in the prime of life and appearing in innumerable ugly forms, are correctly to be classified as evil. Yet death in and of itself, as a phenomenon of Nature, is not an evil. There is nothing mysterious about death, nothing supernatural about it, that could legitimately lead to the interpretation that it is a divine punishment inflicted upon men and other living creatures. On the contrary, death is an altogether natural thing and has played a useful and necessary role in the long course of biological evolution. In fact, without this much-maligned institution of death, which has given the fullest and most serious meaning to the survival of the fittest and thus has rendered possible the upward surge of organic species, it is clear that the animal known as man would never have evolved at all.

Man could not exist, either, were it not for the helping hand of death in making available the most basic means of human living. Man's fuel, food, clothing, shelter, furnishings and reading materials all depend to a large extent upon the operation of death. Coal, oil and peat originate in decomposed organic substances; wood for fuel, building, furniture and the manufacture of paper comes from dead trees; the death of plant life provides man with the food in the form of vegetables, grains, cereals and fruits, and with clothing in the form of cotton, flax and rayon; the death of animal life brings him not only birds, fish, fowl and meat to eat, but also fur and wool for clothing and leather for shoes.

Living and dying, birth and death, are essential and correlative aspects of the same biological and evolutionary processes. Life affirms itself *through* death, which during an early era of evolution was brought into existence *by* life and derives its entire significance *from* life. In the dynamic and creative flux of Nature the same living organisms do not go on indefinitely, but retire from the scene at a certain stage and so give way to newborn and lustier vitality.

The novelist Anne Parrish enlarged upon this thought. Each one of us, she writes, "must die for the sake of life, for the flow of the stream too great to be dammed in any pool, for the growth of the seed too strong to stay in one shape. . . . Because these bodies must perish, we are greater than we know. The most selfish must be generous, letting his life pour out to others. The most cowardly must be brave enough to go."[23] So it is that death opens the way for the greatest possible number of individuals, including the descendants of our own families, to experience the joys of living; and in this sense death is the ally of the unborn generations of men down through the untold ages of the future.

Of course there are living forms like trees, far more simply organized than human beings, that endure for centuries and tens of centuries. In his novel, *After Many a Summer Dies the Swan,* Aldous Huxley, in satirizing the desire for immortality, stresses the ability of certain species of carp to live on for hundreds of years. He pictures an English lord attaining a hideous, subhuman prolongation of life beyond two hundred years, by means of eating the intestinal flora of this fish. The point is that apparently one price of the organic complexity and specialization, including the valued assets of mind and sex love, that make man's career so exciting, so many-sided and so vividly self-conscious is death for the personality at the end of a relatively brief time span.

"The individual has, so to speak, made a bargain. For the individual comes out of the germ-plasm and does and lives and at length dies for the sake of life. It is a bit of the germ-plasm which has arisen and broken away, in order to see and feel life instead of just blindly and mechanically multiplying. Like Faust it has sold its immortality in order to live more abundantly."[24] For me, at least, one of the best antidotes to the thought of personal extinction is to understand fully the naturalness of death and its indispensable place in the great life-process of evolution that has given rise to increasing individuality and finally to the uniqueness and splendor of man himself.

Another consideration that may help to counteract the prospect of oblivion is that every man carries literally all eternity in his being. I mean by this that the ultimate elements of the body, as the Law of the Conservation of Mass implies, have always existed in some form or other and will go on existing forever. The indestructible matter that makes up our physical organisms was part of the universe five billion years ago and will still be part of it five billion years hence. The infinite past comes to a focus in our intricately structured bodies; and from them there radiates the infinite future.

The *social* meaning of death also has its positive aspects. For the occurrence of death brings home to us the common concerns and the common destiny of all men everywhere. It draws us together in the deep-felt emotions of the heart and dramatically accents the ultimate equality involved in our ultimate fate. The universality of death reminds us of the essential brotherhood of man that lies beneath all the bitter dissensions and conflicts registered in history and contemporary affairs. John Donne phrases it perfectly; "No man

is an *Iland,* intire of it selfe; every man is a peece of the *Continent,* a part
of the *maine;* if a *Clod* bee washed away by the *Sea,* Europe is the lesse,
as well as if a *Promontorie* were, as well as if a *Mannor* of thy *friends*
or of *thine owne* were; any mans *death* diminishes *me,* because I am involved
in *Mankinde;* And therefore never send to know for whom the *bell* tolls;
it tolls for thee."[25]

When we attain the realization that death finishes the story, we know
the worst. And that worst is not really very bad. It is, in fact, relatively
so far from bad that traditional Christianity and other religions have always
insisted that for us sinful humans to escape with mere extinction at the end
of our lives would be a terrible violation of justice and would throw grave
doubts on the existence of cosmic morality. To understand that death is
the necessary and inevitable conclusion of our personal careers enables us
to look this fateful event in the face with dignity and calm. Such understanding
provides an invaluable stimulus towards that high art of dying which should
be an aim of all mature and civilized men.

Today in the world large numbers of persons find themselves in a state
of unhappy suspense over the idea of immortality. They are unable either
to believe or disbelieve. They feel that personal survival is a rather doubtful
proposition; yet the possibility of it continues to haunt them. A definitive
settlement of the issue cannot but be for them a psychological gain. And
there can be no question that their resolute acceptance of the fact that
immortality is an illusion would be all to the good. It is best not only to
disbelieve in immortality, but to *believe in mortality.* This means not only
to believe positively that death is the end, but also to believe in the worth-
whileness of human life on this earth and in the high intrinsic value of men's
ethical and other attainments during that life.

Those who possess such a philosophy and who implement it by devotion
to some significant work, profession or cause are best able to rise above
the emotional crises engendered by death. Bertrand Russell gives good advice:
"To bear misfortune well when it comes, it is wise to have cultivated in
happier times a certain width of interests. . . . A man of adequate vitality
and zest will surmount all misfortunes by the emergence after each blow
of an interest in life and the world which cannot be narrowed down so
as to make one loss fatal. To be defeated by one loss or even by several
is not something to be admired as a proof of sensibility, but something to
be deplored as a failure in vitality. All our affections are at the mercy of
death, which may strike down those whom we love at any moment. It is
therefore necessary that our lives should not have that narrow intensity which
puts the whole meaning and purpose of our life at the mercy of accident."[26]

Where the impact of death may be lessened for many is in a change
in the accepted manner of disposing of dead bodies and in the customs of
mourning. In these matters we are still to a large extent barbaric. The sombre,

silent cities of the dead have grown hand in hand with the crowded, restless cities of the living. Already it becomes a serious problem to find sufficient space for graveyards; already the dreary reservations of the departed, ever-present reminders of ever-present death, constitute a heavy economic burden. Cremation would appear to be a far more rational and healthy method of disposing of the dead than burial beneath the ground. For those who wish it, the ashes may always be preserved in an urn and the urn put in a suitable place. Those, on the other hand, who like to think of their bodily elements commingling with the active forces of Nature, can leave instructions for their ashes to be scattered over some favorite sector of land or body of water.

There can be no doubt that cremation would do much to weaken those unpleasant and morbid associations that inevitably arise when the dead body is preserved intact and put in a visible coffin and a visitable grave. In this connection it might be wise to discourage the viewing of the corpse by relatives or anyone else. As for mourning, while individuals will here always follow out their own particular bent, the more extreme and public displays are clearly to be deplored. And it is much to be hoped that the wearing of black, which is a hold-over from primitive superstition, will in due course disappear. That simplicity and dignity should prevail in the matter of funerals is also devoutly to be wished. Today vulgarity and costliness frequently go together. The high cost of dying is only too well known and only too often implies a financial exploitation of death which should not be tolerated. If a husband or father dies, it is bad enough for the family to lose its chief provider without bankrupting itself in giving him an expensive funeral and burial.

The proposal, however, to do away with funeral services entirely does not seem sound. Regardless of the religious and philosophical views of the deceased, his family and his friends, some final gathering and ceremony would appear appropriate and wise. A socially-minded community, keenly aware of the value of the individual, will wish to do honor to its dead, to show its compassion toward them, or at least to give all who die, no matter how slight their earthly achievements, the most democratic recognition implicit in a funeral or memorial service. Also those who loved the departed must have a chance to express their feelings and to participate in a kind of last farewell. And if they have that familiar sense of unreality about the loss of a person whom they have known well, they should be given an opportunity fully to convince both their conscious and subconscious minds that death has actually occurred. Neither dignity nor psychological wisdom calls for suppression of the emotions in the face of death. The normal expression of grief is not inconsistent with reasonable self-control and can serve as a healthy release and purge of emotional tension. What is to be definitely deplored is the expansion of sorrow over a loved one's dying into a little cult of perpetual mourning.

Rituals concerned with death are a form of art and should embody the quality of beauty. In my opinion they ought to stress man's fundamental kinship with Nature and the deep social ties of experience; they ought to avoid sentimentality, showiness and somberness. Funerals or memorial services need not, of course, be connected with any church nor conducted by a clergyman. Various individuals and groups have already developed funeral ceremonies in harmony with the belief that there is no immortality and devoid of all supernatural references.[27]

Yet whatever improvements we make in human customs, to whatever extent we cut down the ravages of premature death, however intrepid and mature we become in our philosophies, however calmly we face the prospect of our own individual end, the loss of our near and dear will always deal a heavy blow, particularly if it is sudden or untimely. It would be mere shallowness to desire or pretend otherwise. When Jonathan Swift heard that Stella, the love of his life, was dying he wrote in a letter: "I am of the opinion that there is not a greater folly than to contract too great and intimate a friendship, which must always leave the survivor miserable."[28] It is understandable how Swift, distracted by grief, could give expression to such a sentiment. But as a serious suggestion it is not to be entertained; we cannot consider surrendering the highest human relationships simply in order to avoid the cruel partings of death. Between human beings there will always be the most ardent feelings; and where these prevail, it might as well be recognized once and for all that death can never be nonchalantly accepted with a shrug of the shoulder. Intense love, when death comes to force a separation, inevitably means intense sorrow. And men and women who are unafraid of the deeper experiences of life will not choose to evade the emotional consequences of mortality.

"Love-devouring death" is one of Shakespeare's aptest phrases. When a parent loses a son or daughter in the full flush of youth, or a lover a wife or husband in the prime of life, all the philosophies and religions in the world—whether promising immortality or not—cannot offset or veil the poignant tragedy. It is only possible to suffer and endure; to be, so far as strength allows, an unflinching Stoic. It is true that gracious Time will gradually soften the shock of death. It is true that wide interests and deep loyalties beyond the circle of friends and family can do much to cure the hurt. All this is true. But the tragedy remains. The sting of death may be tempered, but it cannot be removed.

3. Conclusion

Unsurpassed among the glories of man is his mind. This it is that enables him to know that there is such a thing as death and to reflect upon its meaning. The animals cannot do this; they do not consciously foresee that some day they will perish. When their time comes, they simply lie down and die. There is no problem or tragedy of death for them. They do not discuss the resurrection and eternal life. Men can and do. And it is a high privilege. That the outcome of that discussion and reflection should be the recognition that this life is all does not make the privilege less. "Man alone knows that he must die; but that very knowledge raises him, in a sense, above mortality, by making him a sharer in the vision of eternal truth. . . . The truth is cruel, but it can be loved, and it makes free those who have loved it."[29]

The truth about death frees us from both debasing fear and shallow optimism. It frees us from self-flattery and self-deception. To say that men cannot endure this truth is to abdicate to the weaker elements in human nature. Not only can men endure it, but they can rise above it to far nobler thoughts and acts than those centering around everlasting self-perpetuation. It is said that the denial of immortality leads to a philosophy of "eat, drink and be merry; for tomorrow we die." We hope that men will always be merry; but there is no reason why at the same time they should not be intelligent, courageous and devoted to the welfare of society. If this earthly existence is our one and only chance to have a good time, it is also our one and only chance to lead the good life; or, better still, to combine good time and good life in one integrated whole. If it is our one and only chance to enjoy personally the fruits of existence—and why should we not enjoy them?—it is also our one and only chance to establish a high and honorable record among our friends and fellow-men. There will be no second chance; no fresh opportunity in some immortal realm to redeem ourselves and alter the irreversible imprint of our lives. This is our only chance.

Finally, the knowledge that immortality is an illusion frees us from any sort of preoccupation with the subject of death. It makes death, in a sense, unimportant. It liberates all our energy and time for the realization and extension of the happy potentialities of this good earth. It engenders a hearty and grateful acceptance of the rich experiences attainable in human living amid an abundant Nature. It is a knowledge that brings strength and depth and maturity, making possible a philosophy of life that is simple, understandable and inspiring. We do not ask to be born; and we do not ask to die. But born we are and die we must. We come into existence and we pass out of existence. And in neither case does high-handed fate await our ratification of its decree.

Yet between that birth and death we can live our lives, work for and enjoy the things that we hold dear. We can make our actions count and endow our days on earth with a scope and meaning that the finality of death cannot defeat. We can contribute our unique quality to the ongoing development of the nation and humanity; give of our best to the continuing affirmation of life on behalf of the greater glory of man.

NOTES

1. Quoted in the *Encyclopedia Britannica,* 11th Edition, Vol. XIV, p. 339.

2. The Rt. Rev. William T. Manning as reported in *New York Times,* April 2, 1934.

3. Albert Einstein, "What I Believe," *The Forum,* Oct. 1930.

4. *Encyclopedia Britannica,* 14th Edition, 1929, Vol. VI, p. 239.

5. *Ibid.,* Vol. IV, p. 326.

6. Quoted in *The Hibbert Journal,* Vol. II, p. 725.

7. James H. Leuba, *The Belief in God and Immortality,* Open Court, 1921, Ch. IX.

8. James H. Leuba, "Religious Beliefs of American Scientists," *Harper's Magazine,* August, 1934.

9. Translated by Alfred E. Zimmern, *The Greek Commonwealth.* Oxford University Press, 1924, p. 207.

10. Santayana, *Reason in Religion,* Scribners, 1926, p. 247.

11. Leonard Huxley, *Life and Letters of Thomas Henry Huxley,* Appleton, 1900, Vol. I, p. 237.

12. Kirsopp Lake, *Immortality and the Modern Mind,* Harvard University Press, 1922, pp. 21-23.

13. Quoted by Irwin Edman in *The Uses of Philosophy,* Simon and Schuster, 1955, p. 153.

14. See Corliss Lamont, *The Philosophy of Humanism,* Philosophical Library, 1957.

15. See Sellars, McGill and Farber (eds.), *Philosophy for the Future: The Quest of Modern Materialism,* Macmillan, 1949.

16. See Y. H. Krikorian (ed.), *Naturalism and the Human Spirit,* Columbia University Press, 1944.

17. Don Marquis, "Transient," by permission of Bernice M. Marquis. First published in *The Saturday Review of Literature,* Oct. 22, 1932.

18. Harlow Shapley, *Of Stars and Men: Human Responses to an Expanding Universe,* Beacon Press, 1958, pp. 74, 144.

19. *The Journal of Philosophy,* July 22, 1909, p. 415.

20. Edwin M. Slocombe, "Lantern in the Storm," *Atlantic Monthly,* Vol. 151, No. 5, May, 1933, p. 552.

21. Quoted in John Haynes Holmes, *Is Death the End?* Putnam, 1915, p. 345.

22. Diogenes Laertius, *Lives of Eminent Philosophers,* Putnam, 1925, Bk. X, 125.

23. Anne Parrish, *Golden Wedding,* Harpers, 1936, p. 343.

24. H. G. Wells, Julian Huxley and G. P. Wells, *The Science of Life,* Doubleday, Doran, 1938, p. 551.

25. John Donne, *Devotions upon Emergent Occasions.*

26. Bertrand Russell, *The Conquest of Happiness,* Liveright, 1930, p. 230.

27. See F. J. Gould, *Funeral Services without Theology,* Watts, London, 1923, and Corliss Lamont, *A Humanist Funeral Service,* Horizon Press, 1954 [Prometheus Books, 1977]. Also in this connection the funeral ceremonies of the Ethical Culture Societies are well worth studying.

28. Quoted in John Morley, *Recollections,* Macmillan, 1917, Vol. II, p. 114.

29. Santayana, "Introduction" to *The Ethics of Spinoza,* Dent, London, 1925, p. xix.

Science and Spiritualism

Edward Clodd

Edward Clodd (1840-1930) lived a mysterious double life. By day he was a banker who had worked his way up the ladder from the position of clerk to that of director of the Joint Stock Bank of London. At night and in his spare hours, he was a student of the sciences, especially anthropology, and eventually he became a best-selling author of books interpreting science for laypeople. Almost completely self-taught, his writings won high praise from scientists, and he was welcomed as a colleague by many of the notables of the age, both in science and in literature. In spite of the fact that there exists both an autobiography (*Memories,* 1916) and a biography (*Edward Clodd: A Memoir,* by Joseph McCabe, 1932) of Clodd's life, neither book contains anything at all about his business career. Rather, Clodd himself talks about his famous friends, devoting a chapter to each. McCabe is more interested in Clodd's literary output, and focuses almost exclusively on that topic. The result is that we know nothing about Clodd in his banking career.

Clodd's first book was *The Childhood of the World,* published in 1873. It was a popular account of anthropology, and went through a number of editions and translations. In 1880, he published his study of Jesus (*Jesus of Nazareth*), which was more a study of what was *thought* of Jesus in early times than a biography. Clodd's *Story of Creation* (1888) was a popular interpretation of evolution. In 1906 Clodd became chairman of the Rationalist Press Association, a British organization dedicated to publishing freethought books and periodicals, while organizing nonbelievers into local groups. In 1915, at the age of seventy-five, he retired from banking. He lived nearly fifteen more years and produced several additional books (making a career total of eighteen).

The present selection comes from Clodd's only book on spiritualism. It was first published in 1917, under the ungainly title of *The Question—If a Man Die, Shall He Live Again?* The book has been out of print since the early 1920s.

"Obscurum per obscurius." Whatever we know nothing about, let us make the explanation of everything else.

Vain is the effort to persuade ourselves that no bias or prepossession determines our view of things concerning which two opinions are possible. Impartial attitude is a delusion, especially when we deal with the marvellous; "nothing," as Montaigne says, "is so firmly believed as that which is least known." Every generation, in its own way, seeketh a sign, and the spiritualists believe that a sign has been given; that the door is opened; the veil lifted; the silence of the ages broken by voices from the Beyond.

With the dawn of self-consciousness—the knowing that he knows—man reached the plane where conceptions of himself as something apart from his surroundings were possible; and, with this, hazy wonderment on his destiny. The lust of life, the impulse of the "glory of going on and still to be," possessed and has never left him: while the belief that death is not the end of man had powerful impetus from the dreams of the night and the shadows of things cast by the day. On such and like unsubstantial phenomena the fabric of belief in immortality has been raised: a fabric built on the emotions and, seemingly, as unstable as its foundations. Out of the incomprehensible has risen the illusive: specious feelings have begotten the belief that what is desired must needs have fulfillment; that "being weary proves that man has where to rest." Even the poet from whom this line is quoted, in apostrophizing his dead father, must needs speculate:

> O strong soul, by what shore
> Tarriest thou now? For that force
> Surely has not been left vain!
> Somewhere, surely, afar,
> In the sounding labor-house vast
> Of being, is practiced that strength,
> Zealous, beneficent, firm![1]

It is especially at séances that the emotions, compact as they are of fear, hope and wonder, and when undisciplined, parents of countless evils, have unchecked play. The attitude of the sitters is receptive, uncritical; exaltation of feeling strengthens the wish to believe; the power of suggestion, whose continuous influence in social evolution from a remote past cannot be over-estimated, is dominant, and the senses are prepared to see and hear what they are told. As needful today as when he gave it more than sixty years ago is Faraday's warning against the "tendency to deceive ourselves regarding all we wish for, and the necessity of resistance to those desires."[2] As with his fellow conjurer, sense-deception is the medium's chief tool, the attention and concentration of the befooled onlookers are diverted by his patter, while dim light or total darkness as essentials of his trade effect the rest. Added to these there is the fatigue which in time overcomes the power of the sense-organs to report truly. Surely one can trust one's senses: we say, seeing is believing; whereas the story of man's advance is the story of his escape from the illusions of the senses, especially when they stimulate a dominant idea or obsession. If we believed what we saw, we should hold to the error that the earth is flat and that the sun revolves round it. We still talk of sunrises and sunsets.

And there is no safety, only peril, in numbers; the medium can more easily hypnotize or hallucinate a circle. In their inquiry into Mesmer's methods the Committee laid stress on the fact that performances in which excitement and contagion have full play are more successful than private ones. There is active what M. Gustave le Bon calls "the psychological law of the mental unity of crowds," as manifest, for example, in the recurring epidemic mental disorders of history, from, to name no earlier one, the choromania or the dancing hysterics of the fourteenth century to the religious revivals of our own time.

Concerning the amazingly clever Davey, who so deceived the very elect as to obtain from them certificates as to the supernormal character of his tricks, "the feature is not," says a writer quoted by M. le Bon, "the marvellousness of the tricks themselves, but the extreme weakness of the reports made with respect to them by the noninitiated witnesses. It is clear that witnesses even in number may give circumstantial relations which are completely erroneous, but whose result is that, if their descriptions are accepted as exact, the phenomena which they describe are inexplicable by trickery."[3]

So long as man lives on this planet he will be hoaxed and hocussed. ... Shrewd Thomas Hobbes of Malmesbury—himself a timid man—says in his *Leviathan*, "the most part of men, though they have the use of Reasoning a little way, as in numbering to some degree, yet it serves them to little use in common life in which they govern themselves, some better, some worse, according to their differences of experience, quickness of memory and inclinations to severall ends."[4] Parallel with this is Herbert Spencer's remark that "men are rational beings in but a very limited sense, that conduct results from desire,"[5] and a similar comment by Dr. Henry Maudsley that "it is a plausible but quite false presumption that mankind in general act on rational principles."[6] The tendency in each one of us is to travel along the line of least resistance; the apparent solution of a problem, especially when the problem deals with matters of gravity, is welcomed, as relief from the labor of thinking and from the pain of new ideas. As Giordano Bruno said: "Ignorance is the finest science in the world, because it is acquired without labor and pains and keeps the mind free from melancholy."[7]

Hence, to quote the late Professor William James: "Our faith is faith in someone else's faith, and in the greatest matters that is most the case." Apposite to this are the lines which Henry Sidgwick composed in his sleep, or at least awoke thinking of:

> We think so, because, other people all think so,
> Or because—or because, after all, we do think so;
> Or because we were told so, and think we must think so.
> Or because we once thought so and think we still think so;
> Or because, having thought so, we think we *will* think so.[8]

A stock argument of the easy-going believers in Spiritualism is: How can we deny the genuineness of the phenomena, from raps to messages through "controls," when some eminent and learned men declare their belief in them? Writing to my wife, the distingiushed author, Eden Phillpotts, remarks: "At Birmingham the attitude towards Sir Oliver Lodge is rather amazing. He seems to be regarded as an intellectual giant at the University, which I visited. A railway foreman with whom I had a talk argued thus about Sir Oliver. He admitted that his ideas and opinions were remarkable, but, he said, 'he's a great man and wise and learned, so who are we uneducated, common men that we should think we know better than him?'" The foreman spoke for the multitude who do not and cannot discriminate: they assume that the man who can speak with unchallenged authority on the subject of which he is master is entitled to speak with the same authority of anything and everything else. "When," says Hobbes, "a man cannot assure himself of the true causes of things, he supposes causes of them, or trusteth to the Authority of other men, such as he thinks to be his friends and wiser than himself."[9] An expert in physics may be ignorant of biology and psychology; he may never have read a book on anthropology and hence remained ignorant of the invaluble material bearing on the history of Spiritualism in such classics as *Primitive Culture* and *The Golden Bough,* wherein are supplied antiseptics to Spiritualism. The physicist and the mathematician are not competent witnesses to the truth or falsity of what lies outside their province. They deal with what is exact, definite, and in unvarying relation, which begets in them a serious limitation. On the contrary, the biologist and psychologist, whose concern is with living things, are confronted with variations and exceptions which cannot be confined within any formula. Something to check any cocksureness is always manifesting itself in the phenomena which they investigate. . . .

On one of the rare occasions when that champion trickster and acutest of women, Madame Blavatsky, spoke the truth, she said: "I have not met with more than two or three men who knew how to observe and see and remark on what was going on around them. It is simply amazing! At least nine out of every ten people are entirely devoid of the capacity of observation and of the power of remembering accurately what took place even a few hours before. How often it has happened that, under my direction and revision, minutes of various occurrences and phenomena have been drawn up; lo, the most innocent and conscientious people, even skeptics, even those who actually suspected me, have signed *en toutes lettres* as witnesses at the foot of the minutes! And all the time I knew that what had happened was not in the least what was stated in the minutes."[10]

Adverse comment continues to be made on the aloofness of attitude of the larger number of scientists towards Spiritualism. In *Modern Spiritualism* the late Frank Podmore criticized with some asperity their refusal to take the thing seriously.[11]

Science knows no finality. As M. Duclaux finely said: "Because science is sure of nothing, it is always advancing." If telepathy can be proved; if the "hitherto unknown force" which Sir William Crookes assumed as the only explanation of Home's levitation and fire ordeals can be demonstrated to exist; science will welcome it as a further unveiling of the arcana of nature. Up to the present no such verification has come, and investigation, thus far, warrants no invocation of the supernormal to explain so-called "spiritual" phenomena. It is, as Hobbes wrote two hundred and sixty years ago: "Ignorance of naturall causes disposeth a man to Credulity, so as to believe many times impossibilities: For such know nothing to the contrary, but that they may be true, being unable to detect the impossibility. And Credulity, because men loved to be hearkened unto in company, disposeth them to lying, so that Ignorance itself, without Malice, is able to make a man both to believe lyes and tell them: and sometimes also to invent them."[12]

But what are the facts? The table-turning mania spread to this country in 1853, and the hold which it had on the public mind, especially when attributed to spiritual agency, caused both professional and scientific men to investigate the phenomenon. Amongst the latter Faraday took the leading part in an inquiry, the outcome of which was the conviction that the movements were due to unconscious muscular action of the hands upon the table. To prove this, he devised a very simple apparatus in the shape of two sheets of mill-board, between which he placed two glass rollers and fastened the whole with two elastic bands, an index-pointer being fixed to the apparatus to indicate whether the upper board moved on the lower one—*i.e.* whether there was pressure towards one side or the other. The upper board was freely movable upon the rods when the tips of the fingers or one or both hands were placed lightly on it. "Such a 'planchette' (as it was subsequently termed) was placed on the table beneath the fingers of each operator in a 'table-turning' experiment, and it was found that whereas in previous experiments without a planchette the table had been made to move by the hands lightly resting on it, now there was no movement of the table but a slight forward displacement, more or less conspicuous, of the upper board of the planchette as it moved on its glass rollers under the gentle pressure of the operators' fingers. In this way Faraday showed that it was possible for honest experimenters to apply unconsciously a slight push to the table, and so for their united unconscious efforts to cause it to move or turn in a manner which was to them mysterious and supernatural, whereas when their fingers were separated from the table by the mobile planchette, the 'push' in each case merely caused the upper board of that little intermediary to move instead of acting upon the table itself."[13] Complete proof of unconscious muscular action was supplied by the fact that when the sitters understood the purpose of the apparatus and kept their attention on it, no movement followed; when they looked away from it, it wobbled, though they believed that they kept it in position.

In his lecture on "Mental Education," Faraday says: "A universal objection was made to it by the table turners. It was said to paralyze the powers of the mind—but the experimenters need not see the index, they may leave their friends to watch that and their minds may revel in any power that their expectation or their imagination can confer. So restrained, a *dislike* to the trial arises, but what is that except a proof that whilst they trust themselves they doubt themselves, and are not willing to proceed to the decision, lest the trust which they like should fail them, and the doubt which they dislike rise to the authority of truth."[14]

Sir Ray Lankester adds that "By the irony of human fate, Faraday's detective 'planchette' was subsequently fitted with a pencil and used by 'occultists' to obtain writing caused by the unconscious, though sometimes conscious, direction of its movements by the hands of an inquirer lightly laid on it. Such writing was interpreted by the 'occultists' as 'messages from the spirit world.' On the other hand, 'planchette-writing' and similar experimental methods offer to the psychologist a valuable means of exploring the directive movements given unconsciously to the muscles of the body by the brain in many persons when thus subjected to properly guarded and well-devised experiment."[15] The "planchette" is still taken seriously by spiritualists. Mr. J. A. Hill, while admitting that no success attended his experiments with it, discusses its possibilities as to supernormal results.[16]

After the action brought by the widow Lyon against Home, in 1868, it transpired that Faraday had accepted an invitation from the defendant to a séance, but that Faraday had imposed conditions of investigation which Home would not accept. Little wonder therefore that, choosing his own terms, he was never detected by his dupes.

In 1864 Tyndall was present at a séance at the house of Mr. Newton Crosland, a prominent spiritualist. He tells the result in his *Fragments of Science:* "Nothing occurred which could not have been effected by fraud or accident."[17] In January, 1874, Darwin went to a séance at the house of his brother Erasmus, Mr. (afterwards Sir Francis) Galton, G. H. Lewes and "George Eliot" being also present. The notorious Williams was the medium. After describing the "fun in the dark, chairs, flutes, bells and candlesticks flying about," Darwin concludes: "The Lord have mercy on us all, if we have to believe such rubbish."[18] Huxley attended "a carefully arranged séance" at the same house. A full report of this is given in the *Life and Letters.*[19]: "My conclusion is that Mr. X is a cheat and an impostor." Huxley had already been present at several séances at the house of his brother George as early as 1852, given by Mrs. Hayden, the first medium imported from America; also at the houses of various friends, meeting mediums "by whom he was most unfavorably impressed." Hence his justification, after such sifting of the matter, for declining to join a committee of investigation promoted by the London Dialectical Society in 1869. "If anybody would endow me with the faculty of listening to the chatter of old women and curates in the nearest cathedral town, I should decline the business, having better things to do. And if the folk in the spiritual world do not talk more wisely and sensibly than their friends report them to do, I put them in the same category. The only good that I can see in the demonstration of the truth of Spiritualism is to furnish an additional argument against suicide. Better live a crossing-sweeper than die and be made to talk twaddle by a medium hired at a guinea a séance." At a sitting with Mr. Vout Peters, held on 3rd March 1916, Mr. J. A. Hill says there came this message, apparently from Raymond Lodge, through "Moonstone": "I have come into touch with Huxley." Then Moonstone says: "Who's the old man got funny whiskers? Square forehead, hair caught away here (indicating temples), nose full, clean-shaven lips, upper lip hangs over, scientific, cold. Not a man you would tell your heart troubles to. Very clever. Cold, scientific aspect. (It is fairly certain that this is meant for Huxley; the description is good, though the coldness—a popular view— is probably exaggerated.)" The words in parentheses are Mr. Hill's comment. Huxley seems to have escaped talking the "twaddle" which he dreaded. But we ask with Geronte in Molière's *Fourberies de Scapin,* "Que diable allait-il faire dans cette galère?"

In Mrs. Piper's trances "some few of the persons mentioned were obviously dream-creations. For example, an Adam Bede as well as a George Eliot[20] are alluded to as real individuals on the other side! The controls through whom Mr. Hill receives communications appear to be a spiritual democracy: at least they reach a low plane in one who says: "Now, I'm only an uneducated man—I'm owd Billy—and I can only talk Lancashire dialect, an' tha mayn't understand it." (In the flesh he was Billy Matthews.) Billy adds that he has seen Richard Hodgson, who says to him,"I've brought my old friend, Henry Sidgwick, with me."[21]

Lord Kelvin, whose attitude towards belief in the supernatural was sympathetic, said that fraud or bad observation explained belief in Spiritualism. Professor Clifford, after examination into the genuineness of the phenomena, put his conclusion with brevity: "The universe is made up of matter and motion, and there's no room for ghosts." More weighty, because of his position as the first President of the American Branch of the Society for Psychical Research, is the deliverance of the late distinguished astronomer, Simon Newcomb. "Nothing," he said, "has been brought out by the research of that Society and its able collaborators except what we should expect to find in the ordinary course of nature."[22] Mr. Podmore says that in the fifteen years which have elapsed since, in 1882, Professor Henry Sidgwick, in his Address to the Society for Psychical Research, felt warranted in assuming that a mass of evidence to justify impartial examination would be forthcoming, the hope has not been realized. "While few opportunities have been afforded to the Society's representatives for continuous investigation of any sort, no positive results have been obtained worthy of record. All spiritualist manifestations appear indeed to have become less frequent, not only in private circles, but with professional mediums. The Spiritualist papers no longer teem with records of marvellous séances. There has been little to encourage the Society to investigate the performances of professional mediums."[23] Its main service has been, as Mr. Haynes says, "to extend the region of experimental psychology,"[24] and to make evident that the mind is of far more complex nature than had been suspected.

Save in raps and in table-tiltings and leapings, the decline in the presentment of the physical group of phenomena is continuous, and there is even a slump in materialization and spirit photographs. Evidence, if it deserves the name, centers more upon communications from the departed through a control. The change is one for which spiritualists are coy at giving an explanation.

No eminent man of science since Huxley has dwelt more insistently on the limitation of human faculties and on the insoluble eternal problem of the Why, the Whence, and the Whither than Sir Ray Lankester. In an essay on "Science and the Unknown," he demands that all the reputed marvels of Spiritualism shall be brought before the bar of science for examination and testing.

> Lovers of science have never been unwilling to investigate such marvels if fairly and squarely brought before them. In the very few cases which have been submitted in this way to scientific examination, the marvel has been shown to be either childish fraud or a mere conjurer's trick, or else the facts adduced in evidence have proved to be entirely insufficient to support the conclusion that there is anything unusual at work or beyond the experience of scientific investigators.

It is unfortunately true that most persons are quite unprepared to admit the deficiencies of their own powers of observation and memory, and are also unaware of their own ignorance of perfectly natural occurrences which continually lead to self-deception and illusion. Moreover, the capacity for logical inference and argument is not common. The whole past and present history of what is called "the occult" is enveloped in an atmosphere of self-deception and of readiness to be deceived by others to which misplaced confidence in their own cleverness and power of detecting trickery renders many—one may almost say most—people victims.[25]

Sir H. B. Donkin has had considerable experience of many mediums, and speaks with the authority of a mental pathologist of the first rank when, as already cited, he contends that the demonstrative value claimed for the conclusions in *Raymond* as proved "rests upon nothing but assertion."

This is cogently emphasizèd by the eminent neuropathologist Dr. Charles Mercier, in an article on "Sir Oliver Lodge and the Scientific World" in the *Hibbert Journal* of July, 1917. He says that "it is not for the scientific world, or for anyone else, to disprove Sir Oliver Lodge's assertions, his doctrines, his interpretations, or his facts. The *onus is on him to prove them.* He is to bring forward evidence of fact, not of interpretation of fact; and if he asks us to accept his interpretations, *they must be of such a nature that no other interpretation can be placed upon the fact.* As long as his facts are susceptible to interpretation by the operation of natural laws, he has no right to ask us to follow him in supposing that they are supernatural. As long as he offers us interpretation of fact in the place of fact, he is not entitled even to a hearing. As long as his facts are observed only by himself or by those who have already avowed their desire to interpret them in a certain way, he has no right to ask us to accept them as indisputable."[26]

This irrefragable argument was anticipated by Faraday. He says "that the asserter of any new thing has no right to claim an answer in the form of *Yes* or *No,* or think, because none is forthcoming, that he is to be considered as having established his assertion. So much is unknown to the wisest man that he may often be without an answer; as frequently he is so, because the subject is in the region of hypothesis, and not of facts. In either case he has the right to refuse to speak. I cannot tell whether there are two fluids of electricity or any fluid at all. I am not bound to explain how a table tilts any more than to indicate how, under the conjurer's hands, a pudding appears in a hat. The means are not known to me. I am persuaded that the results, however strange they may appear, are in accordance with that which is truly known, and, if carefully investigated, would justify the well-tried laws of nature. . . . Let those who affirm the exception to the general laws of nature, or those others who, upon the affirmation accept the result, work out the experimental proof."[27]. . .

[In an article entitled "Thought-reader" by Mr. Stuart Cumberland in

The Daily Mail of 5th January 1917, he writes] "In a word, I have never yet in any land or with any medium or adept discovered any alleged occult manifestation that was not explicable upon a perfectly natural basis and which in the majority of instances could not be humanly duplicated under precisely similar conditions. This, as the true believer would say, has been my misfortune. But there it is. So inherent is this hankering after the supernatural in human nature that many would much rather seek for a supernatural than a natural explanation of what may seem mysterious or out of the way to them.

"It is just this longing in human nature upon which these professional psychic frauds are preying today.

"Today, with its heavy death toll and fateful uncertainty so closely affecting every section of the community, is indeed the moment for the practitioners on the shady side of spiritism. There is a natural desire among the bereaved, or those in doubt as to the actual facts surrounding the 'missing,' to seek for news and guidance unobtainable through the ordinary channels. These credulous folk are told that this or that medium is a real wonder, who has given such and such a person the most astounding revelations. So what has been vouchsafed others can quite as well be revealed to them. Hence the run upon the plausible 'crooks,' who so readily trade upon their credulity.

"The foolish, credulous dupes never for a moment consider the utter incongruousness of the association of their beloved dead or missing with these professional 'spookists.' It never enters their heads that if the spirit of anyone dear to them could return at all, it would be to them direct that his return would be manifested, and that to have to go to some strange 'crook' and part with money for the privilege of being put in touch with the spirit is the height of absurdity. They are told that they themselves are not *mediumistic,* and that it is only through the truly *mediumistic* that such communications are possible. Besides, it is the fashion of 'the thing' to go to these mediums, who, 'poor dears,' must live and who are entitled to payment for the exhaustion they frequently undergo in getting in touch with the spirits. No laborer, in fact, is so worthy of his hire as one in the spiritual vineyard.

"And the wine he presses, as he rakes in the notes, is the flow of tears from the sorrowful and distressed.

"It is not only a shady business, but it is a mean and cruel one and should be put an end to. If the foolish cannot or will not protect themselves, they must be protected against their own folly."

"Again and again," writes Dr. Furness, "mediums have led round the circles the materialized spirits of their wives and introduced them to each visitor in turn. Fathers have taken round their daughters, and I have seen widows sob in the arms of their dead husbands. Testimony such as this staggers me. Have I been smitten with color-blindness? Before me, as far as I can detect, stands the very medium herself, in shape, size, form and feature true to a line, and yet, one after another, honest men and women at my side, within ten minutes of each other, assert that she is the absolute counterpart of their nearest and dearest friend; nay, that she *is* that friend."[28]

Sir Oliver Lodge cautions the bereaved against devoting so large a portion of time and attention as he has given in setting and recording communications from the spirit world. He bids them accept his assurance—he settles once and for all by an *ipse dixit* the momentous question—that those who have departed this life "are still active and useful and interested and happy—more alive than ever in one sense—and to make up their minds to live a useful life until they rejoin them."[29]

Bowed down with grief and clutching, like drowning men, at straws, these mourners, while respecting Sir Oliver's precept, will hasten, if their purses permit, to follow his example. They will desire to be themselves assured that those who have departed this life can confirm what he says. Hence no caution that he can give can lessen his unenvied responsibility in causing a rush of sorrowing parents and relatives to mediums, preferably to the woman through whom he sought news from his dead son. Mrs. Leonard and the rest of them will bless his name for the harvest of fees thereby reaped. Bookings "in advance" are reported by the newspapers as active. . . .

This assumption of unbroken relations between soul and body is one of several points on which Spiritualism is in conflict with orthodox teaching, although this is vague enough as to the state and location of the soul between death and resurrection. With an ingenuity which has never failed it, the Roman Catholic Church solves the difficulty by putting the soul in purgatory. In what mental muddle a Protestant Doctor of Divinity plunges himself has example in an answer to the problem given by the Rev. Professor David Smith to a correspondent in *The British Weekly* of the 18th January 1917. "We shall not," he assures his querist, "lack embodiment in the Hereafter. There awaits us a nobler vesture, 'a habitation built by God, a house not made with hands, eternal in the heavens.' This is the resurrection-body, 'a spiritual body (*cf.* 1 Cor. xv. 44) fashioned like unto our Lord's glorious body' (Phil. iii. 21). The comfort, however, is only partial, or, rather, it is ultimate and not immediate. For it is at the Second Advent that the dead will be raised incorruptible (1 Thess. iv. 16), and meanwhile their souls must remain naked, divested of their earthly tent-dwelling, and yet unclothed with their 'habitation from heaven.'. . . Here then lies the comfort of the Christian revelation of the resurrection of the body. It is our assurance that heaven will be no cheerless world of unsubstantial ghosts, but a kindly and homely scene where we shall meet in the fullness of an ennobled humanity and resume the old affections with a deeper and warmer intimacy."

.   .   .

Dwelling for a moment on the overwhelming feeling aroused in the presence of the revelations of astronomy, especially in their correction of the geocentric theory in which the sun was conceived of as an appendage to the earth, and the stars as a subordinate detail—"He made the stars also"[30]—we find in spiritistic teaching a survival of the anthropocentric theory. This, as is well known, had an ardent exponent in the late Dr. Alfred Russel Wallace and, implicitly, has support from Sir Oliver Lodge, who sees in each of the temporary occupants of this speck, one of others as the sand of the seashore innumerable, "an infinite worth and vital importance." It may be so; we know not; in this, as in all the problems that confront us "we may handle the veil as much as we please; but we cannot raise it."[31]

It involves no small stretch of the imagination to envisage a procession of millions upon millions of individuals of such "infinite worth and vital importance," from the semi-brutal, proto-human ancestors to the noblest specimen of *Homo sapiens,* pouring in continuous stream from an ageless past to an eternal future under conditions where, in Sir Oliver's words, "they are more alive than ever," each one of these myriads—for there can be no exceptions—remaining in touch with earth. Each one: the myriad babes who opened their eyes here only to close them in death; the aged gathered as "shocks of corn, fully ripe"; the idiots; the lunatics; the crippled; the untold hecatombs of the slain, the starved, the tortured; the eaters and the eaten—victims of ruthlessness and rapine; awakening the reflection whether human existence has not been more a curse than a blessing in this tear-stained, blood-soaked world. Mingled with that motley crowd, "in that equal sky," so Raymond tells us, for himself and others, are their "faithful dogs to bear them company." This is confirmed by no less an authority than "Owd Billy," who communicates through a medium, Tom Tyrrell, that "the lower brute creation passes into spirit life, same as us."[32] . . .

. . . For myself, the only heaven for which I might indulge desire is renewal of communion with those who have been, and who are, dear to me in this life—if this is not to be, then grant me "a right long, endless, and unawakening sleep."[33]

Certainly one result of the nauseous communications dredged from the subconsciousness of mediums in feigned or genuine trance cannot be the revival of interest in the minds of the thoughtful concerning a future life, an interest which, among such, is waning to vanishing point. Happily the void thereby created is filled by the sense of obligation to the past, of duty to the present, and of responsibility to the future; of realization of the conditions under which we live and which are not of our seeking. But whatever their cause, they supply opportunity for service to, and advancement of, the humanity of which we are parts, and whose joys and sorrows it is our destiny to share.

It may even, as the sense of these responsibilities grows, be incumbent to combat actively a "belief which may easily become an unhealthy occupation, preventing us seeking our salvation here"[34]: a belief against which Sir J. G. Frazer brings this powerful, this true indictment:

"It might with some show of reason be maintained that no belief has done so much to retard the economic and thereby the social progress of mankind as the belief in the immortality of the soul, for this belief has led race after race, generation after generation, to sacrifice the real wants of the living to the imaginary wants of the dead. The waste and destruction of life and property which this faith has entailed are enormous and incalculable . . . disastrous and deplorable, unspeakable the follies and crimes and miseries which have flowed in practice from the theory of a future life."[35]

It should be needless to disclaim that any charge against the integrity of Sir Oliver Lodge and his fellow-spiritualists is made in the animadversions passed on their credulity in these pages. But when he affirms "I am as convinced of continued existence on the other side of death as I am of existence here. It may be said, you cannot be as sure as you are of sensory experience, I say I can,"[36] such plainness of speech must be met by equal plainness.

You, Sir Oliver, knowing, as you must have known, the taint which permeates the early history of Spiritualism, its inception in fraud and the detection of a succession of tricksters from the Fox girls onwards, and thereby cautioned to be on your guard, have proved yourself, on your own admission, incompetent to detect the frauds of Eusapia Palladino. You and Sir William Barrett, who says that "there *is* evidence of his supernormal knowledge,"[37] accept and quote, as parts of a "new revelation," from the automatic writings of the Rev. Stainton Moses. Your faith in the integrity of Mrs. Piper, despite her failure, crowned by her confession, withdrawn, it is true, but none the less a fact, remains unshaken. You lose a dear son in the holiest of causes for which a man can die; you forthwith repair to a modern Witch of Endor to seek, at second hand, consolations which assuredly he whom you mourn would, in preference, pour direct into your attuned and sympathetic ear; you—one of the most prominent and best known of men—are simple enough to believe that your anonymity and that of your wife and family was secure at the early séances which Mrs. Leonard and Mr. Vout Peters gave you. And with what dire result—the publication of a series of spurious communications, a large portion of which is mischievous drivel, dragging with it into the mire whatever lofty conceptions of a spiritual world have been framed by mortals.

What is more serious, your maleficent influence gives impetus to the recrudescence of superstition which is so deplorable a feature of these days. The difference between the mediums whom you consult and the lower grade of fortune-tellers who are had up and fined or imprisoned as rogues and vagabonds is one of degree, not of kind. The sellers of the thousands of mascots—credulity in which as life-preservers and luck-bringers is genuine—

the palmists, and all other professors of the occult, have in you their unacknowledged patron.

Thus you, who have achieved high rank as a physicist, descend to the plane of the savage animist, surrendering the substance for the shadow. Surely the mysteries which in your physical researches meet you at every turn, baffling your skill to penetrate, should make you pause ere you accept the specious solutions of the momentous problems which lie on the threshold of the Unknown Hereafter.

You, and those who credit you and other notable men of science as speaking with authority, will not be shaken in your convictions; but there may be some who, through reading these pages, will agree that when—it may be, I fear, in no near future—the ghost of Spiritualism is laid its epitaph should be:

BEHOLD, I WAS SHAPEN IN INIQUITY
AND IN SIN DID MY MOTHER CONCEIVE ME.

The Question may be, and should be, asked: Granted that the evidence which the spiritualists adduce in support of their belief be of a nature which cannot be submitted to the conditions of observation, experiment and proof required by science, are there not materials by which it may arrive at some undogmatic conclusion as to soul-survival? There are, and these are supplied by comparative psychology: the science of mind.

Comparative anatomy has demonstrated the fact of correspondence of bodily structure, bone for bone, muscle for muscle, nerve for nerve, between the highest mammals and man; his fundamental relationship to the anthropoid apes being further proven by the fact that the same kind of blood flows through the veins of the two. And comparative psychology has proved that there is no break in the chain of mental evolution. "The development of the mind in its early stages is revealed most adequately in the animal."[38] There are not two processes of evolution, one of the body and the other of the mind; there is only one process in one series of graduated stages; hence the history of the evolution of brain and nerve is also the history of the evolution of mind.[39] And it is in the evolution of the brain that the mammals have scored; man, as the "roof and crown" of all living things, thereby securing that lordship in the animal realm of which he has made terrible abuse. His dumb subjects, could they have faculty of human speech, would curse that dominance.

This proof of physical continuity, that ardent and most credulous dupe of mediums, Dr. Alfred Russel Wallace, disputed. His conception of the denizens of the Beyond excluded animals: "No ravenous beast shall go up thereon; it shall not be found there." Co-formulator with Darwin of the doctrine of natural selection, he argued that it did not explain the origin of man's spiritual and intellectual nature which, he contended, must have had another origin, an adequate cause to be found only "in the Unseen Universe of Spirit." The question, which he did not attempt to answer follows:—At what stage in man's evolution was this "spiritual essence of nature" superadded?[40] Was it, once and for all, in the proto-human creatures who represent both apes and men, being a blend of both ere their divergence from a common ancestor; or is there a special creation of the soul in every human being at birth? To put the question is to submit a problem the solution of which rests with its propounders.

To Job's question, "If a man shall die, shall he live again?" science can answer neither "yes" nor "no"; all that can be said is that the evidence supplied by comparative psychology does not support the belief in a future life. It leaves it unsolved.

> Into this Universe and *Why* not knowing,
> Not *Whence*, like Water willy-nilly flowing:
> And out of it, as Wind along the waste,
> I know not *Whither,* willy-nilly blowing.

One fact is clear: there has been no evidence in ideas of the soul, and advance in knowledge of the conditions of existence in any after life, from the dawn of thought to the present day. Spiritualism is the old animism "writ large."

NOTES

1. *Rugby Chapel.* By Matthew Arnold.
2. *Science and Education*, p. 50.
3. *"Annales de Science Psychique." The Crowd,* p. 49. By G. le Bon.
4. *Leviathan,* Part 1., chapter v., p. 31. (Oxford, 1881. Reprint of the first edition.)
5. *Autobiography.* Vol. ii., ,p. 366.
6. *Natural Causes and Supernatural Seemings,* p. 65.
7. *Giordano Bruno.* By W. Boulton.
8. *Henry Sidgwick: a Memoir,* p. 124.
9. *Leviathan,* Part I., chapter xii., p. 79.
10. *A Modern Priestess of Isis,* p. 156. By V. S. Solovyoff. Translated by Walter Leaf. (1895.)
11. *Modern Spiritualism.* Vol. ii., p. 145.
12. *Leviathan,* Part I., chap. ii., p. 77.
13. *Science and Education,* p. 69.

14. *Ibid.*, p. 51.

15. *Ibid.*, p. 69.

16. *Psychical Investigations*, p. 221.

17. Pp. 314-322.

18. *Life and Letters.* Vol. iii., p. 187.

19. Vol. i., pp. 419, 420.

20. *Psychical Investigations*, p. 208. By J. A. Hill.

21. Ibid., p. 145.

22. *Nineteenth Century*, January, 1909, p. 139.

23. *Studies in Psychical Research*, p. 83.

24. *The Belief in Personal Immortality*, p. 108. An admirable treatise, compendious and adequate.

25. *Diversions of a Naturalist*, p. 364.

26. P. 613. And see Dr. Mercier's *Spiritualism and Sir Oliver Lodge*, pp. 59, 131.

27. *Science and Education*, pp. 61, 62.

28. *Fact and Fable in Psychology*, p. 163. By Joseph Jastrow.

29. *Raymond*, p. 342.

30. Genesis i. 16.

31. *Freethinking and Plain Speaking*, p. 157. By Sir Leslie Stephen.

32. *Psychical Investigations*, p. 147.

33. Moschus: *Lament for Bion*, idyll iii.

34. *Evolution of Religion.* Vol. ii., p. 243. By Edward Caird.

35. *Psyche's Task*, p. 52.

36. *Raymond*, p. 375.

37. *Psychical Research*, p. 227.

38. *Story of the Mind*, p. 35. By Prof. Baldwin.

39. "The power of building up appropriate cerebral mechanism in response to individual experience on what may be called 'educability' is the quality which characterizes the larger cerebrum and is that which has led to its selection, survival and further increase in volume."—Sir Ray Lankester's *The Kingdom of Man*, p. 123.

40. *Darwinism*, p. 474.

Review of Popular Arguments

Robert Cooper

Robert Cooper (1819-1868) was born near Manchester, England. As the son of a political radical, Cooper made the acquaintance of many of the radicals of his day when he was still a child. At the age of fourteen he became a teacher and an assistant to the elderly Robert Owen, the Socialist. Soon Cooper was delivering Socialist lectures of his own. Four years later, he had his first pamphlet (on original sin) published. His *The Holy Scriptures Analyzed* was published when he was just twenty. Over the years that followed, he was to continue his critical analysis of the Bible, a theme that runs through many of his publications.

After several years as a Owenite lecturer, he went to London as a freethought lecturer and editor of the freethought magazine *The London Investigator*. His health began to fail, and more than once he collapsed on the lecture platform. He was forced to abandon his public speaking in 1858. Fortunately, at about that time he was the beneficiary of a large legacy (probably the one that was originally to go to Charles Southwell). He lived fairly quietly until his death in 1868. Cooper's major work was the book *The Infidel's* [later *The Inquirer's*] *Text-Book,* a work that enjoyed considerable popularity among freethinkers in the nineteenth century.

The present selection comes from Cooper's work on *The Immortality of the Soul, Religiously and Philosophically Considered,* first published in London in 1852. It had been originally delivered as a series of lectures. It was reprinted once in an American edition in the 1860s, and has been out of print since then.

Friends,—On this occasion it is our pleasing duty to consider the more able and popular arguments usually adduced by theologians in favor of the immortality of the soul. Those having reference more particularly to spiritualism *versus* materialism we shall notice in subsequent lectures, when debating that question. . . .

Probably the most esteemed position in favor of immortality is the following:—"It accords with the fondest hopes and wishes of man; and God would never have implanted in us a desire so predominant, were it not ultimately to be gratified." I reply, it is by no means curious that such a view should be enforced, for, if life is a pleasure, it is far from astonishing that men would wish to prolong that pleasure. But because we *desire* an object, are we *therefore* to infer, as rational beings, that our inclinations will be realized? By what canon of logic are we warranted in affirming that an event cannot fail to happen because we *desire* it? Are our anticipations to be taken as a measure of reality—our hopes as a criterion of fact? As an *argument,* the question amounts simply to this—"All men *desire* to live for ever, therefore they *will* live for ever." I have heard of "jumping to conclusions," but this exceeds anything on record. If we take an illustration, its gross fallacy will be palpable. The desire to become *rich* is a strong feeling in every human breast. *Therefore* every human being will some day be rich. I might with great propriety maintain that this desire "accords with the fondest hopes and wishes of man; and God would never have implanted in us a desire so predominant, unless it were ultimately to be gratified." The argument is a parallel one, and equally conclusive and legitimate. . . . The skeptic, it is alleged, deprived of the cheering hope of a future life, desires to be annihilated. Very well. May not *he* conclude, from his desire, that he *will* be annihilated, as the Christian, from *his* desire, that he will live for ever? If "desire" be a test in one case, it is in both. Allowing for a moment such a nonentity as the soul to exist, we know that man seeks the everlasting vigor of his *body.* Nevertheless, that desire, "powerful and predominant" though it be, is frustrated. Why, therefore, should not the illusive hope for the eternity of the *soul* be frustrated too? The sophistry of this favorite argument is so transparent I need not pursue it further.

We are told, however, that the doctrine of the immortality of the soul is a "consoling" one. "Though it *may* be a delusion, it is a pleasing one. Is it not a blessing to man to believe that he will enjoy hereafter that happiness which is denied him upon earth?" I submit nothing can be a permanent blessing to mankind which is not true. It is the *truth,* and not the *comfort,* of the doctrine we are combatting. Would it not be wiser to fortify yourselves with the stern realities of fact, rather than delude your imaginations with the empty dreams of conjecture? Which course would be the most noble and useful? Which the best calculated to secure the *real* happiness of mankind? I am sincerely of opinion that this belief, instead of being a blessing, has been a *curse* to the human family, inasmuch as it has induced the mass of mankind to remain content with the miseries and oppressions around them, under the vain promise of continuous joy in a world to come. By thus cajoling the masses into apathy and ignorance, popular liberty, enlightenment, and prosperity have been impeded, and this beautiful world of ours enslaved by tyrants and impostors. But more of this anon. It must not be forgotten that there are two sides to this question. If heaven be "inviting," hell, I apprehend, is *rather* "uninviting." Heaven, too, is very difficult, and hell very easy to be merited. The way to the latter is "broad and open"— any person can find that—in the dark, I suppose; but the road to the former is "straight and narrow, and few there be that find it." Probabilities, therefore— a million to one—are that you will get on the *wrong* road. Surely *that* is not very "consoling." Why is it, if this doctrine be so delightful, it is not taken advantage of more promptly? Even the ultra-orthodox are loathe to leave this world for a "better." They always manage to remain in this "vale of tears" as long as practicable. They seem determined to stay on the *sure* side of the hedge as long as they can, placing less reliance on their pet dogma than the good old Saxon maxim that "a bird in the hand is worth two in the *bush.*" The religious community, indeed, give an emphatic negative to this argument every moment of their lives. Instead of offering a premium for the most "express" mode of celestial locomotion, they all seem to entertain an "inward" *doubt* which induces them to have a "longing," not after immortality in a *future* state, but to remain amongst "the pomps and vanities of this wicked world," to the latest possible date.

We now pass to other arguments. A very popular position in confirmation of the doctrine of futurity is, that "it is *necessary* to correct the inequalities of this." Theologians declare that "virtue is not always rewarded and vice punished in this world, and, therefore, there *must* be a future life of rewards and punishments, where the good will meet with their due reward, and the wicked their full punishment." What! because Deity cannot or will not reward virtue and punish vice sufficiently in this world, is that any assurance that he can or will do so in a world to come? Because he allows *injustice* to be perpetrated here, is that a security that he would permit *justice* only to be administered hereafter? If the orthodox are so "impious" as to assert that he fails to see justice rewarded in this life, I dare be so audacious to aver that he would fail to see it enforced in any other. Christians, in their ordinary transactions, act on the very opposite principle. If a man is dishonest on one occasion, they believe he will be dishonest on another. They do not consider that *because* he is a rogue today, that *therefore* he will be an honest man tomorrow. The argument of the unequal distribution of happiness proves too much. It shows that the *brute* creation ought to have a heaven as well as ourselves. There are as great inequalities—as unequal a distribution of happiness amongst them, when compared with each other, as amongst men.

Who will venture to pronounce that *they* have a longing after immortality? Eternal rewards and punishments, instead of "correcting" these discrepancies, enhance their disparity most immeasurably. It would inflict *everlasting* punishment for *temporary* error, and confers endless favor, not so much for an uniformly steady career of practical virtue and usefulness, as mere doctrinal and equivocal belief—and that, too, when avowed only at the eleventh hour, upon the bed of death, or on the steps of the gallows. . . .

We beg your attention to an argument very convenient for those who are unwilling or incompetent to *reason*. "Never mind your skepticism or your logic," they say. "I *feel* something here that tells me I shall live in another and a better world. It is the divinity that stirs within us." Condescending to notice such rant, I need only rejoin, "Never mind your orthodoxy and your faith, your Bible and your priest. I *feel* something here that tells me I shall"—*not*. One argument is just as legitimate as the other. They both prove the same thing—*nothing*. The *argumentum ad hominem* is usually suicidal. It cuts both ways.

"The very circumstances," it is confidently put, "of man conceiving of a future state, is an evidence in its favor. Where did the idea come from if it be not true?" The very circumstances of man *not* conceiving of a future state, I might argue, was an evidence *against* it. The truth is, it is no testimony either way. The mere fact of a man imagining or believing in a thing, is no proof at all of its authenticity, or *vice versa*. Reasoning of this kind would demonstrate every exploded absurdity to be correct. The circumstances of man conceiving of witchcraft, alchemy, astrology, etc., is an evidence of their "truth!" Nay, if this popular argument be conclusive, there can be NO error in the world, because every one has an "idea" upon some subject; and if it be true *because* he entertains it, there is an end to all doubt or discussion. Some parties have an idea there is only *one* God, others *three*, and yet *both are right!* Theologians are strange logicians! I might retort, I have the idea there is nothing but matter in existence. Quoting our opponents' own words, "Where did the idea come from if it be not true?"

The Rev. J. Aldis, in his able lecture on the Immortality of the Soul, states the following as a strong position against the skeptic: "The infidel adduces no *positive* proof in refutation of the doctrine of a future state—that is, he does not *know* man will *not* live again." The position is equally effective against the other side. The reverend gentleman and his brethren adduce no "positive" proof in *favor* of immortality—that is, they do not *know* they *will* live again. With them, indeed, it is mere faith, belief, hope, however amiable and sincere. Not so the skeptic; he is supported by the universal experience of mankind. All *know* this—that when the organization of a human being is decomposed, we never see him again *in propria persona*. To say I must wait till I am dead and *then* I shall behold him, is only asking me to wait till my eyes are destroyed and then I shall *see*, my tongue and then I shall *speak,* my legs and then I shall *walk!* When the world is turned "upside down," when black means white, fact fiction—when everything means exactly what it does *not* mean, I may endorse such "reasoning"—not *till* then.

Our reverend opponent remarks, with an air of dogmatism characteristic of his order, "till proof, *demonstrative* proof, can be adduced that this hope is futile, it is madness to surrender it." I reply, "till proof, *demonstrative* proof," can be adduced that this hope is well founded, it is mere folly to cherish it. What stronger indication in a rational being of mental weakness than to foster a hope, however pleasing, that cannot be shown to be dependent upon fact or reality? Let it be remembered that the *onus probandi* lies with my opponent, and those who think with him. It is for the Christian to *prove,* *"demonstrably* prove," the doctrine of immortality is true, before he can justly call upon the skeptic to accept it.

"Curiosity of man after remote things," is another highly popular argument. The celebrated professor, Dugald Stewart, seemed very partial to it. It is thus developed. "If man was intended only to be an inhabitant of this globe, and if the principle of curiosity was bestowed on him only in subserviency to his accommodation here, whence is it that he is, in general, led to inquire more anxiously about distant and singular phenomena than about those which, from their nearness and frequency, we should expect to be the most interesting?" Unfortunately this reasoning is not based upon truth. It is not a fact that man takes more interest in distant than in proximate objects. What is the real state of the case? How is it in the scientific world. The great majority of our illustrious countrymen are interesting themselves in what concerns *this* world—geology, chemistry, zoology, natural philosophy, mechanics, etc. And what of *ordinary* life? People manifest the most intense interest in things immediately around them, especially if they can get a *profit* by it. All eyes are open to catch what they can, and let the rest go to the wall. It is only when individuals cannot get what they want in *this* world that they become anxious to "emigrate" to *another.* The clergy may act, or rather, *profess* to act, upon this philosophy, but even they, while they pretend to take such solemn interest in things *above*—"distant"—keep a sharp eye to what is around them. Their first "curiosity" is to procure a good fat living. What *may* be "hereafter" is an *after* consideration. Curiosity in relation to objects immediate or remote is no proof of immortality. Because man is curious to know his destiny after death, are we thence to conclude that he *will* know. An inference more gratuitous and unwarrantable from such premises could not be conceived, and unless such a conclusion be drawn the argument is irrelevant. . . .

We are informed that it is "contrary to divine wisdom and goodness to suppose that good men will be annihilated, when, by close and deep study for seventy or eighty years the mind has treasured up vast stores of knowledge and virtue." I reply, that if "divine wisdom and goodness" are to be the standard of *truth*, the theologian will not improve his ground; for why is it, if there be *infinite* intelligence and power regulating our destiny, it should be so ordained that a human being should be taken from amongst us *at all*, much less at the very period when his "knowledge and wisdom" would be of the greatest service to his fellow man? To chide me, and say I ought not to institute such inquiries—that God's ways are not our ways, etc.— is only to rule that we ought not to form *any* judgment of the "wisdom and goodness" of the deity, and that thus the orthodox stultify themselves. It is only begging the question to introduce such an agrument in reply to the skeptic, as it is assuming, as the basis of your reasoning, the influence of a power which is equally questioned by him.

The remainder of the time allowed us must be devoted to the consideration of unquestionably the most popular argument now current in theological literature. *Why* it should be so esteemed I cannot understand. Its fallacy is singularly apparent. "An opinion," reasons Dr. Dick and other divines, "so generally accredited in all countries and in all ages, *must* be true. It is morally *impossible* to be a delusion. The universality and antiquity of the belief is pronounced irrefragable. We submit, however, without hesitation, that the universality of an opinion does not necessarily establish its validity. In the most absolute sense may it be universal, and yet erroneous. History affords abundant instances in confirmation of this view. The trite example of the solar system is a case in point. Prior to the era of Pythagoras, the impression that the earth was flat, and a fixture, was "generally accredited in all ages and all countries." *Yet it was fallacious.* How absurd it would have been for the Grecian priesthood to have met the science of the illustrious sage by stating—"Sir, the belief that this earth is flat is generaly accredited in all ages and all countries, and therefore must be true." Pythagoras would have smiled at their simplicity, as did Galileo before our modern inquisition. The argument of universality and antiquity has been propounded in support of every exploded fallacy, both in science and theology. If legitimate, it would demonstrate the existence of witches, sorcerers, alchemy, astrology, and all phases of delusion and imposture that, in various epochs of development, have deluded the human mind. Antecedent to the Reformation, belief in the infallibility of the pope was "universal" in Christendom. Was it *therefore* true? Was Luther silenced by such reasoning? . . . Why, then, should the skeptic be content with similar fallacies?

. . . Though Moses is said to have been inspired, he makes no reference to a doctrine deemed so valuable. Bishop Warburton, a very orthodox prelate, shows that a future state of rewards and punishments is not taught in the whole of the Pentateuch. Similar admissions are made by Ensor, Wilkins, Tillotson, Geddes, and other eminent divines. How strange that the *"chosen people"* of Deity should have been uninformed upon a tenet declared to be so essential to the eternal welfare of mankind! The punishments Moses held out were not "everlasting damnation," but to "visit the sins of the father upon the children to the third and fourth generation." His remarks were simply such as "their corn and their wine shall abound." His rewards and punishments, indeed, were merely *temporal.* Very strange is it that heaven, through its vicegerent, should be so emphatic in warning the Jews against temporal dangers, and not against those infinitely more serious in a world to come, *if such a world really existed.* The Jews, during their captivity at Babylon, heard for the first time of this fashionable creed. Zoroaster, the founder of the Chaldaic philosophy, had long enunciated it. But even *then* the whole of the Jews did not accept it. On their deliverance, they were divided into two great sects—the Pharisees and the Sadducees. The former endorsed, and the latter ignored it. The Sadducees, who *denied* the doctrine, were the "real original" Hebrews—the true followers of Moses. They took the *Pentateuch* only to be the genuine word of God, rejecting the rest of the books as spurious. It was *because* Moses did *not* teach a future state that they rejected it.

It is to no avail to assert that, in other writings of the Old Testament, passages can be found confirming a futurity. Did *Moses* teach it, the authorized lawgiver of the "chosen people"? As I have stated, the primitive Jews considered that *he* alone was inspired. Moreover, there is no contemporary evidence to establish the fact that the remainder of the books of the Hebrew Bible were known before the captivity in Babylon, where the Jews became acquainted with the immortality of the soul. This event occurred only some 350 years before Christ, and upwards of 1100 *after* Moses. Allowing these writings to be genuine, they are far from conclusive on the subject. Solomon, the "wisest" of his age, expressed great contempt for the doctrine. In Ecclesiastes, chap. iii., he asks, almost in the language of the modern skeptic, "*Who* knoweth of the spirit of man that goeth upwards, and the spirit of man that goeth downwards to the earth? Wherefore, I perceive that *there is nothing better than that a man should rejoice in his own works, for that is his portion:* for who shall bring him to see what shall be after him?" This is precisely the philosophy of the secularist of our own day. Solomon, to render the matter above all doubt, emphatically affirms that "a man hath no pre-eminence above a beast"—"as the one dieth, so dieth the other"—"all go unto one place, all are of the dust, and all turn to dust again." Had *I* so expressed myself, no terms too offensive could have been hurled against me. Even David, in Psalm xlix., v. 12, avers that man "is like the beasts that perish." And again in Psalm cxlvi., v. 4, he declares that on the "very day man goeth to the grave his thoughts *perish!*"

Perhaps the most significant circumstance connected with our present dispute is, that though our modern Christian speaks with such pride and exultation of the "spirit" living for ever, *even some of the early Christians did not believe in immaterialism.* They were decided materialists. Tertullian, Jerome, Justin, and others were among this class. Though the Platonic notions of immortality were introduced amongst Christians at an early date, it was not till the year 249 that the immaterialists became predominant. I find that about this period they succeeded in condemning, at an Arabian council, some Christians as heretics "who maintained that the souls of men perished with their bodies." It was not, however, till the middle of the *sixth* century that the final adoption of Platonism *as a leading and fundamental doctrine* of Christianity took place. Gregory the Great ascended the papal chair. This learned pontiff, highly ambitious, and desirous of rendering the see of Rome independent of the civil power, clearly saw the advantage of giving prominence to such views. The revenues of the church were extremely low. Hence he decreed that the living should pray, and *pay,* for the souls of the dead, making remission for their sins by *purchasing* their expiation.

My friends, I have long been firmly of opinion that the dogmas of theology were first established by the clergy, and subsequently upheld by them in order to promote the supremacy and emoluments of their order. The above fact confirms it. The priesthood of all ages have told the multitude that they are a body of men set apart by Providence to prepare our depraved and miserable souls for "another and a better world." . . .

Part Five

Debates and Dialogues on Unbelief

Introduction

A debate is an attempt to expose an audience to the best arguments on both sides of an issue, and to challenge the arguments put forth by one side with those of the other, or to expose logical gaps or fallacies in each side's statements. As might be expected, there have been many debates between believers and nonbelievers in God or religion. Some of these debates have been in writing over several issues of a publication or journal, while others have taken place before a live audience, and still others have been conducted as interviews on radio or television.

The basic differences between atheists and theists are not going to be resolved in favor of either party, or for the vast majority of their audiences, merely because each side has set forth a number of points in its own behalf. From personal experience as a debater on these topics, I can assure you that the best one can hope for is to initiate some thought processes in all participants. If there are some points raised that seem to be inexplicable or contradictory to your established outlook, perhaps you will give that outlook some additional thought. That extra effort and reading *may* eventually lead to a change in your view. I have seen it happen, but it is not all that frequent. Most people give up before they have resolved all of the points that don't quite fit into their philosophies.

In light of the fairly small number of defections from one side to the other, why have a debate on religion at all? I think the answer is that it serves the useful function of providing the audience with a short and encapsulated version of the major arguments of both sides, thus allowing observers to judge how well the debaters have supported those arguments and the appropriateness of the conclusions that have been drawn. To do that for as many as 2,000 people is indeed a service.

One of the readings in this section does not fit well into any of the three categories outlined above. It is a *fictional* discussion between two characters invented by Diderot. He uses the format to present his own ideas in the mouth of one of the characters, and to let the other react to these ideas. This tactic was much safer than proclaiming the ideas oneself in revolutionary France.

The topics most often debated by atheists and theists are the existence of God, the truth or falsity of the Bible, the truth or falsity of Christianity, the messianic claims of Jesus, and the justification for atheism. Sometimes the debate has been between different factions of the freethought movement, as one of the selections will illustrate. In it Charles Bradlaugh and George Jacob Holyoake disagree about what secularism means. The fact that the same topics are still being debated after more than 100 years once again shows that debates do not settle the enduring issues. Although the medium for dialogues has changed somewhat in the last century with the invention of radio and television, the format is invariably one in which an atheist is questioned by a nonatheist; the latter usually tries to get the former to explain and/or justify his or her position. In the present selections, this is represented by Joseph Lewis's television interview with Mike Wallace.

Historically, the first published debate between a believer and a nonbeliever on a religious issue pitted Robert Owen against Alexander Campbell in Louisville, Kentucky, in 1820. They were supposed to be discussing the "Evidences of Christianity," but neither debater seems to have stuck much to the topic. The result is a rambling and virtually unreadable set of two published volumes. During the rest of the nineteenth century, there were many published debates, mostly in England, although there were some American and Canadian ones as well. It is truly unfortunate that America's greatest orator, Robert G. Ingersoll, never debated before a live audience. He did participate in several written exchanges with the better-known supporters of Christianity, but he turned down all offers to debate "live." Most of these invitations came from run-of-the-mill clergymen, who probably had an inflated sense of how they would do against "the master." They were lucky in most cases that Ingersoll refused their challenge. Across the Atlantic, perhaps the best debaters in England were Charles Bradlaugh, Charles Watts, and G. W. Foote. Although there were a number of public debates in the United States, no one person seems to stand out as the best debater. B. F. Underwood seems to have participated in the largest number of debates in the past century, only a few of which were published. The freethought periodicals often published these debates, but rarely were they issued in book or pamphlet form.

The art of debating freethought topics is not yet dead. There has been a revival of these debates on religion in the past years, with regular exchanges occurring in New York during the Great Depression. The 1970s and 1980s have also seen renewed activity on the public debate circuit. Antony Flew and Wallace Matson, both noted philosophers, have debated Thomas Warren, an arch-fundamentalist. All of these debates have been published in book form by Christian publishers. Evidently the Christians thought that Warren got the better of his opponents, but my reading of the debates leaves me with the feeling that Warren only showed his rigidity. Nevertheless, the art of freethought debate still lives.

Between 1984 and 1986, a series of debates on the existence of God was held on college campuses in California between Gordon Stein and assorted theologians. The debates attracted standing-room-only crowds in almost every case. The student interest in debates on the fundamental issues of religion and atheism runs high. These debates were made available on audio and sometimes on video tape, but have not yet been issued in printed form.

One topic that aroused considerable interest but now appears to be out of favor is the existence of an historical Jesus. The entire controversy over this issue has cooled down, but has not, of course, really been resolved. For a summary of the main points involved, please see the first *Anthology of Atheism and Rationalism.* Many debates that are available in print on the historicity issues have been held between G. A. Wells (against historicity) and his opponents.

Conversation of a Philosopher
with the Maréchale de —

Denis Diderot

Denis Diderot (1713-1784) is best known as the editor of the first modern encyclopedia, *L'Encyclopédie,* and became known as a man of many talents: philosopher, novelist, dramatist, art critic, and a very important figure in the French Enlightenment. Born in Langres, France, he was a brilliant student and was soon sent to college in Paris. He wanted to get a general education, refusing to specialize in any one subject. As a result, he had largely to educate himself, for his family refused to support his eclectic career choice. Diderot lived in poverty for many years, but finally accomplished his aim of knowing something about everything. He earned a living first as a translator, but published his first work *Pensées Philosophiques* in 1746. That was also the year in which he began the *Encyclopédie,* a project which would continue for twenty-five years.

It was entirely due to Diderot's persistence that the *Encyclopédie* was ever completed. He ran into immediate opposition from the authorities, who confiscated parts of the manuscript, censored others, and suppressed the published volumes. The printer also refused to publish parts of it, and changed sections without permission. While the *Encyclopédie* was being published, Diderot wrote a number of other philosophic works, which brought him notoriety as a materialist and an atheist, both dangerous reputations at the time.

Although the *Encyclopédie* was not in and of itself atheistic, it did contain a strong infusion of religious toleration and democracy, both of which were upsetting to the powers running France at the time. Freedom of the press and of thought were also stressed. Throughout the work he assumed a rationalist approach to religion. Taken together with all of his other works, Diderot's output was immense. Many of his books were not published for years after his death, though his reputation continued to grow.

The present selection was first published in 1777. It is set forth as an idealized conversation with Maréchale de Broglie, and contains a strong attack on persecution. It seems to have been first translated into English in 1927, and infrequently reprinted thereafter.

I had some business or other with Maréchal de —. I went to his house one morning. He was out. I was shown in to Madame la Maréchale. She is a charming woman, beautiful and pious as an angel: and she has a tone of voice and a naiveté of speech which entirely suit her face. She was dressing. A chair is drawn up. I sit down and we talk. As a result of some observations on my part which edified and surprised her (for she holds that the man who denies the Blessed Trinity is a ruffian who will end on the gallows), she said to me:

Are you not M Crudeli?

CRUDELI: Yes.

MARÉCHALE: The man who believes in nothing?

CRUDELI: I am.

MARÉCHALE: But your morals are the same as a believer's.

CREDULI: Why not, if that believer is an honest man?

MARÉCHALE: And you put that morality into practice?

CRUDELI: As well as I can.

MARÉCHALE: What! you do not steal, or kill, or pillage?

CRUEDELI: Very rarely.

MARÉCHALE: Then what do you get out of not believing?

CRUDELI: Nothing; but does one believe in order to get something out of it?

MARÉCHALE: I do not know. But a little self-interest comes in useful both for this world and the next.

CRUDELI: I am a little sorry for our poor human race, to be no better than that.

MARÉCHALE: So you do not steal at all?

CRUDELI: I promise you, not.

MARÉCHALE: But if you are neither a thief nor an assassin, you must admit you are hardly consistent.

CRUDELI: Why so?.

MARÉCHALE: Because I think if I had nothing to fear or to hope, after death, I should allow myself a good many little pleasures here below.

I admit I lend to God at a stiff rate of interest.

CRUDELI: So you think, perhaps.

MARÉCHALE: It is not a matter of thinking. It is a fact.

CRUDELI: But one might ask, What are those things you would allow yourself, if you did not believe?

MARÉCHALE: One might not. They are only for my confessor's ears.

CRUDELI: For my part, I never expect any return on my money.

MARÉCHALE: All beggars are in that situation.

CRUDELI: You would rather I were a usurer?

MARÉCHALE: Why, yes. One can be as usurious with God as one pleases. He cannot be ruined. It is hardly delicate, I know. But what does that matter? As the essential thing is to get into Heaven either by cunning or by force, we must use every means, and neglect no source of profit. Alas! whatever we do, we shall get but scanty recognition compared with what we had looked for. And you, you look for nothing?

CRUDELI: Nothing.

MARÉCHALE: But that is very sad. Agree then—you are either a rogue or a madman.

CRUDELI: But I cannot.

MARÉCHALE: But what motive can an unbeliever have for being good, unless he be mad?

CRUDELI: I shall tell you.

MARÉCHALE: I shall be most grateful.

CRUDELI: Do you not think a man can be born with a such happy disposition as to find real pleasure in doing good?

MARÉCHALE: I do.

CRUDELI: And that he may have received an excellent education, which will strengthen his natural leaning towards benevolence.

MARÉCHALE: Certainly.

CRUDELI: And that, in later life, experience may have convinced us that on the whole it is better for one's happiness in this world to be an honest man than a rogue.

MARÉCHALE: Why, yes. But how can he be an honest man, when evil principles united with the passions involve us in evil?

CRUDELI: By inconsistency. And is there anything commoner than inconsistency?

MARÉCHALE: Alas! Unfortunately not. We believe, yet every day we behave as though we did not.

CRUDELI: And without believing, one behaves very much as if one did.

MARÉCHALE: If you like. But what can be the harm in having one reason the more, religion, for doing good, and one reason the less, unbelief, for doing wrong?

CRUDELI: None, if religion were a motive for doing good and unbelief for doing wrong.

MARÉCHALE: But can there be any doubt about it? What is the essence of religion but to check our vile corrupted nature, and that of unbelief but to abandon it to its own wickedness by relieving it of fear?

CRUDELI: That is going to involve us in a long discussion.

MARÉCHALE: What of that? The Maréchal will not be back for a bit. And we are better employed in rational discussion than in slandering our neighbors.

CRUDELI: Then I must go back a little.

MARÉCHALE: As far as you like, provided you make yourself understood.

CRUDELI: If I do not, it will be entirely my fault.

MARÉCHALE: That is very polite of you. But you must know I have hardly read anything but my Prayer Book, and I do almost nothing but study the Gospels and breed children.

CRUDELI: Two duties you have admirably filled.

MARÉCHALE: As regards the children, yes. Here are six round me and in a few days you will be able to see a seventh on my knee. But begin.

CRUDELI: Well. Is there any good in this world which has not got its drawbacks?

MARÉCHALE: None.

CRUDELI: And any evil which has not got its advantages?

MARÉCHALE: None.

CRUDELI: What do you call a good or an evil?

MARÉCHALE: An evil is that which has more drawbacks than advantages, and a good that which has more advantages than drawbacks.

CRUDELI: I hope you will be good enough to remember your definition of good and evil?

MARÉCHALE: I will. But do you call that a definition?

CRUDELI: Yes.

MARÉCHALE: Then it is philosophy?

CRUDELI: And very good philosophy, too.

MARÉCHALE: So I have made philosophy!

CRIDELI: So you are convinced that religion has more advantages than drawbacks. Hence you call it a good?

MARÉCHALE: Yes.

CRUDELI: And for my part, I have no doubt your bailiff robs you a little less just before Easter than he does a few days afterwards, and that from time to time religion prevents a number of evils and produces a number of small goods.

MARÉCHALE: Little by little, that totes up.

CRUDELI: But do you think that these poky little advantages make up adequately for the terrible ravages religion has caused in the past and will cause in the future? Remember it has created and now perpetuates the most violent national hatreds. No Mussulman but believes he is doing an action agreeable to God and the holy prophet in exterminating every Christian. And the Christians on their side are scarcely more tolerant. Think how it has created and still perpetuates in the same country divisions rarely suppressed without the shedding of blood. Our own history offers us examples all too recent and too tragic. Think how it has created and still perpetuates, in society between citizens, and in the family between relatives, the most violent and most lasting of hatreds. Christ said he had come to separate husband from wife, mother from children, brother from sister, friend from friend. And his prediction has been all too faithfully fulfilled.

MARÉCHALE: These are abuses, not the essentials, of the thing.

CRUDELI: It is, if abuses and essentials are inseparable.

MARÉCHALE: And how can you demonstrate that religion and its abuses are inseparable?

CRUDELI: Very easily. Suppose a misanthrope had set out to harm the human race, what could he have invented better than belief in an incomprehensible being about whom men should never agree and to whom they should attach more importance than to their own lives. Now is it possible to separate from the notion of a Divinity the most profound incomprehensibility and the greatest importance?

MARÉCHALE: No.

CRUDELI: Your conclusion, then?

MARÉCHALE: My conclusion is that it is an idea which might well be disastrous, if lunatics got hold of it.

CRUDELI: And you may add that lunatics always have been and always will be in the vast majority; and that the most dangerous lunatics are those made so by religion, and that the disturbers of society know how to make good use of them when occasion arises.

MARÉCHALE: But we must have something with which to frighten men off those actions, which escape the severity of the laws. Destroy religion, and what will you put in its place?

CRUDELI: And suppose I had nothing to put in its place, there would always be one terrible prejudice the less. Besides, in no century and with no nation have religious opinions been the basis of national morals. The gods adored by the ancient Greeks and Romans, the most virtuous of people, were the merest scum: a Jupiter who should have been burnt alive: a Venus fit for a reformatory: a Mercury who ought to be in a jail.

MARÉCHALE: So you think it does not matter at all whether we be Christians or pagans; that we should be none the worse for being pagans and are none the better for being Christians?

CRUDELI: Honestly, I am certain of it, unless we should be slightly merrier for being pagans.

MARÉCHALE: That cannot be.

CRUDELI: But are there any Christians? I have never seen one.

MARÉCHALE: And you say that to me?

CRUDELI: No, not to you, but to one of my neighbors, who is as honest and pious as you: who thinks herself a Christian in all sincerity just as you do.

MARÉCHALE: And you made her admit she was wrong?

CRUDELI: In a moment.

MARÉCHALE: And how?

CRUDELI: I opened a New Testament, which she had used a great deal, for it was very worn. I read her the Sermon on the Mount, and after each article I asked her—Do you do that? Or that? Or even that? I went one further. She is very beautiful, and although most good and pious, she is well aware of the fact. She has a very white skin, and although she does not attach any great importance to this slender merit, she does not mind it being praised. Her throat is as handsome as a throat can be; and although she is very modest, she thinks it as well that this should be noticed.

MARÉCHALE: But if only herself and her husband know it?

CRUDELI: Certainly, I think her husband knows it better than anyone else. But for a woman who prides herself on being such a tremendous Christian this is not enough. I said to her: "Is it not written in the Gospel that he who lusts after his neighbor's wife has committed adultery in his heart?"

MARÉCHALE: And she answered Yes.

CRUDELI: And I said: And is not adultery committed in the heart as surely damned as adultery of the most thoroughgoing kind?

MARÉCHALE: And she answered Yes.

CRUDELI: And I said: And if the man is damned for the adultery he has committed in his heart, what will be the fate of the woman who invites all those who come near her to commit this crime? This last question embarrassed her.

MARÉCHALE: I understand; for she did not, very carefully, cover up this throat of hers, which is handsome as a throat can be.

CRUDELI: That is so. She replied it was a convention, as if anything were more conventional than to call oneself a Christian and not be one. And that also that one must not dress absurdly, as if there could be any comparison between a trifling little absurdity and one's eternal damnation, as well as the damnation of one's neighbor. And also that she was in the hands of her dressmaker, as if it were not better to change one's dressmaker than to throw over one's religion. And that it was the whim of her husband, as if a husband were sufficiently insensate to demand from his wife the forgetfulness of decency and duty; and as if a true Christian should push obedience to a preposterous husband to the point of sacrificing the will of God and despising the threats of her Redeemer.

MARÉCHALE: I knew all those childish answers before you mentioned them. And perhaps I should have employed them like your neighbor. And we should both have been insincere. But what line did she take after your protest?

CRUDELI: The day after our conversation (it was a festival of the Church), as I was going up to my room, my beautiful and pious neighbor was coming down, on the way to Mass.

MARÉCHALE: Dressed as usual.

CRUDELI: Dressed as usual. I smiled. She smiled. We passed each other without speaking. And she, an honest woman! a Christian! a pious woman! And after this sample, and one hundred thousand others exactly like it, what real influence can I allow religion to have on morals? Practically none, and so much the better.

MARÉCHALE: What! so much the better?

CRUDELI: Yes. If twenty thousand Parisians took it into their heads to base their conduct strictly on the Sermon on the Mount . . .

MARÉCHALE: Well, there would be a few handsome throats better covered.

CRUDELI: And so many lunatics that the commissioner of police would not know what to do with them: for our asylums would never hold them. There are two moralities in Inspired Books. One general and common to all nations and all religions, which is more or less observed: the other, peculiar to each nation and each religion in which people believe, which they preach in church and praise up at home, but which is not observed at all.

MARÉCHALE: And to what is this preposterous state of affairs due?

CRUDELI: To the impossibility of subjecting a nation to a rule which suits only a few melancholiacs, who have imposed it on their characters. It is with religious as with monastic institutions; they relax with time. They are lunacies which cannot hold out against the constant impulse of nature, which brings us back under her law. See to it that private good be so closely united to public good that a citizen can hardly harm society without harming himself. Promise virtue its reward, as you have promised wickedness its punishment. Let virtue lead to high offices of state, without distinction of faith, wherever virtue is to be found. Then you need only count on a small number of wicked men, who are involved in vice by a perversity of nature which nothing can correct. No. Temptation is too near: hell too far off. Look for nothing worth the attention of a wise law-giver from a system of fantastic opinions, which imposes only on children: which encourages crime by its convenient system of penances: which sends the guilty man to ask pardon of God for harm done to man, and which degrades the order of natural and moral duties by subordinating it to an order of imaginary duties.

MARÉCHALE: I do not follow.

CRUDELI: Let me explain. But I think I hear the Maréchal's carriage coming back just in time to prevent my saying something silly.

MARÉCHALE: Say it. I shall not understand you. I am an adept at understanding only what gives me pleasure.

CRUDELI: I went up to her and said quite low in her ear: "Ask the vicar of your parish, which of the two crimes is, in his opinion, the more heinous—to piss into a sacred vessel or to blacken the reputation of an honest woman. He will shudder with horror at the first, and the civil law, which scarcely notices calumny while punishing sacrilege with fire, will complete the confusion of ideas and the corruption of the intelligence."

MARÉCHALE: I know more than one woman who would never eat meat on a Friday and who . . . I was going to make my silly contribution. Go on.

CRUDELI: But I simply must speak to the Maréchal.

MARÉCHALE: One moment more, and then we will go and see him together. I do not quite see how to answer you, but you have not made me change my opinion.

CRUDELI: I did not set out to change it. It is with religion as with marriage. Marriage, which has wrecked so many lives, has made for your happiness and for that of the Maréchal. You have both of you done well to marry. Religion, which has made, does make, and will make so many men wicked, has made you better still: you do well to keep it. It is sweet to you to imagine beside you, and above your head, a great and powerful being who sees you walk upon the earth, and this idea strengthens your steps. Continue to be happy in this august guarantor of your thoughts, in this spectator, in this sublime model for your actions.

MARÉCHALE: I see you have not got the proselytizing mania.

CRUDELI: Not in the least.

MARÉCHALE: I think the better of you for it.

CRUDELI: I allow everyone to think as he pleases, provided I am allowed to think as I please. And then those who exist in order to free themselves from these prejudices are scarcely in need of being catechized.

MARÉCHALE: Do you think man can get along without superstition?

CRUDELI: Not as long as he remains ignorant and timid.

MARÉCHALE: Well then, superstition for superstition, ours is as good as another.

CRUDELI: I do not think so.

MARÉCHALE: Now tell me sincerely. Does the idea of being nothing after death not distress you?

CRUDELI: I would rather exist, though I do not know why a Being who has been once capable of making me wretched for no reason should not enjoy doing so twice.

MARÉCHALE: But if, despite this drawback, the hope of a life to come appear to you consoling and sweet, why tear it from us?

CRUDELI: I do not entertain this hope because desire for it has not blinded me to its hollowness; but I take it away from no one else. If anyone can believe they will see without eyes, hear without ears, think without a head, love without a heart, feel without senses, exist without being anywhere, and be something without place or size, very well.

MARÉCHALE: But who made this world?

CRUDELI: I ask you.

MARÉCHALE: God.

CRUDELI: And what is God?

MARÉCHALE: A spirit.

CRUDELI: And if a spirit makes matter, why should not matter make a spirit!

MARÉCHALE: And why should it?

CRUDELI: Because I see it do so every day. Do you believe animals have souls?

MARÉCHALE: Certainly I do.

CRUDELI: Could you tell me, for example, what happens to the soul of the Peruvian serpent, hung on the chimney and exposed to the smoke for two years together while it is drying?

MARÉCHALE: How can it matter to me what happens to it?

CRUDELI: So you do not know that this serpent, after being dried and smoked, is resuscitated and reborn?

MARÉCHALE: I do not believe it for a moment.

CRUDELI: Yet a very clever man, Bouguer, asserts it.

MARÉCHALE: Your clever man is a liar.

CRUDELI: But suppose he were telling the truth?

MARÉCHALE: I should get off with believing that animals are machines.

CRUDELI: And man, who is only a machine a little more perfected than any other. . . . But the Maréchal.

MARÉCHALE: One more question, and it is the last. Does your unbelief leave you calm?

CRUDELI: As calm as it is possible to be.

MARÉCHALE: But suppose you were mistaken?

CRUDELI: Suppose I were?

MARÉCHALE: Suppose everything you believe false were true and you were damned. Monsieur Crudeli, it is a terrible thing to be damned. To burn through eternity. It is a long time.

CRUDELI: La Fontaine thought we should be as comfortable as fishes in water.

MARÉCHALE: Yes, yes, but your La Fontaine became very serious at the end, and I expect the same of you.

CRUDELI: I can answer for nothing when my brain has softened. But if I end with one of those illnesses which leave the dying man in possession of his powers, I shall be no more distressed at the expected moment than I am now.

MARÉCHALE: Your fearlessness amazes me.

CRUDELI: I am much more amazed at the fearlessness of the dying man who believes in a severe judge, in one who weighs our most secret thoughts, and in whose balance the justest man would be lost through vanity if he did not tremble to find himself too light. If this dying man could choose between being wiped out and going before this tribunal, I should be much more amazed by his fearlessness if he hesitated to choose the first: unless, indeed, he were more insensate than the companion of Saint Bruno or more intoxicated with his own merits than Bohola.

MARÉCHALE: I have read the account of the associate of Saint Bruno, but I have never heard of your Bohola.

CRUDELI: He was a Jesuit of the College at Pinsk in Lithuania, who left at his death a casket full of money with a note written and signed in his own hand.

MARÉCHALE: And the note?

CRUDELI: . . . was as follows: "I want my dear colleague, to whom I hand over this casket, to open it when I have performed miracles. The money inside will go to the expenses in connection with my beatification. I have added some authentic memoirs in confirmation of my virtues which will be useful to those engaged on writing my life."

MARÉCHALE: But it is a roaring farce.

CRUDELI: To me, yes; but not to you: your God has got no sense of humor.

MARÉCHALE: That is so.

CRUDELI: It is very easy to sin grievously against your law.

MARÉCHALE: I agree. It is.

CRUDELI: The justice that will decide your fate is very stern.

MARÉCHALE: True.

CRUDELI: And if you believe in the oracles of your creed, the number of the saved is small.

MARÉCHALE: Oh, I am no Jansenist: I look only at the bright side of the medal. In my eyes the blood of Jesus Christ has flowed far. I should think it very odd if the Devil, who never sacrificed his son, nevertheless got the lion's share.

CRUDELLI: Do you damn Socrates, Phocion, Aristides, Cato, Trajan, Marcus Aurelius?

MARÉCHALE: Gracious me, no! Only wild beasts can believe that. Saint Paul said everyone will be judged by his own law and Saint Paul is right.

CRUDELI: And by what law will the unbeliever be judged?

MARÉCHALE: Your case is rather different. You are one of those cursed inhabitants of Corozain and Betzaida who shut their eyes to the light that shone on them and put wax in their ears so as not to hear the voice of reason which spoke to them.

CRUDELI: But these Corozainians and Betzaidans were unique if they were free to believe or not to believe.

MARÉCHALE: They saw prodigies enough to have raised the price of sackcloth and ashes in Tyre and Sidon.

CRUDELI: These inhabitants of Tyre and Sidon were intelligent, but the Corozainian and Betzaidan mere fools. But is it for him who made them fools to punish them for their folly. Just now I related to you an actual occurrence. Now I want to tell you a story: A young Mexican . . . But the Maréchal?

MARÉCHALE: I will send to find out if we can see him. Well then, your young Mexican?

CRUDELI: Tired of his. work, walked one day upon the seashore. He saw a plank with one end in the water and the other on the beach. He takes his seat on the plank; and turning his gaze on the huge space stretched out before him, said. "It is certain my grandmother is talking nonsense when she romances about some inhabitants or other who, God knows when, came here heaven knows where from, but from some country beyond the seas. Why, there is no commonsense in it. Cannot I see the sea merging in the sky? And can I believe, against the evidence of my senses, an old story of unknown date, which everyone rearranges to suit himself, which is a mere farrago of preposterous incidents over which men eat their hearts out, and tear out the whites of their eyes." As he reasoned thus, the undulating waters rocked him on his plank and he fell asleep. As he sleeps, the wind gets up, the waves carry the barque away, and behold our young reasoner started on his voyage.

MARÉCHALE: Alas! that is just like us. We are each on his plank: the wind blows and the waves carry us away.

CRUDELI: He was already far from the mainland when he awoke. And who was mighty surprised to find himself on the open sea? Why, our young Mexican. And who was more surprised still? He again, when the sea seemed to merge in the sky on every side, now that he had lost sight of the beach where he had been walking only a moment before. Then he began to suspect that he might have been mistaken, and that if the wind continued in the same quarter he might be carried on shore, amongst those inhabitants of whom his mother had talked to him so often.

MARÉCHALE: But you say nothing about his agitation.

CRUDELI: He felt none. He said to himself: "What does that matter to me, as long as I get on shore? I have argued like a fool, certainly. But I was sincere with myself, and that is all that can be expected of me. If it be not a virtue to be intelligent, it is not a crime to be a fool." Meanwhile, the wind went on blowing, the man and the plank drifted along, and the unknown shore began to appear. He touches land, and there he is!

MARÉCHALE: We shall meet again there one day, M. Crudeli.

CRUDELI: I sincerely hope so. Wherever it may be, I shall always be flattered to pay you my addresses. Scarcely had he left his plank and set foot on the sand when he perceived a venerable old man standing by his side. The Mexican asked him where he was and whom he had the honor of addressing. "I am the sovereign of the country," answered the old man. At once the young man prostrated himself. "Get up," said the old man; "you have denied my existence?" "I have." "And the existence of my empire?" "I have." "I forgive you that because you acted in good faith. But the rest of your thoughts and actions have not been equally innocent." Then the old man, who held him by the ear, recalled to him all the errors of his life. And at each article the young Mexican bowed his head and beat his breast and prayed for pardon. . . . There now. Put yourself a moment in the place of the old man and tell me what you would have done. Would you have taken this insensate young man by the hair and joyfully dragged him along the beach for ever?

MARÉCHALE: To tell you the truth, no.

CRUDELI: And if one of your six pretty children, after escaping from the paternal roof, and committing every conceivable sort of folly, came home repentant?

MARÉCHALE: I should run to meet him. I should clasp him in my arms and bathe him with my tears. But his father the Maréchal would not take the thing so lightly.

CRUDELI: The Maréchal is not a tiger.

MARÉCHALE: Far from it.

CRUDELI: He would make rather a scene about it. But he would forgive in the end.

MARÉCHALE: Certainly.

CRUDELI: Especially if he came to reflect that, before becoming the father of the child, he had known all that was going to happen to it, and that punishing him for his faults would be of no use to himself, the guilty one, or his brothers.

MARÉCHALE: The Maréchal and the old man are two different people.

CRUDELI: You mean to say that the Maréchal is better than the old man?

MARÉCHALE: Heaven forbid! I mean to say that if my notion of justice is not the same as the Maréchal's perhaps the notion of the Maréchal will not be the same as the old man's.

CRUDELI: But you cannot have realized the consequences of that answer. Either the general definition applies equally to you, to the Maréchal, to me, to the young Mexican and the old man, or I can no longer say what is what, or how one pleases or displeases the old man.

We had reached this point when we were told that the Maréchal expected us. As I gave his wife my hand, she said: It is enough to make one's head go round, is it not?

CRUDELI: Why, if one's head is a good one?

MARÉCHALE: After all, the simplest course is to act on the assumption that the old man exists.

CRUDELI: Even when one does not believe it?

MARÉCHALE: And when one does believe it, not to rely too much on his good nature.

CRUDELI: That is the safest way, if not the politest.

MARÉCHALE: By the way, if you had to state your principles to the magistrates, would you make a clean breast of them?

CRUDELI: I should do my best to hinder the magistrates performing a brutal act.

MARÉCHALE: Oh, you coward! And if you were at the point of death, would you submit to the ceremonies of the Church?

CRUDELI: I should not fail to do so.

MARÉCHALE: Oh, you wretched hypocrite!

Was Jesus an Impostor?
A Debate with Agnes Rollo Wilkie

Arthur B. Moss

Arthur B. Moss (1855-1937) was born in London, the son of a successful businessman. Moss had a good education, and was a Christian until his sixteenth year, when his brother discussed astronomy with him, asking whether Jesus had also come to all other inhabited planets in the universe. After this encounter he began reading such works as Paine's *The Age of Reason,* and Bishop Colenso's works. His shift to freethought was underway. When Moss's former minister heard about this he told the young man's mother, a teacher in his Sunday School, that he would not have the mother of an infidel teaching there. She was dismissed.

At the age of twenty Moss began giving freethought lectures. It was the heyday of British freethought, and Moss knew all of the big names, including Charles Bradlaugh, G. W. Foote, Charles Watts, Annie Besant, and George Jacob Holyoake. To support his lecturing, Moss taught public speaking. At one point, his outside activities were brought to the attention of his school employers, and a long hearing was held to determine whether he should be dismissed. The school officials ruled that he could continue to teach only if he gave up his freethought lecturing. An appeal was supported by many well-known civil libertarians, and eventually Moss was allowed to continue his lectures. Moss also contributed articles to most of the British freethought magazines. He died in 1937.

The present selection is a written exchange first published by Watts & Company circa 1890. Agnes Rollo Wilke was a minor Scottish novelist whose best known book was called *Rosa* (1881). This debate is presented here nearly a century after its first publication.

MR.MOSS'S FIRST PAPER.

A courageous lady has challenged the fierce Saladin to debate; that gentleman, however, is busily engaged in a dialectical encounter which is likely, if I know aught of the argumentative nature of English Freethinkers, to last for some considerable time. It would be a pity, in the meantime, if the distinct challenge of Agnes Rollo Wilkie should go unnoticed; it would imply want of courage on the part of Freethinkers. I, therefore, who am of a gentler nature than the writer of "Sparks and Splinters," advance and gracefully take up the glove. What does the brave lady, who has fearlessly entered the religious arena, wish the Freethinker to prove? And from whence are the proofs to be deduced? The lady herself shall answer these two questions. Here are her exact words as to the issue to be raised in the discussion: "If he can prove from any or all of the reported sayings of Jesus that he was an impostor, or a teacher of unsound doctrine, I shall have much pleasure in reasoning with him or replying to his arguments." This is plain enough. There are two points to be argued—1. Was Jesus an impostor? 2. Did he preach unsound doctrine? Logically considered, there are only two positions that can be taken in respect to the person of Jesus. Either he was God, with attributes and powers infinitely superior to those possessed by human beings, or he was but a poor, frail man, with all the imperfections indigenous to humanity. I know not which of these views Agnes Rollo Wilkie accepts, or whether she rejects both; but this I do know, that, if anybody were to declare that Jesus was God, it could very easily be proved from the Four Gospels that such an idea was totally absurd, and that a human being who said that he was God must either have been an impostor or a lunatic, or both.

If it is conceded that Jesus was a man, are we to accept the Four Gospels as containing an authentic account of his conduct and teachings? If yes, my task is clear. Taking the Gospels as the true account, in every particular, of the life and teachings of the Prophet of Nazareth, I accept the lady's challenge and make essay to demonstrate that Jesus was an impostor and preached unsound, and often very injurious, doctrine. Let me not be misunderstood. I admire, in parts, the real character of Jesus—his fearlessness, his intrepidity, his hatred of all sorts of hypocrisy, his unselfishness, his single-mindedness; but, then, I eliminate from the Gospels the fictitious supernatural element—repudiate entirely all that is inconsistent and contradictory in the narrative, and erect out of all that remains the real and ideal man. In this eclectical process I may not be acting up strictly to the canons of logic; but I err in good company, for I find that Mill, Renan, Ingersoll, and other Freethinkers, adopt the same course in arriving at an idea of the true character of Jesus. But once accept the Four Gospels as inspired records, and we have a very different view of the character and teachings of Jesus. We have an enthusiast as arrogant as a modern Salvationist; a preacher who talks in parables, that his hearers "may hear and not understand;" a charlatan who pretends to heal the sick, give sight to the blind, and raise the dead to life.

Was Jesus an impostor? Can a man work a miracle? Can a law of nature be suspended at the command of man? Can five thousand hungry persons be fed with five loaves and a few fishes? I deny the possibility of miracles. They never have happened, and never can happen. He who knows anything about causation must know that for a miracle to happen would mean that the whole chain of causes through infinite ages—nay, through all eternity—would have to be undone. Undoubtedly, Jesus professed to be able to work miracles, and, since all experience demonstrates that the laws of nature are invariable, he who asked his followers to believe that he was possessed of supernatural power must have been an impostor, or insane. . . .

But I proceed to the next point. Did Jesus preach sound doctrine? Many extol the Sermon on the Mount. A good deal of nonsense every week is preached from the pulpit by learned divines, who do not understand the moral harmfulness contained in some of the teachings of Jesus. "Blessed are the poor in spirit" is by no means sound doctrine. "Lay not up for yourselves treasures upon earth but lay up for yourselves treasures in heaven, where neither moth nor rust doth corrupt." "Take no thought for your life what ye shall eat, or what ye shall drink; nor yet for your body what ye shall put on. Is not the life more than the meat, and the body than raiment? Behold the fowls of the air; for they sow not, neither do they reap nor gather into barns; yet your heavenly father feedeth them. Are ye not much better than they?" All this, in the light of modern requirements and common sense, is very unsound doctrine.

When was it ever praiseworthy to manifest poverty of spirit? The poor in spirit, so far from being blessed, have been the cursed victims of tyranny and injustice in all ages. Poor in spirit! They have been the slaves in all the nations of the earth. Upon their backs have been the whips of knaves and kings; their lips and noses have been slit; they have been bound in chains, and mocking tongues have scornfully spat upon them. And where shall we find the man who "takes no thought for his life, what he shall eat," etc.—where shall we find him? He is to be found in our workhouses; and Christian magistrates describe him as "a rogue and a vagabond." If all men were to imitate the fowls of the air, and take no thought for their lives, this world would be a howling wilderness of starving paupers.

To demonstrate the unsoundness of this doctrine, one has only to practice it for a single week. Nothing that I can write, I hope, will induce my lady disputant to try the experiment. But perhaps Agnes Rollo Wilkie will be disposed to consider the following sound doctrine:—"Unto him that smiteth thee on the one cheek offer also the other; and him that taketh away thy cloak forbid him not to take thy coat also." It is sound enough for the ruffian and the thief, for the conqueror and the oppressor; but for the victim it is most unfortunate. "Blessed are they that hunger now, for they shall be filled." When? In the next world? That is a little too late. Men who starve in this world are not likely to get a front seat in the next. "Blessed be ye poor." I deny it. The poor are never blessed. Poverty is the forerunner of almost every crime and iniquity in this world. It is poverty that begets ignorance; it is poverty that fills our gaols and workhouses; it is poverty that causes maidens to sell their virtue for a morsel of bread; it is poverty that breeds disease; it is poverty that prompts to theft, murder, suicide, and death. Jesus taught that poverty and hunger were blessings; and such I declare to be positively harmful doctrines.

But what shall we say of Jesus when he says that "every one that hath forsaken houses, or brethren, or sisters, or father, or mother, or wife, or children, or lands, for my sake, shall have an hundredfold, and shall inherit everlasting life."? Such a teaching I despise; and the man or woman who would accept "everlasting life" upon such conditions I pity. With all its fault, I love Humanity, and in doing my best to assist my struggling brothers and sisters I get the only reward I want or deserve.

MRS. WILKIE'S FIRST PAPER.

Mr. Arthur B. Moss has taken up the glove for Saladin, and it now devolves upon me to endeavor to prove that Jesus was neither an impostor nor a teacher of unsound doctrine.

If I mistake not, historians and biographers, when analyzing and criticizing nations and individuals, generally admit that the nation or individual whose virtues excel their vices, whose justice and magnanimity far overbalance injustice and meanness, whose aspirations after the higher and healthier vastly preponderate over the ignoble, unsound, and more questionable, are considered as being worthy of all admiration and emulation—nay, to stigmatize such a nation or such an individual as a spurious imposition or an imposter would be to ruthlessly trample on the justice, wisdom, and beauty of true intellectual criticism, and to throw broadcast destructive hyperbolical sophisms which considers anything fair and clever which wins a momentary victory for a favorite sect, ism, or doctrine. It appears to me that too many Secularistic writers and lectures adopt the latter unjust form of criticism in regard to the Nazarene Prophet; not, however, ignorantly, nor yet, I fear, owing to a zeal not according to knowledge, but merely for the ignoble purpose of a momentary victory, which in the end is rottenness to the cause they have at heart. The truth is, all rational thinkers and reformers might do well to regard Jesus as he did the man who was reported to be casting out devils in his name—viz., to affirm or confess that all who are not against are for. On the contrary, however, many so-called pioneers of righteousness are like the blind leading the blind, thereby bringing contempt on their cause by stigmatizing as an imposter, etc., him who was essentially the founder of the authority of the human soul as well as of the Religion of Humanity. Does such a mode of injudicious summarizing and criticizing really forward the noble cause which I honestly believe most of them have at heart? Unquestionably not. And if ever the vast cathedral, in which the universal heart of humanity will sing songs of peace and goodwill—songs of happy deliverance from all forms of creed superstition, Papal corruption, and Monarchical oppression—is to be built, whose towering spire will be lost in cloudless light, its foundation must not rest on any unjust accusation or onesided judgment, either of Jew or Greek, bond or free, black man or white, but on the perennial pillars of justice, knit together by the imperishable cement of brotherly love and charity.

My noble opponent, after stating the two points to be argued, says: "Logically considered, there are only two positions which can be taken in regard to the person of Jesus. Either he was God, with attributes and powers infinitely superior to those possessed by human beings, or he was but a poor frail man, with all the imperfections indigenous to humanity." In reply to the above quotation, I remark that I utterly repudiate the former position. My belief, therefore, in regard to the person of Jesus is, that he was a man possessed of attributes and powers which are in varying degrees indigenous to humanity. Seeing, however, that I know nothing of the logical position of humanity's indigenous inheritance of poverty, frailty, and imperfection, and especially as it smells a little of the catechism doctrine of original sin, my friend will perceive that I do not exactly accept or take either of the two mentioned positions. Moreover, while I regard Jesus as a man possessed of attributes and powers indigenous to humanity, as one gifted with very large and lofty powers and attributes, I neither claim for him absolute perfection nor yet entire sinlessness. If I read the Gospels aright, he never claimed to be either perfect in goodness, or to be without sin, but merely affirmed that he had done many good works, and that none of his followers or adversaries could convince him of sin—*i.e.,* he claimed to be blameless as touching the law and far in advance of all his contemporaries. Nay, even to this day he stands forth a giant among men as the divinest and purest representative of all manly excellence, and only a few here and there are spelling out the first letters of the higher life of truth and goodness which he lived and taught.

Conceding that Jesus was a man, I now say that I do not regard the Four Gospels as containing an authentic account of the teaching and work of one who, whatever his previous knowledge of books and ancient lore, for years was a travelling missionary, associating freely with all classes of people, sharing their joy and sorrow, marking their motives, actions, impulses, rewards, and punishments. Nevertheless, seeing these Gospels, such as they are, contain the most we know of this most remarkable personage, and especially as Mr. Moss and other Secularistic teachers have stigmatized Jesus as an impostor, etc., from the said Gospels, it appears to me that our position, according to the light within us, and as seemeth to each a fair and rational manner, is to deal with the reported sayings of the Nazarene prophet as we find them in the Four Gospels.

In passing, my friend says: "I admire in parts the real character of Jesus—his fearlessness, his intrepidity, his hatred of all sorts of hypocrisy, his unselfishness, his single-mindedness; but then, I eliminate from the Gospels the fictitious supernatural element, repudiate entirely all that is inconsistent, etc., and erect out of all that remains the real and ideal man." Then the Jesus of the Gospels had a real and ideal character worthy of all admiration. Logically, he must either have been an impostor or a real man. If the Gospel Jesus assumed a character and power whereby he cheated and deceived the people, Mr. Moss may erect out of the Gospels a real and ideal man, but not the real and ideal man Jesus, for I hold he must either find in the Gospels an impostor, a cheater, and a liar, or the real ideal man Jesus, full of grace and truth.

. . . Therefore, as I fail to find either the supernatural or the miraculous in the sayings or doings of Jesus, I deny that he ever professed to work miracles. Neither can I find in the Gospel sayings or doings of Jesus anything approaching to charlatanism or arrogant assumption; and my learned opponent must be a little more definite in examples before he pours out such sweeping condemnation. An enthusiast and a parabolical preacher I certainly find, whose acts and wise sayings were to his followers life and liberty, and to his opponents a stumbling-block and blasphemy; and I, moreover, find a real human benefactor, who healed the sick and gave sight to the blind, not by any mountebank jugglery, but by an infinitude of human sympathy and accurate knowledge of the laws of healthy life; and even to this late year of grace the beautiful curative sympathy of Jesus, the Son of Man, is for ever coming in power and great glory in the clouds of pure air and tender pity for the afflicted, and as an almighty power to all real human benefactors; and also with withering condemnation upon the orthodox humbug of prayer, miracle, and quack nostrum of opiate and purge depletion and blister torture. If I mistake not, in every reported case of healing and sight restoring, or imparting, we find Jesus, as a man, by the power of knowledge, the potent force of sympathy, and unwavering faith in the curative power of nature, arousing and calling into healthy action diseased or dormant faculties; and I trust Mr. Moss believes that, when the majority of men and women have learned to know and practice the science of holy or healthy living, all the devils of disease and insanity will be subject to humanity. Happily for the race, there are many who know and believe that pathology is yet but a very imperfect art, struggling and thriving, through much error, prejudice, ignorance, and strife of tongues, towards a correct knowledge of the science of healing.

In regard to the dead-raising, I do not think, in the three reported Gospel cases, that we find anything like positive death or actual decomposition. Jesus is simply reported to have restored the widow's son, and to say that he was going to awake Lazarus out of sleep; and, in regard to the ruler's daughter, he said she was not dead, but sleeping. It is a well-known fact that most drugs used by medical men for assuagement of pain, or with a view to cure disease, produce many and strangely-varying effects and results, according to the different temperaments and constitutions of patients. It is likewise a well-known fact that even in our so-called civilized times there is too much reckless tossing of the supposed dead into coffins or on to the dissecting table; and in the dead-houses of our infirmaries and hospitals more than once the supposed dead son has slowly opened his eyes in response to his widow mother's sharp wailing cry of bereaved anguish; and, if we can believe the newspapers, ever and anon, somewhere in Europe, we read of a sad case of buried alive. "If, therefore, these things can be done in a green tree, what would be done in the dry?"

Thus it will be seen that I hold that there is no sure evidence of death unless where there are positive signs of decomposition. It is evident that Jesus simply believed that Lazarus was either in a trance, the result of physical exhaustion, or under the benumbing power of some poison administered with a view to ease pain or cure disease. Whatever conflicting opinions there may be in regard to Lazarus, one thing is evident, that Jesus did not call on God to suspend any or one law of nature. The Nazarene Prophet was certainly a believer in a parental providence, and, as on all previous occasions of eating, drinking, and healing, we read that he besought his Father God to recognize the work he was to do as for the glorifying of the Father and the Son as co-workers in blessing humanity. Prayer is no supernatural act. Is it not true that every earnest, holy wish is a prayer? It appears to me that, in the Gospel narrative of the raising or restoring of Lazarus, we find neither the supernatural nor the miraculous, but simply the heroic forth-putting of enlightened human intelligence chasing away the death-like darkness of evil and terror. By no word or deed did Jesus indicate any interference with the laws of nature, neither did he address one word to God calling for his special supernatural aid. However, if Mr. Moss will insist that Jesus pretended to be greater than human when restoring Lazarus, he must admit that he simply spoke and acted as a man. If the supernatural and miraculous were called into operation in the restoring of Lazarus, why did Jesus cry with a loud voice (made intensely pathetic and touching by his sympathetic sorrow on account of the sufferings of the victims of ignorance) to Lazarus to come forth? Why did he ask the people present to roll away the stone from the cave, and to untie the grave clothes? It must indeed have been a very clumsy, as well as a very weak, supernatural power which required so much human assistance. Surely the mysterious, miraculous power which gave life to a putrified corpse would also have rolled away the stone and freed the prisoner of the trammels of grave clothes without the aid of a loud voice, or weak, trembling hands, quivering with grief and suspense. And why, if Lazarus was four days absent from the body, have we no account of his wonderful experience? . . .

Mr. Moss asks, "Was Jesus an imposter?" and although he has quoted a few of the figurative and more mystical sayings of the Nazarene Prophet in support of his charges against him, and in a most unfair manner divorced said passages from their relative context, thereby to a degree despoiling them of their original meaning and harmonious consistency, he has, nevertheless, signally failed to convict the Gospel Jesus of imposition. Even granting that modern requirements pass by and despise a good part of his teaching, and that the majority fail to rightly interpret the ideal beauty of his doctrine of self-renunciation, that in no way takes from the soundness of his doctrine, the reality of his character, or the grandeur and beauty of his ideal standard of life and conduct; and, if Secularism build on any other foundation than truth and righteousness, it will only be one more delusive *ism* which the inflowing tide of progression will sweep away. One consolation, however, to all who believe that the human mind is the one divine miracle, moulding circumstances and events to its will (that if the majority of nations are full of puniness and pugnacity—that although the majority of men, even in our times, are mere pigmies in intellect, wrangling over word definitions and the worm-eaten husks of obsolete creeds—are but mere smoke and cinders, without the creative genius which, by an act of spontaneous generation, spread beauty and grace, and crowns with authority), is the consciousness that man can fall back on the irrefragable fact that Jesus, pre-eminently conspicuous among all the martyrs for truth and righteousness, stands forth as an immortal manifestation of all the graces and virtues which bend our entire manhood and womanhood in reverent adoration.

"Can a man work a miracle?" Before answering this question I must first know what my learned opponent considers a miracle. Is it not true that what is easy and perfectly natural to the enlightened student of any science appears incomprehensible and miraculous to the ignorant, benighted, and uneducated? The words, the ideas, the actions, and power of a thinker, a logician, and rhetorician, appear to the mute spectator like miracle, which he or she cannot explain, save by saying that the God-spirit of the universe flows into him and through him. Again, that which appeared miraculous and supernatural to the ancients has in our times become common property and power, raising mankind higher and higher in the scale of intellectual existence; and it may be that that which appears to the majority in our day as mystical, miraculous, and supernatural will, in the future, be irrefragable facts, and that mind, the only incomprehensible and limitless phenomenon, will ever more continue advancing in its natural ascent of upward and onward progression in the infinite cycles of endless evolution. If it be true that in nature there is no finity, but only infinity, to speak of a miracle and create ghosts of the miraculous and supernatural may be simply expressions of ignorance. The truth is, before we absolutely prove to what extent or limit it is possible for the human mind to apprehend, know, understand, utilize, and make subservient to the will, we are not in a position to definitely affirm where the natural ends and the supernatural begins.

"Can a law of nature be suspended at the command of man?" If we are to believe in the acknowledged achievements of science, unquestionably yes. What said Professor Simpson to the orthodox bigots who questioned the morality of chloroform administration under certain conditions or circumstances? Is it not an established fact that the natural laws of conscious thought or feeling are suspended by the administration of chloroform, and that by the command of man? If, therefore, in one instance, man can, by his inventions or discoveries, suspend one or more of the natural laws of sentient life, may it not be possible to multiply or increase such power and knowledge?—and the morality of such a philosophy can only be determined according to the amount of good or evil results. If mercy be exhibited, pain and suffering lessened, and happiness and health increased by such scientific suspensions of natural laws, I conclude all sensible people will recognize such power and knowledge as positive good. Why, then, apply a different standard of criticism and judgment in regard to Jesus? If to some of us his great intellectual and moral power (by which he revised the whole of the social structure of his times, by which he restored the original grandeur of the mental and moral constitution of humanity, and readjusted the disorganized will) appear as supernatural and miraculous, we must admit that he only exerted such power and knowledge in curing the diseased, healing the sick, vitalizing the paralytic, and in chasing away, or casting out, devils of insanity. If, therefore, a man only puts forth innate or acquired power in lessening pain, diminishing suffering, and increasing happiness, I hold that, even if his power appear magical and miraculous, he is no impostor, but a real friend and savior of mankind.

In passing, I remark that, if a man can by the power of scientific knowledge suspend one or more of the natural laws of conscious thought or feeling, and that without injury either to the permanence of law or law-respecting nature, it is surely reasonable and logical to suppose that God's perfect knowledge of the constitution and laws of solar systems will enable him, if he choose, for some beneficent purpose, to suspend one or more of said natural laws without injury to the permanent and invariable nature of law. Why speak of laws as if these were greater than nature? Logically, law must succeed and not precede the law-giver. If nature manifests its energy and power through the medium of law, law must have proceeded and come forth from nature; and, therefore, it is surely both reasonable and logical to suppose that nature can suspend or alter the operations of law, so that the various laws of matter and mind harmonize with the growth and requirements of nature. To conclude that nature has no power or dominion over law is to concede law the originator and absolute sovereign of nature.

"Can five thousand hungry persons be fed with five loaves and a few fishes?" We simply read that Jesus divided the little store of provision, and that all did eat and were filled. The truth is, the whole seeming miraculousness of this (so-called) miracle consists in the grandeur displayed by Jesus' power to rise superior to all outward circumstancess. If we consider the circumstance with an unbiased mind, we shall find that it was neither by miraculous multiplication of provisions, nor yet by weight or measure of meat consumed, that the enthusiastic crowd were filled and strengthened, but by the charity, the considerate care, brotherly love, and rich beneficence of the man who appeared a very God to the weltering masses, feeding them with the imperishable bread of truth and wisdom. The secret or seeming mystery of the wonderful power of Jesus simply lay in his absolute self-trust. His unfettered mind knew nothing of hindrance and limitation, and he never forgot that nature is greater than all law, operation, or force, and thus with fearless intrepidity he exercised the divine power and right of man. What appeared to his followers an impossibility was to him a grand occasion. If the loaves were few and the fishes small, he, the Son of Man, will infuse into the frugal repast the strength and purity of the immortal bread of life. To me, therefore, neither here nor yet in any other case did Jesus pretend to work a miracle. His supreme mastery over circumstances and his serene self-trust filled the crowd with wonder, faith, courage, and hope. They had been invited to partake of a commonwealth, and the exhilaration of joy which filled their grateful hearts made the smallest mouthful more to them than a feast. He is not great who can alter matter, or who spreads out lavishly from his store-houses and wine-cellars; but he alone is great who revolutionizes a corrupt social structure, and who liberates the mind and gives to it unbounded empire over every circumstance and event. . . .

Again, Jesus is said by my opponent to be an impostor because he asked his followers to believe he possessed supernatural power. If I read the Gospels aright, I do not think that Jesus in one instance used the word supernatural, and Mr. Moss might have been nearer the truth had he said that, through ignorance or superstition, Trinitarian believers have assumed that Jesus possessed supernatural power. He certainly claimed to be a revelation sent out from God, and again and again said his words were life and truth. I am inclined to think that Jesus knew more of nature in its immeasurable infinity than to babble about the supernatural. Judging from his life and teaching, and his complete oneness with the spirit of nature, I conclude that he believed the supernatural can neither be understood by man nor yet imparted or revealed to him by God. If the human mind only knows infinity, if it can penetrate into the laws of the phenomena of matter, and beyond those into the more mystical realms of sentient life-beats throbbing within the inner core of nature, then enlightened reason, finding only an infinity of nature, concludes the supernatural a mere mythical creation of ignorance and superstition.

If M. Jules Soury's psychological critical acumen be measured according to his knowledge of prognosis of disease, we shall have very little difficulty in showing that his own mental hallucinations prevented him from perceiving the sober sanity of Jesus.

"Did Jesus not profess to cast out devils?" "What are they?" "Science knows nothing of them." Science simply calls them by another name. I at once admit that Jesus professed to cast out devils, and, judging from many of his sayings, he believed in a personal Devil. Such a belief, however, in no way proves him to have been an impostor. It was something to the credit of the Jews that, if they believed all help in time of trouble and deliverance from evil came to them specially from Jehovah, Israel's God, they likewise attributed all outbreaks of social anarchy, family calamities, and physical diseases to the supernatural interference of evil spirits or devils. For a personal Devil we have substituted a principle of evil, and for demoniac, foaming devils we have varying forms of insanity—epilepsy, convulsions, and paralysis. . . .

"Did he [Jesus] not profess that he was the only medium through which God could be approached?" "Did he not say, I and my Father are one," etc.? It appears to me that Jesus simply claimed to be the only medium through which God as a father could be approached—*i.e.,* through sonship with the Eternal Spirit. It may be that the conception or idea of God as a universal, beneficent parent had dawned on the human mind prior to the advent of Jesus. Nevertheless, he was the first who publicly taught such a doctrine as the way to a knowledge of mankind's origin and oneness with the infinite—the absolute and perfect; and thus the perfect man, both obeying and commanding the laws of nature, is the way, the truth, and the life; and for Jesus to say, No one cometh to the father save by me or my doctrine, was neither an earnest of imposition nor an evidence of insanity, but simply an enlightened, heroic man, with the courage of his opinions and the bravery to die in their defense. . . .

If the doctrine Jesus taught was to him everlasting life, his saying, "Whosoever believeth on me shall not perish, but have everlasting life," was simply an assertion that he believed that the doctrine which was life to him would, if believed in and acted upon, save nations and men from perishing by the various forms of evil which prey on the credulous ignorance of the poor and oppressed, and which lay in wait to hunt him to death as a heretic and blasphemer.

"Can belief in a man save humanity?" If I mistake not, Mr. Moss has himself again and again written that man, and not God, can and will save humanity. If he really believes what he writes, will he not indignantly repudiate the charge if some less Rationalistic believer stigmatize him an impostor? Why cannot Secularistic teachers deal with Jesus as they expect others to deal with them? Is it not true that all higher knowledge, all increase of moral and mental power, all apprehension of solar and sentient laws, and all imperishable life, flow into humanity through man—*i.e.*, that man is the organized eater of the subtle exhalations of life; and this life, manifested in words and deeds, is salvation to the race; and thus the word-made flesh is the life and savior of humanity?

There may have been, both before and after Jesus, men who suffered more for truth and righteousness, riper scholars, more subtle philosophers, and more eloquent orators, but none more earnest and more real, more pure and comprehsnive in conception of the love and charity which alone can knit men together in amicable industry and enterprise, and none more sublimely great with the strength of wisdom and the beauty of tenderness; and although, in the future, science, art, and poetry make our earth a very Eden, in which love, wisdom, and justice continually chant a rhythmical trio, no more cosmopolitan foundation can any priest, prophet, or reformer lay than that which has been already laid by Jesus, the founder of the brotherhood of Humanity.

. . . If my friend conscientiously rejects the doctrine and dogmas of Christian orthodoxy, I do not see how he can consistently call in its evidence as an authority in pronouncing judgment on any other prophet, priest, or system of religion. The truth is, if we reject the supernatural, miraculous, and infallible in orthodox Christianity, we cannot accept its judgment as a standard of integrity whereby to arrive at a true conception of the character and teaching of any religious prophet or priest. Therefore, when Mr. Moss cites any religious sect as an authority in natural religion and moral ethics, so he reveals the weak side of his argument that reason and common sense at once perceive it to be a mere bundle of heterogeneous sophistry. In fact, to stigmatize Jesus, Buddha, and Mohammed as impostors bespeaks a want of intellectual comprehensiveness and destitution of sympathetic insight and perception, which disqualify such a one from fairly criticizing or appreciating men whose aspirations followed after the infinite and eternal, and whose emotions centered in God and the placidity of life, unmixed by carnal passion or sensual desire. Without comprehensive sympathy it is impossible to criticize the past, or even to attempt to touch and vitalize the hidden springs of the present. We may prate of progress, and eloquently denounce all save our pet theories; but the master power which moves the world one mile forward in true progression enters sympathetically into the very inmost being of society, and, with wonderful affinity, feels the aggregate of its needs, sufferings, and undeveloped capabilities, and, fusing the light of a new mind, creates a diviner atmosphere and imparts fresh power. Enthusiasts and specialists Jesus, Buddha, and Mohammed may have been; but the devout fervor of an enthusiast and the passionate earnestness of a zealot differ as widely from the self-seeking impudence and cool audacity of an impostor as truth from falsehood. Therefore, I once more say that Secularistic writers who stigmatize Jesus as an impostor either fail to understand the meaning of the word, or fancy the majority of their readers one-sided ignoramuses, ready and willing to swallow any pill of sect-nostrum they may choose to compound.

If I rightly interpret Secularism, it has higher aims than mere sect propaganda. It is not true that it aims at the enlightenment, liberalization, and sanctification of the entire mental, moral, and emotional nature of mankind? Does it not burn with holy enthusiasm to unswaddle the conscience of every form of benumbing dogmas and dwarfing superstition, and to exterminate the supernatural sanction of priestly dominion? Methinks the giant martyrs of Freethought (whose bloody sufferings of Inquisition torture, lonely imprisonment, and cruel death purchased for us a free platform and a free Press) followed after some such ideal; and, if ever Secularism became an intellectual monarch, merging error and superstition into natural religion, scientific wisdom, and moral grandeur, it will cease throwing its mud and dirt of scurrilous ridicule at the thorn-crowned brow of Jesus of Nazareth, and set itself to the grander and diviner task of reading and preaching his gospel through the enlarged enlightenment and learning of advanced civilization. The work of the true reformer is not to destroy or defame the New Testament, but to read its gospel with a diviner vision, and preach it with more rational comprehensiveness and more cosmopolitan sympathy than the illiterate Galilean fisherman or the learned Paul, fresh from the ponderous ritual of Judaism; read and preach it to the weary, heavy-ladened, and hungry, so as to remould and modernize all that is permanent and saving in Christ's gospel of sonship with eternal truth and brotherhood with humanity; and so gather up and conserve all the imperishable and perennial of every prophet, priest, and apostle, and every system of religious, social, and political life. Mr. Moss will, therefore, perceive that I do not object to a remorseless and impartial application of logic in regard to the character and teaching of Jesus, but simply refuse to accept any cited authority or standard of criticism save the unfettered reason of an unbiased mind, moving in harmony with sympathetic insight and the finely-touched perception of a pure moral will.

After asking if Jesus preached sound doctrine, Mr. Moss quotes a string of the more extreme and transcendental sayings, extracted from what is termed the Sermon on the Mount; and although, as heretofore, he has wrested these from their context, as examples of unsound doctrine, I will deal with the passages quoted as if standing alone without any modifying or qualifying context, and endeavor from these alone to demonstrate Jesus as a teacher of sound doctrine, far exceeding the wisdom of the Stoics, or the milk-and-water piety of the adultered rushlight of modern requirements.

1. "Lay not up for yourselves treasures upon the earth, but lay up for yourselves treasures in heaven." It may sound rather strange in the ears of modern scribes and pharisees; nevertheless, this so-called unsound doctrine appears to me the very acme of social and political prosperity and harmony. It is the perennial trunk of the tree of life, from whence shall continually spring the gigantic branches of wisdom, love, and beauty, the leaves of which will be for the healing of the people. Is it not true that laying up of treasure for self upon earth has been and is the accursed bane of true civilization? Is it not the benumbing incubus which crushes out the godlike energies of millions in every nation, and breeds within their starving-rebelling bosoms the viper brood of despair, insanity, assassination, rapine, and every form of anarchy and murderous revolution? What is the monstrous iniquity of entail land possession, perpetual pensions, legacied princes, and every form of unequalled distribution of labor and reward, but the unsound doctrine of laying up treasures upon the earth? If this be the light of modern requirements, it is a pernicious, positive evil; and it appears to me that our modern unsound doctrine, or iniquitous systems, are the impositions which specially call for reform; and I trust that nothing Mr. Moss can advance will tempt me to forsake "the true light which lighteth everyone who cometh into the world." The light of modern requirements, forsooth! Surely it cannot be that one bearing a pioneer's torch and wearing the crown of a martyr's reproach points me to the dim, misty light of modern requirements: "when light is darkness, how great is the darkness." The truth is, the light of modern requirements bends the knee and prostrates the conscience before an expensive mummy crown, and steels its heart against the piteous wail of millions of ill-clad, half-fed paupers: on Sunday it whines prayers to God to send a plenteous harvest, and on Monday, in its synods, assemblies, and legislative courts, it cries away with the Jesus men who seek to restore a commonwealth of religious and social rights, and restore to us the titled treasure-holders, the common Barabbases. The light of modern requirements has many scribes and pharisees, who wrangle and squabble over "tithes of mint and cumin," over oaths and affirmations, but who pass by the weightier matter of the law—justice, mercy, and righteousness; scribes and pharisees who form a majority to close the doors of Parliament against all who aim at the abolition of perpetual pensions and the reforming and remolding of land laws. Here again, however, as with miracle-working, Mr. Moss evidently interprets the sayings of Jesus in the light of mere sect bigotry and prejudice. Jesus again and again told his followers that the kingdom of heaven was within them,

and not in a far country, nor yet in any "lo here or lo there;" and I am inclined to think Mr. Moss believes it is better and nobler to have an inward possession of right-feeling and right-doing than to trample over the weak, or, in any prudential manner, make use of their money or necessities for self-glorification or self-bettering; that he believes it better to spend and be spent in the cause of Humanity than to selfishly leave the oppressed and ignorant in bondage, and lay up for himself an abundance of material treasure which can only pamper the physical wants of his nature.

2. "Take no thought for what you shall eat and what you shall drink," etc. Most, I think, will admit that mere instinct will manage the eating and drinking business—*i.e.,* provided those who lay up treasures for self upon the earth will allow the millions of ill-clad, half-fed masses, destitute of houses, lands, wine-cellars, barns, store-houses, or bank accounts, to get a bird's privilege of gathering an ear of corn, or carrying off a ripe apple or cherry. The truth is, if the light of modern requirements has no diviner or higher theme to suggest as a stimulant for earnest thought than eating and drinking, I hardly think we have reached an era of enlightened civilization essential for pronouncing a positive judgment in regard to the character and teaching of one who, while humbly associating with all classes, healing the sick and teaching the ignorant in filial trust, claimed sonship with the eternal spirit, and, while reverently spanning a past eternity of marvellous infinity, also bridged over a future eternity of still more marvellous infinity, and, gathering up the sins, sorrows, joys, aspirations, and capabilities of mankind, lived a tender, sympathetic brother of every race and tribe, and died a meek, willing martyr for the divinest truth which can dawn on the mind of mankind.

3. "Behold the fowls of the air, for they sow not, neither gather into barns;" and I add: "Consider the flowers of the field; they toil not, neither do they spin," etc. By such sayings it is evident Jesus wished to inculcate the beauty and purity of a natural life, untrammelled with artificial wants and more sensual desires; and not, as Mr. Moss seems to think, to encourage or teach a destructive theory of mere speculative abstract piety, or to establish any form of monastic or recluse asceticism. His own active practical life demonstrated the fact that his religion touched, vitalized, and sanctified all the springs and relations of daily life. Again, what do we learn when we behold the fowls of the air? If we wisely read, this beautiful illustration teaches no unsound doctrine, but rather life and truth. Beholding the fowls of the air, we neither learn idleness, sensualism, artificiality, nor yet any other form of inactive and selfish morbidity. They rise with the sun, and soar and sing; they love, marry, and bring up their young, and tenderly nurse and feed them; they cheerfully revel in all the joy and beauty and liberty of their natural life; they only breed young in times of plenty, and build for them cosy nests, around which the pure air of heaven blows health and purity; they have no fever hovels, no dens of crime and pinched paupers, no work-

houses or penal imprisonment; and, were it not for the powder and shot of lords and princes, who lay up treasures for self upon the earth, terror and desolation would not come nigh their dwellings.

In summer, too, the roses and lilies preach to us their sacrament of beauty and sweetness; and, if stern fate doom them to die in winter, they neither leave the funereal gloom of Atheism, nor yet the night-shade of Pessimism, to obscure the coming spring, whose mystic power calls them forth to a resurrection of ever-evolving life.

I grant, however, that all this, in the light of modern requirements, may appear very unsound doctrine. Nevertheless, seeing we are still far from perfection, it is surely monstrous folly to set up the light of modern requirements as an absolute umpire in matters pertaining to the eternal well-being of every unit of sentient life. We have glanced at some of the results of the light of modern requirements, and a mere cursory analysis discovers the sad fact that we have very little real light or wise understanding to dispute about. There is, without doubt, a vast amount of misspent energy and misused power; but the acme of the present light and learning seem to thrust humanity to the wall, and set to a teeth-and-nail fight over national prestige and an electing God.

4. I am inclined to think the humble or poor in spirit are the true aristocracy of earth. Physically, they may be fettered by the injustice and imperfections of our social and political structures; but surely we shall not condescend to measure the stature or freedom of our men and women by mere external surroundings, or the quantities or qualities of their food and raiment. It is the arrogant, the superciliously proud, and the tyrannical dominant classes who, in all ages and in every nation, make slaves of the unprotected and ignorant. It is the poor righteous man who saves the cities, and the proud mountebank kings, grasping landowners, and selfish capitalists who bind the poor and ignorant in chains. It is the mocking revelry of such sensual knaves which, in all ages, drowns the righteous complaint of the masses, who must either take the kick and the crumb, or die of starvation, like a dog, unpitied and unmourned. Had Mr. Moss more real knowledge of the inmates of workhouses and the national plagues which eat out the heart of society, he would find, in most cases, that it is those who have taken too much thought for eating, and especially for drinking, who fill our workhouses. Drunkenness, wasteful improvidence, and our corrupt social and political systems are the evils and impositions which make workhouses and heavy taxation grinding curses on honest poverty. There are a few cases of sheer poverty in all workhouses; but, if we only had honest poverty to deal with, society would soon right itself. It is idleness, drunkenness, ignorant wastefulness, prostitution, and thousands of illegitimate waifs of children (promiscuously begotten and fiendishly denied by the rogues and vagabonds too clever and well versed in the light of modern requirements of laying

up of treasures for ever passing through the purgatorial fires of workhouse bed and board), which constitute a large majority of the inmates of charity institutes. The modern rogue and vagabond is a beggar on horseback, and our princes and king-men have bleeding feet, torn hearts, a smoky garret, and one meal a day.

If all men imitated the fowls of the air, the plentiful bosom of the earth would supply rich nourishment for all her children, and this world would be a very Canaan, flowing with milk and honey; and pauperism and the howling wail of starvation would be unknown. Poverty certainly is an evil; but it is not the greatest, and no right-minded man or woman will ever advocate poverty as essential to godliness, or any form of noble living; and to affirm, or even suppose, that he—who spent his life in aiding and blessing the poor, who commended the earnest charity of the widow, and uttered withering woes at all who laid on heavy taxes and oppressed burdens—either directly or indirectly commended poverty as an essential good, is to wantonly misrepresent the meaning of his life, teaching, and mission. It is not at poverty where the axe requires to be first laid, but at the evils and impositions which render it an inevitable condition of unjust laws and bad government. Undoubtedly, poverty makes many a gem of purest ray to blush unseen; nevertheless, poverty gave the Jews a Jesus, the Greeks a Homer, and voluntary poverty the Eastern nations a Buddha; and stern poverty, in modern times, gave Britain a Burns; and all over the face of the earth many homes of honest poverty suggest to the poet the sublime picture of the "Cottar's Saturday Night."

5. If Mr. Moss sneer at the doctrine of forbearance and the punishment of forgiveness, I suppose he simply believes in dethroning one Caesar to anoint another, or the god of the *golden calf* with a man's head. Epictetus no doubt concluded he would put himself on a level with the stealer of his lamp had he uttered a weak complaint, let alone punish the thief. It is surely a wiser and more humane doctrine to allow the coatless thief to carry away our over-cloak than enrich a lawyer to convict the poor wretch and burden the State keeping him in gaol. Better allow a poor contractor— it may be, driven desperate by dull trade—to charge a little extra than go to court and thereby both become bankrupt. (It is individual cases which are here indicated, and not national or general codes of rectitude.)

6. Down in the lowest slums of vice and crime the profane rascal, saturated through and through with seared iniquity, will give manly, scientific rounds of blows with any belted knight, cultured Secularist, or pugnacious Calvinist; "but he that ruleth his own soul is greater than he who taketh a city." If giving blow for blow be the sound doctrine of modern requirements, then, judging from the present attitude of nations and sects, both secular and sacred, we may expect a war-millennium some time in the autumn. . . .

In conclusion, Mr. Moss says he despises the teaching which asks a man to forsake the sympathy of social relationships and social comforts;

nevertheless, I do not imagine my friend so narrow, in mental acumen as to suppose Jesus here meant his followers to ruthlessly sever or neglect the duties of husband, father, brother, or son. There is a deeper and far more significant forsaking here implied—a forsaking which takes place every day in many homes in every city—viz., the forsaking of the unsound doctrine and ignorant prejudice of fathers, husbands, wives, brothers, and sisters; and, I fear, if we have the bravery to be true to conscience, we shall, whether we desire it or not, have to forego a good deal of earthly possession. I do not suppose, judging from his own life, that Jesus preached the doctrine of rewards as a stimulus or reason why men should do good or be good, but simply because he knew that reward always follows in the footsteps of noble action and lofty aspiration, as surely and naturally as light chases away darkness. However, if Mr. Moss will despise such teaching, why traduce the poor creed-bound minister who loves his wife, children, glebe, house, and bread and butter, better than poverty and an unfettered conscience? If it is better for the peer, the pope, the prince, and the monarch to love their earthly possessions more than the general good, then let us be done with cant, and allow the motley farce to play on.

I do not question my friend's love for humanity, and know nothing of the nature of the reward he receives for his service to the brotherhood; but this I say, that the man or woman who expects to inherit everlasting life, and to transmit it to posterity, is unworthy of such a Divine gift if he or she put more value on individual joys and comforts than universal good. While society is imperfect, and the majority ignorant and unprotected, every martyr for righteousness, every true social and political reformer, and every bringer-in of higher scientific light must, to a great extent, forsake the comfort of property, the enrapturing pleasures of love and friendship, and the blessed joys of connubial endearment. From the tiny babe in the cradle (slain by impure gases and murdered by the legalized wholesale poisoning of compulsory vaccination) up to the giant martyrs of all ages and nations who, like Jesus, go bravely forward to every form of reproach, torture, ignominy, and death, the bloody anguish of suffering innocence is the Divine sacrifice which taketh away sin. There may, however, come a time when true progression will require no more sacrifice—a time when holiness will be inscribed on our horses, when peace and goodwill shall wave on the front of our war-ships, when righteousness, like a mighty river, shall run down our streets—a time when fraternity and brotherhood will be the ensign on every breast, the motto on every Parliament house, and the password of all social organizations; but, then, all the impositions of the light of modern requirements and the unsound doctrine of sectism will have been merged into the true light of the human gospel of love, truth, and charity inaugurated by Jesus of Nazareth.

MR. MOSS'S SECOND PAPER.

My acceptance of the challenge of Mrs. Agnes Rollo Wilkie seems likely to involve me in a discussion of considerable length; but, as it has always been a source of great delight to me to discuss with an opponent whose sole desire is to arrive at truth, not to win a mere dialectical victory, I proceed to the task of examining the position taken by my lady disputant with no small degree of pleasure.

At the outset let me say that my opponent has not adhered strictly to the points at issue in this debate, and that, although her exhaustive and able reply may be justly regarded as an admirable piece of composition, alike creditable to her head and heart, its logic, in many respects, is extremely weak. For instance, the question in dispute is not whether a man named Jesus ever lived, who was a noble, intrepid, magnanimous soul, towering high above his fellows, and possessing many admirable qualities of nature rarely blended together in one man, but whether, taking the Four Gospels as authentic, the Jesus therein described is such a man, or a Being claiming higher attributes than those belonging to humanity, and teaching doctrines that are absolutely faultless; or whether, after all, the Jesus of the Gospels is merely a charlatan, a pretender claiming to work miracles, professing to be on an equal with God himself, and preaching doctrines that common sense repudiates as unreasonable, impracticable, and morally harmful.

If I understand my graceful opponent aright, there is a perfect argument between us in one respect. We are both agreed that Jesus was not God. In erecting for our admiration an ideal or real Jesus, who, my antagonist says, "stands forth a giant among men, as the divinest and purest representative of all manly excellences," Mrs. Wilkie should, at least, have given us some idea of the sources of evidence accessible to her from which she formed her opinion. . . .

It is perfectly obvious, then, that my friend adopts the same process in arriving at a just estimate of the character of Jesus as I do myself; all she objects to are "the unjust accusations which some leading Secularistic teachers ever and anon heap on the memory of the noblest and purest martyr of Freethought and pure religion." With that, however, I have nothing to do. Agnes Rollo Wilkie goes further; and here I join issue. "The truth is," she says, "unless we read the Gospels through the jaundiced optics of Roman and Protestant Trinitarianism, we shall find nothing of the supernatural or miraculous in the sayings or doings of Jesus." Not only do I strongly dispute this statement, but I think I can prove to demonstration the very opposite. And upon this the whole question turns. If Jesus was a man, did he profess to work miracles? If yes, then, indeed, must he have been an impostor, since the whole of human experience goes to show the impossibility of their happening. A miracle is not the suspension of one law of nature; it is a violation of the whole of the laws of nature.

With a marvellous lack of plausibility, my opponent seeks to show that the cases of recorded "raising of the dead" were not miracles, after all; that there is no evidence of actual death, no proof of decomposition. True, there is no proof that Lazarus was dead, except the statement of the Gospels. But is not the testimony of Jesus to be considered reliable? Is his veracity to be impugned? In John xi. 14 my opponent will find these words: "Then Jesus said unto them plainly, Lazarus is dead." Could anything be more emphatic? Why should Jesus deceive his disciples? Why should he "weep" at the grave, if Lazarus was not dead? Why should Martha say, "Lord by this time he stinketh, for he hath been dead four days," if he were in reality not dead, and not in a state of decomposition? But when my antagonist says that Jesus "never pretended to work miracles," Does she mean to imply that making the blind to see, the deaf to hear, the lame to walk, feeding thousands with five loaves and two fishes, casting out devils, walking upon the sea, ascending into heaven, were natural occurrences? Or is it her contention that Jesus never pretended that he did these things, but that the writers of the Gospels, who did not know the real character of the "divinest and purest of men," asserted it for him?

Are the Gospels altogether unreliable when they state that Jesus performed miracles, and pretended not only to cast out devils himself, but to give his disciples power to do likewise? And if the Gospels are unreliable in this respect, why should their account of the sayings of Jesus be considered reliable? But let us dwell for a moment on this question of the miracles of Jesus.

Mrs. Wilkie endeavors to show that Jesus did not wish it to appear that he had miraculously raised Lazarus from the dead. Well, suppose I allow, which I certainly cannot, that sort of explanation to suffice in this case, what of the other alleged miracles? Mrs. Wilkie would find some of them much more difficult to explain away than the one which serves the purpose of illustrating her argument. When Jesus rebuked the wind and commanded the waves to cease beating so roughly against the ship in which he and his disciples were sailing, would my antagonist have us believe that Jesus only did what anybody else might easily have accomplished, if they possessed the requisite amount of faith? Or would she say that, just at the moment Jesus rose to rebuke the winds and the sea, the tempest subsided? Are all the wonderful doings of Jesus to be explained away in this sophistical fashion? Did the five loaves and two fishes expand so enormously as to satisfy the appetites of thousands of people? Were the two blind men who had their eyesight restored to them merely intellectually blind? When Jesus pretended to walk upon the sea, was it upon a large piece of floating ice? Certain I am that I have not read the Gospels through the "jaundiced optics of Roman and Protestant Trinitarianism;" yet I undoubtedly find that the sayings and doings of Jesus are enveloped in the miraculous and supernatural.

Mere word jugglery I detest: clear thinking and clear expression of our thoughts are inculcated as important duties by Secularists; and, if my opinions are unreasonable, I shall certainly refuse to distort the plain meaning of language for the purpose of bolstering up any pet theory which I may hold in regard to Jesus or any other religious reformer. The Gospels seem to me to be little else than a long record of the miraculous performance of Jesus; his teachings are embraced in a very small compass, and, were it not for the atmosphere of supernaturalism surrounding him, the religion of which he was the founder could never have wielded the power it has in the world.

If Jesus did not perform miracles, he deceived his disciples; he deceived the multitude who followed him; he deceived himself, and through him the masses have been deceived ever since.

The Folly of Jesus.

In a London asylum at the present time there is a man who declares himself to be a king, and that all the people about him are conspiring to keep him out of his rights. Of course he is not a king; he is merely a pretender, and a lunatic. His pretension, that of being a monarch, is the result of a disordered mind; he is, nevertheless, an impostor. Certainly his imposition is not of so bad a character as that of him who knowingly deceives his fellow man; but unconscious deception is often as disastrous in its results. In the religious world of today there are hundreds of earnest men who believe themselves to be the special "favorites of God," and to be filled with the "Holy Ghost." The fact that they are mistaken does not prevent them from deceiving others, and this imposition frequently has for its result the filling of our lunatic asylums. In like manner, I declare that Jesus thought himself capable of working miracles; thought and said that he was a veritable God, and that belief in him determined the posthumous destiny of every person born into this world. He was wrong; but that did not prevent thousands of people believing in his pretensions, many declaring that, if Jesus were in fact not God, he was the greatest impostor that ever lived. Now, I do not go so far as that; I merely say that Jesus of the Gospels never lived—that is, I deny the Jesus who was born of a virgin, who was tempted by a devil, who performed a number of miracles, and who, as a climax to an extraordinary career, was crucified, and, after lying in the grave about two days, rose from the dead, and in the presence of a multitude of spectators ascended upwards through the clouds into heaven. If, however, I believed in the Gospels, I could see no alternative but to accept one of the two positions named above. Inasmuch as I do not believe in the Gospels, it is still open for me, if evidence is forthcoming, to believe that a man named Jesus lived, who did the best he could in his day to preach what he believed to be true, and to assist in removing many of the evil influences by which the people of his day were surrounded. My able opponent, Mrs. Wilkie, is not satisfied with this opinion; and, while she does not regard the Four Gospels as authentic, she goes to them, diligently reads them, and seeks to demonstrate from them that Jesus never pretended to be God, or to be on an equal with God; that he did not believe in the supernatural; that he did not pretend to work miracles, though he did cast out devils; and that, above all, Jesus "stands forth as an immortal manifestation of all the graces and virtues which bend our entire manhood and womanhood in reverent adoration." It is against this that I protest; and I sincerely object that these exaggerated descriptions of the moral excellence of the life and teachings of Jesus are as misleading and erroneous as the contentions of the priests, who exalt the poor Carpenter of Nazareth into an infinite God. While Mrs. Wilkie goes to the Gospels for the purpose of showing Secularists what an erroneous impression they have formed of Jesus, I go to the Gospels to demonstrate that Jesus was not the kind of individual she, in all the generosity of her heart, would like him to be, but a man who made claim to extraordinary powers, which it was utterly impossible for him to possess; and, if it be objected that Jesus believed he was in possession of this power, it does not follow that he was not an impostor, for the greatest impostors that ever lived have been deceived themselves, as well as deceiving the masses who followed them.

My antagonist does not seem to attach the same meaning to words that I do, when frequently the whole force of the argument rests on the interpretation to be given to one single word. I asked, "Can a law of nature be suspended at the command of man?" and my graceful opponent at once replies: "If we are to believe in the acknowledged achievements of science, unquestionably yes." To illustrate what she means by this, she observes: "What said Professor Simpson to the orthodox bigots who questioned the morality of chloroform administration under certain conditions and circumstances? Is it not an established fact that the natural laws of conscious thought or feeling are suspended by the administration of chloroform, and that by the command of man? If, therefore, in one instance, man can, by his inventions or discoveries, suspend one or more of the natural laws of sentient life, may it not be possible to multiply and increase such power and knowledge? And the morality of such a philosophy can only be determined according to the amount of good or evil results." Here it is clear that my opponent has fallen into an error. Her illustration is not that of the suspension of any law of nature; it is only that of using one law of nature to counteract the effect of another. On this point it will not be out of place to quote John Stuart Mill, who says ("Essays on Nature," page 5): "The nature of a thing means its entire capacity of exhibiting phenomena. And since the phenomena which a thing exhibits, however much they vary in different circumstances, are always the same in the same circumstances, they admit of being described in general forms of words, which are called the *laws* of a thing's nature." Further on he observes: "Though we cannot emancipate ourselves from the laws of nature as a whole, we can escape from any particular law of nature, if we are able to withdraw ourselves from the circumstances in which it acts." That is all that is done in the case of a person who is chloroformed before an operation is performed upon him; he is deprived of his consciousness by one law of nature, which counteracts another which would cause him to feel agonizing pain. A miracle means much more than this. To satisfy five thousand hungry persons with "five loaves and two fishes" is a very different thing from benumbing the brain with chloroform, in order to painlessly remove a limb. One is a physical impossibility; the other a perfectly natural event. . . .

Another folly of the Nazarene Carpenter was the erroneous notion he propagated concerning himself. He thought he was God, and said so. "I and my Father are one," "Before Abraham was I am;" and when tempted by Satan, Jesus answered: "It is written again, Thou shalt not tempt the Lord thy God" (Matt. iv. 7). To say that Jesus elsewhere declared that he was not God does not strengthen my opponent's position; it only weakens it; for, if the declarations of Jesus were of such a strangely contradictory nature, what reliance can be placed upon them? My learned antagonist tries to explain away the statement of Jesus, that he and his father "were one." Her explanation, however, that Jesus simply "claimed to be the only medium through which God as a father could be approached—*i.e.*, through sonship with the eternal spirit," is rather unsatisfactory, in view of the fact that Mrs. Wilkie acknowledges that Jesus was merely a man.

The language of Jesus is so misleading and mystifying that a thousand different interpretations have been put upon it; and I say, in the language of Mr. B. F. Underwood, that "clear thinking is quite as important as correct living, and that the man who helps to make men think aright thereby helps to advance, not only intellectual but moral progress, and to augment the sum of human happiness; and that he, on the contrary, however unexceptionable his conduct and pure his motives, who helps to befog, mystify, and confuse the minds of men by his shallow, dreamy thought is quite as much the enemy of moral as of intellectual advancement."

Belief and Salvation.

In making bold to grapple with my question, "Can belief in a man save humanity?" Mrs. Wilkes launches forth into an argument which she appears to think quite unanswerable. "If I mistake not," she says, "Mr. Moss has himself again and again written that man, and not God, can save humanity. If he really believes what he writes, will he not indignantly repudiate the charge if some less Rationalistic believer stigmatize him an impostor?" Let the matter be looked at fairly, and what does this argument amount to? Every earnest reformer claims for the principles he advocates fair, candid, and impartial consideration, and warns his hearers that the rejection of these principles is likely to be fraught with great danger, ultimately perhaps leading to the moral ruin of those who repudiate them. To the mind of Mrs. Wilkie this is tantamount to a preacher saying: "He that believeth on me shall be saved, and he that believeth not shall be damned;" and this, my antagonist avers, was all that Jesus did. He announced his doctrines to the world: of their truth and moral value he at least was in no kind of doubt, and he left them for the people to accept or reject, with the full responsibility as to consequences, whichever way they decided. And so Mrs. Wilkie confidently declares that, "if the doctrine Jesus taught was to him everlasting life, his saying, 'Whosoever believeth on me shall not perish, but have everlasting life,' was simply an assertion that he believed that the doctrine which was life to him would, if believed in and acted upon, save nations and men from perishing by the various forms of evil which preyed on the credulous ignorance of the poor and oppressed, and which lay in wait to hunt him to death as a heretic and blasphemer." This reads well, and looks plausible enough, until taken in conjunction with other declarations of Jesus. What were the hearers of Jesus to be saved from? Not from ignorance, nor vice, nor crime, but from "the wrath to come." When? Not in the present life, but in the next world. The people were to believe that Jesus came to save them, and that he alone could successfully prevent the damnation of all mankind. And so, when instructing his disciples to go forth to preach, Jesus distinctly charged them to tell the people that "the kingdom of heaven is at hand." This was one of the chief doctrines of the Nazarene. With him the "day of judgment" was "at hand," and he frequently described the awful fate that awaited those who disbelieved in him. The goats were to go away into "everlasting punishment," but the sheep were to enjoy "eternal life."

There is a wonderful difference between the doctrine of belief as taught by Jesus and that propagated by Rationalistic teachers. With Jesus belief in him and his pretensions meant salvation. The man who said "I believe," was insured against all risks as far as the next world was concerned; but he who doubted, and said so, was condemned, and unheard in his defense. Nay, when the disciples went into any city to proclaim Jesus as the Savior of mankind, if they were not cordially received, they were directed by the "meek and lowly Jesus" to "shake off the dust of their feet," and it would be "more tolerable for Sodom and Gomorrah in the day of judgment than for that city." Could human folly or wickedness go further than that? No Secularist ever preached damnation in the next world for those who disbelieved his teachings in this. The Rationalist merely says that certain actions in life are attended by certain consequences, and urges, with all the ardor of his nature, that men should adopt true principles, in order that they might know how best to promote the highest happiness for all. I am a Secularist; but I do not say that Mrs. Wilkie will be damned if she does not believe me or my doctrines. Right belief, of course, I hold to be of great importance;

but good conduct I consider to be of infinitely higher concern to man. A man with a wrong belief may often do noble deeds, prompted thereto by the love of humanity. But, as a matter of fact, it is wise to "learn what is true, in order that you may practise what is right." A man's belief alone will never save him; it is his actions that will do that. And, though his belief may be egregiously wrong, if his life be pure, his aspirations lofty, his actions just, he will deserve condemnation neither in this world nor in any possible world beyond the grave.

Doubtful Morality.

. . . Though I cannot lay claim to the possession of the "finely-touched perception" referred to, I dare declare that I have considered the life and character of Jesus, as recorded in the Four Gospels, with an unbiased mind, and that I do not see any reason for concluding that Jesus was, as Mrs. Wilkie affirms, the "divinest and purest of men"—nay, the free exercise of my reason leads me irresistibly to the opinion that he was no better than some men who lived before him, and in many respects inferior to many who have lived since. I do not say that the doctrines he taught were not very good, considering the time in which he lived. What is wise or good in one age is not necessarily so in another; and it would be just as unreasonable to suppose that the teachings of the present time will be considered as wise and useful a thousand years hence as they are today, as to imagine that the truth and moral value of the utterances of Jesus will be equally acknowledged through all time. Everything in this world is a growth, including the knowledge of truth and morality. The intellect of Jesus was not equal to that of Socrates or St. Paul; and each of these teachers was intellectually very far removed from a Bacon, a Mill, or a Spencer. And who can expect otherwise, except those of "biased mind"? "Sympathetic natures" are naturally disposed to elevate Jesus to a position far above his deserts; but logical minds are bound to judge his character and teachings in comparison with others, and not to allow feeling to usurp the position which is only properly filled by reason.

Among the unsound doctrines of Jesus I named, "Lay not up for yourselves treasures upon earth, but lay up for yourselves treasures in heaven," etc. So far from this doctrine appearing unsound to the "sympathetic nature" of my antagonist, it is to her "the very acme of social and political prosperity and harmony." Imagine social and political prosperity being dependent on those who lay up their treasures in heaven.

My opponent charges me, somewhat ungenerously, with wresting passages from their context; yet in this very case I gave the full quotation, while Mrs. Wilkie only gives it in part; and she should remember that the illustrations supplied by Jesus for the purpose of assisting his hearers in understanding his teachings go to support the position which I have taken in this debate, and not that which my antagonist has maintained with such conspicuous ability. Not only were men to "lay not up treasures on earth," but they were to "take no thought for their life;" they were not to make any more provision for themselves than the "lilies of the field," but to "seek first the kingdom of God and his righteousness," and all else would be added. When was social or political prosperity advanced in the smallest degree by practice based on such teaching? I know that it is not wise to think solely of hoarding up wealth in this world and neglecting to fulfill our manifold duties, as citizens, parents, brethren; but to take as little "thought of the morrow" as the lilies of the field, leaving each day's difficulties to come upon us without previous consideration or prudential forethought, is to allow ourselves to be buffeted about by wind and storm, and to drift aimlessly to inevitable destruction. What would be said of a young husband who should make no provision for his wife in the case of accident or illness befalling him in the performance of his daily labor? What would abundance of "treasure in heaven" avail him in such sad time of need? Though he ardently and in true sincerity performed all his religious duties, experience demonstrates that heaven is blind to his misery and deaf to his most passionate appeals. But man is not always wanting in sympathy. . . . If my antagonist affirms that some selfish creatures—and they are frequently to be found among the so-called admirers of Jesus— devote themselves to the acquisition of wealth, that they may tyrannize over the starving millions, I agree with her in her statement, and deplore the fact. But I say that, because some people abuse the good things of the earth, others should not be condemned because they propose to make the wisest use of them. Because bad laws exist, and some men avariciously monopolize thousands of acres of land, while others "have not where to lay their head," that is no reason why men should not make wise preparation for future contingencies on earth, when earth and the things of earth are all they have any knowledge of. . . .

It is easy enough for Mrs. Wilkie to say that Jesus wished to "inculcate the beauty and purity of a natural life, untrammelled with artificial wants and more sensual desires;" but how could Jesus imagine that people in towns or cities could do aught else than live an artificial life? As populations increase, and the struggle for existence becomes more keen, the "beauty and purity of a natural life" can be experienced only by the very few. To the masses, therefore, the doctrine of Jesus must be quite impracticable, even if we allow this new interpretation of the text. The doctrine of "Resist not evil" Mrs. Wilkie thinks is much better than "Resist evil, no matter from whence it may come." "It is surely," she remarks, "a wiser and more humane doctrine to allow the coatless thief to carry away our overcloak than enrich a lawyer to convict the poor wretch, and burden the State by keeping him in gaol." Is it, indeed? If my graceful antagonist were robbed of her purse by some half-starved wretch, would she say: "Well, it is far better that the poor thief should have it than the hard-working solicitor whom I should have to employ to get him convicted"? Speaking for myself, I do not think it is. If one thief got off in this easy way, the thieving profession would increase its staff wonderfully. This reminds me of an opponent I had at one of my lectures at Manchester a short time since, who said that the turning to one's assailant "the other cheek," after having been smitten on the one, was a "good educational process;" it taught a man to bear injustice with great fortitude. I then told my opponent that if, when he went outside the hall, somebody were to strike him in the face and rob him of his watch, he should not complain; he should rather exclaim: "What a splendid educational process I have gone through; it does one a world of good!" And, if it were not ungallant, I would fain say the same to my friend, Mrs. Wilkie. If the "coatless thief were allowed to go scot free," it would put a premium on such thefts, and neither my accomplished antagonist nor I would be able to walk the streets in safety.

Mrs. Wilkie does not believe that Jesus meant what he said when he declared that those who forsook husband, father, mother, brother—nay, all— should get a hundredfold in the shape of reward in heaven; and I am sincerely glad to learn that Jesus merely meant that these persons should "forsake their parents' ignorant prejudices." What a pity it is Jesus did not say so; he would have saved mankind no end of pain and sorrow. But Mrs. Wilkie is silent as to the declaration of Jesus: "If any man come to me and hate not his father, and mother, and wife—yea, and his own life also—he cannot be my disciple." In the generosity of her heart I feel sure she would say that Jesus did not mean hate. Unfortunately, we cannot allow Mrs. Wilkie to make new doctrines for the Nazarene; he must be judged on what he is alleged to have said, from the only record we have of his utterances, and not from any teachings my antagonist may generously manufacture for him.

In conclusion, let me say that the disposition to exaggerate out of all reasonable proportion the merits of the character and teachings of Jesus is fraught with great danger to truth; and, though I have been profoundly impressed with the beauty, force, and wisdom of Mrs. Wilkie's remarks, I cannot help thinking that she has signally failed in her attempt to demonstrate the soundness, practical nature, or moral worth of the doctrines of one whom she does not hesitate to describe as the "divinest and purest of men."

Is Secularism Atheism?

George Jacob Holyoake and Charles Bradlaugh

Although George Jacob Holyoake first coined the word "secularism," he would probably be surprised at being remembered for that accomplishment. Holyoake was a fighter, and in spite of his meek and unimpressive physical appearance, outlived and was more influential than many of his more vocal contemporaries. Holyoake was born in Birmingham, England, in 1817 at just about the time Richard Carlile started the revival of militant British freethought with his defiant republication of Paine's *The Age of Reason.*

Holyoake came from a poor family. His early aptitude for mathematics led him to become a teacher of mathematics and logic in a vocational mechanic's school. He was soon attracted to the socialism of Robert Owen. Owen was, of course, also a freethinker, urging a "rational religion" on his followers. Although Holyoake did not have a strong speaking voice, he supplemented his modest income by lecturing in support of Owenism. At one of his lectures in Cheltenham, he was baited with a question from the audience about man's duty to God. Holyoake's response was that England was too poor to have a God, and that it would not be a bad idea to put Him on "half pay" (i.e., retire Him). For this remark Holyoake was arrested, tried, and convicted of "blasphemy." Shortly before his own death, Richard Carlile testified at Holyoake's blasphemy trial. Holyoake was sentenced to six months in jail. After being released he defiantly returned to Cheltenham and publicly repeated the very words which had originally gotten him into trouble.

Holyoake went to London and founded a magazine, *The Reasoner,* with some money won in an essay contest. At all times he was a gentleman in his writings and lectures. His coining of the word "secularism" was an attempt to give atheism some respectability. Holyoake defined it as concern with the problems of *this* world.

Holyoake wrote prolifically, founding and editing about ten magazines as well. He was one of the founders of the Cooperative Movement, in which the producers of the goods also own shares in the retail outlets for those goods. This movement has been very successful in England. Holyoake wrote four books on the history of cooperation, a number on theology and secularism, plus two two-volume autobiographies—*Sixty Years of an Agitator's Life* and *Bygones Worth Remembering.* In addition, Joseph McCabe wrote a two-volume biography—*Life and Letters of George Jacob Holyoake.* Holyoake died in 1909 after leading a very productive life. For biographical material on Charles Bradlaugh, the reader should refer to pages 73 and 74 of this work.

The present selection is a verbatim account of a debate held in London on March 10 and 11, 1870. It was printed later that year by Austin & Co., and has never before been reprinted. The debate was an unusual occurrence because it pitted two members of the freethought community against each other, rather than the more traditional combination of a freethinker and a clergyman. In this debate two freethinkers are arguing about what such terms as "atheism," "secularism," and "skepticism" mean. It provides a rare look inside the freethought camp. Austin Holyoake chaired the debate.

PROPOSITION: "The Principles of Secularism do not include Atheism."

THE CHAIRMAN: Ladies and gentlemen, at the request of both disputants, and I trust with your approbation, I shall have the honor of presiding over this debate. The proceedings tonight will be of a somewhat unusual character. The disputants, as you are aware, are not exactly opponents; they are both Freethinkers of the extremest school. But I believe there is a confirmed difference of opinion in what may possibly be termed a matter of policy in advocacy. Since 1852, or the early part of 1853, when the word Secularism was first adopted as a general term for Freethought, there has been some difference of opinion amongst Freethinkers generally as to the full scope of its meaning. Matters have been disputed several times during the years that have elapsed, and it is intended by this debate tonight and tomorrow night, if possible to settle once and forever those differences. Mr. Holyoake represents what may be called one school of Freethinkers, Mr. Bradlaugh represents another. But as they are both Freethinkers, I feel certain that on this occasion there will be very little work for me to do. Mr. Holyoake pursues the impersonal policy in debate, Mr. Bradlaugh the same, excepting when persons attack him in a personal manner, then he is apt to strike out somewhat strongly; but as there is not likely to be any irritation of that kind, I feel quite sure my office will be a sinecure. I shall, to the utmost of my ability, act strictly impartially between the two, and if you will quietly listen to what is said by each disputant, I am sure we shall all spend a pleasant evening, and I am also sure we shall go home instructed. Now the proposition which will be discussed follows: "The Principles of Secularism do not include Atheism," that is the proposition for this evening. . . . Mr. Holyoake maintains the affirmative. . . . Mr. Bradlaugh will reply. . . .

MR. G. J. HOLYOAKE: Mr. Chairman, ladies and gentlemen.—This discussion might, perhaps, be aptly termed an explanation of the views which each of us takes of principles which we appear in common to hold. I shall be quite ready to consider such explanations as may be offered on the other side, and I shall hope that such explanations as I have to offer may be considered there in a perfectly friendly spirit, with a view to arrive, if possible, at a common understanding on the subject. Parliament is now, and will be for some time to come, occupied with an endeavor to adjust for us some system of national education. Now the greatest impediment in the way of its being made Secular education is the prevalence of the imputation, and as I think the misconception, that Secularism necessarily involves Atheism and Skepticism. I think that an injurious misconception. I have, as the Chairman has announced to you, for many years, ever since we began first to talk upon the subject of Secularism, had distinct views as to the meaning which that term ought to bear. It never was in my mind, as it appears to have been in the mind of the Chairman, a matter of policy. I never was able to understand, or to encourage, or to avow, or to sanction any enunciation of principles as a matter of policy, irrespective of their being actually and intrinsically true. (Hear, hear.) I have spoken often elsewhere to the same effect, and I find upon looking over again the writings of years ago, I have always insisted upon the distinction which I am going to insist upon tonight. I have continually said that Secularism was not proposed as a new name for an old subject, not as a new name for old Freethinking, or for the old antagonistic and ofttimes ferocious Atheism, but that we proposed a new name for a new form of Freethought, in which we would deal with the agreements at which Freethinkers had arrived, maintaining those propositions about which we have agreed in common, and which were perfectly independent of Atheism or Theism. Now Secularism, presupposing the existence of Atheistical Societies and Freethinking Societies, built partly upon the results attained by them. It proposed to go farther than that—to be distinct from them—to be affirmative instead of negative—to act upon what free inquiry had discovered—to occupy the ground criticism won—to set up principles of nature in the place of principles of theology, and found, if possible, a kingdom of reason, for those who found the kingdom of faith inadequate and unreliable. Atheism still has its place; it still has its unfinished work in hand. Anti-christianism has its hands full, leaving Secularism with duties which have long waited, and are still needed more than ever. Now to present to you briefly the principles of Secularism, as we have ofttimes tried to explain them, that you may compare them with the principle of Atheism, and judge whether they are connected or not, I will, in a few words, state the case— I mean first the case of Secularism. In every generation of men there have been original thinkers, with whom alone progress has had birth, but who, owing themselves no allegiance save to truth, have been subjected to the resentment of all who from ignorance, or custom, or fear, think as their neighbors think. In addition to these, a dangerous class has arisen, and established themselves in every country, who, assuming to be the delegates of God and his sole representatives, have charged individual conviction with guiltiness, and met its expression with intimidation, both opprobrious and penal. Against these combined forces of folly and fatuity, of policy and presumption, there is no defense except by entrenchment within the absolute and impassable barriers of Secular truth. It is this which Secularism attempts by founding a dominion of reason where all who think are free, and all who are true are sure; asserting its own principles, but not assailing others, needing neither to assail, nor condescending to assail, theological systems. Secularism keeps its own ground by studying the means which nature places at the disposal of man. It commands resources of self-help—in a Utilitarian rule of morals it finds guidance. It establishes personal desert by service and veracity. In all these principles there is perfect independence of Atheism. If you desire a brief summary, which may be given in a few words, of what the principles to which I have adverted point to, so far as meets the object of this discussion, I would state them thus: 1. Secularism maintains the sufficiency of Secular reason for guidance in human duties. 2. The adequacy of the Utilitarian rule which makes the good of others, the law of duty. 3. That the duty nearest at hand and most reliable in results, is the use of material means, tempered by human sympathy, for the attainment of social improvement. 4. The sinlessness of well-informed sincerity. 5. That the sign and condition of such sincerity are—Freethought—expository speech—the practice of personal conviction within the limits of neither outraging nor harming others. I presume you see the purport and meaning of those principles, and therefore will scarcely detain you to explain them further. Their scope you will gather from the statement I have made of them. To maintain the sufficiency of reason is absolutely indispensable, or you give no authority to any human being to form his own conclusions on any proposition submitted to him. That is not an orthodox proposition. It partakes undoubtedly of the nature of heresy, and I shall readily admit throughout, that the Secularist, standing apart, does not include himself among Christians, does not need to profess Christianity, but holds himself quite independent, occupying his own ground, and asserting his own principles for the purpose of his own guidance. Mr. Mill has luminously, since we first began to talk on the subject, explained the adequacy of the Utilitarian rule as a guide in all matters of morality. Another point we insist upon which marks Secularism, is the employment of material means—the proposal and the assertion that this world is capable of indefinite improvement by the wise use of those material agencies which are at our command. The theology may have its professions; there are many who rely on them, and find consolation, and, as they believe, security, in their appeal to them; but we know that the Theologian and the Atheist alike, whatever opinion each holds, if he employs the material agencies, masters the processes of nature, and passes his life in accordance therewith—it will be well with him whether he believes any creed-wise way or not. (Cheers.) It is a heterodox opinion to maintain the sinlessness of sincerity. I think it is the distinctive mark which distinguishes Secularism from what is called Secular instruction. By it Secular justice would be done to the conscience, it satisfies the expectations, it satisfies what the religious man would call the special instincts of a man's spiritual nature, that his conscience shall be justified whether God exist or not,—shall be justified to himself, and his fellow man, and to any future tribunal before which he may be brought in another world. If he justifies his course of conduct, his conscience arms him and prepares him for every issue which can happen to him. I am here to maintain that neither the existence of God, nor the nonexistence of God, neither the mortality, nor the immortality of the soul—that none of these doctrines are in any way necessary—that they are separate and independent from these Secular tenets. A man should hold the opinions I name, not as a matter of policy, but as a matter of truth—(hear, hear)—because there is a distinction between them, because they are as separate as it is possible for separate things to be. What I have always maintained is, that it is the ordinary mistake made to consider that if you separate yourselves from anything: for instance, stand apart from theology, and do not consult it, and do not rely on it, and do not deal with it, and do not condescend to discuss it—that you therefore deny it. I say you are not in the position of a person who is necessarily antagonistic to it. Now, what I maintain is this, that to ignore is not to deny, to go one way is not to deny that there may be, to other persons, another way. To travel by land I think is not to deny the water. The chemist ignores architecture, but he does not deny it. The geologist does not keep a singing class, but he does not therefore deny music; and so the Secularist concerns himself with this world without denying or discussing any other world, either the origin of this, or the existence of that. (Cheers.) . . .

Now just for one moment see what Atheism is. I will take my own statement on it, because I have long been, not only inclined to that opinion, but have used the word *Cosmist* when I describe myself. When anybody uses the word Atheist, what does it mean? One who is not only without God, but without morality. I mean without that conclusive knowledge which the Theist assumes about Deity. Therefore, since I make it a rule of my life to limit what I will say by what I know, I have nothing to say on that subject of which I know no more than my neighbor, and he knows far too little to satisfy himself. I have always stated Atheism was this. The Atheist is one who says I see reason to believe in the self-existence, self-subsistence, self-action, eternity, infinity, materiality of nature, and he makes this affirmative declaration about the world which he knows, and that nature of which he is part. But he says, I do not recognize the fact of the personal consciousness of the universe, as the Pantheist does, or conceive satisfactorily of the existence of a separate Being over it, as the Theist does, and I maintain that the proper attitude to take, is a Secular and affirmative one, and to say of neither theory, I affirm this or that. The theologian who sets up his theory treats matter as an unintelligent tool of God, as something almost disreputable; he treats matter as some carnal thing. These people, without meaning it, blaspheme against nature, and against the universe of which they are a part. (Loud cheers.) You see how wide and vast a topic that is to enter upon. That is distinct from Secularism, and the world will never have time to stand still to listen to Secular propositions, if you have to settle the Atheistic first. Professor Huxley is supposed to be the most philosophical type of the Atheist whom we have among us. The *Spectator* says, "Professor Huxley, it is well known, avows a belief that the processes of scientific inquiry, if strictly pursued, will yield results not consistent with certainty, as to the existence of a sentient final cause. The final cause may be nonsentient, or may not exist—cause being as infinite as effect, so absolutely beyond human ken, as to be clearly unknowable and untraceable." If that is the highest expression to which Atheistical speculation has attained, how can you, of that which is "untraceable," make a basis of any part of a statement which you propose for universal acceptance among the people? I will advert just for a moment or two to some opinions which induce me to enter into these explanations, because in the *National Reformer,* and in those Secular Societies which we have in various parts of the country, the public are so little able to see any distinction between Atheism, or between Freethinking and Secularism, that they naturally conclude they are identical. You see as I go along what I maintain. We ought in these societies to have a Theological department, if you please an Atheistical department, to which these questions should be referred, and that which bears the name of a Secular Society ought to deal with Secular subjects in its public and official proceedings. Years ago, the *National Reformer,* in 1865, had a passage criticizing the Rev. Mr. Thomas in a leading article in the beginning of the number. I thought it at the time, and I have no reason to doubt, it was editorial. It said: "Mr. Thomas at the very threshold of his discourse falls into the common error, confounding Secularism with Atheism. This is unfortunate on the part of one who came, or rather rushed forward, to instruct his flock. Once more we will recapitulate that Secularism is not Atheism, although many Secularists are Atheists." That I hold to be sound doctrine. Mr. Bradlaugh will allow me to say of another article, the older the *Reformer* grows, the more it degenerates. It was written by my brother, the Chairman, at a much later date, in 1868, with reference to some articles of mine which appeared in the *Reformer*, in which I have uttered, what I am uttering here tonight, and which I am now to substantiate. He undertook to say, "he deemed it impossible to advocate Secular principles apart from Atheism." This is the qualification, "it was impossible to advocate them in such a manner as to influence people without stating the difference between the Secularist's view and those of his opponents, and when that is done, 'the murder is out!'" If there is a murder in it, it had much better be out. (Laughter.) If Atheism be the murder which is in Secularism, then it would be dishonorable for us to keep it back. I would have put it myself in the front. I would have in the beginning put it in front, if it had been the case. The writer goes on to say, "There is no man or woman who is willing to listen to Secular views, knowing they are intended to set up a system entirely apart and devoid of all religion"—that I take to be altogether begging the question. You set up Secular principles for their own value. Many persons are Secularists who can see religion even in this. The provision is not to set up a thing "devoid of all religion," but to set up a thing distinct in itself, and you have no more right to say it is set up apart from the religion, than the clergyman has a right to say, when you set up Secular knowledge apart from his creed, that you intend thereby to set it up devoid of religion or public piety. This is the remark urged over and over again in the *Reformer,* and it is made the most serious charge against the opinions I hold. The writer goes on to say, "You cannot betray persons into Freethought." If it were possible that any of us could be betrayers—if we had principles which we withheld treacherously, which we concealed knowing well their true knowledge, and we intended "to betray" persons into Freethought, then Mr. Bradlaugh need not waste his time to come here, for that policy would bear on its front so much discredit, and so much disgrace, that nobody would stand up, even in this country, to protest against it. They (Mr. Adams is one) speak of me as a person who held formerly clear and distinct views on this subject, but now for the purpose of policy, or with a view to conciliate opponents, make representation that Secularism is not Atheism. I say, for the purpose of policy or conciliation, I never coined a phrase or withheld an explanation in my life. (Loud cheers.) And I come here tonight for the express purpose of making that as clear as possible, that if these principles are not in themselves honest and distinct, then they ought to be placarded and known as Atheistic, and let that declaration be made at whatever peril or whatever cost. I have always maintained that you never can conciliate anybody by unfairness, by deceit, or by compromise. You can only conciliate a man by justice, by implicit truth, by the most transparent courtesy. I will tell you how you can conciliate him. You can conciliate him by fairness of speech, by paying some attention to his feelings, by not willfully or wantonly outraging him: not outraging his sincerity as you wish him not to outrage yours, by supposing that if he differs from you, it is because he does not see your truth in the same light as you see it. You can only conciliate any human being by fairness, frankness, and an explicit statement, which leaves those who hear it in no doubt whatever as to the honest meaning of those who employ it. (Loud cheers.) My time is over. You have seen distinctly what my view is, and I wish Mr. Bradlaugh to discuss that. If he can show that intellectually the two things are not distinct, if the two things are to be confounded, if Secularism involves Atheism, I shall be as ready as any person in this country to make the declaration; but what I maintain is, that they are essentially distinct in themselves—that to confound them, is not to see their truth, and whoever does confound them has an injurious and public misconception of them.

MR. BRADLAUGH: I do not stand here tonight to urge any view in relation to Secularism, or to the meaning of the word, which is not in every way consistent with every argument that I have urged for the last twelve years; and I think it will be in the memory of some of you, and I am sure within the memory of my friend Mr. Holyoake, that the very views I am about to contend for tonight, I contended for, at some length, at least thirteen years ago, in debate with him at Philpott Street, in precisely the same way we are arguing tonight, so that the line I take is not a new one. (Hear.) I put my view with considerable deference, because, undoubtedly, any man who selects a name, and makes a fame for it, has the fair right to ask the people who adopt that name to adopt his meaning with it; and unless there be some special reason for not adopting the meaning and definition which he has chosen to put to it, it is generally better to take the one he has put. But in this case, I shall submit to you that there is such a reason; and I shall submit to you that, consciously or unconsciously, Mr. Holyoake himself has adopted a definition and explanation which is not a logical one. Now, it should never be forgotten that in all sorts of differences of opinion, or questions of meaning, that Mr. Holyoake has great right to be heard from our platform, and to be listened to with the most earnest attention (cheers), because long before I ever spoke in the movement at all, he paid—with the penalty of imprisonment—for his testimony in favor of Freethought in this country. (Cheers.) And if I could imagine that one word would fall from me, tonight or tomorrow, that would savor of personal depreciation, then I certainly should not permit myself to continue that which I trust is, and will be, an explanation of each of our views, rather than a discussion for mere victory in word-play. (Hear, hear.) I am quite sure Mr. Holyoake means it so, from the character of the speech to which we have listened; and before putting forward any views of my own, I will take the liberty briefly to run through what he has said to you. And at the outset I feel a little difficulty. He says that it is misapprehension that Secularism involves Atheism. He says that Secularism occupies ground independent alike of Theism and Atheism. The position which he himself chooses to maintain is, that the principles of Secularism do not include Atheism. Certainly I am an Atheist. Certainly I have been one for the last eighteen years of my life at any rate, and if the principles of Secularism do not include Atheism, then I am— supposing Mr. Holyoake's definition of Secularism to be a proper and conclusive one—excluded from the Secular ranks. (No, no.) Permit me to deal with the debate in my own way. (Hear, hear.) The proposition which Mr. Holyoake himself worded, was that "The Principles of Secularism do not include Atheism." Then they must exclude Atheism. (No, no.) I can only make arguments. I cannot make patience in my listeners. I will endeavor to deal with the matter to the best of my ability, and I can only understand "include" to mean "include:" that which is not included in any given set of opinions, is excluded. It is possible I may be wrong. I am sure those who hold the contrary opinion had better leave it to Mr. Holyoake to set it right. That would be much better than to interrupt one another as we go on. I do not see any ground that can be taken independently of Theism and Atheism. Theism, if it claims anything, claims to be everywhere. How you can take the ground outside everywhere, I do not know. The Theist claims that there is no thought, no phase of thought, that is not determined by Deity. You have to challenge this initial groundwork before you can make any way with your Secularism at all. (Hear, hear.) However, following the very able speech to which we listened, I have another difficulty occurring to my mind. Mr. Holyoake says that Secularism was not a new name for old Freethought, but a new name for new forms of Freethought in which Freethinkers were agreed. Now, I confess that I have hitherto misunderstood Mr. Holyoake. I thought the position he took, and took most effectively, in the debate with the Rev. Brewin Grant some seventeen years ago, was in fact that Secularism was rather a new name adopted in avoidance of the odium cast on the old names of Infidel and Atheist, and was not intended as the name of a new party at all. I dare say I am wrong in that, because that is what Mr. Holyoake is best able to explain; but I certainly should like to have that made more clear to me in the course of this debate. And I understood Mr. Holyoake then not to put the very harsh meaning on the word Atheist that he does tonight, but to describe himself then as a non-Theist, which for all meaning is precisely the same as Atheist, except that one is in one langauge and the other in another; one is Latin, the other is Greek. I understood him to say I am non-Theist, simply because men have associated with the word Atheist associations of opprobrium which I do not choose to have put on me, and which I do not deserve, and therefore I think the new name is not open to the bad character already wrongly associated with the old one. I understand Mr. H. tonight to take higher ground; I understood him to put it, that Atheism means not only without God, but without morality. That this is the fair meaning of it. If that be so, then Mr. Holyoake would be quite right in contending that the principles of Secularism could not include Atheism, because certainly they could not include that which was without morality. But I deny that Atheism ever did mean that in any fair way in any age of the world. I deny it has ever meant it with the best thinkers. Why, to use a quotation rendered almost old to you, by the many times I have repeated it lately on the top of the *Reformer*— Samuel Taylor Coleridge said, "There is not one in a thousand who has either strength of mind or goodness of heart enough to be an Atheist." He says, "I repeat, not one in ten thousand has either goodness of heart enough or strength of mind enough to be an Atheist." Bacon, in his famous essay on Superstition, speaks of an Atheist as being more moral than many other men. So that at any rate there is one thinker of a recent date, and one not so long ago, who entertained a different opinion as to the meaning of the word Atheist. The word Atheist does mean to be without God, but it does not mean to be without morality. To me every idea of God is such that as a Secularist I am bound to deny. I find the preached ideas of God interfering with the children in their cradles, with the children in their schools, with the grown-up children in their churches, and in their daily avocations of life, and I am obliged to destory Theism to make way for Secularism. (Cheers.) Mr. Holyoake says, and says truly, that he would never allow policy with him to supersede principle, nor do I suppose that any man who has paid the penalties in early life that he has for advocating a principle, would do so; but I am not at all sure that in the endeavor to take ground which, according to his own view, should neither anger nor outrage your opponents, that he has not taken a ground which is indefensible. Who is to be the judge when you outrage the Theist? According to my view I never outraged the Theist. According to my view, his irritation is the natural consequence of having an indefensible position, which I attack, and I cannot help it. If he calls it outrage, so much the worse, and I must keep on with the outrage until the repeated administration of common sense compels him to capitulate. To attack the Theologian's position is an outrage, because he does not admit your right to be anywhere—except under his dominion. But my friend, Mr. Holyoake, says, the Secularist's position is the substitution of a kingdom of reason for those who find the kingdom of faith impossible. Ah! the Secularist finds the kingdom of faith impossible, he finds belief in God impossible, he finds belief in religion impossible. What is the difference between finding belief in God impossible, and being an Atheist? I do not say there is no difference, but I confess I should like to understand it. Then my friend very ably puts it to you, in addition, that in every age where there have been men of progress, there has been a dangerous class who have claimed to be delegates from God, and there has been no defense against this class, save in the entrenchments of Secular and positive truth. Where are you to dig your entrenchments? This dangerous class have claimed to occupy all the ground, they do not permit you to have the slightest spot on it. You are obliged to try your right to that "everywhere," before you can begin to form your entrenchments at all; but our friend says Secularists do not need to assail, nor should they condescend to assail theology. Why not? If you want positive truth it can only be obtained by the eradication of falsehood. We may dispense with the word "positive" before truth, because all truths are positive, all principles are positive. I do not like to take a certain word which may carry with it some kind of meaning to some, and be misleading to others. All truths are positive, all principles are positive, but you cannot get truths except by eradicating falsehoods. How can you have your Secular entrenchments, for what is your Secularism going to do? It is going to teach men, as Mr. Holyoake explained in his very able exposition of Secularism in the Cowper Street debate with Mr. Grant, "the Physical Laws on which health depends; the Moral Laws on which happiness depends; the Intellectual Laws on which knowledge depends; the Social and Political Laws on which material prosperity and advancement depend; the Economic Laws on which wealth depends." Now to do this, you must challenge the theological doctrine that God regulates health; and in fact in this very discussion Mr. Holyoake himself says, that "the position is the position of a denial of a Special Providence, and a distrust of it." This is true. So that in fact before you can be a Secularist, to take the position Mr. Holyoake takes, you must reject all supernatural supervision, reject all Theistic control, and if that is not in reality and fact being an Atheist, whatever you may call it, then I confess I have yet to learn the meaning of words. My friend says he would put to you the sufficiency of reason for guidance in human duties. Yes, here we will agree; and that he would put to you the Utilitarian test and explanation of morality as given by Mr. Mill. Yes, to an extent also I agree. As far as Mr. Mill expresses his views on Utilitarianism, he and I would both adopt those into the Secular Text-book; but he goes a little further, and he talks of the sinlessness of well-informed sincerity. As to the word "well-informed," I am not sure whether it is not a later addition to the text by my friend, probably for some good reason.

MR. HOLYOAKE: It is.

MR. BRADLAUGH: Yes, I thought so. Do not understand me as meaning any sort of catch. I want to understand what we are about. I believe I have clear and definite views which I can put before you. Mr. Holyoake has the right to his opinions, and the right to express them, for we are not bishops of a party, we are not leaders of a party, we are only men in a party, who have a wide circle, the members of which desire that what we do say shall be clear and definite. I object to the phrase altogether, I object to the phrase because it is open to anyone to say, you pretend to be sincere, but your sincerity is not well-informed, I am better informed than you are, and your sincerity is sinful. . . . Although at present it may be perfectly true that all men who are Secularists are not yet Atheists, I put it to you as also perfectly true, that in my opinion the logical consequence of the acceptance of Secularism must be that the man gets to Atheism, if he has brains enough to comprehend. (Loud cheers.) I cannot say I followed out sufficiently carefully to reply to it, although I tried to do so, that portion of my friend's speech in which he spoke of conduct being justified to conscience, after he came to some question of the possibility of that conduct being submitted to some possible tribunal after life. I say it is absolutely immoral and absolutely unsecularistic— against the whole principles of Secularism, as I understand them—to admit the possibility of conduct in this life being the subject of trial, judgment, and sentence after death, and in some future world; and I urge that the whole basis of our Secular cause is in direct ignoring and denial of the possibility of any such state of existence at all. Now my friend says to ignore is not to deny, and the illustrations he gave were curious. Let us see whether the illustrations fit in, for illustrations are sometimes dangerous. The traveller by land is not to travel by water; to study geology is not to study music; therefore you may travel in this world without denying the possibility of travelling in the next. That I take to be the true meaning of Mr. Holyoake's argument. Unfortunately you cannot, because the Theist says there is only one conveyance, and if you make a good journey by land, so much the worse for you if you do not get your water passage with a corresponding ticket. "What if you gain the whole world and lose your soul?" You have to challenge the Theist's position, and you have to say we do not believe, we do not accept it, we do deny a theory of morality which you as theologians propound to us, for we take the Utilitarian theory of morality; we declare we find that conduct carries with it its rewards or its punishment now at once, and we have nothing whatever to do with the position you take of a judgment by-and-by. Mr. Holyoake says that is his position, and that this has nothing to do with Christianity. But the Christian's position, the Theist's position, is, you cannot find the outside ground, you are obliged therefore to at once give the denial, and you are obliged to challenge the very initial stage of the march. Now, I find the time is going, and I have only three or four minutes left. I shall not be able, until my next speech, to put before you Secularism as I have endeavored to shape it, so as to give the widest scope for anyone, but I may say you will find it clearly put in the principles, objects, and rules of the National Secular Society contained in the Almanack, edited by myself and Mr. Austin Holyoake. Oh, says Mr. G. J. Holyoake, take the *National Reformer* in 1865, there is an editorial article, and in that you put the position which I accept, the position that Secularism is not Atheism;

but that it is an editorial article by a disciple of Mr. Holyoake's, not by me, it is an editorial article when I was not editor. You may remember there was an interregnum of eighteen months or two years in consequence of my ill health, when, although I contributed to the *Reformer,* I was not its editor. It was edited by Mr. John Watts, who was taught by Mr. Holyoake, and who held in most respects the views that the latter held. Mr. Holyoake meant nothing unfair—it probably escaped him that the *Reformer* was edited by Mr. John Watts at that time. I only put it to you that my views have always been the same all through. I hold the views which Mr. Austin Holyoake has put before you, though I must regret that Mr. G. J. Holyoake's researches in the *National Reformer* have not led him to read some of the articles I have penned on Secularism myself. I have penned many short papers, and there is my "Plea for Atheism," in which I have put my views as strongly and clearly as possible before the world by refraining from doing that which I intend to do now, because I concede to Mr. Holyoake the right and place to give the principles of Secularism to the Atheist, because of the position he has taken in it. I have grown now to have a circle of hearers who have grown into it, perhaps, during the last eight or ten years. At times it is necessary that one should speak plainly and distinctly, and it is for that reason I want that this debate shall go forth to the parties who meet our views—the views of an older man, and the views of a younger man—so that you may judge for yourselves what is this Secularism which is put to them. I do not urge, and I shall be sorry to urge, that there is any attempt on the part of a man like Mr. Holyoake to betray anybody into the acceptance of anything, but I do urge it as a betrayal of a man into your principles if you tell him we can take a ground which it is utterly impossible for human thought to take, a ground which it is utterly impossible for any thinker even in mind for a moment to put himself upon independently of Theism or Atheism. Our friend is a non-Theist. He never was independent of Theism. He struck at it boldly; he is in the position of being without God, and the position of independence of God; his denial of God's omnipotence, denial of God's omniscience, denial of special providence, denial of the efficacy of prayer to Him, denial of special interference—and given these denials, what becomes of the independent position after? I think I have occupied my time, and I leave it for our friend to continue the explanation he has begun. (Loud cheers.)

MR. HOLYOAKE: I perfectly remember the ancient debate that I and Mr. Bradlaugh had together many years ago, and it is quite true that his views remain now substantially what they were on that occasion; but it is not less necessary on that account to repeat before new hearers and at a new time, in, if possible, more vivid terms, those distinctions of opinion which I think would give strength and clearness, and more public utility to Secular opinion. Mr. Bradlaugh had then, as he has still, that notion which I think attaches to nearly all theological reformers, that they must take a clean sweep in this world before they can bestow on it the illumination of their own special insight into truth. In a little book on the principles of Secularism, which was published a short time ago by Mr. Charles Watts—there were two little pamphlets, one entitled "The Philosophy of Secularism"—as though it would appear that good sense runs in the family—(laughter)—in this "Philosophy of Secularism" Mr. Watts, who is now the accredited lecturer to the National Secular Society, says very distinctly, "that the question of the existence of God being one of conjecture, Secularism leaves it for persons to decide for themselves. Atheism includes Secularism, but Secularism does not exact Atheistical profession as the basis of cooperation; it is not considered necessary that a man should advance as far as Atheism to become a Secularist." (Cheers.) Now that is an admission of the essential distinction between the two things, that you may become a Secularist without it being necessary to advance as far as Atheism. It can only be because Secularism is in itself a distinct thing as far as it goes. Although you may go beyond it, you are not called on by the profession of Secularism to adopt Atheism, and go further and beyond Secularism. When Mr. Watts had opponents, he wrote again on Secular principles, and lost sight of the perspicacity which he previously employed, and he adopted that sort of philosophy of which Mr. Bradlaugh has tonight given us so energetic an expression. He says, "it is necessary to prepare people's opinions for the reception of distinct views by clearing the human mind from the weeds of error." Now Mr. Watts appears in the character of a world-clearer—like my friend and teacher, the late Robert Owen, who had an opinion that he was called upon to take some immense broom, and sweep the world clean before he could set down his theory of human progression in it. Mr. Watts goes on to state, "the province of Secularism is not only to enunciate positive principles, but also to break up old systems which have lost their vitality, and to refute theologies which have hitherto usurped judgment and reason." Here is an immense sweep. None of us will live to see the day when the man who has made it, will be able to give us the secular information which we are waiting to receive now. This "province" is too wide. There must be in human nature, and in the department of human thought, distinctions such as I am contending for. Mr. Bradlaugh seems to think because Secularism excludes Atheism, therefore Secularism excludes the Atheist. I return to "dangerous illustrations" again. A man may be a geologist belonging to a Geological Society—geology does not include chemistry. If you study geology ever so long you will not be taught chemistry, but it does not exclude the man as a student of geology who is also a chemist. A man may be what he pleases beside that which he comes to study, only upon the plan and the principle upon which you enter, you can get no other instruction than that which fairly and properly belongs thereto. A Secularist Society would admit Mr. Bradlaugh, or any person, although he might be an Atheist or Deist, provided he holds distinctive principles as to the materiality of human progress. My friend's hearing did not serve him quite accurately. I did not say "alarm" anybody. I never troubled myself with alarm. I said, "you are bound not to outrage or harm them." Your opinions should be within those limits. By "outrage," I mean what I have many times stated; no imaginary thing, no subtle principle. Not outraging a man, means you shall not impugn his sincerity—you shall not deny his truthfulness, you shall not impute to him bad motives: you shall take him altogether as a responsible and honest disputant. If you do that, you may state your opinions in whatever way you please, and I believe you will never outrage, and never offend any honest mind that listens to you. If you attract disputants, do not discredit them, do not have bitterness; for the moment you say in a party of Englishman, that a man has some base or false motive, that he is a hypocrite; the moment you so assail him, there is an end to controversy about the truth. You never, in a sensible disputation, should discuss personal worth or personal motives. Mr. Bradlaugh is quite right, I did point out to Mr. Grant that I did use the word "non-Theist," because non-Theist was without opprobrium, and opprobrium was associated with the word "Atheist." I also did point out to him that the word "Secularism" did get rid of it, and also put before the mind moral objects we had in view. His charge was that of infidelity, which means apostacy to the truth, and my observations were for the purpose of bringing into sight those moral, and positive, and practical considerations which Secularism puts down as cardinal and leading principles. Positive truth— Mr. Bradlaugh thinks the word "positive" should be got rid of. I use it in the sense of Comte, in the sense that a positive truth is a provable principle; thus he distinguishes between the principles which are speculative and those which are provable. We endeavor to entrench ourselves in princples which are provable (by an application to nature, to experience, and to human reason), whether the Bible is true or not, or whether God exists or not, as Mr. Binney states in his book, *How to Make the Best of Both Worlds.* This world is here, and there is all the possibility of making it better or worthless whether there be a God or not, or whether there be a heaven above or a hell below. (Cheers.) Now as to the meaning of the term "Atheist." I agree with Mr. Bradlaugh, as I have put it in my "Limits of Atheism," by saying with Mr. Mill, that with every age Atheists have been men remarkably distinguished for their personal integrity and morality: but I speak of the theological meaning of the term, and because my own information of ancient things and old languages is not reliable, I went to Professor Newman, whom I knew to be capable of speaking on the subject, and a person of not very narrow theological views as you know, and I asked him what the word "Atheism" meant. Did it connote immorality? He said, "Among the Greeks, among whom the term arose, a man had no power of conceiving he could disbelieve in the Gods and be moral, and they connoted the word as being without morality, and so the word came down to us." It is a different thing to say that the connoting is true. I agree with Mr. Bradlaugh that it is false, but we have to deal with the sense in which the public use the term. Therefore I repudiate the word Atheism in that sense, although I do not repudiate the principles which it represents. I do not conclude that Atheism does embody a system of morals. It is a purely speculative question as to the origin of the universe, and the principles which underlie the whole of it, as Theism accounts in some way for all its mysteries and marvels. And that speculation, although a magnificent one, although one I believe of imperishable interest to the human mind, although one to exercise our highest faculties, it can only teach the humility with which we should judge so great a question. And although this pertains to the question of Atheism, there is no system of morality in it. By Secularism is meant that we cleave to nature; we try to search out the facts of nature, and if we are not afraid of curtailing our creed within the limits of our knowledge, it may include the discovery that he is more moral than the Theist may prove to be, who travels further from nature, and from that experience which best teaches us morality. (Hear, hear.) . . . Now, I want to know why it is when a man's attention is directed to these principles of morality which are found in the process of nature, and he shall study this vast world of physical science, which shall make him master of his destiny, giving him that information which shall guide him and guard him from error—he should as a Secularist be disqualified from looking beyond this life, or from having any speculation about it? Why should he not conjecture whether God is at the bottom of this mystery of existence, whether there is not a future world? A man must ask himself something about the unknown world, or life into which he may be going. Suppose we regard death as I regard it, as some last venture on an untried existence; you cannot prevent a man putting the question—"If I am a moralist, and if I do good to the utmost of my power, will not that be my justification?" You can found no system, and have no party, and have no followers— you will deserve none, unless you teach men that while reason is sufficient for them, perhaps it is as well to use it; and that as long as they are well-informed in their sincerity, and have striven to know the truth with all their power, if they find themselves in a future world and at a future judgment, they will be the first persons who will stand well there, and be well received. If the world is to be cleared, if we are not to get rid of the delusion that there is no room in this world for new truths until you have combatted every theological error in it—far be it from me to say there is no necessity for denying theological error and meeting it boldly face to face—but to say you must clear the world from all these delusions first, if you must do that, when will you begin to reform the world? It is one of those delusions, one of those figures of speech as to which an untrained mind seems to be full. Has the mind no opening, no thought, no care, no thirst for some new light, some new view? A man rests in superstition in which he has been reared, because another man has not shown to him a clearer, better, brighter, and purer way. I say the world is waiting for a new view and new principle. What said Dr. Hooker, when President of the British Association? What a splendid view did he not present to the great assembly there, when he said, "There is this vast kingdom of science, we who are philosophers and students are masters of it. We have won it in spite of the Church. We have won it without their consent. We have won it in spite of their opposition; and now we hold it independently of them. The priest may speak with authority upon those subjects communciated to him in the domain of theology; the wonders of this world, its mysteries and its marvels are ours. With the science we have used we have conquered these secrets; they are our own. No priest can call them in question as against us; no priest can be heard on them, because on this subject they have no knowledge, because they speak without authority, and no man ventures to rely on what they say." How was science conquered? Did philosophers sweep the world first? Did they enter the lists against every warring theologian? Did they not conquer in silence, peace, and patience? And though I am as ready as any man to come face to face with theologians, and not shrink from them, yet I think it is impolicy for party writers not to see the distinction between these things, not to have one time for one thing, and another time for another, and to devote the larger portion of your exertions to giving information in a world always willing and waiting to receive it. When I go into the provinces, I find various societies and associations all over the kingdom are occupied with a negative form of Freethought. I find some score of young orators who are mere negationists. If a man is a negationist he can trade without any capital in principles. His stock-in-trade is the simplest possible. He has only to deny what somebody else holds, and he is set up in the art of controversy. That is not Secularism in any possible sense in which you can regard it. If you regard that which is Secular as that which pertains to this life, the issue of which can be tested in this life, all is clear practice. It is the old and ancient idea of the word "Secular"—that which belongs to life and time. I propose to take nature as the subject of study, and to take the study of its process and master its principles, in order to attain to the results, which the mastery of life will give us for the conduct of human affairs. When I take the different societies of the theological caste and see what they are doing, they are trying to discover—not what theories are to be overcome, not what addresses are to be delivered, they have no conception of so distinct a duty; they are trying to discover the Northwest passage of theology, which every priest is in search of, but of which nobody attains to any satisfactory discovery. That would not matter much. But these idealists say the whole ocean cannot be traversed for the purpose of navigation, but you must still linger in some corner of the world trying to discover the mystery of the world's existence. I say the broad face of nature—this wide world in which we live, this boundless expanse of which we might avail ourselves, ought to be made fruitful for works of instruction for human guidance, for the inculcation of Secular principles. The present life may be assumed to be worth having, since we resist any attempt to end it. Being worth having, it is important to improve it, for our sakes and others. Since experience shows it is possible to improve life, and since this improvement is a benefit to others, any divergence from the straight path is, I think, a waste of time. When I look on the wrong which exists in the world, not only with regard to that question to which I alluded—the ignorance in which the people of this country are—to concentrate the powers of Secular societies mainly for the inculcation of those matters which are material, is essential. Then we shall need no longer the consolation of the priest, because we shall anticipate his consolation by getting rid of the evil upon which he would console us. While using science to its utmost, humanity would deliver itself. My plea is this, in these societies you should have a department of theology, a department if you like for the inculcation of Atheism; I have not the slightest objection to that. If you choose to have a department where persons wish to make loud and demonstrative speeches, why, I would add, if you please, a Howling department. I have said, if a man thinks the plain law of courtesy is a violation of his conscience, I would rather that he was brutal than base and dishonest. It is better to be brutal if you cannot else be true, than to gloss over the truth, or to hide it under any pretense of courtesy. My meaning is with regard to Secular criticism, that we should entrench ourselves in the inculcation of purely Secular principles, making it our main object, and that every Secular Society should discuss Secular subjects: and when you talk Theology or Atheism, the people should have indications that those matters were about to be discussed, so that those persons might have fair opportunity. On all other occasions you should make clear to the public what you are engaged about as to Secular principles. I believe if this were done, there would be no compromise of truth, no conscience would be distressed, no truth would be withheld, no plainness of speech prevented; but there would be more clearness, more confidence, more security; and the members of a Secular Society would be morally responsible for the principles they really hold, and not made responsible for any wandering speech made by any speaker, who on the platform may open his mouth. I want Freethought—Freethought with courage and perspicacity, and with so much good sense as that the public shall know what we mean, whether they like to know it or not, that they may be able to say—"We know what the Secularists mean; we see the definition of principles accepted among them; we know they are principles of candor, and not intended to mislead or to misdirect. We may dislike their principles, but we know how to confront them; at least we see they have this merit, right or wrong, they are masters of their own principles, and their principles are not masters of them." (Loud cheers.)

MR. BRADLAUGH: The principles, objects, and rules of the National Secular Society, so far as they relate to this debate, I will take the liberty of reading to you; and it is rather unfortunate, as far as I am concerned— I have no doubt it arises from what I have written, not having been so clearly expressed as to render it possible for Mr. Holyoake to use it—but it does happen that during the last eleven years I have written some seventy little papers on Secularism, and I wrote one or two pamphlets which, although not direct expositions of Secular principles, contain my views in relation to the matter, and Mr. Holyoake has not thought it wise in debating with me in any way to quote one single word from anything I have said. I do not wish to detract from the value of what my friend, Charles Watts, has said. On the contrary, I think what he said very good; and if Mr. Holyoake will oblige me with the pamphlet I think that I can show that Mr. Watts has stated the case somewhat differently to what our friend supposes. Mr. Holyoake read to you a passage; he might have read a sentence lower down, in which Mr. Watts said, "It is true that many Secularists believe that if their principles were logically reasoned out, it would show the fallacy of all supernatural faiths." That is just the position one would be contented with; but the principles of the National Secular Society are these:—"This Association declares that the promotion of human improvement and happiness is the highest duty. That the theological teachings of the world have been, and are most powerfully obstructive of human improvement and happiness; human activity being guided and increased by a consciousness of the facts of existence, while it is misguided and impeded in the most mischievous manner, when the intellect is warped or prostrated by childish and absurd superstitions. That in order to promote effectually the improvement and happiness of mankind, every individual of the human family ought to be well placed and well instructed, and all who are of a suitable age ought to be usefully employed; for their own and the general good. That human improvement and happiness cannot be effectually promoted without civil and religious liberty; and that, therefore, it is the duty of every individual—a duty to be practically recognized by every member of this Association—to actively attack all barriers to equal freedom of thought and utterance for all upon political and theological subjects." Having read that which I presume Mr. Holyoake has noticed, and to which I presume he finds no objection, permit me to say I have not come across the class of advocates in the movement to whom he refers as mere negationists. The men I have worked with for ten years have done positive work. They have not talked about it, but done it—assisted me in the Reform movement, and in freeing the shackles of the press. They have sent in petitions from every part of the country to assist in passing the last Evidence Amendment Act, and they have sent in seventy petitions which will increase to some two hundred before another week or two is over, to amend the Act this year. They established schools in different parts with great difficulty, because many of them are very poor indeed; but I know none of them who are mere negationists. I do not know of any and most certainly none of those with whom I have the honor and pleasure of working, and with whom I shall work very long I trust, fall under that category at all. There is no prominent improvement they have not taken part in. They have done more with reference to the question of capital and labor, and the laws of population, to have those matters discussed and understood in every factory and workshop throughout the last six years, than any other set of men at all. Talk of Social Science Associations devoting themselves to it. To make it possible, such men as Carlile and Paine went to jail, and laid the foundation for those associations which are now acting on their principles. Just the same as you, Sir, and Charles Southwell going to jail twenty odd years ago paved the way for the Sunday lectures, which are now being heard in St. George's Hall, and other places. Let us follow step by step. Mr. Holyoake puts it that the Atheist holds the self-existence of nature, the self-subsistence of nature, the self-action of nature, the eternity of nature, the infinity of nature, and the immateriality. I could not comprehend that in the first speech, because immateriality is a word I do not understand.

MR. HOLYOAKE: Materiality, not immateriality.

MR. BRADLAUGH: I apologize for misunderstanding. I also misunderstood the word "harm" as "alarm"—it was not a defect of memory, but a defect of listening. It is immaterial, except that I do not know there is any difference between self-existence and self-subsistence—otherwise we should agree—and that may pass without any discussion at all. But Mr. Holyoake says Secularism has nothing to do with Atheism, any more than geology has to do with chemistry. Geology is one department, chemistry is another. Secularism is one department, theology another. But suppose the chemist said to the geologist, you must not break the rock with your hammer— you must not go down to examine the strata—you must believe as I shall explain it: there is water, under that the fire, then granite, then brimstone, and you must not examine it at all. The geologist would have to say to the chemist, I must get rid of your chemistry, I need to examine the earth, and I must examine it. Take what the theologian says to the Secularist. You must not study the laws of health, because they are in the hands of God. He warps the mind of the child in the cradle, and it is only by unlearning and retraining, that you make good the ground you take. Nor do I think Secularism can have a Howling department. Ranting, and religious howling, have nothing in common with Secularism. I would say Church of England people have no place in our ranks; Wesleyans and Methodists have no place in our ranks; people who hold salvation and faith have no place in our ranks; we cannot have a howling department in our ranks. Let us clear it away at once. (Cheers.) We have seen the lesson of morality. I say you cannot get your lesson of morality without Atheism. Atheism does not talk of the origin of the universe. It teaches the "how" and not the "why." It is on the facts of the universe it gives its lessons. It is by the diffusion of real knowledge among the people, and the improvement of the people that Atheism does put out its scheme of morality. You cannot have a scheme of morality without Atheism. The Utilitarian scheme of morality is a defiance of the doctrine of Providence and a protest against God. But let us see, is it quite clear that a Secularist taking the position of a teacher of Secular views, should stand up and say to those around him, I regard death as a last venture on an untried existence? I think not. I do not think that the teacher whose views are in such a state of uncertainty on that subject, while he might be a Secular scholar, ought to be a Secular teacher. I think the Secularist is one who has learnt enough of the "how" of his existence, to know that instead of death being a last venture on an untried existence, it is an entire cessation of his individual existence altogether. This is the broad ground I will take. I hold that the logical consequence of Secularism is the denial, the absolute denial of a Providence. See what wide elements come in. What is the use of applying the utility or test of morality, if the question is not to be the health of your body here, but the possible advantage in some untried state of existence—some supposed state hereafter? The theory of morality may be entirely overruled. But we will take it a little more, because in quoting the words of Robert Owen and of my friend Mr. Watts, Mr. Holyoake really put before you that for which I should contend, namely, that there is need of an enormous broom to sweep the world clear of human error. But my friend says the province is too wide, and you cannot do it. The man who pretends he can sweep the whole world is a madman, but he may take a little piece of the broom in his hand and sweep some portion of it clear, and he may believe in human ability to sweep some other portion, and his example may encourage the sweeping. I think it is true Secular morality, and true Secular duty to teach and to do the clearing away of human error. I hold you have no right to pass by error. Wherever you find it, as a Secularist you are bound to make war on it, whether you succeed or fail. I hold you are not a true Secularist if you do not, even accepting the definition of Secularism that Mr. Holyoake would have given you. But he says there must be a special department for that. What does that mean? What does Secularism claim to do? It claims at any rate to have a theory of morals. What does theology claim to do? It claims to have a theory of morals. What does theology claim? That its theory of morals excludes every other. What does Secularism claim to do? To fight for standing room and beat the other back. To gain the standing room, it must make war on the monopoly claimed by theology of control over human thought. Then it is said we are not to impute bad motives to our opponents, and not to impugn their sincerity. Is that so?

Suppose we find our opponents absolutely false. Suppose I am of the opinion, as in the case of Tischendorff, that he invented the manuscripts which he professed to have found at Sinai, am I not right in giving my reason why I think so, and imputing it to him, while I feel that the production of this MS. unchallenged, will be a piece of evidence that will shake the minds of the people with whom I come in contact? I am bound to impute bad motives if I feel they ought to be impugned. I do not mean where you find a man whom you believe to be sincere, you shall insult him. I never have done that. Where I find an honest man, and I have met many true and honest men, I have never insulted them. I have never outraged them, nor have I been accused of it. But where I have met a charlatan, and there are many of them, I have never hesitated to thrust the sharpest piece of irony through him, and to expose him and nail him down. (Loud cheers.) Nor do I think that our friend was quite fair or quite logical when dealing with the words of Robert Owen, and dealing with the words of my friend Charles Watts. He argued that the province was too wide. He says if you set out with clearing away error, you will have never done; and when will you begin your work? When? We are beginning it now. When you have the forest of error before you, with each tree you hew down and root and grub up, you have begun the work; because you have prepared the ground, for the seed of the many science sowers around us. The fact is, it is positive work to clear away—work which must be done—which you cannot avoid doing; and how can my friend find his independent spot in the ground, while it is ground in which there grows, as he more effectively and more clearly than myself describes, a Banyan tree? He says—"Religious error is like the Banyan tree: every branch has taken independent root in the soil of superstition, and must be cut through before the tree will fall." He was right—it must be cut through—it is positive work cutting it through—it is no negationist's work. Each falsehood you knock out of a man's head, leaves room for a fact to grow. Each stain of error cleared from the human mind is like the dirt you take from the old painting to enable the natural picture to be seen. I do not think it is fair or wise to the workers in the movement, to put it in the way Mr. Holyoake has done. The work you have to do is double work: the destruction of error, with the consciousness that no error is entirely destroyed until it is replaced by the truth. When you have discovered an error you have done but little, because when one error is destroyed another error may be taught, until you have replaced it by the truth. That is secular work, and that is what we have been doing, as may be seen by our programme of action as published in the National Secular Society's Almanack, which is as follows:

1. A system of Compulsory Secular Education, so that each child may, at starting in life, be placed in a fair condition to form more correct opinions,

and be fitted for more useful conduct.

2. The disestablishment and disendowment of the State Church, and the placing all religions and forms of speculative opinion on a perfect equality before the law.

3. Specially the improvement of the condition of the Agricultural classes, whose terrible state of social degradation is at present a fatal barrier to the formation of a good state of society.

4. A change in the Land Laws, so as to break down the present system by which enormous estates are found in few hands, the many having no interest in the soil, and to secure for the agricultural laborer some share of the improvement in the land he cultivates.

5. The destruction of the present hereditary Chamber of Peers, and substitution of a senate containing life members, elected for their fitness, and therewith the constitution of a National Party intended to wrest the governing power from a few Whig and Tory families.

6. The investigation of the causes of poverty in all old countries, in order to see how far unequal distribution of wealth or more radical causes may operate. The discussion in connection with this of the various schemes for social amelioration, and the ascertainment if possible of the laws governing the increase of population and produce, and affecting the rise and fall of wages.

This is not a programme of work in words, it is the programme of work we have done for the last twelve years. We have some results to show for it. We have not done all we should like to do, but we are doing more every day, and instead of discouraging men and talking of negative work, instead of telling them there is independent ground when there is not, tell them what the truth is—tell them that Church, Chapel, Bishop, Rector, Independent Minister, would all unite to crush our Freethought if they could. (Loud cheers.) Tell them we must carry the war into every Church and Chapel. Where will you take your Secularism—into the agricultural districts—without the advantages of the negative men? Go to Wiltshire, Dorsetshire, and Devonshire—you will not get the independent ground. You can only get the work done when we have knocked the Bible leaves off the eyes of the people. (Loud cheers.) If today we number ten times as many as we numbered in England ten years ago, if Freethought literature has a circulation it never had before in the history of England, if the Bishop of London and those about him are obliged to come and ask for assistance of funds to counteract Infidelity, and if from one end of the land to the other there are woeful lamentations, why is it? Is it because we are recognized as a political party in the State. Mr. Stanhope, at a meeting in the West Riding of Yorkshire, was pleased to connect my name with them, although I there hardly deserve it; but he was pleased to say that he found them the most active and energetic reformers in the country. He called them the most dangerous. Why? Because they were doing good work. I ask my friend, if in the whole history of the Freethought movement, we ever took such a position in England before?

Take the Reform agitation—it was called an Infidel movement. It was an Infidel movement, an Atheistical movement. The papers wrote against it as such. It was based on the laws of Society, on those elements of existence which disregard preaching. It had no fair words with empty meanings, it put real truths; it only outraged those who deserve the outrage for their manifold stupidity; and I feel that the cause for which Robert Owen worked so hard, I feel that the cause for which Carlile went to jail, I feel that the cause for which Paine wrote so manfully, I feel that the cause for which men were burnt a long time ago, I feel that that cause is now making its way, and in a few years will stand in equal rank at least with any other party in the country. I feel in a few months we shall tear from the statute book the infamous Blasphemy Laws that have laid on it so long. I know there is strength enough in our party now to back me up in every effort I may make in dealing with these things. It is because I want your thoughts and my speech to go together to the public, that they may no longer question your views and mine, and for that purpose let us understand and speak distinctly to the people this great truth, that there can be no Secular system-maker, no Secular priest, no Secular Pope, because all we can do is, as Mr. Holyoake will tell you, to talk Science as our Providence—science only—the codification of the facts of existence up to today, and today's knowledge. We can give no system with defined limits, never to be surpassed, because men may, and do, find out new truths, and usefully afford such knowledge, that the system of today is outgrown by the teaching of tomorrow. No church and no creed, no priest, no altar—there is only the best knowledge of all men to which we can point you, and from which we ask you to select. . . . My friend Mr. Holyoake says, with regard to the words Infidelity and Atheism, that he objects to them because of the opprobrium which has gathered round them. The people who fight for old Nationalities, remember the words of opprobrium that have been heaped on their country and their cause, but only to fight to redeem cause and country from that opprobrium. They do not admit the opprobrium to be deserved, but they fight to show that the whole is a lie. And I maintain the opprobrium cast upon the word. Atheism is a lie. I believe Atheists as a body to be men deserving respect—I know the leading men among them who have made themselves prominent, and I do not care what kind of character religious men may put round the word Atheist. I would fight until men respect it. I do not quarrel about the word Secular, if it is taken to include this body of men, but I do object to it if we are told Atheism has nothing to do with it. I object when I am told that Atheism is not its province, because I say the moment you tell me you have to deal with the affairs of this life, to the exclusion of the rest, you must in effect deny the rest. If you do not deny the rest, if you admit it is an untried future, you leave your Secularism in doubt, you partially paralyze the efforts on your own side. If you tell our people "you must not impugn the sincerity of your opponents, that you must not impute bad motives to them" when they read the foul lies heaped on the graves of the great dead, and hear the base calumnies used against the hard-working living, I say you are teaching to them that which I do not consider their duty. You should never lightly impute, never rashly urge against any opponent motives, you should never do it without full proof to justify your imputation. But I say if you have a liar, mark him; if you have a thief, mark him; if you have a robber, mark him; if he be an opponent, do not spare him on that account. All you have to do is to take care when you strike, you have your sword of proof and truth in hand to strike with, and be sure that you will not break down when the blow falls. (Loud cheers.) Half a minute more, and my time is gone. I regret in this debate I have not had the opportunity of hearing Mr. Holyoake's objections, which no doubt would be well maintained, founded on my own views of Atheism in connection with Secularism, especially as put forward in my "Plea for Atheism." This plea is my manifesto to the world—this I am ready to defend, and I will not have Atheism erased from our propaganda. (Loud cheers.) . . .

Mike Wallace Interviews
Joseph Lewis on TV

Joseph Lewis (1889-1968) was at one point the leading American spokesman for atheism, from about 1940 to 1965. During that period he served as president of the Freethinkers of America, and as the publisher of the Freethought Press Association. Lewis was born in Alabama, into a very poor family. He left school after the third grade and went out to help support his family. Eventually he came to New York City, where his invention and marketing of the one dollar men's shirt made him a wealthy man by the 1920s. He also dabbled in publishing, founding the Eugenics Publishing Company, which was largely responsible for bringing inexpensive birth control and sexual information to the American people at a time when there was a great deal of ignorance on both topics.

Lewis was a great supporter of Thomas Paine, and helped to rehabilitate his image. He paid for and had erected statues of Paine in Thetford, England; Paris, France; and Morristown, New Jersey. He also published new editions of works by Paine and Ingersoll. Lewis formed the Thomas Paine Foundation and named his Freethinkers of America magazine *The Age of Reason* (among other titles). Lewis wrote a book claiming that the true author of the Declaration of Independence was Thomas Paine. Although the thesis has been discredited, his was still an interesting piece of work. Lewis also wrote a number of books, all of which were published by his Freethought Press Association. Among them were *The Bible Unmasked, An Atheist Manifesto,* and *Atheism and Other Addresses.* Lewis's style is marked by a great deal of emotionalism: he is always outraged and shocked at something religious or some passage in the Bible. In fact, his "masterpiece" was a large volume called *The Ten Commandments,* in which he tried to show that the Commandments are impossible to follow and poor moral guides.

The selection presented here is a television interview that Lewis participated

371

in with Mike Wallace, who hosted the "Night Beat" program over station WABD, New York City. The program aired the interview on May 22, 1957, from 11:00 to 11:30 p.m. Both Lewis and Wallace seem somewhat unable to follow each other's thinking; this is *not* a debate, but it represents the more modern analog of a debate, the television interview. The text was published in Lewis's magazine, *The Age of Reason*, in July 1957.

———

WALLACE: Our first guest tonight is the President of the Freethinkers of America, self-described as a society organized for maintaining the separation of Church and State. He is Joseph Lewis—a man who not only denies the existence of God, but says that "the Bible has been the most detrimental influence upon the social and intellectual progress of Man." What are Mr. Lewis's views on Sunday Schools, Communions, religious wedding ceremonies? Why does he say that prayer is a form of self-humiliation, and what code of morality does Mr. Lewis live by himself? We'll ask these questions of atheist Joseph Lewis in a moment.

Atheist Joseph Lewis has been disenchanted by religion almost all of his life. Born in Montgomery, Alabama sixty-eight years ago, he was educated for a while in the public schools, leaving them when he was nine. At twenty-five he wandered into a Freethinkers of America forum, took the floor and made such a vigorous speech, that he was elected President on the spot. He has held this post ever since, publishing a monthly magazine called, *The Age of Reason*. During his life Mr. Lewis has initiated at least fifteen legal proceedings against what he termed "the encroachment of religion upon the public school system." He is the author of such books as, *The Bible Unmasked* and *An Atheist Manifesto*. Mr. Lewis is a man of decidedly unpopular views. He is expressing his own views here tonight. They should not be construed as my own, those of the station or of our sponsors.

Mr. Lewis, first off, let me read to you from the Old Testament for just a moment. Chapter One, verses one, two, and three: "In the beginning, God created the heaven and the earth, and the earth was without form and void, and darkness was upon the face of the deep and the spirit of God moved upon the face of the waters. and God said 'Let there be light' and there was light." Do you believe that?

LEWIS: No sir, I do not. That's a fairy tale.

WALLACE: It is a superstition?

LEWIS: It is, sir. No such creation took place. A creation predicates a time and place when and where there was nothing. Such a concept is impossible to an intelligent mind.

WALLACE: And the Bible is a fraud?

LEWIS: I say so. Yes, sir.

WALLACE: More than a fraud?

LEWIS: I think it is worse than a fraud because it has been the cause of untold misery to the human race and has arrested intellectual progress for the past two thousand years.

WALLACE: I understand that you say that the Bible is full of obscene and revolting stories.

LEWIS: It is. I need but mention a few if you'd like to hear them. The story of Lot being made drunk by his two daughters and then committing incest with him is one of the most revolting stories that I know of.

WALLACE: I don't think that it's necessary to go on. Do you consider the Ten Commandments to be a good code of morality for mankind?

LEWIS: No, sir. I do not.

WALLACE: For what reason?

LEWIS: Because they're outdated. They're outmoded. They're primitive taboos that were made into a religious system. The very first Commandment has no meaning or significance whatsoever. In fact, the three religious systems which accept the Ten Commandments do not list them the same. The Hebrew, the Protestant and the Catholic differ as to the First Commandment.

WALLACE: I understand you feel that the Ten Commandments rather than having any value are a detriment?

LEWIS: I say, so. Yes, sir. I can give you many instances of their detrimental influence upon mankind.

WALLACE: Well, before we go any further, may I read to you what Rabbi William Berkowitz of the Congregation B'nai Jeshurum here in New York told us today regarding your attacks on the Bible and on the Ten Commandments. First of all, on the Bible. The rabbi said, "The theme and the aim of the Bible is to elevate—the theme and the aim is to elevate man to his noblest purpose through its ethical teachings and moral doctrines, making man partners with God in the creation and maintenance of the Universe. It has and shall always withstand the test of time and the attack of cynics and of atheists." And as to the Bible containing what you have called obscene stories, Mr. Lewis, the rabbi said as follows: "Within its pages are, of course, stories of human beings which tell of both their greatness and their shortcomings." He said, "My answer to Mr. Lewis's charge would be simply to repeat 'to err is to be human, but condemning the entire Bible as a work of obscenity is foolish and unintelligent.'" Any further comment before we get into the rabbi's answer on the Ten Commandments?

LEWIS: On the contrary, he's defending his position and of course he wants to find out or say something that's going to be beneficial to him; but he is not right. He is entirely wrong about the matter. If obscenity is in the Bible, then there must be some reason for it, and the reason was not for elevation, nor to inspire goodness.

WALLACE: What in that case, in your mind, is the reason for what you call the obscenity in the Bible, Mr. Lewis?

LEWIS: It is a collection of obscene stories gathered together solely for the purpose of expressing the lasciviousness of human nature, and that is why they are put in the Bible. If it were one or two instances it would be different; but the Bible is filled with these obscene stories.

WALLACE: Isn't that what the rabbi says? He says, "it points out the shortcomings and the greatness of man and points out that 'to err is human.' "

LEWIS: The stories as related in the Bible and the narratives themselves do not point to such a moral. The rape of Tamar by her brother Amnon does not show anything that's good or point out a moral that might come from such a narrative. It is a story of the satisfaction of a vicious, lustful desire.

WALLACE: On the Ten Commandments, Rabbi Berkowitz said, "No document has ever exercised as great an influence on the religious and moral life of man. It not only civilized an uncivilized people—the Jews—but remained as the core of a moral code for all peoples. The present-day problems and moral crises can best be met in terms of the categories described in these commandments." Any comment on that, Mr. Lewis?

LEWIS: Of course, I don't believe it. It is not true. As I told you, the First Commandment is not accepted by all the religionists in the same manner.

WALLACE: Would you . . .

LEWIS: For instance . . .

WALLACE: I beg your pardon.

LEWIS: . . . the First Commandment states, "I am the Lord, thy God, who brought thee out of the land of Egypt out of the house of bondage." Now, the Catholics and the Protestants do not accept that part of the Commandment about out of the house of bondage and out of Egypt because they were never in Egypt, and they were not even in existence at the time this Commandment was written.

WALLACE: Would you also discard the Sermon on the Mount—the code adhered to by people of Christian denomination?

LEWIS: You can take what's good in the Sermon on the Mount, but the parts that are certainly not good and are too silly for words should be eliminated.

WALLACE: Such as?

LEWIS: Such as if your eye should offend, pluck it out; or if your hand offends you, cut it off. I think that's an utterly ridiculous code to follow.

WALLACE: We talked with Dr. Langmead Casserley, an Anglican of the General Theological Seminary today. He told us as follows: "Living up to the Sermon in an obvious literal sense is of course impossible, but when men do great and noble deeds, the Kingdom of Heaven will be at hand. People follow the Sermon every day, everywhere. These deeds do not get publicity. You do not turn to a newspaper and see 'Extraordinary Devotion of Accountant in Toledo.' Sanctity lacks news value," Dr. Langmead Casserley said, "but these are the moments when men live up to the Sermon on the Mount that makes life worth while." You disagree?

LEWIS: I disagree most emphatically, sir.

WALLACE: All right. Just . . . I have gone through this as you can understand, just to get the difference of opinion.

LEWIS: That's right.

WALLACE: Mr. Lewis, let me ask you this. There are undoubtedly thousands of atheists in the United States today, but very few of them launch attacks as you do on the Bible, the Ten Commandments, the Sermon on the Mount, on all organized religion. They seem, most of them, to be perfectly happy to live by their own beliefs and let others live by their own. What I would like to get at is, why this bitterness, this destructiveness on your part? Why are you so passionately opposed to religion and desirous of tearing down the house of religion?

LEWIS: Well, because I think it has done a great deal of harm and when you have the ability to do something, I think it's your duty to do it. You might say the same thing about Abraham Lincoln. He looked upon slavery as an institution that he thought was harmful, he thought it was detrimental, he thought it was reprehensible. And so he devoted his life to the abolition of slavery, which, by the way, has Biblical sanction.

WALLACE: What crimes—what harms have been done in the name of religion, sir?

LEWIS: Oh, religion has committed so many crimes it would take an encyclopedia to record them.

WALLACE: All right, then, let me ask you this question. Let me put it to you this way. Is not the good that organized religion—or for that matter disorganized religion—is not the good that religion has done over the years—has it not outweighed the bad that has been done in the name of religion by possibly a thousand to one?

LEWIS: No. I think the contrary is the truth. I would say the harm that it has done outweighs the good by ten thousand to one. Religion invented Hell, it invented blasphemy, it invented witchcraft. Why those three things alone, if you recorded the crimes committed in those names, would be sufficient to condemn it before the world.

WALLACE: Mr. Lewis, let me find out, if I may, about your own code of morality—the precepts that you live by. Mr. Lewis, would you kill?

LEWIS: I would be very reluctant to kill.

WALLACE: That's not answering the question.

LEWIS: Ah, probably in extreme self-defense I would, but otherwise no.

WALLACE: You would not kill, except in self-defense?

LEWIS: I believe so. I hesitate to kill an insect.

WALLACE: Would you commit adultery?

LEWIS: No, sir. I would not.

WALLACE: Would you steal?

LEWIS: No, sir. I would not.

WALLACE: Would you bear false witness against someone—would you testify in court falsely—commit perjury?

LEWIS: No, sir. I would not.

WALLACE: Well, Mr. Lewis, you say that you will not do any of these things. Would you tell me then, what is the difference between your code of morality and that of the Ten Commandments whose content essentially I have just read and whose content you say that you condemn?

LEWIS: Because you haven't given the full meaning of the Ten Commandments. When you ask me whether I would bear false witness—if the Commandment read, "Thou shalt not bear false witness," if that were all to the Commandment, it would be a very good commandment, but the Commandment reads, "Thou shalt not bear false witness, against thy neighbor." That reduces it to a provincial code of conduct. That means only your neighbor—you must not bear false witness against him.

WALLACE: Well you're . . . aren't you . . .

LEWIS: It's a primitive concept—it was a primitive taboo. But to the stranger beyond the gates or to other peoples, it was perfectly all right to bear false witness, and the biblical testimony is in support of that premise by the conduct of the primitive Hebrews themselves.

WALLACE: Well I think that in the standards by which we interpret the Ten Commandments today, the bearing of false witness is not only against the neighbor who may be next door or sitting next to you but against your neighbor in the broader sense. But that does not . . . you say would not kill, I would not commit adultery, I would not bear false witness, I would not steal; these are the same things. Is not your morality exactly the same as that set forth in the Ten Commandments?

LEWIS: No, it is not, because these things that you mention are basic and were in existence long before the Ten Commandments were ever written or even printed. The basic rule of life is that you protect yourself in society.

WALLACE: Well, then, the Ten Commandments are reflective of what is right in life and you condemn them.

LEWIS: No, they're merely repeating some of the old codes that are as ancient as man himself.

WALLACE: Well, it's not bad to repeat old codes if old codes are valid.

LEWIS: No, but you separate those which have very little value, very little significance, very little influence. Take those about creating a Sabbath Day. Do you realize what that has done to man? People have been beaten to death—people have been killed. Take the third Commandment, "Thou shalt not take the name of the Lord, Thy God, in vain." That has brought about blasphemy. People's tongues have been ripped out. People have been burned at the stake. You must take them all. You can't take just a few. And when you say, "Thou shalt not kill," what do mean when you say, "Thou shalt not kill"? Moses, himself, the so-called lawgiver, killed a man without the slightest provocation. Does anyone suppose that a God of the Universe would give a murderer a Commandment to tell other people, "Thou shalt not kill."

WALLACE: Mr. Lewis, an author by the name of F. Scott Fitzgerald once wrote as follows: He said, "The easiest way to get a reputation is to go outside the fold, shout around for a few years as a violent atheist or dangerous radical and then crawl back to the shelter." Would this, in any way, describe the motivation or the possible future of Joseph Lewis?

LEWIS: No, sir. I don't like to say this but he may have been inebriated when he made that statement, because it's not true.

WALLACE: What did you say?

LEWIS: I said that when Fitzgerald made that statement he was inebriated, I would much rather quote Coleridge—Samuel Taylor Coleridge, who said, "Not one man in a thousand, yes, I repeat it, not one man in a thousand has strength of mind or goodness of heart to be an atheist."

WALLACE: Strength of mind or . . .

LEWIS: . . . goodness of heart.

WALLACE: . . . goodness of heart. Would you explain . . .

LEWIS: Samuel Taylor Coleridge . . .

WALLACE: Would you explain what you mean or what Coleridge— Samuel Coleridge Taylor—Samuel Taylor Coleridge . . .

LEWIS: Samuel Taylor Coleridge . . . that's right.

WALLACE: . . . meant and what you mean when you interpret . . .

LEWIS: Because he was then associating with the English atheists who were the leaders of their time. They were the finest men of England, and he made that statement because it takes a great deal of courage to express your thoughts in this particular philosophy.

WALLACE: Uh-huh. I'm certain that that is true. I'm certain . . . How did you become an atheist? Your parents were Jewish, is not that a fact?

LEWIS: They were. Yes, they were Jewish.

WALLACE: Orthodox?

LEWIS: No, sir, they were not. One of my brothers brought a copy of Ingersoll's lectures into the house. It was left for me, when I found the book, to read those lectures to my mother.

WALLACE: At the age of . . .

LEWIS: I started about the age of fifteen or sixteen; probably seventeen. They impressed me very much. They impressed my mother very much. One thing led on to another. After I read Ingersoll, I began to read Thomas Paine and between the two they became my educators.

WALLACE: As a boy, before you got to Ingersoll, had you attended synagogue or Sunday school?

LEWIS: I have a very slight recollection of having attended Sunday school probably once or twice in my lifetime and at a very early age.

WALLACE: You were not Bar Mitzvahed? Confirmed?

LEWIS: No. No, sir. I was not.

WALLACE: We asked Rabbi Berkowitz to tell us his earliest recollection of going to temple and he recalled as follows. He said, "When I was nine years old, I went—to shul—I went to shul with my parents and grandparents. I remember watching the beauty of the worship and listening to the choir. I remember feeling a wonderful sense of solidarity with my family and feeling a link between myself and all my peoples through the ages. It gave me great peace." Now, that is Rabbi Berkowitz' rememberance of religious feeling when he was just a boy of nine. Do your remember, prior to Ingersoll, your . . . any religious feeling in your life prior to the time when you began to read these . . . Ingersoll lectures?

LEWIS: No, sir.

WALLACE: None whatsoever?

LEWIS: None whatsoever.

WALLACE: When, as many intelligent people as do subscribe to various religions, when they do subscribe to these religions, get as much solace, as much comfort, do as such good in the name of religion, how in the world can you . . . we are not here questioning your belief, your desire, your understanding of yourself as an atheist; what we are questioning here is your desire to tear down the house of religion. Why do you want to take away from these people something they find so fulfilling, so comforting?

LEWIS: I don't believe they find it comforting. I believe that they live in great fear. I believe they suffer from some form of fear complex. I believe that they tell you that they get some kind of a consolation because they love God. Why the necessity of loving God? (If there is such a thing as God.) Does He need our love? What can we do for God? How does He know that we love Him? They love God because they fear Him; their so-called love is based upon a deep-rooted fear of a jealous and vindictive God. They fear that He's going to inflict some punishment upon them, and therefore they devote themselves to prayers or supplications and fastings and what not to appease Him. They fear the wrath of God. I want to emancipate them from this frightful fear.

WALLACE: But if these people, if these people need this, want this, why do you want to legislate against them? Why don't you just leave them alone and then you go your own way independent?

LEWIS: Oh, no, on the contrary. I want them to let us alone. I don't want them to encroach upon the educational system. They're constantly hammering to break down the secular public schools of this country. The public schools were established, they were thriving, they were doing very fine, and all of a sudden you get released time. For what purpose? To send the children to religious school. Now they want to bring in some other things, like Bible reading. They want the people to bring the preacher into the public school. They want to teach religion in the schools. They want to get control of the public school system. What was the matter with the public school system when it was first established? When it was first started, it was perfectly satisfactory to everybody. It is they—the religionists—who are pressing themselves upon the body politic. We want to hold inviolate that wonderful Constitution of ours, and particularly that first article of the Bill of Rights. We don't want them to violate it. We also want them to pay their rightful share of taxes.

WALLACE: Mr. Lewis, have you ever in your life felt a real desire to pray, did you want to turn to somebody, some thing, some one and therefore want to pray?

LEWIS: I have never had the desire to pray. I may have gone to people in times of uncertainty and asked their advice about the matter, or talked to them about the problem, but as to praying, no sir.

WALLACE: No . . .

LEWIS: Absolutely not.

WALLACE: You abhore prayer?

LEWIS: I think it's wasted words on the desert air. I don't know to whom they're praying. No prayer in the whole history of mankind has ever been answered.

WALLACE: You say, I understand, that prayer is a form of humiliation.

LEWIS: I do sir. I believe a man who prays humiliates himself because he hasn't the strength to fight his own battles, and he's calling upon some mythical force to help him.

WALLACE: In other words, you regard prayer, as used by those of us who are religious more or less, you regard it as a crutch.

LEWIS: I would say that self-reliance is a better staff than the crutch of religion. I think I can put it that way, and that would express it very well. I'd say no prayer has ever been answered and I say it's a humiliating gesture to get on your knees or raise your hands in prayer. No results can come from it, and it defeats its purpose by preventing you from using your own energies to solve your problems.

WALLACE: We talked with the Jesuit, Father La Farge about your ideas about prayer. He said, "Mr. Lewis's idea of prayer is rather crude. Prayer is not just asking for something, but being attuned with God." and Dr. Langmead Casserley, whom we quoted earlier, said, "Prayer is not to get God on our side, but to get us on God's side."

LEWIS: I think what they are saying is utterly ridiculous and without foundation. What do they mean by getting on God's side? It's too silly for words. There's no such thing. They're talking in riddles. They're talking of things about which they know nothing.

WALLACE: Well, it is evidently . . .

LEWIS: Getting on God's side or God getting on your side, is just a lot of nonsense.

WALLACE: It is evidently something that they understand.

LEWIS: I don't believe that they do. If they say they know, then I believe that they are under some kind of a delusion. I don't think they can demonstrate in the slightest degree what they're talking about when they say they want to get on God's side or they want God to get on their side.

WALLACE: When was the last time that you stepped inside a church or a temple to witness a service, Mr. Lewis?

LEWIS: I have been invited to speak at many churches and I was in one in Miami two years ago. I spoke from the platform at a Wednesday night Forum, but not to attend services.

WALLACE: That is the last time that you went to a service?

LEWIS: Yes, sir.

WALLACE: What kind of a service was it?

LEWIS: That's a Unitarian Church.

WALLACE: The Unitarian Church. They asked you to speak at their Wednesday night forum, not at a service?

LEWIS: That's right.

WALLACE: How can you remain a conscientious atheist if you do not know more of what is going on inside the opposition, so to speak?

LEWIS: I think I am perfectly acquainted with what goes on inside the opposition. I think I know all about the services and much of the ritual that takes place. It can be described as a form of post-hypnotic impressions upon the people who have been inculcated with this idea of God, and the religious ceremony, when they were children. The child would know nothing about these ceremonies unless the parent, or the preacher, had inculcated these things in his mind when it was in an impressionable state.

WALLACE: Mr. Lewis, let's up-date the story a bit now. There's a fellow in town, an Evangelist preacher by the name of Billy Graham, a man you've publicly attacked. In an open letter to Mr. Graham, you charge as follows: You say, "Your campaign is purely a mercenary undertaking. The only thing spiritual that you're interested in, in this New York crusade, is the religious motto on the money you get."

LEWIS: That's true. I did charge him with being mercenary.

WALLACE: What leads you to believe that you understand Billy Graham's motives so well and credit them so little?

LEWIS: Because it seems incredible to me that an honest man would preach such an obviously false doctrine, and he certainly has given no evidence to support his claim and is not performing what he says he performs. He cannot fulfill his promises.

WALLACE: What's that?

LEWIS: And that is, he claims he is giving spiritual value to the people who come to hear him. He's preaching a doctrine that has no evidence to support it, and as Ingersoll said so many years ago, he's "hooting the same hoots that have been hooted for hundreds of years," and I don't know of a single instance where results have been obtained from it. He is preaching a false doctrine.

WALLACE: And you still cannot understand why thousands of people, tens of thousands of people, are coming to Madison Square Garden to listen, to pray, and some of them to come at his call?

LEWIS: I think I can explain that. Only yesterday, I got a newspaper clipping from Detroit stating that Billy Graham's Crusade here has recruited 250,000 people who are being brought here by train and bus and other forms of conveyances to attend his meetings at Madison Square Garden. In other words, in plain language, he's packing the Garden with these people who are already believers in order to make it appear that he is a big success. To most of them it is an excursion to New York.

WALLACE: You mean these are people who are already there and he's . . .

LEWIS: Yes, he is bringing them here in "truckloads," he's bringing them here in trains; they're stopping in hotels and he arranges for their transportation. There is no doubt that they are coming to New York for a visit and they're obligated to go visit Billy Graham at Madison Square Garden. I say that's packing the meetings.

WALLACE: We spoke with Billy Graham's office today and they reply to your charges this way: First, that he "packs" the Garden, illegally, so to speak. "Untrue and our files are open to the public on the bus accommodations we have made; all chartered buses are for groups from

Brooklyn, Staten Island and elsewhere in New York. Middle Western people—only 40 have come from Chicago." Second, that he is making money from the crusade. "He's paid a salary of $15,000 a year from the Minneapolis Evangelist Foundation. All offerings at the Garden are taken only for defraying expenses of rental and publicity. They are handled by a gentleman who is an executive director of Macy's Department Store who volunteered to be our Treasurer."

LEWIS: I defy him to open his books to the public. I say that Mr. Billy Graham probably found preaching the gospel more profitable than being a Fuller Brush salesman. That is what he was before he became an Evangelist. I say that there is absolutely no proof, and particularly when he tells you that he wants people to accept Christ as their redeemer, there's no proof that a character such as Jesus Christ of the New Testament ever existed. He has no such proof. He is preaching a doctrine that has absolutely no foundation whatsoever spiritual or otherwise. He is preaching a false doctrine.

WALLACE: One final question, Mr. Lewis. When you are on your deathbed, do you think that it is barely possible that you might call either for a rabbi or a priest as so many, I think you will agree, as so many professed nonbelievers have done before you?

LEWIS: No, sir, that is not true. I don't know of any nonbeliever that has ever called for some clergyman to come to him. I was on my deathbed twice . . .

WALLACE: You were on your deathbed twice?

LEWIS: Yes, sir. I had two heart attacks. In both instances, I was given up and I had no intention then of calling for any priest or rabbi or any other clergyman. I believe with Thomas Paine that in silent resignation there is more consolation than the murmuring wish of a prayer. What is the purpose of calling for a clergyman? He can't do anything for me. He can't do anything for himself. He will suffer from the same ills of the flesh. He'll die just as I will, as all others will die. He doesn't possess powers other than any ordinary human being. And the muttering of a prayer is as useless a thing as I can imagine.

WALLACE: Mr. Lewis . . .

LEWIS: Let me say this: It's often said that Thomas Paine and Voltaire recanted before they died. It is not true. Neither did Robert G. Ingersoll.

WALLACE: Mr. Lewis, are you bitter, perhaps, because there is no God in your belief?

LEWIS: Oh, to the contrary. I'm perfectly satisfied. I am an emancipated human being, completely free from a belief in a tyrant God. It wouldn't make a particle of difference to me if there is a God or not. In fact, I would really feel sorry for an Omnipotent Being who couldn't make a better universe than we have. If, with all the resources at my disposal, I could not make a better world, I would be ashamed of myself.

WALLACE: Thank you, sir, for coming and explaining your point of view to us tonight, Mr. Lewis. In his book, *The Bible Unmasked,* Joseph Lewis has written, "It is our duty to expose the Bible. We must continue to tell the truth about the Bible. We must continue to enlighten the people." And he goes on, "And if after the true facts are known, there are some who still insist the Bible is good enough for them, they are welcome to it." What would a religionist answer? In the Book of Common Prayer, these words are set down: "We have erred and strayed from Thy ways like lost sheep." For those who disagree with Mr. Lewis, his challenges to religion may possibly be worth while. For, possibly, many of us tonight will re-examine and, chances are, reaffirm our own religious beliefs.

Part Six

Ethics and Unbelief

Introduction

Many theists base their belief in God upon an untested thought. They think that without a God there could be no absolute or objective ethics. Without a God man would make all ethical judgments subjectively, by consensus in many cases. What these theists fear about this approach is that when circumstances change, there will be no way of preventing a particular society from changing its consensus as to what is ethical. The result, they say, would be the horrors of another Holocaust: the possibility that a given society would make such actions as infanticide, cannibalism, and incest ethical. Even worse, these theists feel, would be the loss of ethical guidance to people in their daily lives. Stealing and killing would be permitted in any circumstance in which a given individual thought he was warranted.

We need to examine carefully whether the theist's fears are justified. In addition, we need to show how the *theist* really comes to have his ideas about good and evil, and whether *that* source is any better or different than the atheist's source. Is a theistically-based ethic immune from the same charges that the theist hurls at an atheistic system of ethics?

Perhaps the simplest and most important question that an atheist can ask a theist about ethics is "Why do you do good?" The theist would probably reply, "Because God wants me to." The next question to the theist would be "Why do what God says?" To this the standard theistic answer is "Because God is good." If we stop at this point and look at what the theist has said, we see that he has just asserted that "God is good" *before* God has even told him to do anything. This assertion means that the theist has made an ethical judgment about what is good and what is evil *without having heard about that subject from God.* In other words, the theist has just demonstrated that there *is* a way of making at least some correct ethical judgments *without* turning to God for advice. Once the theist has admitted this fact, it should not be so difficult to convince him that an atheist can do the same thing for *all* ethical judgments. "Wait," interrupts the theist,

"I know God is good because God tells me that He is good." But this answer won't do, because the justifications for believing something is true (i.e., that God is good) cannot come from the very source being evaluated. If person A wanted to know whether he should do what person B says, and we ask him *why* he should listen to B, person A would not have a very convincing set of reasons for listening to B if the only reason he had was that B said of himself that he was good. If *someone else* provided evidence that person B was indeed good, or had good character "references," then the evidence would appear more compelling. Of course, the theist can always say that, by definition, God is good, but this is also not a compelling argument. After all, there are plenty of gods who have been worshiped by various religions and who were *not* good, or who were only partly good. A god is not necessarily good *by definition*.

Having established that the theist makes at least some ethical judgments without asking God, we can now move on to the question of whether *correct* ethical judgments can be made without God's help. The first problem we have to face is what makes an ethical judgment correct. A theist would say that *all* ethical judgments that come from God are, by definition, correct. The atheist may well reply, "What do you do about judgments that have to be made about new situations for which God has never given any answers?" The theist may reply that he merely prays or looks inside himself and the answer becomes apparent to him. The atheist may reply: "I can do exactly the same thing when faced with a novel ethical dilemma, and I can also come up with an answer. In my case, at least, that same process did not produce an answer from God, and I doubt whether it did in your case either." In other words, our conscience can give us guidance. Surely during these introspective times man is making ethical judgments without relying upon God (regardless of what the theist may think).

We now come to the evidence for whether the theist *ever* gets ethical advice directly from God. Let us try to examine this issue with an open mind. We will assume that there is an all-powerful and all-knowing God, just for the sake of argument. How does the theist claim to be able to obtain advice from this God, and what are some examples of that advice (and its quality)? I think that the theist would not claim that he had a direct "pipeline" to God, but rather that God had revealed his ethical advice largely through the Bible. While no one doubts that there is some good ethical advice in the Bible, much of it is very general. For example, "Thou shalt not steal." Does this mean that there are absolutely no cases in which one can steal, or does this prohibition mean that every instance of taking something from someone else is stealing? What if a person were to take back the very thing that had been stolen from him in the first place? Similar ambiguity is found in the advice not to kill. Is killing in self-defense or on the battlefield immoral?

Some moral advice in the Bible is downright unhelpful and dangerous. For example, Mark 10:9 states that all divorce is wrong, yet in Deuteronomy 24:1-3, we learn that divorce is not only acceptable but accomplished by merely writing a bill of divorcement and sending one's wife away. In Matthew 5:28 we learn that a man who has merely looked upon a woman with lust in his heart has committed adultery. And in the very next verse Jesus says, "If your right eye causes you to sin, pluck it out and throw it away from you." If anyone were to follow this last piece of advice, he would be a one-eyed sinner, for one's eye can never cause one to sin, even if one believes in sin. Perhaps one's brain can, however. It should also be mentioned that the idea that a "sin" committed *in* the mind is as wrong as a sin committed in actuality is both foolish and obviously untrue.

When examining the other methods by which theists have claimed to get information from God, we must consider revelation. This is the direct passing of information from God to a living person, or so it is claimed. A cursory look at some of this divine communication will soon uncover confusion and contradiction. If we are to believe all those who say that they experience direct revelation, then God has evidently asked people to found religions that fight with other, established religions; he has ordered wars among his followers; gone back on his promises; and denied what he already had said. It seems probable that *all* people who claim to have had a revelation are simply mistaken.

Without direct, on-the-spot information from God about how to make ethical decisions, what does a theist do when faced with a novel moral situation? He makes a decision based upon past experience, knowledge, peer observation, parental teachings, and societal pressure—which is exactly the way an atheist would decide. If these prove inadequate, there are always experts available to consult.

Theism provides no adequate moral guidance in and of itself. In reality, the theist obtains the vast majority of his information about ethical decision making from exactly the same nontheistic sources as the atheist. This realization will quiet the fear of even the strongest theist that an ethic without God will lead man down the garden path to self-destruction. This simply is not so, because *all* operational ethics is based entirely upon nontheistic principles, which include doing unto others as you would have them do unto you, seeking the greatest good for the greatest number, proceeding in the way that hurts the least, and exercising simple expediency (a course not generally recommended). These are really the only tools we have to solve ethical dilemmas, and we nonbelievers are glad to share them with theists.

There seem to be four major ethical principles. In order for an action to be considered moral (ethical, if you wish), the answer must be yes to each of four questions that frame the principles. That is, there must be four yeses. When there are only three or two the situation becomes more ambiguous, and when there are a couple of "I don't knows," things can become complicated. We will look at a simple case after listing the four questions and their corresponding principles: (1) Would I want someone else to do this to me (the Golden Rule, which is found in almost every culture, including those far older than Christianity)? (2) Will this action spare the infliction of pain on people who don't want to suffer pain? (3) Will this action produce the greatest good for the greatest number (the Utilitarian principle)? and (4) Will this action allow people to realize their full potential (to be self-actualizing)?

If affirmative answers can be given to these questions, the particular behavior is ethical, given current information. However, if we have incorrect information (as may happen when testing a new drug for which no long-term toxicity studies have been done), we may make a wrong judgment. If we *know* that we do not know the answer to one or more of the questions, it may be best to defer an answer until later. If we have to give an answer now—if the situation won't permit delay—then we can only make an educated guess about future harm to people, and proceed cautiously.

When we are faced with a situation in which all four of the questions can be answered yes, but one is answered no, what do we do? Well, it depends upon which one is no, and how positive we are that the others are yes. For example, suppose we know with confidence that our new policy guidelines, which we will announce soon at work, will improve efficiency. That will make the company more profitable, and *that* will please not only stockholders but those employees who have retirement programs tied to the price of our stock. The guidelines would not involve anything that we would not want others to do to us. It will allow some additional employees to realize their potential. However, since the policy strictly enforces promptness in arriving at work, and penalizes those who do not arrive on time, then some people will be hurt. It may hurt those who simply cannot get going in the morning or who have to do certain chores before departing for the office (e.g., dropping their child off at a day care center). In this case, we could argue that an employee has the responsibility to arrive at work on time and, barring an occasional emergency exception, anyone who is not giving their full required time to the company is not playing by the rules to which they agreed upon being hired.

Of course, there are many cases in which the weight of the no answers may be greater than the weight of the yes answers. Often we simply cannot evaluate the weight of either. In these cases, we can either defer an answer or take a risk that we will be wrong and will have to correct our actions in the future. There is a moral requirement to correct any unethical behavior we may do, in any case. This is one reason that concept of forgiveness of sin in Christianity is so inherently immoral to the atheist. Sin can only be forgiven *by the person injured by the action.* For example, a thief can only be forgiven by returning the object, apologizing, and asking forgiveness from the person he wronged. A priest isn't the proper party to forgive, and even God (if there is a God) is not the offended party, at least not the *only* offended party. By taking corrective action against the actual party who has been injured by one's actions (whether intentional or not), the atheist is more in touch with reality than is the Christian.

The final question that the theist always asks the atheist is, *why* be moral if there is no God? The answer is simple in the short-term but complex from the long-range perspective. The short-term answer is self-preservation. If everyone were allowed to kill or rape or rob at will, one's person, property, and safety would be at risk. So it is for self-preservation and survival that one is moral. The long-term answer is that first, the survival of the human race is an assumed good. Every species "tries" to survive. If the human race desires to survive, then it must have societies that survive (humans are social animals), and in order for societies to survive, the people who make up those societies must survive. The only way they can help assure their survival is by being moral. In addition, each generation has incurred a moral obligation to continue to make the world a better place, because previous generations worked to make the world a better place. The world can only become a better place when its members are acting morally. This morality includes feeding the starving, educating the ignorant, raising the standard of living of the poor, and so forth. That is the moral (the good) thing to do. Why? Because feeding a person is intuitively better than allowing him to starve.

In conclusion, we can see that it is not only possible for a nontheist to be moral, but the method by which an atheist can decide about moral issues is also explainable. The criteria the atheist uses are logically justifiable, and the goal of survival is understandable. In short, theists who attack atheists on moral grounds have once again been shown to stand on a shaky foundation themselves.

Is Religion the Necessary Basis of Morality?

E. Haldeman-Julius

Emanuel Julius (1889-1951) grew up as the son of poor immigrant parents in Philadelphia. At the age of thirteen, Julius left school and started a career in newspaper work (as a copy holder), which was to be his life's work. At the age of seventeen, he was a reporter on the New York *Call*, a Socialist newspaper. After working on several other newspapers, Julius became Sunday Editor of the *Call*. While in New York, he met Marcet Haldeman, a banker's daughter from Girard, Kansas, who was an aspiring actress. In 1915, Julius was asked to become an editor on *The Appeal to Reason*, of Girard, Kansas, then this country's largest Socialist paper. Since Marcet Haldeman's father had died, she had gone back to Girard to run the family bank. In Girard, Julius courted Marcet, and they were married, whereupon they hyphenated their names into Haldeman-Julius.

In 1919, Haldeman-Julius bought the *Appeal,* with money partially advanced to him by Marcet. He remembered that as a child he had been delighted with a little booklet of Oscar Wilde's *Ballad of Reading Gaol.* He ordered the linotyper to set up this poem and *The Rubaiyat* by Omar Khayyam, and print them as small booklets. These were advertised in *The Appeal* at twenty-five cents each, and were the first two of the Little Blue Books that would make Haldeman-Julius famous. The series eventually reached more than 2,000 titles, and sold over 500 million copies, at prices as low as five cents each. There was also a series of Big Blue Books selling for twenty-five cents each.

Many of the titles were freethought books. Robert Ingersoll, Thomas Paine, J. M. Robertson, Chapman Cohen, Bertrand Russell, Clarence Darrow and Voltaire were among the authors included. Joseph McCabe wrote hundreds of Big and Little Blue Books, and made his living for a number of years almost exclusively from writing for the Haldeman-Julius company, which also published a number of magazines and a newspaper, *The American Freeman*. Emanuel Haldeman-Julius was responsible for giving the famous cultural historian Will Durant his start, and for helping the struggling Simon & Schuster company to acquire its first bestseller. Tragically, Emanuel drowned in his swimming pool in 1951.

The present selection comes from an article that Haldeman-Julius wrote for one of his own short-lived publications, *Know Thyself*. William Fielding was the editor, and the article first appeared in January 1925.

Let us glance for a moment, my friends and fellow-skeptics, in a spirit of scientific curiosity at the claim that religion is the necessary basis of morality; that religion and morality are indeed one, being merely different aspects of salvation by the grace of God; that there can be no morality without religion. Aside from the phantasmagoria of the Bible, this is the biggest lie the Christians try to put upon us. It is among the most stupid, pretentious and bald, brazen assumptions of the bally-hooers of holiness. This gibberish of sacred and supreme morality is a familiar defense of the Christian when his more technical and transcendental hocus-pocus is hit heavily in the solar plexus. When theology is groggy from the shattering blows of reason: when the miracles are miserably used by laughter and logic: when the Apostles' Creed is rejected with a hoot and doctrine collapses fatuously like a slit bladder: in short, when religion cannot confute nor convince, nor absolutely terrorize the sinner, by crying up the pregnant, dire, delirious possibilities of another life: then, with a smirk and a shuffle the Christian utters the hoary lie that religion is morality, and morality is religion, and never the twain shall be found separate.

I say this is a lie. I say it is well to speak plainly about this self-righteous, arrogant, insulting, utterly false claim of the churchmen. It is not even plausible. One cannot pay it the polite observance that one would grant to clever sophistry. Outside of religion, such a claim would instantly be heaped with the scorn it deserves. No other institution, no movement, no philosophy, no form of human belief or activity except that of religion would claim to be the origin and essence and sole assurance of morality. Were such a claim advanced in behalf of any nonreligious system of belief or conduct, what sensible man would believe or even give it a courteous nod of recognition? Yet outside of religion there are superior moral forces that have a more valid title to the importance that religion claims for itself out of sheer, unmitigated gall.

This claim of Christian morality is not only a lie. It is a kind of pious theft. The Christian would steal the credit that belongs to all other influences of life. With one sweep of sanctimonious plunder, the churchman would expropriate the ethical values of the ages of human evolution. The whole structure of social law, and the whole body of individual ethics, he would falsely identify as the property of himself and his peculiar *God.* He would rob the philosopher of his ethical goods. He would rob the artist. He would rob the scientist. He would rob the moralist untrammeled by theological notions. He would rob the builders and lawgivers, who wrecking not of the fantastic demands of another life, have tried to erect institutions and mark safe paths for the purposes of this life. He would rob the teacher and the thinker. The Christian would rob man himself who, in the age-long struggle with natural forces and the adjustment of his social interests, has learned a few things that were not originally written in any book sacred or profane, about the business of life.

There is a material basis of morality which the Christian finds it convenient to ignore. When man learned how to provide himself more easily with food; when he learned how to build for himself a better kind of shelter; when he learned how to labor more intelligently, how to formulate laws for the better protection of his life and goods, how to enter into mutual arrangements for his safety and social well-being; when man, his wits sharpened by necessity, learned how to manage these simple but fundamentally important material things, he achieved a very practical and potent sort of morality. And religion did not help man to achieve this morality. Man had to solve these very material and very moral problems of existence or perish. Not how he was to die, but how he was to live, was the question. As a matter of good sense, if man had been less superstitious, less religious, less borne upon by dark and terrified speculations about another life, he would have progressed much faster in arranging sensibly the affairs of this life. Man, for example, would have learned more quickly how to use fire had he not worshipped it in fear as a portent of the gods. He would more quickly have mastered the elements had he not seen in them and shrunk trembling before them as the awful, mysterious operations of the gods. The builder, I say, is a pioneer of morality. As man builds, so does he grow in civilized and ethical stature. And what has religion built? It has built idols. It has built churches. It has built torture chambers and dungeons and bonfires for heretics. It has diverted man's energy and imagination from moral to frightfully immoral things.

The truth is that religion, far from being a moral force, has given its sanctifying allegiance to the greatest immoralities in the history of man. There has been no "custom of fell deeds," no proud wrong of oppression, no baseness of sham that religion has not blessed. The thinkers and humanitarians and liberators have always recognized the church as their great enemy. The moral, the intellectual evolution of the race has been harried and impeded in every age by priestly force and craft. And religion has been defeated, on first one ground and then another, by the growing ethical sense of mankind. The churchman trips himself upon his own quibble. He protests, in a most aggrieved tone, that the abuses and iniquities of religion were the fault, not of religion *per se,* but of the undeveloped mind and morals of the race. So in a dark age of mankind religion, helpless and blameless, has been guilty of dark practices. What is this but a confession that religion is not the great light, the great moral regulator of society? We can see that there has been much religion with little morality. It is written plainly for all to read that religion, instead of leading man to higher morality, has followed man to the lowest depths of immorality. If religion has simply reflected the age, then it has been no more significant as a moral guide and arbiter than man's habits of love and war, of eating and drinking. Religion, by the churchman's own admission, is not the creator and custodian of pure ethics: it but fawns upon, pours ointment upon, and throws its robes around the current practices of sinful man—not so much his individual peccadilloes (though it has ever been prone to wink an eye at the triflings of saints) as his social *mores*. *God* has always been strong for the custom of the country. He is a patriot of densest ray serene, a reactionary, a one-hundred-percenter, the most antique and be-whiskered of the old fogies.

Men have believed strange things—they have performed strange deeds—and, however given by folly and wickedness, religion has said these beliefs and deeds of man were holy. When man believed in slavery, religion backed up this article of the age's morality with a mighty and prolonged "Amen." The church has defended human bondage in every form. The priest, the soldier and the lord of lands and serfs have worked in complete, pious accord to bind and rob the stupid, praying masses. The Bible has furnished innumerable texts for the tyrants and slaveholders. The medicine men of religion have in every age brewed doses to stupefy the herd into hugging its chains. The church has upheld the institution of slavery in slave countries: and—oh! most moral, most noble, most courageous priestcraft—it has dared to oppose slavery in free countries. We no longer believe in slavery: a man, chiefly propelled by economic forces, has passed on to more subtle and efficient institutions. So today the witch-doctors do not preach of the righteousness and blessings of slavery, although they worship the same Bible that, in other ages when this supremely moral religion was less moral, was quoted liberally by the soothsayers to prove that to be a rebel was wickedly human, to be a cringing slave divine.

The immoral record of religion is immense. History is full of it. We read of religious wars: and what can be more terribly immoral than to drive men into killing one another for the sake of conflicting ideas of Godolatry? We read of the stake—of the fires lit by Christian zeal, of the roasting of right-honest heretics for the glory of *God*. We read of men stretched on the rack. We read of men thrown into dungeons. We see everywhere man set against man, the human race divided into numbers of bloodthirsty, warring sects: all for *Jesus*, all for religion, all for this thing that calls itself the only symbol and safeguard of morality. We see men trying to bring knowledge to their fellows—trying to improve the intelligence, and therefore the true morals, of the race: and persecuting these men, striving with all its power to keep men in darkness so that they might more easily remain in subjection to the superstition-mongers, we find that moral-religious band of the churchmen. Crime of crimes—most dark and damnable of all immoralities—we see religion binding the intellect of man: we see religion with whip and gag and bundles of Bible-blessed fagots denying men the right to speak and punishing men for the slightest honest motion of the lips: we see religion forcing scholars to recant their intelligent teachings, burning with hoodlum holiness the books of the thinkers; hounding, with spies and thugs, the educators as if they were criminals. We see that, under the absolute sway of this holy, most moral religion, it was regarded as a crime to think. It was the age—ah, yes, the *very religious* age—the age in which there could be no ignorance without religion, and no religion without ignorance. The morality of the church bade men wade through slaughter to the altar of the true *God.*

There were moralists in those days; or you may call them intellectuals; or skeptics, as indeed they were. They spoke for morality against religion. They denounced as highly immoral this enslavement of the human mind. They condemned the hanging of witches. They declared that massacres— *religious* massacres—were *immoral.* They insisted that man should respect his thinking faculties and dignify them by sane, free usage. They cried out to men that it was a glory, not a crime, to think. They held that knowledge, not blind belief, was the higher moral force: that man should cultivate and follow the leading of his intellect rather than follow his mad, fanatical, pious emotions into bloody ditches. Voltaire wrote his magnificent essay on *Toleration* as a protest against a most Christian butchery—a veritable, vile commonplace of that most Christian moral age. The scholars, the philosophers, the real *irreligious moralists,* under the leadership of the lofty-minded anti-church Diderot, labored heroically, with infinite moral earnestness and self-sacrifice, to assemble knowledge that would triumph over the immorality of religion. These men—these moral-intellectual skeptics—were on one side. The church— religion—was on the other side. Choose between them, my friends, on the ground of simple morality! Will you have the light spread by the torch of the bigot or the light spread by the pen of the heretic? The man of God on the warpath or that old skeptic, Voltaire, in his study?

We have spoken of the past. A great deal of water has passed under the bridge since the days when no sinner was safe and only marauding, murdering saints could lay down the moral law to mankind. This water has been less and less reddened with the blood of heretics. As man has grown in morality—guided by intelligence, by the arts and sciences, by the gradually perceived necessity of making the world a little safer for progress—the ignorant immoralities of religion have lost the power they once fearfully held; and these immoralities, although they have survived in spirit and theory in the holy of holies of the tabernacle, have been abated in practice. Religion, for all its babble of morality, has appeared in history as an immoral force that has been compelled, from age to age, to accommodate itself to the progressive morality of the race: a morality growing up outside of the church and perforce asserting itself generally in opposition to the church and to religion.

What article of morality, social or individual, can we hail as the blessed gift of the church? What has religion given to man in the way or morality? Nothing—not a Presbyterian jot nor a Baptist tittle. We owe to the thinkers and scientists, to the artists and inventors and builders—and to the operation of social forces as nonreligious, as undiscriminating between preacher and publican, as the forces of nature—the moral and material gifts that are ours today. Our age, for its more obvious great advantages, is chiefly indebted to science. I am not thinking simply of the mechanics of our civilization—of better communication, transportation, sanitation, illumination—though surely in this more efficiently ordered world there is the stuff of morality growing out of material things. We are safer, cleaner, more productive—in short, we are, in external habit at least, more civilized—and we cannot thank the church for our situation. We have to thank, not religion, but science—science, which religion assailed furiously as the foe of righteousness, before which religion has reluctantly retreated, and which, emboldened to a last desperate stand, religion is fighting today under the leadership of the braying Bryans of prairie pews. We have no longer the institution of serfdom or of chattel slavery—pleasant little hells on earth that were blessed by the church: we have the wage-system, not as the gift of the Mother of God (or the Father or the Son or the Holy Ghost), but as the gift of necessity, the mother of invention. We no longer witness the spectacle of witch-hanging, nor see demons in human form, because science has taught us that insanity is pathological rather than theological. It is no longer a crime to think—not a crime in the eyes of the law, nor a crime that bigots, however wild-eyed in godliness, are free to punish. Shall we thank the church? No: we must thank the skeptics.

There are other ways in which we see that morality has been a process of destroying old religious ideas. Consider, for example—in this day of feminism triumphant or at least within sight of its goal—the teaching of religion, of Christianity, regarding woman and sex. When men speak of morality, they are apt to think of sex—as if sex were the only phase of life that held moral implications. And in this very particular and delicate moral sphere, what is the record of religion, that holy mother of morality? Woman was regarded by the church as the slave of man—the slave of his domestic and social economy, the slave of his desires. Under the beneficent, bright, moral light of religion, it was seriously debated whether woman had a soul. Woman was the temptress in the eye of God, as the divine orb was cocked in those days. The very function of sex was regarded as unclean, shameful, a thing to be hidden. Talk of sex, thought of sex, knowledge of sex in any guise and purpose, was taboo by the most smirking, itching, pious Christian morality. This Christian doctrine, this stupid, dirty ethic of religion, obscured for ages any just and proper consideration of the rights of woman and the civilized, intelligent function of sex. The sexual life of man, under this rule of Christian immorality, was not free nor candid nor sensible. Christianity, on this subject of sex, was a "cistern for foul toads to knot and gender in." Today sex has lost its holy, ignorant shame. It has come out of the darkness. It is trying to assume its wholesome, natural, joyous place in the life of man. Women are coming to be free—companions of man in moral freedom and equality, not creatures of man in immoral, religious bonds. We are learning the truths, the laws, of sex that we may live more intelligently: that there may be less disease, less misery, less terror, less of the atmosphere of Christian unctuousness and uncleanness in this vital relationship of man and woman. And with no thanks, by your leave, no religion. Here, as elsewhere, religion has simply been driven from post to post of retreating orthodoxy by the evolution of society, the light of science and the growth of the nonreligious moral sense of mankind.

When we hale religion before the bar of immorality, we find that it has sinned in so many ways that it were vain to ploddingly enumerate them. We are startled, then repelled, and at last bored by the appalling, endless record of Christian immorality. However, let us turn a casual eye upon another outstanding example of religion on canting mischief bent. It is due to religion that we have had ever with us, and have with us not less blatantly and irritatingly today, the most immoral of tendencies: the pseudo-moral desire to reform the morals, compel the beliefs and dictate the habits of other men. The Christians (and on this score we cannot wholly exculpate one Jesus of Nazareth, who came preaching from the provinces) saddled upon mankind the evils of proselytizing. They started—introduced to our Western World at least—that evangelical rage which has swept amazingly down the ages; which has grown until it has assumed a multitude of forms and spread like a subtle poison into all man's intellectual activities; which has split our ears, robbed us of sleep, interrupted our mediations, pricked our unoffending skins, singled us out, each and every one in his turn and in his mind, as a fair mark for any meddling fanatic with a dyspeptic, bilious call to preach and convert and save.

We wish to be let alone. We wish to think. We wish to seek out, to work out, our own little plan of salvation—or, as one of the brethren blithely puts it, we wish to go to hell in our own way. We wish to retreat into our libraries, into our workshops, into the quiet and freedom and peace of our own personalities—and there seek God or the Devil, or philosophy or fun, the positive joy of exaltation or a merely negative relief from the boredom of God's mad, grievous, stupid world. Alas! it is little of this private, unbothered, freely hell-bent joy that we can snatch away from the smoke and din of this and that "ism," "ology," and sacred, saving plan of thought. The soul-savers are constantly on our trail: if they are not actually tracking us to our selfish, bookish, meditative lairs, still their cries are all about us and it is the God of battles (of spiritual battles no less terrible than that physical warfare that God blesseth through the lips of patriotic ecclesiastics) rather than the God of peace who rules in our world of holy, helpful-handed babble. Preachers, preachers everywhere, and not a moment nor a quiet spot in which to think. Preachers of humbug (instead of statesmen) in politics: preachers of freakishness and salvation and impertinent moral purpose (instead of artists) in art: preachers of fantastic systems and super-religious (instead of real thinkers) in philosophy: preachers of faith, folly and fantasy, of cure-alls and cosmic trifles, of uplifting and go-getting: Fundamentalists preaching the religion of gestation and Modernists preaching the religion of gesture.

Preach! cried Jesus. Go everywhere and shout into the ears of every damned sinner the glad tidings of salvation. Let no man escape. Tell the heathen that Jesus died. Make it hot for the skeptics. Shout the holy word until the heavens crack and the stars fall affrighted into the jarred depths of space. Lift the gigantic megaphone of missionary purpose, and rock the very walls of Time's corridors with the bawlings of holiness, fill the shrinking ages with apostolic noise until history jabbers and staggers like a drunken thing; split with the mournful, bloody-eyed wail of war-dancing piety the eardrums of all the generations, born and unborn, of the great Sun. So spake Jesus, or words to this general, excruciating effect. And religion through the ages has tried impertinently and violently to save men—often by the method of massacre.

And from religion this proselytizing fever has spread to all the other interests and pursuits of life. So that the preachers of this, that and the other are as the sands of the seashore, and their combined babel is as irritating and distracting as a sandstorm. And we are not simply preached at—blasted with an unearthly, pious noise. We are subjected to actual interference—and faced with threats of greater interference. Puritans spy upon our books and pictures. Bigots plot to get control of our schools. The Christians itch to lay their hands upon our very personal habits—as they have already told us what we shall drink. Societies "pro" and "anti" swarm in the social atmosphere like fleas, each with its neat little pestiferous program of how we should live and think, swear or pray. The intolerance of the preacher and the censor and the moral reformer—this shall rank, with the historian of these hectic-holy ages, as one of the greatest immoralities of religion. It is a big noise. It is a bore. It is a pest, Horatio.

Morality Without God

Mangasar M. Mangasarian

M. M. Mangasarian (1859-1943), as he was invariably known, was born in Turkish Armenia. He came to the United States to attend Princeton Theological Seminary, from which he graduated in 1882. After a period as an independent minister, he seems to have become much more liberal in his theology, and to have taken a position as a lecturer at the Ethical Culture Society in Chicago, where he served from 1892 to 1897, after which he founded the Independent Religious Society of Chicago. Mangasarian remained as "pastor" of this rationalist group from 1900 to 1925. He then became pastor emeritus and lived in retirement in Los Angeles until his death in 1943. He was the author of fifteen books, some of which were collections of his lectures. The story of Mangasarian's mental travels from orthodoxy to rationalism is told in his psychological autobiography, *The Story of My Mind,* published in 1910.

The present selection was first published in two issues of a magazine called *The Rationalist,* which Mangasarian edited in Chicago, on July 15 and 30, 1913. To my knowledge it has never appeared in print elsewhere.

The question, Can there be any morality without a belief in God? is a fundamental one, and the fact that we are willing to study it proves that we take a real interest in radical problems. To this question the first answer is that given by philosophy, and the second is that of history. We will confine ourselves to the theoretical or philosophical aspect of the question.

What is there in the belief in a God which should be deemed indispensable to the moral life? Why should the moral life be inseparably associated with a belief in God? The theological position, in which you and I were brought up, is that morality is impossible without a belief in God. As opposed to this is the scientific position that morality is independent of the supernatural. The scientist does not deny dogmatically the existence of one or many gods; he is far from denying even that there is at the heart of the universe a mystery,—an insoluble problem, at least a problem that hitherto has refused to reveal its secret to the human mind,—but he contends that to associate the moral life with this mystery, this insoluble problem, is to envelop it in darkness and uncertainty, which would hurt more than it would help the cause of morality.

"No God, no morals," says the theologian. He even desires earnestly that all unbelievers in his creed may be immoral. He is really grieved and disappointed when he finds goodness among unbelievers. He knows that people cannot get along without morality, and hence the only way he can give *his* creed a prestige is to make it indispensable to morality. If he can get everybody to think that they cannot have morality without his creed, the future of his creed would be secure. To establish this intimate relation between the supernatural and morality, the clergy either deny that goodness without their creed is goodness at all, or they try to show that the credit of it really belongs to the religion they preach. "Decent" unbelievers, if there are any, are really believers without knowing it, argues the theologian. Accordingly, if the Japanese, for example, are patriotic and honest, it is due to Christian missions; if they are not, it is the fault of Shintoism, the ancient religion of Japan. If Darwin and Huxley were splendid men, it was because they lived in a Christian atmosphere; if they were bad men, it was because they were not Christians. In short, directly or indirectly, the theologian claims all the credit for whatever goodness there is in the world. We shall not stop to inquire, for the present, how so parsimonious a spirit can be reconciled with morality; but it is evident that in associating belief with morality the preacher is trying to save *the belief,* and not morality. When the Czar of Russia says to his subjects: "You cannot have either order or peace in Russia without the autocracy," he is trying to save his throne by associating it with the essentials of civilized government. The people must have order and peace. "I am the only man who can guarantee you these blessings," says the autocrat. Of course, his main object is to render autocracy indispensable to the people. It is much like the Republican party going before the country and saying, "You cannot have prosperity in America unless you keep us in power," or like the Democratic party claiming that it alone can save the country. In the same way the theologian says, "You cannot have morality unless you have my creed." He is playing politics, just as much as the Czar of Russia, or the Tammany "boss" in New York, and, like his fellow-politicians, he would see the country ruined if that would advance his party or church.

We wish to test the position of the theologian which makes morality impossible without *his* creed. If he is a Turk, then it is the Moslem creed; if he is a Jew, then it is Judaism; if he is a Christian priest, then it is Christianity which is absolutely indispensable to morality. And even as he couples his creed with reality, he joins unbelief in it with immorality. He insinuates that to doubt his doctrines is a crime, and as a Czar hurls the epithets of "rebel" and "traitor" against all who question his right divine to do as he pleases, the priest denounces the heretic as a monster of iniquity, to be burned alive here, if the laws permit it, but in the hereafter, whether the laws permit it or not. But to call a man who questions the existence of the clergyman's God a criminal does not make him so. When you have no way of meeting the argument of your opponent, and you attack his character, you only exhibit temper. To call a man whose questions you cannot answer names, such as "blasphemer," "monster," "devil," is, if I may have permission to say it, the policy of cowards. If you cannot answer him, why do you attack his character?

But the theologian knows what he is about. If he can get people to believe that whoever questions his creed is a scoundrel, he will succeed in associating inquiry with immorality, and by so doing he will be strengthening his contention that only believers in his creed can be reputable people. Furthermore, if he succeeds in defaming the character of the inquirer, people will avoid him,—it will not be respectable to be seen in his company, or to think as he does,—all of which will protect the church against the disturbing investigator.

But for the sake of argument be it conceded that every one who questions the existence of God is a villain,—would that relieve clergymen from the obligation to produce their evidence for his existence? The other day a mass meeting was held in one of our public schools to denounce reckless driving. One of the speakers, a clergyman, said that Darwinism and infidelity were responsible for criminal driving. This was the clergyman's way of refuting Darwinism. He thought that if he could prove that the evolutionists kill people he would be disproving Darwinism. But Darwinism is a scientific theory, and if it is true, even if it killed people, it would still be true. If Darwinism is false, on the other hand, all the painstaking and respect for human life on the part of Darwinian automobilists would not make it true. Darwinism does not stand or fall with the characters of riders in autombiles. But this clergyman had no other way of answering Darwinism, so he called it names. This is the argument of sheer desperation. It is not discussing a subject; it is trifling with it. To call the man who asks for the evidence about the trinity a "monster," instead of giving him the evidence, is a proof that the preacher finds it handier to abuse than to reason. He has epithets, but no arguments. That is all it proves.

The Christian religion in which we were educated teaches that to believe is a virtue, and not to believe is a crime. Is that sound? If I were to say to you, "You must believe that George Washington was the first President of America," would you deserve any credit for believing it? Is there any merit in subscribing to a proposition which cannot be reasonably doubted? But suppose I were to say, "You must also believe that George Washington invented the theory of evolution," could you be blamed for refusing to credit a statement for which there is no evidence? You believe in the first statement because it agrees with the facts. You reject the second because it contradicts the facts. In other words, you believe or question according to the evidence presented. Religions are just as much subject to evidence as anything else. To deny this is to ask for blind relief. Where there is no light there is no sight. Where there is no evidence there can be no faith. The preacher says, "God made the world in six days;" if he can prove it we have got to believe it. If he cannot prove it, we are not to be blamed for saying, "Not proven." The priest says Jesus was born of a virgin. We ask for the evidence. If religious doctrines should be accepted even in the absence of convincing evidence, then why is not Mohammedanism as true as Christianity? Why is not a bit of blue glass as good as a God? To believe intelligently one must have the evidence; to believe blindly, one religion is as good as another.

The existence of God, let it be the Christian, the Jewish, or more modern ones, has always been in dispute. A hundred books are written to prove his existence; a hundred others question his existence. A great thinker in the eighteenth century said, "That which is the subject of eternal dispute cannot be a foundation for anything." That eliminates disputed questions from the list of fundamentals. The scientist, therefore, in striving to separate morality from theology renders a great service to morality. He removes it from the sphere of uncertainty and controversy by making it independent of debatable doctrines.

But it is not only about the existence of the deity that there is uncertainty; the world is equally in the dark about his character. It is not enough to say there is a God,—we must also be sure of his parts. Yet that question is even more in dispute than his existence. If the mere belief in a God is enough, why will not an African black god answer the purpose? The Christian god has a son, and no man may approach him except through the son. The Mohammedan god has no son. They cannot both be the same god. The God of the Christian demands the atoning blood of his son before he will make terms with man. The Mohammedan god repudiates such an idea. How can they be the same being? What are we going to do about it? Is it safe to associate morality with a being whose character is undecided?

Even when we have decided that the Mohammedan god is no god at all, and agreed upon our own deity, are we sure that his character as represented to us in creed and Bible is calculated to encourage the moral life? That is an important point. What we know about the divine character is what the priests tell us about it; and what we ourselves infer from the nature of the acts attributed to him, and the stories told about him in religious literature. Now the character of God as painted for us in the Bible is not calculated, in my opinion, to encourage the moral life. The god of the Jewish and Christian scriptures is not at all a moral being. He does not set an example that can be, or should be, followed by man. To begin with, he violates his own commandments. I do not say this hastily or carelessly,—I have looked into the question. Take, for example, the commandment, "Thou shalt not kill." Jehovah breaks that commandment a hundred times, if the Bible is reliable. He has no respect for his own word. No sooner had Moses descended from Mt. Sinai, with the Ten Commandments, than God urged him to get the Jews to kill one another, and fifty thousand were slain in one fit of passion. The repeated commandment of God to the Jews to exterminate their neighbors,—to put men, women and children to the edge of the sword,—shows that he did not mean to live up to his profession. The same is true of the commandment, "Thou shalt not steal." No sooner has he given this commandment than he tells his people how they may spoil their neighbors, destroy their altars and temples, and seize their goods. He says again, "Thou shalt not commit adultery," and then he commands his soldiers to capture the daughters of the Gentiles and keep them forcibly for unlawful purposes.

He says, "Thou shalt not bear false witness," and on every page in the Old Testament everything base is said of the Egyptians, the Babylonians, the Assyrians, whose character modern research has vindicated, for it has been proved that their civilization was far in advance of that of their accusers.

And God says, "Thou shalt not covet"—and then he shows to the people the pleasant lands and homes of their neighbors to arouse their covetousness,—to satisfy which they wade through a sea of blood from Egypt to Canaan.

How can a being who does not live up to his profession,—who breaks his own commandments,—be our moral ideal? In their attempts to reconcile God's conduct with morality, the preachers resort to sophistry. They say, "God is not bound by the same moral laws that we are. He can take away life, land, or property from one man and give it to another. He is above the law. He is good even when he does that which if we did it would make us criminals," and so on. Thus, sophistry becomes a profession. We develop Jesuitical powers; we become intellectual gymnasts,—dancing on ropes and splitting hairs,—to prove that God can break all the moral commandments and still be immaculate.

It is a fact, moreover, that close identification with such a being has contributed to corrupt both the church and the state. Tyrants have claimed the right to violate the moral law whenever it interfered with their personal pleasures. As the anointed of God, kings have tried to answer all protests against their misdeeds by quoting the acts of God. Priests have persecuted and exterminated whole races, and have given the example of God who destroyed the heretics as their justification. The atmosphere created about us by the feeling that our moral teacher has himself done the very things he has forbidden, is an evil one.

But it may be answered that the Old Testament is no longer the authority it once was, and that the New Testament, or rather, the character of God as revealed in Christ, is our ideal. I have the highest reverence for the beautiful things Jesus is reported to have said, but the teachings of Jesus condensed in his commandment, "Resist not evil," is the very negation of morality. We had recently the yellow fever in New Orleans. What did we do? We resisted it with all our might. It is the only way physical evil can be destroyed. There was a time when if the cholera came to a city it was said that God had sent it, and it was useless to fight it. Today we do not care who sent it, we do not want it, and we resist it. Consider the disclosures of dishonest banking houses and insurance companies. What do we do? We drag the guilty into the light; we examine, we investigate, we expose, we punish. We do not say to these people, you have taken so much of our money, take also what there is left of it. We resist evil. In politics, in commerce, in every department of life, we find that in resistance alone is our salvation; and yet Jesus, the Oriental monk, believing the end of the world to be close at hand, undertakes to tie our hands, paralyze our will, and give to evil, physical or moral, a free field. If we did not resist evil we would soon be so incapacitated for effort, so emptied of energy and ambition, that we would become the victims, not only of every physical pest, but also of every moral iniquity. "Resist not" is just what a priest would say to his people, or a king to his subjects. But "Resist" is what the liberator would say to his fellowmen.

But are there not examples of the highest morality in the Christian world? Yes, surely, and I am glad to admit it, but it is in spite of the Christian creed. That such an enervating doctrine has not destroyed goodness shows that theology is listened to only one day in the week; the other six days we listen to common sense. We are better than our beliefs, better than our creeds. The Asiatic theology which we call inspired has not succeeded in perverting Anglo-Saxon human nature. That is what it proves.

What importance did Jesus attach to the moral life? Let us see. You know that when he was on the cross there were two thieves crucified with him. One of them reviled him; the other said to him, "Lord, when thou comest into thy kingdom remember me," and Jesus said, "This day shalt thou be with me in Paradise." Indeed! What had this man done to deserve such a sudden apotheosis? It gives me pain to say, but say it I must, that a greater slight upon morality could not have been placed. Think of saying to a malefactor whom the laws of society were justly punishing,—that his life of guilt and crime, the thefts and perhaps also the murders which he had committed,—were all *forgiven* him! Is the moral life as easy as that? Is it possible that by simply calling Jesus "Lord," and by accepting him as the Son of God, a malefactor can enter heaven, while the man whose life has been above reproach must go to perdition for lacking the faith of the malefactor? Why then be moral at all? All people need to do is to use deferential language to Jesus,—call him "Lord," believe in him,—and all the wickedness they may be guilty of shall not prevent them from entering heaven. If in one moment, and by a mere profession, a thief and a murderer can step ahead of the righteous and the honest, then the Christian religion is correct; righteousness is but "filthy rags." But is such a religion, which welcomes the malefactor into heaven and sends his victims to everlasting destruction, calculated to command the respect of the fair-minded? Charles Spurgeon must have had the example of the Christian thief in mind when he said to his hearers, in the London Tabernacle, "Thirty years of sin will take less than thirty minutes to wipe out in." To him repentance at the last moment was better than a whole life of "godless" morality.

But let us get a little closer to our subject: When the preachers state that morality is impossible without God, they really mean—without the Christian religion. As we intimated above, the Mohammedan God and the Christian God, not being the same, cannot both be true. But it is not enough even to believe in the Christian God; one must also believe in Christ, the Holy Ghost, the atonement, and so on. Hence, the Christian religion is the only power that can save the world, according to the preachers. Let us follow this thought and see where it will lead us. If you have imagination try to bring the whole world before your mind's eye. Think of the millions upon millions of human beings dwelling upon its surface—of the hundreds of millions of Buddhists, Moslems, Brahmans; and to these add the millions who follow Confucius, or profess Shintoism, Judaism, Jainism; and the millions who once followed Zoroaster, Zeus, Apollo, Mithra and Isis. Compare with this tremendous host the number of people who during the last two thousand years have called themselves Christians, and tell me if it would be inspiring to think that the Christians, who are but a handful compared with this innumerable majority, are the only people who can be moral? But if the heathen, so-called by Christians, can be as moral as ourselves, then Christianity is not indispensable; but if it is the only power that can make people good, think of the gloom and despair which must be the portion of every sensitive soul who realizes the hopelessness of the situation! For thousands of years our humanity was denied the Christian religion, and even now, twenty centuries after the birth of Jesus, only a handful, compared with the earth's population have accepted the only true religion, and it is only this handful that can be moral. Could anything be more depressing? . . .

But let us follow the lead of the preacher a little farther. He says there can be no morality without the Christian religion. But *which* Christian religion does he mean? The Catholics denounce Protestantism as a perversion; the Protestants call Catholicism an imposture. Which, then, is the Christian religion, without which there can be no morality? If one sect is as Christian as another, why then do they try to convert each other? Why do the Catholics send missionaries to the Protestants, and the Protestants to the Catholics? The Protestants mean by Christianity *their* creed, and only theirs. If this is true, then there is no morality without the Protestant faith. Now see to what a small faith, and to what a pale and sickly hope the preacher has brought us. Ah! he has led us into an alley! The world is no longer in sight; the sun and stars have disappeared, and the great winds that fan the earth and sky are heard no more.

Now this Protestant religion, which is the only power that can make men good, what is it? A moment ago we asked, Which is the Christian religion? We now ask, Which is the Protestant religion? Is it the Church of England? Is it Lutheranism? Is it Methodism? Is it Presbyterianism? Is it Unitarianism? Is it the Baptist Church? Is it Christian Science? We believe we have mentioned enough to select from. It will not do to say that all these sects are equally Christian. Why, then, are they separated? Why do not the Baptists commune at the Lord's table with the Presbyterians, and why do the Episcopalians claim that they alone have apostolic ordination? A Methodist preacher is not allowed to speak from an Episcopal altar— his ordination is not considered valid, and his church is only a sect in the eyes of the Church of England. Which of these, then, is the true Protestant religion, without which no morality is possible in this world, or salvation in the next? The proposition that there can be no morality without God, when analyzed, comes to this: There can be no morality without the Protestant religion, and it is as yet uncertain which is the Protestant religion. How educated people can find cheer and comfort in an alley, and mistake its darkness for a horizon, or how they can be happy in the belief that no one can be good or brave without believing as they do,—is beyond my comprehension. And when we remember that this Protestant religion did not exist before the sixteenth century—that it is only about three hundred years old, and that, if it is the only true religion, it waited a long time— until mankind had reached middle life—until the world had begun to turn gray—before it commenced to minister to its needs—we begin to realize that there is no thoroughfare to the alley to which the preacher has conducted us. It is a *blind* alley!

Let us hasten out of this darkness! Let us return to the kisses of the sun, and the wind, and the air, and the light! To think that the whole world, past and present, has been, is, and will be irrevocably lost, unless it accepts our three-hundred-year-old, and much-divided, religion! What gentle and refined mind can stand the strain? Who can walk straight under the weight of such crushing pessimism? Is it not fortunate that only one day in seven is devoted to church-going?

When I was a Presbyterian minister, one of the hymns we used to sing in church began with the words, "From Greenland's Icy Mountains," and went on to speak of "India's Coral Strands," and "Africa's Sunny Fountains," ending with this sentiment:

> Where every prospect pleases
> And only man is vile.

Think of the essentially unmoral mind of the man who could write such a hymn, and of the callousness of the people who can sing it! Think of putting so false, so uncharitable, so conceited, so mean and small a thought into music, and then singing it! If they wept over it, if they mourned over it, it would be less incongruous, but to sit in their pews, and with the help of organ and piano, to *sing* about the vileness of the earth's greater population seems to me, in my haste, to lend considerable support to the doctrine of total depravity. The Christian will trade with the "heathen," he will travel into his country, he will trust him in business, but, on Sunday, when he is in church, when he is kneeling at the altar, in the house of his God, he calls him "vile." If the only way we can appreciate our own morality is by defaming the majority of humanity, how immoral must our morality be? Let me ask a question: When we sing that the Hindus, the Chinese, the Japanese and the rest of the non-Christian world are "vile,"—that is to say, that there is no love, no devotion, no patriotism, no honesty, no friendship, no temperance, no philanthropy, no chastity, no truthfulness, no mercy, no honor in heathen lands—I say, when we deny that in any part of the world there can be any morality which our own creed has not created,—do we realy believe it? To preach the brotherhood of man in one breath, and in the next to call those who do not believe in our creed "vile,"—what is that?

A clergyman of Chicago, one of our leading, popular and successful preachers—one who has had phenomenal success as a minister of the Gospel, and who addresses the largest Christian audiences in the country—speaking to the Young Men's Christian Association, declared that "This earth would have been a hell if Christ had not died on Golgotha." There must be something of the nature of a blight in a creed that can force from the lips of an educated and benevolent man such unlovely words! And *there is*. It is so self-centered, so intolerant, so exclusive, that in its eyes the whole world, except its own little corner, is nothing but "a hell." To intimate that the world which gave us our republic; the world which gave us our constitution and independence; the world which has crowded our galleries with works of imperishable beauty, and our libraries with immortal poetry, literature and philosophy; the world which gave to our universities their culture,—and which created Socrates, Plato, Aristotle, Pericles, Seneca, Cicero and the Antoines,—the world whose ruins are more wonderful than anything we possess, and whose dead are more immortal than our living—to suggest, I say, that this pre-Christian world was "a hell" takes my breath away! I never imagined that this fearful Asiatic creed could smite or sting an otherwise wholesome soul into such a contortion. What is there in this Palestinian Hebrew whom our famous preacher worships as his god, that can tempt a man to bear false witness? How can a man with the example of Greece and Rome before him think of this earth as a hell without his "shibboleth"? Victor Hugo says, "It is a terrible thing to have been a priest once"; it is not less terrible to be an orthodox Protestant preacher today. And why? Because for the preacher there is something higher than the truth—his creed.

The proposition that there can be no morality without God, and that the earth would be a hell without Christ, in its final analysis means this: People will not be moral without the belief in a future life. It is the hope of future rewards which gives to the God idea its value. St. Paul himself admitted that if the Christians believed in Christ for this life only "they were of all men the most miserable." Were the clergy to tell their flocks this morning that, although they felt sure of the existence of God, they had their doubts about another life, how many of them would return to worship on the following Sunday? Yes, it is the mingled hope and fear of the future which gives the belief in its God its importance. If there were no death—if men could live here forever, they would not much concern themselves about spirits and invisible beings. It is the idea that when we die we fall into the hands of God, the idea that it is a terrible thing, as the Bible says, to fall into the hands of the living God—it is this idea which lights the altars, bends the knee, and builds churches. To placate the deity that he may reward us in the future is, frankly, the object of all religious ceremonies. If this be true, then the proposition that without God there can be no morality amounts to this: Without future rewards and punishments no man will live a moral life.

This doctrine leads to the following conclusions: First, man is naturally immoral, and the only way he can be arrested in his career of vice and crime is to promise him future rewards if he will behave himself, and to menace him with hell-fire if he will not. Secondly, the proposition implies that morality *per se* is not desirable, that no one could be virtuous enough to desire virtue for its own sake, and that without great and eternal rewards morality would go a-begging. And this is religion! What then is irreligion?

Why do people desire health? Certainly not for any post-mortem rewards. The health of the body is cultivated for its own beautiful sake. Health is joy, it is power, it is beauty, it is strength! Are not these enough to make health sacred? But if the health of the body does not need the prop of future rewards to commend itself to us, what good reason have we to think that morality, which is the health of the mind, is a wretched investment if there be no other life? Morality is temperance. How can our ideas about the unseen world so change the worth of temperance as to make it a stupid and irksome restraint? If it is good to be temperate in the pursuit of pleasure or of wealth, or in the gratification of desire, why should our speculations about the hereafter alter our attitude toward the value of temperance and self-control in everything? God or no God, a future life or no future life, is not temperance better than intemperance? To ask, Why should a man practice temperance, even if it be preferable to intemperance? is to insinuate that man is by nature either a fool or a monster, and that he will not behave well unless he is promised enormous returns in the shape of eternal rewards, or scared to death by eternal torments. Well, if the preachers are right, it is a serious question whether so depraved a creature as man deserves to be saved at all. To have created so contemptible a creature was a great enough blunder, but think of perpetuating his race forever and ever!

But let us see how much truth there is in the preacher's estimate of human nature. Take the example of a father who is devoted to his little motherless girl. Will he be less fatherly without the belief in future rewards? "But to love and care for one's child is only natural morality," replies the clergyman. Of course, it is. And that is why it is genuine and untainted with expectations of a reward. It never enters into his mind that he is going to be paid big wages for loving his own child. It is artificial morality that pines for rewards and sickens and dies when the expected recompense is questioned. If there are no future rewards, will people continue to abstain from meats on Friday, or sprinkle their children, or read the Bible, or listen to sermons? The natural virtues, on the other hand, will spring up like flowers in the human soil, heaven or no heaven, and men and women will love, will sacrifice, will perform heroic deeds, whatever may be their theories concerning the hereafter.

Let us take another case. Why is an employer of labor good to his men? Is it because he expects to be rewarded for it in the next life? Analyze his motives and you will find that if he treats his men well it is because he believes that to be the best way to get along with them, to earn their good will, to keep his own self-respect, and to merit the approval of the community in which he lives. He is not going to change his conduct toward his employees, nor will the motives which now influence his conduct lose their force immediately after he finds out that there is nothing coming to him in the next world for being good and just to his workmen.

The theologians appear to labor under the impression that morality being irksome and undesirable, it would be an injustice not to reward the people who put up with it with a paradise of some kind. They think that the man who does not rob his neighbor, beat his wife and children, or get drunk, ought to be rewarded. Certainly he ought—if it is for a future reward that he does not do these things. If we have any influence at all with the powers that be, we shall see that these people who have denied themselves the pleasure of cutting their neighbors' throats, or of leading an intemperate, dishonest and brutal life, shall receive their reward in the future.

There is no doubt that some people are kept from doing wrong by the fear of a distant hell; and others are provoked to good works by the hope of a heavenly crown. But the mistake of the theologian consists in thinking that anybody actuated by such motives can be moral. A vicious dog is not made gentle by chaining him—he is only prevented from doing harm. It is true that to prevent a savage beast from hurting people is also a service to humanity. It is also true that if by preaching the fear of hell the churches succeed in preventing vicious men from doing harm, they are benefactors. Fear, while not the highest motive, is nevertheless quite effective with some people. Of course, as far as my own preference goes, I would not preach the doctrine of everlasting hell even if I could be assured it was the only thing that could save mankind. I would not care to save mankind under those conditions. There is nothing more immoral than the idea of unending torture. The worst criminals are not half so immoral as the creators and perpetrators of the unquestionable hell of Christian theology. I cannot think of a greater insult to the human conscience than to say that this fearful establishment with its everlasting stench in our nostrils is the parent of all virtue, and that if its fires were to be extinguished there would be an end to goodness. It is equivalent to saying that the only way to prevent this world from becoming a hell is to have a hell in the next. Well, that is the gospel of despair.

"It is quite easy," I imagine the preacher saying, "to talk in this strain now, but wait until you are on your death-bed." But the frightful death-bed scenes we read of in religious literature are generally fictitious. The dying thoughts of a sane and brave man or woman are as free from fear as the sleep which closes the tired eyelids. What does a mother think of in her last moments? She thinks of her dear ones—her children, whom she has to leave motherless in the world! How noble is human nature! And it is this nobility which makes theology jealous. The dying mother should be thinking of her God, of her own soul, with fear and trembling, instead of thinking of her little ones! So thinks theology. And when theology cannot get horrible death-bed scenes it invents them. In *Theron Ware,* the deacons of the Methodist Church say to their minister, "Give us more of the death-bed scenes of Voltaire and Thomas Paine." For a long time it was a part of the vocation of the theologians to postpone the attack upon an intellectual giant until he was dead or dying; and then, with sensational details, the pulpit dwelt upon the supposed agonies and torments of the infidel death-bed. And yet the last cry of Jesus on the cross, "My God, my God, why hast thou forsaken me?" was a cry of unbelief and despair. Neither Socrates with the hemlock, nor Bruno in the flames uttered such a cry. The preachers invent gruesome tales about the unorthodox because the thing is popular, and they wait until the heretic is dead, because the dead cannot defend themselves.

But it is not true that when people come to die they confess that the preacher's hell and heaven are real, after all. The other day a negro shot his wife and babe fatally and then ran away. When the neighbors arrived upon the scene of the tragedy they found the dying mother with her arms around her infant trying to soothe its pains. She had torn a fragment of her bodice to stop with it the bleeding wound in the child's arm. Motherhood! Was she worrying about her own soul—about eternity, about God, about the devil, about heaven, about hell! Oh, no! She had one thought, which puts all preaching to shame—to ease the pain of her dying child. She forgot she was dying herself. She forgot all about her future reward. But she did not forget her child. That is the way mothers die. No believer can die a better death. And when preachers can tell us of a God who can love like this negro mother did, or who, in the words of the English poet, Wordsworth, will

> Never blend his pleasure or his pride
> With sorrow of the meanest thing that feels,

then we shall worship him—not for his heaven, nor from fear of his hell, but for his own sweet self.

Others may be able to tell whether or not there is another life. I cannot. But whether or not there be a life beyond the grave, I know that spring will come every year, that the gentle rains will fall, the sunlight will woo and kiss all it meets, the harvests will wave, and the world will sleep and wake each day. In the same way, I know that whatever the preachers may say about a godless morality, the charities, and the humanities will spring up eternal in our daily lives, and beauty and liberty shall never perish from our earth.

What then is morality? We have confined this discussion to the supernaturalist's answer to that question. Theology makes morality impossible. If God does as he pleases, if he is not under obligation to respect any laws, he cannot be moral himself, neither can he make his creatures moral. Where is the evidence that God wishes man to be better than he is himself? But if man were to imitate God by pleasing himself and seeking his own glory, he would justly expose himself to the charge of immorality. Again, if God is perfect, why are his works, his acts, his world, so full of injustice and suffering? Faith in an unintelligible being, instead of clarifying our thoughts and rationalizing our lives, makes everything a puzzle.

Four hundred years before the Bard of Avon, a Persian poet, the inimitable Omar Khayyam, stung sharply by the problem of evil in a world professedly cradled under the eye of a Heavenly Father, and feeling as keenly as Wordsworth "the weary weight of all this unintelligible world," lifted his musical voice to its full compass and demanded of the dark powers whom men call gods permission to "grasp this sorry state of things entire," that he may "shatter it to bits" and then "remold it nearer the heart's desire." Every thinker and reformer is engaged in making the world anew, which is a criticism of the world as it now is. If God created the world perfect, he could not keep it so; hence the aching effort of man to escape the consequences of this divine failure. To shift the entire responsibility for evil upon man is to vote the deity out of the universe; for if puny man, with his limitations, could defeat the decrees of omnipotence, what is omnipotence good for? Upon what or whom does the deity try his omnipotence? But if man is the chief factor in the government of the world, what economy is there in supporting so picturesque a figurehead as an omnipotent lord? If man is nothing, and God is everything, then the seams and the cracks in the world are *his* doings and not man's. Is the world today as God made it, or has man spoiled it? If it is as God made it, then man has not succeeded in spoiling it; but if man has spoiled it, then omnipotence is a failure, and all our prayers should be addressed to man, for if he has more power than God, he is the one to look up to for help. "Thy will be done in earth as it is done in heaven," prayed. Jesus. Naive soul! If God can impose his will in heaven—in the infinities of the universe—is it only on this atom of dust which we call the earth that he cannot have his way? Supernaturalism snaps under the strain of experience and reason. A blind faith may live forever; but the moment it opens its eyes it dies.

Steady relations with a being "whose ways are past finding out," and who with all his powers, is helpless against his own creatures, is not calculated to make one either reasonable or moral. The virtues which, for example, the great Pagans cultivated are impossible to believers in the supernatural. I am very anxious that you should not misunderstand what I am about to say. There have been Christians, Jewish and Moslem believers, who have been as brave and as sincere as any Pagan we might mention. But—and this is the important point—I am almost afraid to say it, becuase you may not understand me: Greatness of mind and greatness of heart in a Socrates or a Seneca is reasonable; but a Christian or a Moslem who tries to be progressive, tolerant, universal in his sympathies, and who lays more stress upon the deed than the creed, is a contradiction. I repeat that it is impossible to believe in the supernatural and be reasonable or moral at the same time, because there can be no common ground between the supernatural and human life. If the church-goer is honest and reasonable, he is so despite his creed. In books written by cardinals or Protestant theologians, there will be found many sensible things, for example, but for a cardinal or a Protestant to say sensible things is like cutting away the branch from under his feet. A supernaturalist cannot afford to be sensible. Suppose he were to recommend religious tolerance, and earnestly urge its practice. That would be sensible, but if there has been a revelation from God, and it alone is the truth and all other religions are false, how, then, can a believer in revelation recommend tolerance? Would he have us be tolerant to falsehood? Can he afford to disagree with the Holy Ghost? Neither a Catholic nor a Protestant believer in a special revelation can take the sensible view about religious tolerance without self-stultification. If he is tolerant he is not a Christian.

In the same way it would be very sensible of a priest or a preacher to recommend character, and to exalt it as the priceless jewel of life. But how can he do that without discrediting the most fundamental teaching of his church, namely, that the righteousness of man is as "filthy rags," and that God saves whom he will—not according to desert or merit, but according to his grace or pleasure. What, then, is character worth to any man? "He that *believeth* shall be saved." How can a man with that dogma to uphold say anything sensible about character without contradicting himself? Suppose, again, the priest or preacher were to laud freedom and the right of private judgment. That would certainly be a very sensible thing to do. But how can a supernaturalist afford to sing the praises of freedom of thought? If private judgment is right, then the church is wrong when it punishes the heretic, or when it compels people to swear that they will preach only Jesus Christ and him crucified. If freedom of thought is right, why is there an infallible revelation? If we must obey the church, or the Pope, or be lost forever, is it not perfectly foolish to recommend freedom of thought? The supernaturalist, then, cannot be clear and consistent, that is to say, rational, either in a thought or deed without stultifying himself. You understand now what I mean when I say that supernaturalism makes morality unintelligible. . . .

Morality, according to the French Rationalist, M. Guyau, is heroism—the ability to say, *I can*. Morality is plenitude of life. Will a fountain flow unless it can overflow? Morality is the overflowing of the life that is in us. Theology makes goodness synonymous with weakness. The lower a man's vitality, the deader his desires, the more emaciated his body, the holier he was supposed to be. Hence, fasting, retirement from the world, and ashes and sack cloth were recommended. This was also the Buddhist theory, which made of morality a plant to be cultivated only in the wilderness. Both Buddhism and Christianity are Asiatic. They represent the indolence of man. How bracing is the European challenge—*I can!* Why does the lamp light up my room? It can. It is filled with oil. Why should a man be brave, fearless, free? Because he can! Why should he sacrifice comfort, position, reputation, life itself—for a cause? Because he can! Why should he go to the fire rather than subscribe to a lie? Because he can. The story of all the heroes and martyrs who pined away in dungeons or expired at the stake becomes clear at once. Morality is heroism, and the hero is the man *who can!*

Andrew Carnegie offers to devote five million dollars to the cultivation of heroism in the race. By the provisions attached to his gift it is plain that he has in mind physical bravery. Of course, all heroism, even when of the body, is not without a touch of moral and mental grandeur. To jump into the whirling sea to save a life, or to dare the roaring flames to reach the cradle of a child, requires not only nerve, but also soul. We would be glad to have Mr. Carnegie's definition of a hero, but this is ours—The hero is he who *can*. This is also the definition of morality. There is a big difference between people who can and people who *can't*. It is not always easy to drop that little "t," but the hero can. Yet, this alone, would not make one a hero. There is not a man or a woman who can do something; but more than that is required to be a hero. Shall we say: He who can do the *difficult is the hero?* It is easy to glide down the stream, but to sail against the current requires persistence, patience and courage, in one word—effort. To attempt the difficult, then, is one of the necessary elements of heroism. But not even now have we the true definition of a hero. We have all known of men who have attempted the difficult without deserving to be called heroes. Neither the acrobat who balances himself on a tight rope, nor the athlete who performs wonderful feats, could be classified with the heroic men and women whose memory we love to keep green. Is, then, the hero the man who attempts the difficult at the *risk of his life?* Life is the greatest thing in the world. Life is the greatest word in human language; it is the greatest gift we can receive or give. If we lose our money, we may hope to make it up again; if we lose our reputation, our good name, which is more than gems or gold, even this we may live to recover; but if we give our life away, it is given for all time, it can never be recalled. They, then, who, in attempting the difficult, give their lives, give all, for no one can give more. Have we now the true hero defined? I do not think so. Many years ago Dr. Tanner, a New York physician, fasted for forty days. Here was the case of a man attempting the difficult at the risk of his life; was he, then, a hero? The shopkeeper, in running through the flames to save his valuables, attempts the difficult at personal peril; but is his act heroic? From time to time eccentric men have tried to swim across the Niagara River. A man, not long ago, got into a barrel and was hurled from the sharp edge of the precipice into the seething depths below, losing his life in the attempt. He was certainly bold; but was he a *hero?* The hero, then, is the man who attempts the difficult at the sacrifice of his life, for a *noble purpose.* The nobler or larger the purpose for which one risks one's life, the more heroic is the deed. What gives value to the deed is the purity of the motive and the loftiness of the aim. We look *up* to the author of such a deed because he is more than we are; because he did what we could not, because he *is* what we all wish to be. There has not been a country or an age which has not had its heroes. But it is not enough to have had heroes once. The old heroes cannot do our work for us. We need heroes today, men and women, who, for their country and for humanity, will speak only the truth, and do only the right, whatever the cost.

I can, therefore I ought! Behold the moral gospel—sweet, inspiring, and crystal clear as noonday. We do not need a devil to scare us into virtue, nor a paradise to bribe us into the embrace of truth and beauty. Shall the eyes ask a reward for seeing? or the ears for hearing? Humanity has been compared to the passengers on board a great vessel, sailing on the ocean. Some terrific wave, mountain high, in the darkness has swept overboard our captain, or smashed the rudder, if we had one. We are now drifting. It is our pleasure and duty to give this wandering, pilotless, rudderless vessel a direction. It is a great task. Can we do it? Say no, and we are lost. Say yes, and with hope and courage shall swell every bosom. The waves will become charmed, and beautiful shores shall rise before us to cheer our spirits and ennoble our efforts.

Morality is ability. Whatever increases our powers, ennobles us. The freer, braver, and more devoted we are, the better men and women we shall become. "Conscience is born of love," wrote Shakespeare. In the alembic of this glorious truth all the terrors of the Jewish-Christian religion dissolve into nothingness. A word from Shakespeare, and the nightmares of the past are no more. Love!—behold the cradle in which conscience was born! Fear is the mouth of hell. Love is life, nursing into being and maturity all that is good, all hat is true, all that is beautiful. Says Tennyson:

> Perplext in faith, but pure in deeds,
>   At last he beat his music out.
>   There lives more faith in honest doubt,
> Believe me, than in half the creeds.

This *is* music, and it descends over the babel of wrangling creeds, as the sunlight, after a long storm, streams over the spent and weary waves.

Women

Hypatia Bradlaugh Bonner

Hypatia Bradlaugh Bonner (1858-1934) was the younger daughter of the famed British atheist and politician Charles Bradlaugh. Born near London, her role, and that of her elder sister, Alice, was always to be supportive and helpful to her extremely busy and overworked father, for whom she served as secretary. She was quick to defend his memory after he died, and often came to his defense against the tired charge (hurled falsely at every atheist of note since 1700) that he had taken out his watch in front of an audience and given God five minutes to strike him dead if God existed. Bradlaugh always sued when this was claimed, and always won, giving the money to charity.

Alice Bradlaugh died in her early twenties, and Hypatia became the main support to her father. After his death, she wrote the first important biography of him, *Charles Bradlaugh: A Record of His Life and Work,* (with J. M. Robertson writing the section on Bradlaugh's political career). In 1885 Hypatia married Arthur Bonner, a printer and publisher, and together they republished collected editions of Charles Bradlaugh's works, along with a number of other important freethought books under the imprint "A. & H. B. Bonner" of London. She also edited a magazine called *The Reformer* for a number of years, with J. M. Robertson.

Hypatia Bradlaugh Bonner was the author of three books in addition to the biography of her father: *Christianizing the Heathen, The Gallows and the Lash* and *Christianity and Conduct.* She organized the celebration of the centenary of Bradlaugh's birth in 1933. She died the following year.

The present selection is from her book *Christianity and Conduct,* first published in 1919. The book has been out of print since the 1920s.

> Behold, thy mother and thy brethren stand without desiring to speak with thee. But he answered . . . Who is my mother?
>
> *Matt.*, xii, 47.

> Woman, what have I to do with thee?
>
> Jesus to his Mother (*John, ii, 4*).

> Let women learn in silence with all subjection. But I suffer not a woman to teach, nor to usurp authority over the man, but to be in silence. For Adam was first formed, then Eve. And Adam was not deceived, but the woman being deceived was in the transgression. Notwithstanding she shall be saved in child-bearing, if they continue in faith and charity and holiness and sobriety.
>
> *First Epistle of Paul to Timothy,* ii, 11-15.

It is difficult to exaggerate the adverse influence of the precepts and practices of religion upon the status and happiness of woman. Owing to the fact that upon women devolves the burden of motherhood, with all its accompanying disabilities, they always have been, and always must be, at a natural disadvantage in the struggle of life as compared with men. Men have had two courses open to them; in regard to women: (1) to minimize the disadvantages so far as it lay in their power to do so; or (2) to take advantage of the natural disabilities in order to impose artificial ones, and by this means increase their own power and authority. The first course is the moral course, tending to the common good; the second is the immoral course, in which the selfish interests of one part of the community are made to triumph at the expense of the other part. It is the second course which usually has been followed. With certain rare exceptions, women all the world over have been relegated to a position of inferiority in the community, greater or less according to the religion and the social organization of the people; the more religious the people the lower the status of the women.

In ancient Egypt, two thousand years before the Christian era, women were in a position of closer equality with men, and had greater freedom and independence, than anywhere at any time since,[1] at any rate until quite recently. Egyptologists such as Professor Flinders Petrie, M. Maspero, and M. Paturet describe the women who lived in Egypt four thousand years ago as equal with men before the law, inheriting equally and having full control over their property and person. Polygamy existed in theory in ancient Egypt, but seems to have been rare in practice. In Europe under Christianity polygamy has been forbidden in theory, but has been by no means rare in practice—in a clandestine form.

The women of ancient Greece and Rome had no such freedom as that enjoyed by the earlier Egyptian generation. Under the Roman Republic they were, according to law, subject to the absolute control of the father or the husband. In marrying, the woman merely exchanged one master for another. During the days of the later Empire there was a general relaxing of restrictions; this reacted favorably in the case of women, who then reached their position of greatest independence in Europe. They held property, took part in public affairs, had complete control over their own homes and establishments, and even held municipal offices.[2] In a recent book, which professes to see in history the working of Christian principles, it is claimed that "it was in virtue of the faith of Christ, and that alone, that the position of woman was bettered, and respect for woman increased, in the later Roman Empire and in the dark ages that followed."[3] But the records bear witness that on the advent of Christianity, with its doctrine of the inferiority of women, their liberties were curtailed, the range of their activities contracted, and their character lowered.[4]

Christianity is sometimes described as an essentially feminine religion, inasmuch as the Mother of God is a chief object of worship, and women have had a conspicuous place allotted to them as saints and martyrs; and also because in the New Testament there is much which appeals to the peculiarly feminine emotions of tenderness and pity. It is very certain that Christianity has always found its chief supporters among women, although, with a few recent exceptions, they have never been permitted to aspire to the priesthood, and have been strictly forbidden to allow their voices to be heard as Christian teachers.

Tertullian, who lived in the third century, described women as "the devil's gateway," and declared that they ought to go about in humble garb mourning and repentant for the sin of their mother Eve. The Canon law could neither forget nor forgive the seduction of Adam.[5] St. Ambrose, in fact, puts this forward definitely as the reason why woman should take man as her ruler, so that he may not fall a second time through female levity. The saint evidently thought that, with man and woman on equal terms, the man would stand a poor chance. At a Church Council held at Macon at the end of the sixth century there was a bishop who expressed a doubt whether woman was a human being at all; but the Council decided that, in spite of all her shortcomings, she really did belong to the human species. At a Council held at Auxerre, women were forbidden to receive the Eucharist in their bare hands; and some of the Canons of the Church forbade them to approach the altar during the celebration of Mass: in the Middle Ages the Church even employed eunuchs in the cathedral choirs in order to supply the soprano voices, which otherwise belong only to women.[6] In parts of Europe women were obliged to enter the church by a separate door, and to sit and stand apart from the men—a practice which still prevails in certain churches at the present day.

It is notorious that the early Church took a very coarse and detestable view of marriage, and advocated celibacy as a far higher state. Marriage, said the Fathers, prevented a person from serving God perfectly, since it induced him to occupy himself with worldly affairs.

> This antagonism to marriage had a great influence on family life. It is strange how seldom children are mentioned in the Christian writings of the second and third centuries. Almost nothing is said of their training; no efforts are mentioned as being made for their instruction. . . . Tertullian describes children as "burdens which are to us most of all unsuitable, as being perilous to faith."[7]

After a prolonged struggle the Church succeeded in establishing the institution of clerical celibacy, which, with its nominally celibate clergy and its congregations of nominally celibate monks and nuns, was one of the most frightful sources of immorality which it is possible to conceive.[8] This position taken by the Christian Church towards marriage was accompanied by the most odious views concerning women generally. And there is very little doubt that this contemptuous and hostile attitude adopted towards them by official Christianity has been largely responsible for the heavy disabilities under which European women have suffered even in the most progressive Christian States. The Pauline doctrine of the subjection of women is alone answerable for much that is evil in the conduct of society towards women.

This contempt for women, carrying with it their exclusion from active participation in issues affecting the welfare of the community, has not been confined to any one branch of Christianity; it is to be found to a greater or less extent among all sects. Nothing, for example, could be more insolent than John Wesley's attitude towards women as displayed in a rebuke he addressed to his wife:—

> Be content [he wrote] to be a private insignificant person, known and loved by God and me. Of what importance is your character to mankind? If you was buried just now, or if you had never lived, what loss would it be to the cause of God?[9]

If we look at the position of women in Europe at any time between the rise of Christianity and the dawn of Rationalism at the end of the eighteenth century, we find them generally in a very low state of culture and condition. There have, of course, been exceptions. There always have been individual women who, through force of circumstances and sheer driving power, have risen above their fellows; but these were the exceptions, the rare exceptions. Too often, indeed, both men and women of the rural populations were sunk deep in misery and degradation, and then the woman was just the slave of a slave. Too often both lived and died in a condition scarcely better—

in some respects, infinitely worse—than that of the cattle in the fields. Who that has ever read it can forget *La Bruyère's* poignant description of the peasantry of Christian France in the century before the Revolution, in which he speaks of them as having fallen to such depths of misery that only the power of difficult speech distinguished man from beast? Where humanity is sunk so low as this it is the bitterest irony for the Christian apologist to talk of the betterment of the position of woman and the increase of respect in which Christian influences caused her to be held. The "faith of Christ" which could bring wealth to the coffers of the Church and enable its ecclesiastics to live in splendor with huge followings of courtiers and courtesans availed nothing to alleviate the lot of the man and woman who tilled the soil and sowed the seed.

What has Christianity done for the women of Abyssinia? Abyssinia is one of the oldest of Christian countries, and its late ruler, Menelek, traced his descent back to the Queen of Sheba. In Abyssinia there is no development of rationalism to dispute the claims of Christian influence. Whatever unaided faith in Christ could accomplish, we might expect to see it there. The Abyssinians care a great deal about their religion, and believe that they are the only real Christians; they would not admit that the English who visited them were Christians at all.[10] They may be quite right; there are so many varieties of Christians, each professing to be the only true one, that it is difficult for outsiders to decide. In Austria, under the Empire, the Church of England, all-important as it is in Great Britain, was not accepted as Christian. The Abyssinians, at any rate, are described as being extremely religious, and the clergy hold the people in their power by threat of excommunication and other clerical anathemas. A favorite subject for church decoration appears to be martyrdom on earth and torture in hell; all the good people are represented as white, and all the bad people and the devils as black. Education—such as it is—is confined to the Church, the women are regarded as beasts of burden who do all the hard work of daily life, and the people generally are described as being morally lax, while polygamy is a common practice. In Abyssinia, where Christianity has been the prevailing religion for close upon sixteen hundred years, and where Rationalism is utterly unknown, the women folk are no better than beasts of burden.

Russia is another very Christian country untouched by Rationalism until quite modern times. In Russia, among the so-called upper classes, it was the custom two hundred years ago for the husband's horsewhip to hang over the bed of the married couple; and we are assured that it was no empty symbol. The treatment of female serfs was often infamous to the last degree. There were nobles who "plied a regular trade in young peasant girls, whom they sold to brothels. Gangs of serfs were taken to the southern markets, where Armenian merchants bought them for the purpose of exportation to Turkey."[11] Until well within the last century the Russian peasantry lived together in great families composed of twenty, thirty, or sometimes as many as fifty or sixty members, all subject to the absolute authority of the eldest man, usually the eldest grandfather, unless he was too feeble to keep order. The despotic authority in such families fell most heavily upon the women, especially upon the last new daughter-in-law; each generation was a slave to the elders, and the last comer was a slave to all, scolded, cursed, and beaten without mercy.[12] These Russians were intensely pious, living on terms of the closest intimacy with God, the Holy Virgin, and the saints—if one may judge from their folklore, folk songs, and traditions. The gross superstitions of the peasants were kept up and even fostered by the Church.[13] It was the intellectual movement—not Christianity, but the movement away from Christianity—which bettered the condition of the cultured classes and brought them increased respect. Heresy is sometimes fanatical and irrational, at other times rational and temperate; and in so numerous, so varied, and so emotional a people as the Russians it has taken every variety of form. One good result of the movement towards intellectual and personal emancipation was the break-up of the old despotic great family system and the awakening interest in education; but emancipation was still very partial and very tentative when the War came [World War I]; then followed the Revolution, and then chaos, out of which a new and greater Russia may be born.

The case of Russia and that of Abyssinia are extreme instances of the worthlessness of "faith of Christ" as an influence in the betterment of humanity; extreme both in their brutal despotism towards women and in the unquestioning credulity of the people. The Russians doubted neither Christ nor Mary, neither Heaven nor Hell, neither witchcraft nor sorcery; their faith knew no bounds, for it was commensurate with their ignorance.

The rise has taken place recently in the status of women in certain countries is due almost wholly, if not entirely, to the decline in religious belief. Among our own people, where circumstances have been specially favorable to the growth of the spirit of liberty, the independence of women and the equalization of their rights have come only little by little; every step has been gained in defiance of the Church and the teachings of the Scriptures, and in no way through their aid.[14] When women cease to kiss the rod which has chastized them for the past sixteen centuries, their emancipation will be still further hastened, their characters strengthened, and their activities given full scope, not only in England, but in France, Italy, Spain, and in the other of the Christian countries of the world. The wider education of women should do much to improve their condition; it should make them more respected, and, what is of equal importance, it should make them respect themselves more. The more women know, the less they will "believe." And once released from the thraldom of belief, they will be free to prove their own worth. The more heretical women become—*i.e.,* the more they think, criticize, and make up their minds for themselves, instead of humbly asking their husbands, as enjoined by St. Paul—the sooner will they reach a position of dignity and independence.

NOTES

1. For a more detailed study of this subject see *The Religion of Woman,* by Joseph McCabe.
2. Donaldson, *Woman: Her Position in Ancient Greece and Rome,* Bk. II.
3. Mozley, *The Achievements of Christianity,* p. xiv.
4. Donaldson, Bk. III.
5. Ostrogorski, *Rights of Woman,* p. xi.
6. Westermarck, *Origin and Development of Moral Ideas,* I, pp. 663, 666.
7. Donaldson, p. 180.
8. No one can have any real idea of the grossness or the extent of the immorality of the clergy who has not read Lea's *Sacerdotal Celibacy,* or consulted the records of ancient cities, visitations to religious houses, and similar documents. See also Coulton's *Medieval Studies* (first series).
9. Quoted by Morley in his *Diderot,* p. 169.
10. A. B. Wylde, *Modern Abyssinia,* p. 142; H. Vivian, *Abyssinia,* p. 275.
11. Tikhomorov, *Russia: Political and Social,* I, p. 234.
12. "The Little Russians have a very characteristic saying:—
    Who is going to bring the water? The daughter-in-law.
    Who is to be beaten? The daughter-in-law.
    Why is she beaten? Because she is the daughter-in-law."

A song of the Great Russians, in which the young wife laments her weariness, shows that the husband is powerless to protect his bride from the "striking, roaring, striking, roaring," of the angry father-in-law and the upbraiding of the angry mother-in-law (Tikhomorov, *Russia: Political and Social,* I, p. 185).
13. Ibid., p. 180.
14. What irony it is to boast of the respect in which women are held by virtue of the faith of Christ when twentieth-century Christians could defend the establishment of *maisons tolerées,* and a notoriously pious Prime Minister of England could authorize a police regulation under which young women—even decent, modest young women—could be arrested, while their men companions went free. The Rev. A. A. Toms (Hunstanton) actually suggested that "frail women" should be compelled to wear red bonnets. There are no frail women without frail men, but there was no suggestion that frail men should wear red caps as a danger signal to weak women.

Christianity and Slavery

Edward A. Westermarck

Edvard (often anglicized to Edward) Westermarck (1862-1939), who was Finnish by birth, eventually became one of the world's foremost anthropologists. He obtained his early education (through the M.A.) in his native Finland. He then went to the British Museum in London to gather material for his doctoral dissertation, which was eventually expanded into what became his most impressive book, the three-volume work entitled *The History of Human Marriage.*

Westermarck spent most of his adult life as a professor of anthropology or sociology, both in Finland and in England. He was professor of sociology at the University of London from 1907 to 1930.

Among his scholarly works are *The Origin and Development of the Moral Ideas* (2 vols.), *Marriage Customs in Morocco,* and *Ethical Relativity.* He died in Finland in 1939, a self-confessed agnostic.

The present selection comes from his last book, *Christianity and Morals,* first published in 1939 by Macmillan, though not reprinted since. This excerpt is unusual in that it deals with the Christian attitude toward slavery, something that is almost never understood correctly by either Christians or unbelievers.

There still remains a branch of economics where we might expect to find conspicuous traces of Christian influence, especially as the very objects that it is concerned with are human beings—I mean the institution of slavery.

Slavery is essentially an industrial institution, which implies compulsory labor beyond the limits of family relations. The master has a right to avail himself of the working power of his slave, without previous agreement on the part of the latter. This I take to be the essence of slavery; but connected

427

with such a right there are others which hardly admit of a strict definition, or which belong to the master in some cases though not in all. He is entitled to claim obedience and to enforce this claim with more or less severity, but his authority is not necessarily absolute, and the restrictions imposed on it are not everywhere the same. Voluntary slavery is spoken of, as when a person sells himself as a slave, but this is only an imitation of slavery true and proper: the person who gives up his liberty confers upon another, by contract, either for a limited period or for ever the same rights over himself as a master possesses over his slave. If slavery proper could be based upon a contract between the parties concerned, I fail to see how to distinguish between a servant and a slave.

Christianity recognized slavery from the beginning. Paul wrote: "By one Spirit are we all baptized into one body, whether we be Jews or Gentiles, whether we be bond or free." But he also wrote: "Let every man abide in the same calling wherein he was called. Art thou called being a servant? care not for it: but if thou mayest be made free, use it rather. For he that is called in the Lord, being a servant, is the Lord's freeman: likewise also he that is called, being free, is Christ's servant. Ye are bought with a price; be not yet the servants of men. Brethren, let every man, wherein he is called, therein abide with God." Masters are told to give to their servants that which is just and equal; but in the first place servants are commanded to obey in all things their masters "according to the flesh; not with eyeservice, as men-pleasers; but in singleness of heart, fearing God." Peter says that they shall be subject to their masters with all fear; "not only to the good and gentle but also to the froward." There are a few references to slavery in the Apostolic Fathers. Ignatius writes: "Overlook not the men and maid-servants: neither let them be puffed up; but rather let them be the more subject, to the glory of God, that they may obtain from him a better liberty. Let them not desire to be set free at the public cost, that they be not slaves to their own lusts." Barnabas tells masters not to be bitter in their commands towards any of their servants that trust in God. The same injunction is found in the 'Didache,' together with the order that slaves shall be subject to their lords, "as to God's image."

Christianity's acceptance of slavery belonged to its Jewish heritage. Among the Hebrews the slave class consisted of captives taken in war; of persons bought with money from neighboring nations or from foreign residents in the land; of children of slaves born in the house of native Hebrews who had been sold by their fathers, or who either alone or with their wives and children had fallen into slavery in consequence of poverty, or who had been sold by the authorities as slaves on account of theft when unable to pay compensation for the stolen property. Slaves of foreign extraction were not to be emancipated, but should remain slaves for ever. But in no case had the master absolute power over his slave. Whether the latter was an Israelite or a foreigner, his life, and to some extent his body, were protected by law. If a man by blows destroyed an eye or a tooth, or any other member belonging to his man-servant or maid-servant, he was bound to let the injured person go free. And a master who smites his slave so that he dies under his hand, "shall be surely punished"; but if the slave continues to live for a day or two after the assault, the master goes free on the score that the slave is "his money." In the Talmud masters are repeatedly admonished to treat their slaves with kindness; and emancipation of slaves is practically encouraged in various ways, in spite of the dictum of certain rabbis that he who emancipates his slave transgresses the positive precept of Leviticus xxv. 46, "They shall be your bondmen for ever."

Paul also knew the slavery of the Greco-Roman world. The power, originally unlimited, which the Roman master had over his slave was during the Pagan Empire limited in various ways. Claudius and Antoninus Pius put check on his legal right to kill his slave. The Lex Petronia, A.D. 61, forbade masters to compel their slaves to fight with wild beasts. In the time of Nero an official was appointed to hear complaints of the wrongs done by masters to their slaves. But in those days when Roman slavery had lost its original patriarchal and, to speak with Mommsen, "in some measure innocent" character, when the victories of Rome and the increasing slave-trade had introduced into the city innumerable slaves, when those simpler habits of life which in early times somewhat mitigated the rigor of the law had changed—the lot of the Roman slave was often extremely hard, and numerous acts of shocking cruelty were committed. At the same time we also hear, from the early days of the Empire, that masters who had been cruel to their slaves were pointed at with disgust in all parts of the city, and were hated and laothed. And with a fervor which can scarcely be surpassed Seneca and other Stoics argued that the slave is a human being with dignity and human rights, born of the same race as ourselves, living the same life, and dying the same death—in short, that our slaves "are also men, and friends, and our fellow-servants." Epictetus even went so far as to condemn altogether the keeping of slaves. "What you avoid suffering yourself," he says, "seek not to impose on others. You avoid slavery, for instance; take care not to enslave. For if you can bear to exact slavery from others, you appear to have been yourself a slave." These teachings could not fail to influence both legislation and public sentiment. Imbued with the Stoic philosophy, the jurists of the classical period declared that all men are originally free by the Law of Nature, and that slavery is only "an institution of the Law of Nations, by which one man is made the property of another, in opposition to natural right."

Considering that Christianity has commonly been represented as almost the sole cause of the mitigation and final abolishment of slavery in Europe, it deserves special notice that the chief improvement in the condition of slaves at Rome took place at so early a period that Christianity could have absolutely no share in it. Nay, for about two hundred years after it was made the official religion of the Empire there was an almost complete pause in the legislation on the subject. Beyond a law of Constantine, to the effect that a master who put his slave to death in a nonjudicial way was to be punished as a murderer, the Christian emperors seem to have done little to guard the life of the slave. Whilst it was provided that any master who applied to his slave certain atrocious tortures with the object of killing him should be deemed a manslayer, it was emphatically said that no charge whatever should be brought against him if the slave died under moderate punishment, or under any punishment not inflicted with the intention of killing him. Arcadius and Honorius even passed a law refusing protection to a slave who should fly to a church for refuge from his master; but this law was, in the West, followed by regulations of an opposite character. Under Justinian certain reforms were introduced:—enfranchisement was facilitated in various ways; the rights of Roman citizens were granted to emancipated slaves, who had previously occupied an intermediate position between slavery and perfect freedom; and though the law still refused to recognize the marriages of slaves, Justinian gave them a legal value after emancipation in establishing rights of succession. But the inferior position of the slave was asserted as sternly as ever. He belonged to the "corporeal" property of his master, he was reckoned with among things which are tangible by their nature, like land, raiment, gold, and silver. The constitution of Antoninus Pius restraining severity on the part of masters was enforced, but the motive for this was not evangelic humanity. It is said in the "Institutes" of Justinian: "This decision is a just one; for it greatly concerns the public weal, that no one be permitted to misuse even his own property."

It is strange that the inconsistency of slavery with the tenet, "Do to others as you would be done by," though emphasized by a pagan philosopher, never seems to have occurred to any of the early Christian writers. The principle that all men are spiritually equal in Christ does not imply that they should be socially equal in the world. Slavery does not prevent anybody from performing the duties incumbent on a Christian, it does not bar the way to heaven, it is an external affair only, nothing but a name. He only is really a slave who commits sin. Augustine says that slavery is a burden which has justly been laid upon the back of transgression. Man when created by God was free, and nobody was the slave of another until that just man Noah cursed Ham, his offending son; slavery, then, is a punishment sent by Him who best knows how to proportion punishment to offense, and the slave himself ought not to desire to become free. Not one of the Fathers of the Church hints that slavery is unlawful or improper. In the early age martyrs possessed slaves, and so did abbots, bishops, popes, monasteries, and churches; Jews and pagans only were prohibited from acquiring Christian slaves. So little was the abolition of slavery thought of that a Council at

Orleans, in the middle of the sixth century, expressly decreed the perpetuity of servitude among the descendants of slaves. On the other hand, the Church showed a zeal to prevent accessions to slavery from capture, but her exertions were restricted to Christian prisoners of war. As late as the nineteenth century the right of enslaving captives was defended by Bishop Bouvier.

Like the Apostles, Councils and popes reminded slaves of their duties towards their masters, and masters of their duties towards their slaves. The Council of Gangra, about the year 324, pronounced its anathema on any one who should teach a slave to despise his master on pretense of religion; and so much importance was attached to this decree that it was inserted in the epitome of canons which Hadrian I in 773 presented to Charlemagne in Rome. But there are also many instances in which masters are recommended to show humanity to their slaves. According to Gregory IX "the slaves who were washed in the fountain of holy baptism should be more liberally treated in consideration of their having received so great a benefit." Slaves who had taken refuge from their masters in churches or monasteries were not to be given up until the master had sworn not to punish the fugitive; or they were never given up, but became slaves to the sanctuary. Faithful to her principle that human life is sacred, the Church made efforts to secure the life of the slave against the violence of the master; but neither the ecclesiastical nor the secular legislation gave him the same protection as was bestowed upon the free member of the Church and State. Various Councils punished the murder of a slave with two years' excommunication only, if the slave had been killed "sine conscientia judicis"; and the same punishment was adopted by some Penitentials. Edgar made the penance last three years, whereas if a freeman was killed, the penance was of seven years' duration. Facts do not justify Lecky's statement that, "in the penal system of the Church, the distinction between wrongs done to a freeman, and wrongs done to a slave, which lay at the very root of the whole civil legislation, was repudiated." The Church prohibited the sale of Christian slaves to Jews and heathen nations. The Council of Chalons, in the middle of the seventh century, ordered that no Christian should be sold outside the kingdom of Clovis, so that they might not get into captivity or become the slaves of Jewish masters; and some Anglo-Saxon laws similarly forbade the sale of Christians out of the country, and especially into bondage to heathen, "that those souls perish not that Christ bought with his own life." The clergy sometimes remonstrated against slave-markets; but their indignation never reached the trade in heathen slaves, nor was the master's right of selling any of his slaves whenever he pleased called in question at all.

The assertion made by many writers that the Church exercised an extremely favorable influence upon slavery surely involves a great exaggeration. As late as the thirteenth century the master had practically the power of life and death over his slave. Throughout Christendom the purchase and the sale of men, as property transferred from vendor to buyer, was recognized as a legal transaction of the same validity with the sale of other merchandise, land or cattle. Slaves had a title to nothing but subsistence and clothes from their masters, all the profits of their labor accruing to the latter; and if a master from indulgence gave his slaves any *peculium*, or fixed allowance for their subsistence, they had no right of property in what they saved out of that, but all that they accumulated belonged to the master. A slave or a freedman was not allowed to bring a criminal charge against a free person, except in the case of a *crimen lese majestatis*, and slaves were incapable of being received as witnesses against freemen. The old distinction between the marriage of the freeman and the concubinage of the slave was long recognized by the Church: slaves could not marry, but had only a right of *contubernium*, and their unions did not receive the nuptial benediction of a priest. Subsequently, when conjunction between slaves came to be considered a lawful marriage, they were not permitted to marry without the consent of their master, and such as transgressed this rule were punished very severely, sometimes even with death.

The gradual disappearance of slavery in Europe during the latter period of the Middle Ages has also commonly been in the main attributed to the influence of the Church. But this opinion is scarcely supported by facts. It is true that the Church in some degree encouraged the manumission of slaves. Though slavery was considered a perfectly lawful institution, the enfranchisement of a fellow-Christian was deemed a meritorious act, and was sometimes recommended on Christian principles. At the close of the sixth century it was affirmed that, as Christ had come to break the chain of our servitude and restore our primitive liberty, so it was well for us to imitate him by making free those whom the law of nations had reduced to slavery; and the same doctrine was again proclaimed at various times down to the sixteenth century. In the Carlovingian period the abbot Smaragdus expressed the opinion that among the other good and salutary works each one ought to let slaves go free, considering that not nature but sin had subjected them to their masters. In the latter part of the twelfth century the prelates of France, and in particular the archbishop of Sens, pretended that it was an obligation of conscience to accord liberty to all Christians, relying on a decree of a Council held at Rome by Pope Alexander III. And in one of the later compilations of German medieval law it was said that the Lord Jesus, by his injunction to render unto Caesar the things which are Caesar's and unto God the things that are God's, indicated that no man is the property of another, but that every man belongs to God. Slaves were liberated "for God's love," or "for the remedy" or "ransom of the soul." In the formularies of manumission given by the monk Marculfus in the seventh century we read, for instance: "He that releases his slave who is bound to him, may trust that God will recompense him in the next world"; "For the remission of my sins, I absolve thee"; "For the glory of God's name and for my eternal retribution," etc. Too much importance, however, has often been attached to these phrases. For the most trivial occurrences, however, has often been attached to these phrases. For the most trivial occurrences, such as giving a book to a monastery, are commonly accompanied by similar expressions; and it appears from certain formulas that slaves were not only liberated, but also bought and sold, "in the name of God."

Nor can we suppose that it was from religious motives only that manumissions were encouraged by the clergy. It has been pointed out that "as dying persons were frequently inclined to make considerable donations for pious uses, it was more immediately for the interest of churchmen, that people of inferior condition should be rendered capable of acquiring property, and should have the free disposal of what they had acquired." It also seems that those who obtained their liberty by the influence of the clergy had to reward their benefactors, and that the manumission should for this reason be confirmed by the Church. And while the Church favored liberation of the slaves of laymen, she took care to prevent liberation of her own slaves; like a physician she did not herself swallow the medicine which she prescribed to others. She allowed alienation of such slaves only as showed a disposition to run away. The Council of Agatho, in 506, considered it unfair to enfranchise the slaves of monasteries, seeing that the monks themselves were daily compelled to labor; and, as a matter of fact, the slaves of monasteries were everywhere among the last who were manumitted. In the seventh century a Council at Toledo threatened with damnation any bishop who should liberate a slave belonging to the Church, without giving due compensation from his property, as it was thought impious to inflict a loss on the Church of Christ; and according to several ecclesiastical regulations no biship or priest was allowed to manumit a slave in the patrimony of the Church unless he put in his place two slaves of equal value. Nay, the Church was anxious not only to prevent a reduction of her slaves, but to increase their number. She zealously encouraged people to give up themselves and their posterity to be the slaves of churches and monasteries, to enslave their bodies—as some of the charters put it—in order to procure the liberty of their souls. And in the middle of the seventh century a Council decreed that the children of incontinent priests should become the slaves of the churches where their fathers officiated.

The disappearance of medieval slavery has further, to some extent, been attributed to the efforts of kings to weaken the power of the nobles. Thus Louis X and Philip the Long of France issued ordinances declaring that, as all men were by nature free, and as their kingdom was called the kingdom of the Franks, they would have the fact to correspond with the name, and emancipated all persons in the royal domains upon paying a just compensation, as an example for other lords to follow. Muratori believes that in Italy the wars during the twelfth and following centuries contributed more than anything else to the decline of slavery, as there was a need of soldiers and soldiers must be freemen. According to others, the disappearance of slavery was largely effected by the great famines and epidemics with which Europe was visited during the tenth, eleventh, and twelfth centuries. The number of slaves was also considerably reduced by the ancient usage of enslaving prisoners of war being replaced by the more humane practice of accepting ransom for them, which became the general rule in the latter part of the Middle Ages, at least in the case of Christian captives. But it seems that the chief cause of the extinction of slavery in Europe was its transformation into serfdom.

This transformation has been traced to the diminished supply of slaves, which made it the interest of each family to preserve indefinitely its own hereditary slaves, and to keep up their number by the method of propagation. The existence and physical well-being of the slave became consequently an object of greater value to his master, and the latter found it more profitable to attach his slaves to certain pieces of land. Moreover, the cultivation of the ground required that the slaves should have a fixed residence in different parts of the master's estate, and when a slave had thus been for a long time engaged in a particular farm, he was so much the better qualified to continue in the management of it for the future. By degrees he therefore came to be regarded as belonging to the stock upon the ground, and was disposed of as part of the estate which he had been accustomed to cultivate.

But serfdom itself was merely a transitory condition destined to lead up to a state of entire liberty. I have elsewhere discussed the causes of this process. As a quite subordinate one may be mentioned instances of lords liberating their villeins at the intercession of their spiritual confessors, the clergy availing themselves of every opportunity to lessen the formidable power of their great rivals, the temporal nobility. The influence which the Church exercised in favor of the enfranchisement of serfs was even less than her share in the abolition of slavery proper. She represented serfdom as a divine institution, as a school of humility, as a road to future glory. Luther was horrified when the German peasants demanded that villeinage should end, because "Christ has delivered and redeemed us all, the lowly as well as the great, without exception, by the shedding of his precious blood." According to him, the spiritual kingdom of Christ must not be changed into an external worldly one: "An earthly kingdom cannot exist without inequality of persons. Some must be free, others serfs, some rulers, others subjects. As St. Paul says, 'Before Christ both master and slave are one.'" The Catholic Church, again, was herself the greatest serf-holder; and so strenuously did she persist in retaining her villeins, that after Voltaire had raised his powerful outcry in favor of liberty, and Louis XVI himself had been induced to abolish "the right of servitude" in consideration of "the love of humanity," the Church still refused to emancipate her serfs.

Not long after serfdom had begun to disappear in the most advanced communities of Christendom a new kind of slavery was established in the colonies of European states. It grew up in circumstances particularly favorable to the employment of slaves. Whether slave or free labor is more profitable to the employer depends on the wages of the free laborer, and these again depend on the numbers of the laboring population compared with the capital and land. In the rich and underpeopled soil of the West Indies and in the Southern States of America the balance of the profits between free and slave labor was on the side of slavery. Hence slavery was introduced there, and flourished, and could be abolished only with the greatest difficulty.

From the moral point of view negro slavery is interesting chiefly because it existed in the midst of a highly developed Christian civilization, and nevertheless, at least in the British colonies and the United States, was the most brutal form of slavery ever known., First there was the capture of the negroes in Africa, then the "middle passage" with its indescribable horrors, and lastly the miserable existence in the new country. It may be worth while to consider more closely some points of the legislation relating to this particular outgrowth of Christian civilization. . . .

This extraordinary system of slavery was not only recognized by Christian governments, but was supported by the large bulk of the clergy, Catholic and Protestant alike. In the beginning of the abolitionist movement the Churches acknowledged slavery to be a great evil, but with the making of this acknowledgement they believed that they had done their share, and denied that there was any obligation on them, or even that they had any right, to proceed against the slave-holders. But things did not stop here. The lamentations of resignation were gradually changed into excuses, and the excuses into justifications. The Bible, it was said, contains no prohibition of slavery; on the contrary, slavery is recognized both in the Old and New Testaments. Abraham, the father of the faithful and the friend of God, had slaves; the Hebrews were directed to make slaves of the surrounding nations; St. Paul and St. Peter approved of the relation of master and slave when they gave admonitions to both as to their reciprocal behavior; the Savior himself said nothing in condemnation of slavery, although it existed in great aggravation while he was upon earth. If slavery were sinful, would it have been too much to expect that the Almighty had directed at least one little word aganist it in the last revelation of His will? Nay, God not only permitted slavery, but absolutely provided for its perpetuity; it is the very legislation of Heaven itself; it is an institution which it is a religious duty to maintain, and which cannot be abolished, because "God is pledged to sustain it." According to some, slavery was founded on the judgment of God on a damned race, the descendants of Ham (as Augustine said); according to others it was only in this way that the African could be raised to a participation of Christianity and civilization. With the name of "abolitionist" was thus

Part Six: Ethics and Unbelief

associated the idea of infidelity, and the emancipation movement was branded as an attempt to spread the evils of skepticism throughout the land. According to Governor Macduffie, of South Carolina, no human institution is more manifestly consistent with the will of God than slavery, and every community ought to punish the interference of abolitionists with death, without the benefit of clergy, "regarding the authors of it as enemies of the human race." It is true that religious arguments were also adduced in favor of abolition. To hold men in bondage was said to be utterly inconsistent with the inalienable rights which the Creator had granted mankind, and still more obviously at variance with the dictates of Christian love. Many clergymen also joined the abolitionists. But it seems that in the middle of the nineteenth century the Quakers and the United Brethren were the only religious bodies that regarded slave-holding and slave-dealing as ecclesiastical offenses. The American Churches were said to be "the bulwark of American; slavery."

Nobody would suppose that this attitude towards slavery was due to religious zeal. It was one of those cases, only too frequent in the history of morals, in which religion is called in to lend its sanction to a social institution agreeable to the leaders of religious opinion. Many clergymen and missionaries were themselves slave-holders, the chapel funds largely rested on slave property, and the ministers naturally desired to be on friendly terms with the more important members of their respective congregations, who were commonly owners of slaves. It is interesting to notice how slow the anti-slavery movement among the Quakers was towards practical achievement. It was in 1675 that a companion of George Fox, after visiting Barbadoes, delivered a remonstrance to Friends in Maryland and Virginia against slave-holding; but although from that time on sporadic protests against it were made in Pennsylvania, "the Society gave these memorials a cold reception. The love of gain and power was too strong on the part of the wealthy and influential planters and merchants, who had become slave-holders, to allow the scruples of the Chester meeting to take the shape of discipline." Not until John Woolman had devoted the latter part of his life (from 1742 to 1762) to a crusade against slave-dealing and slave-holding was the Society solidly converted to the cause of abolition. But Adam Smith makes the remark that the resolution of the Quakers in Pennsylvania to set at liberty all their slaves, was due to the fact that the principal produce there was corn, the raising of which cannot afford the expense of slave cultivation; had the slaves "made any considerable part of their property, such a resolution could never have been agreed to." As regards the Parliamentary act against the slave trade in 1807 and the emancipation of all slaves in British dominions in 1833, it has been pointed out that "the success of the abolitionists lay, among other things, in the economic aspects of the question. While the long battle for the abolition of the slave trade was being waged, it became evident that it would be far cheaper to increase the number of slaves by propagation than to continue importing fresh supplies from Africa; and later, when the abolitionists turned their attention to the extinction of slavery itself, the change in the economic condition of the West Indies gave added impetus to the anti-slavery cause."

To explain the establishment of colonial slavery, the laws relating to it, and the difficulties in the way of its abolition, it is necessary to consider not only economic conditions and the motive of self-interest, but also the want of sympathy for, or positive antipathy to, the colored race. The negro was looked upon almost as an animal, according to some he was a being without a soul. Even the free negro was a pariah, subject to special laws and regulations. In the Code of Louisiana it is said: "Free people of color ought never to insult or strike white people, nor presume to conceive themselves equal to the whites; but, on the contrary, they ought to yield to them on every occasion, and never speak or answer them but with respect, under the penalty of imprisonment, according to the nature of the offense." The 'Code Noir' prohibited white men and women from marrying negroes, "à peine de punition et d'amende arbitraire"; and in the Revised Statutes of North Carolina we read: "If any white man or woman, being free, shall marry with an Indian, negro, mustee or mulatto man or woman, or any person of mixed blood to the third generation, bond or free, he shall, by judgment of the county court, forfeit and pay the sum of one hundred dollars to the use of the county." In Mississippi a free negro or mulatto was legally punished with thirty-nine lashes if he exercised the functions of a minister of the gospel. Colored men in the North were excluded from colleges and high schools, from theological seminaries and from respectable churches, as also from the town hall, the ballot, and the cemetery where white people were interred. The Anglo-Saxon aversion to the black race is thus expressed by an English writer: "We hate slavery, but we hate the negroes still more." Among the Spaniards and Portuguese racial antipathies were not so strong, and their slaves were consequently better treated.

As the slavery existing in Mohammedan countries has partly served as an excuse for their annexation by Christian powers, it is interesting to compare Islam's attitude towards slavery with that which not long before had prevailed in the Christian world. The slave should be treated with kindness; the Prophet said: "A man who behaves ill to his slave will not enter into paradise." The master should give to his slaves of the food which he eats himself, and of the clothes with which he clothes himself. He should not order them to do anything beyond their power, and in the hot season, during the hottest hours of the day, he should let them rest. He may marry them to whom he will, but he may not separate them when married; nor must he separate a mother from her child. The Prophet said: "Whoever is the cause of separation between mother and child, by selling or giving, God will separate him from his friends on the day of resurrection." To liberate a slave is regarded as an act highly acceptable to God, and as an expiation for certain sins. These rules, it should be added, are not only recognized in theory, but derive additional support from general usage. In the Mohammedan world the slave generally lives on easy terms with his master. He is often treated as a member of the family, and occasionally exercises much influence upon its affairs. This could of course not be expected in the case of colonial slavery; and some of its laws were no doubt inspired by fear on account of the multitude of slaves in a wealthy nation.

Bibliography

These are the original citations of the books and pamphlets from which the selections (except poems) were taken.

Anonymous. *The Question of Method as Affecting Religious Thought.* London: Thomas Scott, 1873.

Benn, Alfred W. *Revaluations: Historical and Ideal.* London: Watts and Co., 1909.

Besant, Annie. *Life, Death and Immortality.* London: Freethought Publishing Co., 1886.

Bonner, Hypatia Bradlaugh. *Christianity and Conduct.* London: Watts and Co., 1919.

Bradlaugh, Charles. *When Were Our Gospels Written?* London: Freethought Publishing Co., circa 1880.

Bradlaugh, Charles, and George Jacob Holyoake. *Secularism, Scepticism and Atheism.* London: Austin and Co., 1870.

Clodd, Edward. *The Question: If a Man Die, Shall He Live Again?* London: Grant Richards, 1917.

Cooper, Robert. *The Immortality of the Soul, Religiously and Philosophically Considered.* London: James Watson, 1852.

Diderot, Denis. *Dialogues by Denis Diderot.* London: George Routledge and Sons, 1927.

"Diderot." *Thoughts on Religion.* London: R. Carlile, 1819.

Haldeman-Julius, E. *Know Thyself.* Girard, Kan.: vol. 2, no. 5 (January 1925): 16-20.

439

Lamont, Corliss. *The Illusion of Immortality*. New York: Philosophical Library, 1959.

Lewis, Joseph and Mike Wallace. *The Age of Reason* 21 (July 1957):1-5.

Mangasarian, Mangasar M. *The Rationalist* (Chicago) 2 (July 15 and 30, 1913):6-38.

McCabe, Joseph. *Sources of the Morality of the Gospels*. London: Watts and Co., 1914.

Moss, Arthur B., and Agnes Wilke. *Was Jesus an Impostor?* London: Watts and Co., circa 1890.

Paine, Thomas. *Extract from a Reply to the Bishop of Llandaff*. Toronto: Belford Clarke, 1879.

Taylor, Robert. *Astronomico-Theological Lectures*. Boston: J. P. Mendum, 1857.

Westermarck, Edward A. *Christianity and Morals*. New York: Macmillan, 1939.

Wheless, Joseph. *Forgery in Christianity*. New York: Alfred A. Knopf, 1930.

The *Anthology*, volume 1 is:

Stein, Gordon. *An Anthology of Atheism and Rationalism*. Buffalo, N.Y.: Prometheus Books, 1980 (paperback, 1984).

Suggestions for Further Reading

Arnheim, Michael. *Is Christianity True?* Buffalo, N.Y.: Prometheus Books, 1984.

Bonner, Hypatia Bradlaugh. *Christianity and Conduct.* London: Watts and Co., 1919.

Brown, Marshall G., and Gordon Stein. *Freethought in the United States: A Descriptive Bibliography.* Westport, Conn.: Greenwood Press, 1978.

Carter, Lee. *Lucifer's Handbook: A Simplified Critique of Popular Religion.* Los Angeles: Academic Associates, 1977.

Foote, G. W., and W. P. Ball. *The Bible Handbook for Freethinkers and Inquiring Christians* (8th ed.). London: Pioneer Press, 1938.

Hinton, Richard [pseudonym of Charles Angoff]. *Arsenal for Skeptics.* New York: Alfred A. Knopf, 1934.

Ingersoll, Robert G. *Some Mistakes of Moses* (most recent edition). Buffalo, N.Y.: Prometheus Books, 1986.

McCabe, Joseph. *A Biographical Dictionary of Modern Rationalists.* London: Watts and Co., 1928.

Mencken, H. L. *Treatise on the Gods.* New York: Alfred A. Knopf, 1930.

Nethercott, Arthur. *The First Five Lives of Annie Besant.* Chicago: University of Chicago Press, 1960.

Paine, Thomas. *The Age of Reason* (most recent edition). Buffalo, N.Y.: Prometheus Books, 1984.

Robertson, J. M. *A History of Freethought in the Nineteenth Century* (2 vols.). London: Watts and Co., 1929.

Russell, Bertrand. *Why I Am Not a Christian.* New York: Simon and Schuster, 1957.

Smith, George H. *Atheism: The Case Against God.* Buffalo, N.Y.: Prometheus Books, 1979.

Stein, Gordon, ed. *An Anthology of Atheism and Rationalism.* Buffalo, N.Y.: Prometheus Books, 1980.

———, ed. *The Encyclopedia of Unbelief* (2 vols.). Buffalo, N.Y.: Prometheus Books, 1985.

———. *Freethought in the United Kingdom and the Commonwealth.* Westport, Conn.: Greenwood Press, 1981.

Tribe, David. *100 Years of Freethought.* London: Elek Books, 1967.